for Jan

BERNARD SHARE first became seriously addicted to travel when, after graduating from Trinity College Dublin and working in publishing and advertising, he sailed in 1954 on a five-week voyage to Australia to become the first lecturer in English at the fledgling university in Newcastle, New South Wales. Returning to Ireland, he set up his own writing/design partnership in Dublin and in 1966, largely on the proceeds of a successful series of books for children, went round the world again. Since then he has been successively, and sometimes simultaneously, the general secretary of CLÉ, the Irish Book Publishers' Association; editor of *Books Ireland* from its inception in 1976 until 1987; and, from 1977 to 1992, editor of *Cara*, the inflight magazine of Aer Lingus, on whose behalf he travelled to Tasmania, Nepal, Argentina and the nether reaches of the then defunct Ballinamore and Ballyconnell canal.

His publications include a travel book, three novels, a book on 'The Emergency' (known outside neutral Ireland as World War II) and a history of Aer Lingus. A socio-historical study of the Shannon Region is due for publication in the autumn of 1992. He has broadcast and scripted programmes for both Irish and Australian radio and written a regular humorous column for *Hibernia*. He lives in County Kildare.

Far Green Fields

FIFTEEN HUNDRED YEARS OF
IRISH TRAVEL WRITING

●

EDITED BY
BERNARD SHARE

THE
BLACKSTAFF
PRESS

BELFAST

First published in 1992 by
The Blackstaff Press Limited
3 Galway Park, Dundonald, Belfast BT16 0AN, Northern Ireland
with the assistance of
The Arts Council of Northern Ireland

Typeset by Textflow Services Limited

Printed by The Guernsey Press Company Limited

British Library Cataloguing in Publication Data
Far Green Fields: Fifteen Hundred Years of
Irish Travel Writing
I. Share, Bernard
820.8032

ISBN 0-85640-489-6

For Bert, Danny, Jim,
Mary and Rai,
compagnons de voyage

CONTENTS

INTRODUCTION

'Your Irishman as a traveller is not a known quantity, as your Englishman is or your German,' wrote Desmond Fennell: 'The Irish become exiles but seldom travellers, except in the service of England, when they have already come to feel themselves as Englishmen. At least, if any native Irish travel, they do not write about it . . .'

This collection of Irish travel writing, by its very existence, challenges Fennell on one judgment whilst confirming him in another. The Irish have been travelling hopefully for at least as long as recorded history, and the account of the voyage of Saint Brendan in search of the Promised Land became a medieval bestseller, as did Tim Severin's modern pilgrimage in his wake. But whether or not Brendan actually reached America, as many believe, it is fairly certain that he did not write his own account of his adventures: there is thus, from the beginning, some justice in the assertion that the Irish have been slow to record their impressions of the far green fields. Many, of course, had other preoccupations: the Scotti Peregrini, who carried the light of learning to Britain and Europe in the Dark Ages, had other matters on their mind than a description of the beauties of Iona or the price of fish in Bobbio; and later generations travelled often by necessity, regarding new landfalls with the disenchanted eye of the possessor of a one-way ticket.

Amongst those who, in Louis MacNeice's words, 'slouch around the world with a gesture and a brogue/And a faggot of useless memories' there have been many, nevertheless, who have deemed the experience worthy of record, and to that record have brought what seems to emerge from these pages as a native sensibility setting them apart, to a greater or lesser extent, from the observers of more geographically, politically or materially favoured societies. Many, as Fennell points out, found themselves for one reason or another in the service of the colonial power which ruled in their own country; and of these, paradoxically, there were a not inconsiderable number who distinguished themselves in the service of the same British Empire they were frequently disposed to castigate in the Irish context. This dichotomy is evident in some of the writers here represented and accounts, perhaps, not only for a refreshingly detached viewpoint

1

brought to bear upon certain curious corners of the colonial world, but for the evidence of a ready sympathy with other subject populations dreaming of being masters in their own land.

Many of these travellers, however, have no discernible political axe to grind. Some made the journey, as in the case of Lord Mount Cashell's grand tour, because it was the done thing: and his experiences would have disappeared into oblivion with countless others of the same mould had it not been for the percipience of a lively young lady – one of a number, it may be said, who happily give the lie to the prevalent image of the home-bound Irishwoman. Others, more recently, travelled as independent citizens of an independent state – historically a novel experience which reflects itself in several of the narratives. But if there is one common quality that can be isolated – a risky business in such a disparate company – it is the abiding Irish concern with people as much as the places in which they find themselves: what might be attributed to the peasant in all of us.

This selection attempts to offer some appreciation of the range – geographical, social, temporal – of Irish travel writing, and of its quality. If much of the material is drawn from the nineteenth and early twentieth centuries, it is because travel writing, as a genre, was scarcely evident until then, at least within the Irish dimension: Ó Cianáin wrote his account of the Flight of the Earls from a background very different from that of the leisured observer; and Wolfe Tone, emigrating – at least notionally – to America in 1796, recorded in his journal little more than random impressions of the country and its people, while expending much ink on plotting and politics. The choice, again, has been governed by that which, excerpted from the body of an often extensive account (those who wrote, wrote frequently at length and at leisure), will stand on its own feet. And the selection has been limited to material which has appeared in book form, as distinguished from periodical journalism: writing that can be said to reflect the matured judgment of the writer rather than the instant impression.

The date of Saint Brendan's birth is generally set at AD 489, which means that, at least notionally, this conspectus extends over a millennium and a half of Irish curiosity about the wider world. As regards the debatable assignation of nationality, I have chosen to follow the criteria suggested by Conor Cruise O'Brien, rather than that adopted by the international soccer team selectors, who would not, one feels, cavil at Mark O'Polo: 'Irishness is not primarily a question of birth or blood or language: it is the condition of being involved in the Irish situation and usually of being mauled by it.' Not many of the selected writers evince clear evidence of that mauling, with the notable exceptions of Ó Cianáin, Tone and Mitchel; but all, in one sense or another, fall within the terms of O'Brien's definition. Some readers may observe that many, particularly among the nineteenth-century travellers, come from what might be described as an Ascendancy or privileged background – but then this would be largely true for the travel literature of many other countries. In the case of Ireland, it derives clearly from an economic and political situation which left those who travelled because they had to with little opportunity or inclination for finding either a voice or a publisher.

Be this as it may, the overriding criterion of choice has been – within the established definition – one simply of good writing on a theme of enduring interest. There were the hard cases: the sentimental journey of Laurence Sterne, born in Clonmel, was difficult to exclude; but Sterne's Irish involvement was little more than one of accidental birth, and due weight had to be given to the dictum of that eminently reluctant Irishman, the Duke of Wellington, that birth in a stable does not make one a horse. As to less justifiable exclusions – such as the explorer Edward Shackleton, of a Kildare Quaker family – the editor can offer as an excuse only the fact that another traveller among ice and snow had already selected himself, and offer him priority in a putative second volume.

Little could be done about those outstanding travellers who chose to exclude themselves through silence: Brendan's voyaging contemporaries, Bran and Mael Duin; the wandering scholars already referred to; and, nearer to our own day and our own experience, men such as the Galwayman Robert O'Hara Burke, who left to his colleague William John Wills – predictably an Englishman – the recording of their doomed journey across the Red Centre of Australia to its quietus at Cooper's Creek. Burke's minimal contribution to the literature of travel remains in the mind, however, when much else has faded: 'I hope we shall be done justice to. We have fulfilled our task, but we have been aban . . .'

If not all the travellers herein represented are cast in such an heroic mould, the majority of them evoke, I suggest, the spirit of what

W.B. Yeats described in another context as 'The indomitable Irishry', largely subscribing to Robert Louis Stevenson's philosophy that to travel hopefully is not infrequently better than to arrive.

BERNARD SHARE
JANUARY 1992

TO THE PROMISED LAND

Saint Brendan, son of Findlug, descendant of Alte, was born among the Eoganacht of Loch Léin in the land of the men of Munster. He was a man of great abstinence, famous for his mighty works and father of nearly three thousand monks.

When he was fighting the good fight, in a place called Clonfert of Brendan, there arrived one evening one of the fathers whose name was Barrind, a descendant of Niall.

When this Barrind was plied with many questions by the holy father, he wept, prostrated himself on the ground and stayed a long time praying. But Saint Brendan lifted him up from the ground and embraced him, saying:

'Father, why should we be sad during your visit? Did you not come to encourage us? Rather should you give joy to the brothers. Show us the word of God and nourish our souls with the varied wonders that you saw in the ocean.'

When Saint Brendan had finished his remarks Saint Barrind began to describe a certain island, saying:

'My son Mernóc, steward of Christ's poor, left me and sought to live the life of a solitary. He found an island near Slieve League, called the Delightful Island. Then, a long time afterwards I heard that he had many monks with him, and that God had shown many wonders through him. So, I set out to visit my son. At the end of a three-day journey, as I was approaching, he hurried with his brothers to meet me. For the Lord revealed to him that I was coming. As we were crossing in a boat to the island the brothers came, like bees swarming, from their various cells to meet us. Their housing was indeed scattered but they lived together as one in faith, hope and charity. They ate together and they all joined together for the divine office. They are given nothing to eat but fruit, nuts, roots and other greens. But after compline each remained in his own cell until the cocks crowed or the bell was struck. Having stayed overnight and walked round the whole island, I was brought by my son to the sea shore facing west, where there was a boat. He said to me:

"Father, embark in the boat and let us sail westwards to the island which is called the Promised Land of the Saints which God will give to those who come after us at the end of time."

'We embarked and sailed, but a fog so thick covered us that we could scarcely see the poop or the prow of the boat. But when we had spent about an hour like this a great light shone all around us, and there appeared to us a land wide, and full of grass and fruit. When the boat landed we disembarked and began to go and walk round that island. This we did for fifteen days – yet we could not find the end of it. We saw no plants that had not flowers, nor trees that had not fruit. The stones of that land are precious stones. Then on the fifteenth day we found a river flowing from east to west. As we pondered on all these things we were in doubt what we should do.

'We decided to cross the river, but we awaited advice from God. In the course of a discussion on these things, a man suddenly appeared in a great light before us, who immediately called us by our own names and saluted us, saying:

"Well done, good brothers. For the Lord has revealed to you the land, which he will give to his saints. The river there marks the middle of the island. You may not go beyond this point. So return to the place from which you departed."

'When he said this, I immediately questioned him where he came from and what was his name. He said:

"Why do you ask me where I come from or how I am called? Why do you not ask me about the island? As you see it now, so it has been from the beginning of the world. Do you feel the need of any food or drink or clothing? Yet for the equivalent of one year you have been on this island and have not tasted food or drink! You have never been overcome by sleep nor has night enveloped you! For here it is always day, without blinding darkness. Our Lord Jesus Christ is the light of this island."

'Straightaway we started on our journey, the man coming with us to the shore where our boat was. As we embarked in it he was taken from our eyes and we passed through the same darkness to the

Delightful Island. When the brothers saw us they rejoiced with great joy at our arrival and complained of our absence for such a long time, saying:

"Why, fathers, have you left your sheep wandering in the wood without a shepherd? We knew of our abbot going away from us frequently somewhere or other – but we do not know where – and staying there sometimes for a month, sometimes for a fortnight or a week or more or less."

'When I heard this, I began to console them, saying to them:

"Think, brothers, only of good. You are living undoubtedly at the gate of Paradise. Near here is an island which is called the Promised Land of the Saints where night does not fall nor day end. Your abbot Mernóc goes there. An angel of the Lord guards it. Do you not perceive from the fragrance of our clothing that we have been in God's paradise?"

'The brothers then replied:

"Abbot, we knew that you were in God's Paradise in the wide sea; but where that Paradise is, we do not know. We have indeed often noticed the fragrance exuding from our abbot's clothes when he returns from there after the space of forty days."

'I stayed on with my son for two successive weeks without food or drink. Yet our bodies were so satisfied that to others we seemed full of new wine. And after forty days I received the blessing of the brothers and the abbot and set off with my companions on the return journey to my cell. I shall go there tomorrow.'

When they heard these things, Saint Brendan and all his community prostrated themselves on the ground, glorifying God and saying:

'The Lord is just in all his ways and holy in all his works. For he has revealed to his servants such great wonders. He is blessed in his gifts, for he has nourished us today with such a spiritual foretaste.'

When they had said this, Saint Brendan spoke:

'Let us go to repair our bodies and to the washing of feet in accordance with the new commandment.'

When that night was over, Saint Barrind, having received the blessing of the brothers in the morning, set out for his own cell.

Saint Brendan, therefore, when fourteen brothers out of his whole community had been chosen, shut himself up in one oratory with them and spoke to them, saying:

'From you who are dear to me and share the good fight with me I look for advice and help, for my heart and all my thoughts are fixed on one determination. I have resolved in my heart if it is God's will – and only if it is – to go in search of the Promised Land of the Saints of which father Barrind spoke. How does this seem to you? What advice would you give?'

They, however, having learned of the holy father's will, say, as it were with one mouth:

'Abbot, your will is ours. Have we not left our parents behind? Have we not spurned our inheritance and given our bodies into your hands? So we are prepared to go along with you to death or life. Only one thing let us ask for, the will of God.'

Saint Brendan and his companions, therefore, decided to fast for forty days – but for no more than three days at a time – and then to set out. When the forty days were over he said goodbye to the brothers, commended all to the man put in charge of his monastery, who was afterwards his successor there, and set out westwards with fourteen brothers to the island of a holy father, named Enda. There he stayed three days and three nights.

Having received the blessing of the holy father and of all the monks that were with him, he set out for a distant part of his native region where his parents were living. But he did not wish to see them. He pitched his tent at the edge of a mountain stretching far out into the ocean, in a place called Brendan's Seat, at a point where there was entry for one boat. Saint Brendan and those with him got iron tools and constructed a light boat ribbed with wood and with a wooden frame, as is usual in those parts. They covered it with ox-hides tanned with the bark of oak and smeared all the joints of the hides on the outside with fat. They carried into the boat hides for the makings of two other boats, supplies for forty days, fat for preparing hides to cover the boat and other things needed for human life. They also placed a mast in the middle of the boat and a sail and the other requirements for steering a boat. Then Saint Brendan ordered his brothers in the name of the Father, Son and Holy Spirit to enter the boat.

While Saint Brendan remained alone on the shore and blessed the landing-place, three brothers from his own monastery came up, following after him. They fell immediately at the feet of the holy father, saying:

'Father, leave us free to go with you wherever you are going; otherwise we shall die on this spot from hunger and thirst. For we have decided to be pilgrims for the days of our life that remain.'

When the man of God saw their trouble, he ordered them to enter the boat, saying:

'Your will be done, my sons.'

And he added:

'I know why you have come. One of you has done something meritorious, for God has prepared a suitable place for him. But for you others he will prepare a hideous judgment.'

Saint Brendan then embarked, the sail was spread and they began to steer westwards into the summer solstice.

from THE VOYAGE OF SAINT BRENDAN, translated by John J. O'Meara

GEORGE A. BIRMINGHAM
1865–1950

Budapest in 1925, when Canon James Hannay (George A. Birmingham
was a pseudonym) was acting as chaplain to the British community. 'I
wanted to know about Hungary', he wrote: 'every Irishman must.
Was it not a pamphlet [by Arthur Griffith] called *The Resurrection in
Hungary* which started our Sinn Fein movement?' Hannay, born in
Belfast, was educated at Trinity College Dublin and became rector of
Newport, County Mayo, in 1892. He began writing fiction, but it was
not until *Spanish Gold* in 1908 that he attracted a wide public; thereafter
he produced a George A. Birmingham novel almost every year. The
production of his play *General John Regan* in Westport in 1913,
following a successful London run, led to his being boycotted locally
when it was discovered that he was the author. He left Ireland and,
after serving as a British army chaplain, lived in Somerset and later in
London, where he took charge of a small parish. This description of
the Hungarian capital is from *A Wayfarer in Hungary* (1925).

—————

PEST

Beyond the Millennium monument lies the Város Liget, the most
important park in Budapest. The approach to it is across a wide
bridge, on each side of which is an artificial lake. Here in winter
Budapest 'society' – and a good many other people who are not
'society' – skate to the music of bands and after nightfall by brilliant
artificial light. Skating is a sport at which Hungarians excel. But even
in Budapest there are beginners, awkward on their skates as swans
are in walking. They are segregated in a pond of their own – very
much, one imagines, to their own comfort – certainly to that of those
who have learnt to swoop and glide, who have accomplished that

poetry of motion which is only possible in skating, which is nowhere seen in more perfect grace than in Budapest.

In this artificial lake, on the right side of the bridge, is an artificial island, and on it a castle, also artificial. This is the Museum of Agriculture, and it is full of interesting things; but the building itself is more interesting than anything in it. It is intended to illustrate the different architectural styles – Gothic, Renaissance, Romanesque and Baroque – which are to be found in Hungary. Actual buildings have been carefully copied. The wing nearest the town, for instance, is a copy of an ancient castle of the Hunyadi's, part of which, at least, was built in the days of the great János. The experiment of a building in such varied styles seems almost foredoomed to artistic failure. It is too fantastic for any purpose under the sun except education, and not very useful for that. But in this case the unexpected happened, and a building of unusual beauty has been produced. It owes something, no doubt, to its picturesque situation and to the moat-like effect of the water round it; but – impossible as this seems – it actually achieves a certain harmony, a measure of dignity and attractiveness. The wanderer gazes at it first with amazement, then with puzzled uncertainty, but at last with admiration.

The north part of the park, on the left hand after crossing the bridge, contains a Zoological Gardens, chiefly remarkable for the entrance-gate, a picture of which might very well serve as a frontispiece to the *Arabian Nights*. Beyond the Zoological Gardens are the great Széchenyi Baths. These and the baths in the Gellért Hotel are the finest and the most luxuriously fitted of the many baths in Budapest. Their supply of hot water comes from Artesian wells bored at the end of the Andrássy-út. They contain huge tanks of beautifully blue, transparent water of various temperatures. In these the bather can wallow for hours, if he chooses, or bathe or dive or swim. There are dry, hot rooms, like those in our Turkish baths; steam-rooms in which it is impossible to see and very difficult to breathe; shower-baths of every possible kind; and, of course, massage-rooms. This kind of bathing is so popular in Budapest that the many establishments are always full – generally too full to be pleasant. In the large entrance-hall at the Széchenyi or the Gellért Baths you find on certain days long queues of people waiting to buy tickets for admission.

Beyond the baths the park disappears, as if no one ever cared to go past them. The roads, well kept and well planned up to that point, degenerate badly. The grass becomes either muddy or dusty. The whole place seems to come unravelled, until the wanderer finds himself, quite unexpectedly, in a broad road with tram-lines running along it. Like so much else in Budapest, this part of the park gives the impression of being unfinished, as if the abundant energy which erected the great monument at the entrance, the composite museum buildings, the Oriental dream-gate of the Zoological Gardens, and the vast bathing-house, had become so completely exhausted that there was none left for the laying down of a simple roadway.

The part of the park which lies on the right side of the lake is finished – *ad unguem*. Like the world in Stevenson's child poem, it is full

> Of such a number of things
> That I am sure we should all be as happy as kings.

Certainly if museums, band-stands, statues, smooth walks, well-kept grass, trees, a fashionable sports club and restaurants induce happiness this part of the park ought to be a paradise. There is even, among the restaurants, a branch of Gerbeaud's, a tea-shop and confectioner's which is famous in Budapest and believed by the Hungarians to be equally famous all over Europe. Certain kinds of small cakes – very sugary, very creamy and jammy, so sticky that they can only be comfortably eaten with spoons – are called Gerbeauds, whether they are actually made by Gerbeaud himself or not. You ask for a Gerbeaud in an hotel after dinner if you want something sticky and sweet. This is fame. The wanderer ought certainly to visit the central Gerbeaud, in Vörös-Marty Tér, which used to be called Gisella Tér. Gisella was the wife of King Stephen the Saint, and, one might suppose, is entitled to a square in a fashionable part of the town. But Vörös-Marty was a poet and a patriot, so poor Gisella had to give place to him, after an immense statue – or rather a whole group of statues – was erected to his honour in the square. I am not at all sure that both queen and poet will not have to give way in the end to the confectioner. Certainly a cab-driver will take you straight to the place you want if, having forgotten the names both of Gisella and Vörös-Marty, you ask simply to be driven to Gerbeaud Tér. This also is fame. The Londoner may be proud of Buzzard's cakes, but it would be useless to ask a taxi to drive you to Buzzard Street when you wanted to go to Oxford Street.

At afternoon tea-time Gerbeaud's is full. Rank, fashion, and beauty assemble there. The rank one takes for granted. It is not a rare thing in Budapest, for a very large proportion of the Hungarian upper classes has titles. The 'fashion' is obvious, and beauty is more than common. I have heard the Hungarians described as a beautiful race. This is not true. The peasants and the lower classes in towns, when not Jewish, are squat, square-faced, with high cheek-bones. The prevailing type is Mongolian. But among the Hungarian aristocracy there is a great deal of physical beauty. The men are often finely built, with well-shaped features and frank, fearless faces. One has no difficulty in believing that they are good soldiers and very good officers. Neither among the men nor women of the upper classes is there much trace of the Mongolian type. Are they of a different race, part of that Nordic stock to which we are asked to believe that all our aristocracies belong? The Hungarians themselves would deny this, and – their pedigrees are unimpeachable – they have certainly been Magyar for a long time.

Owing to the difficulty of getting a table or tea put on it in the afternoon, the wanderer will be well advised to pay his visit to Gerbeaud's about noon. He will find the rank, fashion, and beauty there just the same, only not in quite such large quantities. The Hungarian breakfast (I think I have mentioned this before) is miserable: a tiny ration of coffee with whipped cream in it, and a *semel* or two – the smallest and least satisfying of rolls. The Hungarian luncheon-hour is 2 pm or later. The time between is long, and the Hungarian lady, out for a morning's shopping, finds it necessary to sustain herself with a sandwich and a glass of Tokay. Where can she go – since the popular café is for her humbler sisters – except to Gerbeaud's? The sandwiches are good – so is the Tokay, so is the coffee, so are the multitudinous little biscuits called *te baekkerei*. If she goes away with a box of chocolates in her bag, the chocolates are good too – so good that I have known English people buy them and send them home to England, although there are in England – I must not advertise my favourite confectioner – several people who make good chocolates.

Gerbeaud himself, as his name indicates, was a Frenchman, but his business was not built up on French knowledge of cookery and French skill. Gerbeaud's predecessor was a Hungarian, and it was he who made the shop famous. Old-established residents in Budapest still call the shop and the cakes by the name of the Hungarian.

I have sometimes wondered whether the Hungarians ought not to be given credit for being the originators of the rich and varied little cakes which fill our confectioners' shops now – indeed, cover the counters of pastry-cooks' shops all over Europe. When I was a boy the variety of little cakes was small, and those which existed were plain and unadorned compared to the sticky, sugary, jammy things we have now, each lying in its little white-frilled dish like a precious baby in a cradle. There was a time, in 1888 or thereabouts, when London was suddenly invaded by tea-shops which called themselves Hungarian. They were immensely popular because they supplied little cakes which at that time were quite strange to us – rich, sumptuous and delicious. Were those tea-shops really Hungarian? Did their cakes, or the knowledge of how to make them, actually come from Hungary? On such subjects one seeks information in vain from books, and human memory is a fallible thing. But it would be pleasant to think that in this matter, too, Europe owes a debt to Hungary. The same race which saved us all from Turkish domination hundreds of years ago, and, just the other day, gave its first decisive check to the advancing waves of Bolshevism, may perhaps also have made our afternoon tea-parties the glorious things they are. The *croissant*, now eaten everywhere and at its best in Paris, came originally from Vienna, and the French were taught to make it by Austrian bakers. There is nothing absurd in supposing that the art of making sumptuous cakelets came from Hungary, from that very shop on Gisella (or Vörös-Marty) Tér, where Hungarian ladies are even now digging their pretty teeth into these delicious trifles.

ROBIN BRYANS
1928–

Born Robert Harbinson Bryans in Belfast, Robin Bryans has written under the name Robert Harbinson in the course of an active literary career. As a young man he was employed in the Belfast shipyards and has recorded his early life in his autobiographical *No Surrender: An Ulster Childhood* (1960). Later he lived in Canada where he worked both as a trapper and a teacher. As Robert Harbinson, he has written short stories and autobiography, while his travel books under his pseudonym include accounts of Iceland, Brazil, Morocco, Trinidad and Tobago and *Crete*, from which this extract is taken. The record of a journey made in 1967, it is one of the last full reports from the pre-package era. But the writing was on the wall. 'I had always enjoyed the breakfast of crisp-crusted bread, unsalted butter and the renowned Cretan honey. Now an inferior marmalade is often offered instead . . .'

BRIDES OF THE LIBYAN SEA

Crete's best highway and the busiest is the one running along the north coast, westwards from Iraklion to Rethymnon and Khania, so linking the island's three principal cities. But I try to avoid it whenever possible and head across the island to the south coast where there are not even tertiary roads or footpaths through the White Mountains, but where there is always a fisherman willing to put his caique out and ferry the traveller on to the next village of white houses scattered on the shore like flotsam and jetsam thrown up by the Libyan sea.

To reach the south coast village of Khora Sfakia, however, I had to follow the main road out of Rethymnon as far as Vrises. And as always Cretans and the few tourists were looking out of the bus windows for a glimpse of a small sheet of water on the landward

15

side. This is Lake Kournas, whose 160 acres make it Crete's largest freshwater lake – in fact, the only one, because Lake Voulismeni at Ayios Nikolaos connects with the sea, though Kournas also enjoys a reputation for being bottomless. Some of the legends concerning the freshwater lake read like Greek myths. According to one, the ghost of a girl haunts the lake. To escape rape by her father she turned into Lake Kournas, just as Daphne was transformed into a bay tree to escape Apollo.

At Vrises, one bus must be exchanged for another which then fights its way southward through the mountains and, with as much judgment as luck, finally descends at Khora Sfakia. At Vrises the Rethymnon *nome* has been left behind. With its wide stream of fast-flowing water Vrises is to the Khania prefecture what fountain-filled Spilli is to the Rethymnon *nome*. The river and great trees make it a most attractive village. Immense planes and walnuts overhang the road and dapple the bridge with shade. The water below is unbelievably clear and unsullied in its course down from the ranges of olive-green mountains rising behind the town. Even at midday in summer Vrises remains fresh and morning-like. The whole scene here could easily be mistaken for an English village on a lovely summer's day, although the mountains around have enough trees to lend a Tyrolean touch as well.

An exceedingly pleasant hour passed while waiting for the Khora Sfakia bus to come in. When it did I saw that not only had I exchanged one *nome* for another but also the comfortable new buses of the main road route for a sixteen-seater which had definitely seen better days. Old mountain farmers returning home from market were already installed with a mountain of cloth bundles. Crashing its gears the ancient Volvo shuddered out of Vrises. It took us nearly four hours to negotiate the forty kilometres to Khora Sfakia, not so much because of the bus's advanced years as from the constant turning and rising and falling of an unmade road which in winter is often impassable because of snow that, even in the burning sun of June, still lingers on the peaks.

I presumed the temperature in these high places of the island's interior must drop sharply at night. Though I had nothing other than a thin shirt and shorts on, the mountain men around me were wearing heavy woollen clothes, including white knitted vests of fishermen-ply thickness, as though they were whalers bound for Greenland.

But then the men dressed in these thick white jersies of elaborate design in an afternoon temperature of 90°F. were a law unto themselves. They were Sfakians, a race apart, descended, some say, from the Dorian invaders of the Minoan-Mycenaean city-states. Other and equally learned theorists flatly contradict this. They say the Sfakians are not Dorians but the people who fled *from* the Dorians, to the remote south as well as to the remote east around Sitia, and that therefore they must be descendants of the original Minoan people who kept their 'pure' Minoan ways – the Eteocretans. Whatever theories may try to account for prehistory, at least in historical times, the people of this remote central southern region emerge as 'pure' Sfakians, a name itself that stirs memories of mountain fighters of a hardiness and physique that verges on the mythical, even among other Cretans.

Soon the bus would enter the mountain retreats of the Sfakia province where one ravine is rich in human humus from the wholesale slaughter of thousands of ambushed Turks, and where another shows the stark remains of a Venetian castle built for the abortive purpose of subduing the wild, passionate Sfakians. But mostly these upland parishes are stained with the blood of family vendettas rather than the Muslim corpuscles of pashas and Janissaries. Young men and old may still go after a sheep-stealer with unblunted intentions to take the law into their own hands.

Mountain people are not infrequently blackguarded by lowlanders. Scots are mean, the Welsh wild, the Pathans of the North-west Frontier bloodthirstier than their compatriots on the plains of Pakistan, the Swiss alpine dwellers are inhospitable and unfriendly, and so on. There is no doubt that in byegone times the Sfakians were wilder than they are today, but then so was everybody else. Nor were they alone in settling differences between families by bloodshed. In short, I found the Sfakians little different from country Cretans everywhere in their attitude to the stranger-guest. Kindness and generosity and solicitation for the stranger's well-being did not suddenly disappear in this region of supposed cut-throats and thieves. Indeed, whenever kindly-disposed friends warned me to keep away from a certain district because the inhabitants supposedly disliked 'outsiders' I invariably went there and never suffered any abuse except to my waistline from over-lavish meals. Somebody had forewarned me that shepherds in Sfakia still carry arms, but the only one I knew well

was out with his gun after thrushes and wood larks with whom the
Sfakians have had a long hereditary blood feud, and one which,
oddly enough, is covered by the official game laws.

The driver of the sixteen-seater bus had also seen better days and
as proof he had put a photograph of himself with a big tomato-
loaded lorry over the windscreen for the proud Sfakians to see. It
kept company with a Madonna and Child, the Redeemer, St Barbara,
and a chain across the windscreen with thirty pendant crosses.
Occasionally the driver would stop because he had seen somebody
leaping like a goat down the mountain rocks in order to chat with a
friend in the bus, a chat in which all the passengers joined, none of
them seeming to object to the delay.

Soon we left an Italianate landscape of cypresses and fields terraced
with drystone walls, and the road passed up the north slopes of
mountains seen from Vrises. Almost without realising it, I saw we
had reached the top and were running into a curious, high plateau,
shut in by a ring of mountains, in which a triple-humped hill carried
the ruins of a Turkish castle. This is the Askifou Plain, and the village
up here bears the same name. The fields are very fertile and not
stony. Plane trees on the plain have a strange, dense foliage of dark
yellow-green. Askifou village perches on a rock and commands
views over the plateau. This is so much a world apart that the arrival
of the bus is a major event in the day. Several other patriarchal
shepherds got into the bus with their crozier-like crooks. A German
youth also boarded carrying a rucksack and a large earthenware jar
full of *xyno nero* got from one of the nearby village wells. This 'sour
water' reputedly has curative properties, though I did not care for its
taste. The German had been exploring the ravine called Katrai after
King Minos's eldest surviving son. Alas, Katreus when he became
king of Crete was accidentally speared by his own son, Althaemenes
– Strength of Growth.

In 1941 the remnants of the British force, severely lacking in the
strength of growth, crossed the road the sixteen-seater bus was
bumping along. The Battle of Crete was over and the British troops
were on their way to Khora Sfakia to escape from the harbour which
for centuries had been the port for arriving and departing
revolutionaries. But in 1941 I was an evacuee in the far west of Ireland
and my German fellow-traveller with the 'sour water' was not even
born, and now we too followed the ancient escape route to Khora

Sfakia as the bus passed from the lost-world of the Askifou Plain and began to descend. We now experienced the most thrilling part of the journey, beginning with a run along a deep gorge hung with scraggy cypresses on its upper reaches. After the gorge the road plunged earthwards, revealing miles of majestic coast and the southern mountain barrier against the Libyan Sea. This, above all other road journeys, shows Crete as an island of mountains and mountain people.

Khora Sfakia lodges, just, on narrow rock terraces above the sea, and is wedged into steep and rocky clefts of the mountain cliffs. The harbour is not so much a sheet of water as a pocket handkerchief of water, and water so clear that landing craft sunk during the 1941 evacuation can be seen on its bed. Unlike Ayia Galini, which manages to fit more or less comfortably into its gorge, Khora Sfakia's cove is too small, so the houses go scampering up the mountainsides like goats, and like goats they perch and posture and cling to impossible ledges in apparently inaccessible places. Their walls are white, their doors blue, and in between the houses, precarious trees flourish along with vines, and as always, with the rose too, favourite amongst flowers in Crete right back to Minoan times when it was painted on the palace frescoes. This was the sacred flower from which Aphrodite cured Hector's wounds with its oil of roses. And being the flower of the Greek Goddess of Love (who was also Goddess of Family Life) the rose not surprisingly has become the *rosa mystica* of the Virgin Mary, who gets an ample supply of them at her many shrines in Khora Sfakia's forty-five churches.

This number of churches may strike the visitor as somewhat excessive for such a tiny township, but this is to be in ignorance of the fact that a century ago Khora Sfakia had as many thousands as today it has hundreds of inhabitants. After the rebellion of 1866 and the explosion at Arkadhi Monastery, many of the Sfakians left Crete to escape Turkish reprisals. No doubt they thought it better to live to fight another day. But they did not, and the population dwindled from 3,000 to today's mere 300.

But 'mere' is hardly a term to use of the people of Khora Sfakia as I found when, a little bone-shaken and cramped, and wondering why German youths travel so easily and become naturally accepted even in places where their fathers were the most recent enemy, I got off the bus at the village's little cove. Some of the old warriors had left behind their sturdy farmhouses of an architecture all their own. One such has recently been converted into the inn. Or rather, a part of it has been converted, for in the other half the farmer and his wife still live with their herds and flocks.

It is difficult to imagine a more perfect place than that inn perched on the tiny harbour's edge, basking in the summer heat, remote from madding and maddening crowds, tucked away into the cleft in the mountains' south coast cliffs, and in indisputed command of the Libyan Sea.

The sea at Khora Sfakia has a special quality, a luminous translucence. In mid-afternoon the immaculate, turquoise enamel is decorated with white and perfect Ionic scrolls as waves break in geometrical precision over submarine rocks. And when sundown progresses the sea becomes lighter in hue, but the horizon turns amethyst with cirrus clouds floating like feathers. At this hour, troupes of swifts and swallows swoop over the white-walled houses, their sickle wings slashing the radiant sky. It is wonderful then to sit on the inn's terrace immediately above the millpond sea, and look towards the triple-peaked rock just beyond the harbour which sits like a chocolate cake on a mother-of-pearl plate. On my second evening at the inn I saw a ship far out, the only vessel sighted in two days. It crawled across the horizon, that sharp dividing line between nacre sea and purple sky, like an ant walking warily on a wall.

Far from being vendetta-crazed cutthroat riflers of travellers' bags and baggage I found the Sfakians, at least in the person of the innkeeper, excellent at cooking and generous as hosts and gifted with the normal Cretan genius for hospitality. I sat up late with the owner because a fisherman had taken his caique further along the coast to pick up a party of guests who had telephoned from the next village across the mountains. We sat talking in the loggia dining-room, the night air blowing in sweet and full of flower scents, the lamp casting warm light on the stone arches and round-headed doorways of the cleverly converted building.

The innkeeper had made up five beds as requested on the telephone, and with typical Cretan concern for guests had kept a first class meal that would be ready for the new guests in spite of the uncertain hour of their arrival. When they did at last arrive, I was thoroughly disgusted, ashamed and embarrassed. The four men and one woman, all young and British, sailed into the starlit harbour and the landlord's open hand of welcome on the quay. They saw the best rooms I had so far had in Crete, equipped with Scandinavian-design furniture specially made in Khania for the inn, and then announced they would pay ten shillings – not each but for all five of them in one double room. The owner offered them two of the rooms he had prepared at ten shillings for each room. But these objectionable young people stormed out of the inn, shouting insolent remarks, and made off to sleep on the beach.

Such abuse of Cretan hospitality is infuriating. It happens so often. People from many countries descend on Crete, believing that to haggle over prices is the done thing. So far as hotel accommodation is concerned, it is not the done thing, because all inns and hotels have their charges fixed by law, charges which by British or American standards are extremely low. The back of the bedroom door usually carries an official statement of the price. Those five insulting people would never have dreamed of walking into an English hotel and demanding a double room for five people at two shillings per head. Next morning, the owner showed me one of the rooms in which some weeks earlier the polished wooden floor had been blackened in one area by cigarette stubs. The couple, in fact, had nearly caused a fire, and when told so the girl had simply laughed at the innkeeper. Wild and bloody times past there may well have been on the island. But never was the brutal insensitivity and lack of grace that accompanies the profit-making ethic of the affluent society, part of the Cretan way.

I knew of another couple, a painter and his wife and their child. They arrived at a village outside Khania, and their eye for beauty led them to a fine old barn they thought would make a fine house. They asked the farmer how much he would rent it for. He told them the absurd sum of a hundred drachmas per month, less than thirty shillings a month. When the couple said they could only afford fifty drachmas, the farmer's heart melted for he imagined they were destitute, seeing in them a Mary and Joseph. He let them live in the barn for nothing, and from every ewe milking sent them over a can for their child. Three months later the couple bought an expensive German car, and the poor farmer and his wife, out in their fields from sunrise to sunset, seeing the barn-dwellers race to and from the beach in such style, realised there was another cuckoo in the Cretan nest.

At the time of my visit to Khora Sfakia high summer had come. I knew Iraklion's hotels would be full. Yet here, at one of the island's most beautiful sea villages two double rooms with their own private terrace overlooking the Libyan Sea were dismissed by those five abusive young travellers at rates equivalent to Salvation Army hostels for down-and-outs. My Irish blood boiled at this in the way that passionate Sfakian blood is supposed to. But no melodrama ensued. Instead, the innkeeper sent me over another glass of wine while he helped his wife clear the loggia tables of the five uneaten though ordered meals. As everywhere in the village, there were cats to help in the clearing up. The cats of Sfakia own the place. They are wiry and disdainful, and aristocratic even in their scrounging.

Next morning I was on the road by seven o'clock in order to spend the day at Frangokastello. This most sinister of all Venetian fortresses on Crete was built in 1371 when the Serene Republic tried to break Sfakian resistance. My early start, however, was not in an attempt to catch the *drossoulites* – the 'dew shades' for which this deserted castle on the coast is known. The dew shades undoubtedly occur, though I never saw them, and doubtless they have some perfectly innocent natural explanation. But the local people say that when the *drossoulites* rise from the ground, they can see the ghosts of the 385 Cretan men who were killed defending Frangokastello against the Turks in 1828.

A sinister air surrounds the castle which stands in a lonely place at the sea's edge with nothing but a sun-baked desolate plain of scrubland between it and the mountain wall. On climbing the steep hill out of Khora Sfakia, the fortress's honeyed stones come clearly into view. It looks about an hour's walk away. But this is a deception played by the extreme clarity of the light and atmosphere along this coast. Besides, the villages and the road hug the mountain foothills, avoiding both the sea and the desolate plain and the uncanny 'Frankish Castle', a name used in preference through the centuries to the official Castel St Niketas.

Looking back at Khora Sfakia from the road up the gorge-sides, the little port is screened by pines which resinate the air as their gum resinates the wine. More climbing through the rocky land brings the next village into focus on the other side of the gorge. The bus to and from Vrises passes through the gorge. Beyond it, the road along the coastal mountains leaves the trans-island Vrises road, and trundles traffic-less and deserted to the villages scattered along the foothills.

Compared with the climb up from Khora Sfakia's cove, the going is easy though stony. That was a splendid morning of azure, the sky and the sea vibrant with colour, the air fresh and balmy, and the winding, dusty road below the mountain barrier with its white villages quiet under the sun.

I stopped for breakfast at Komitades, the first of these villages, and had boiled eggs and new-baked bread and succulent tomatoes which were served by a young man just home from national service as a sailor at Soudha Bay. And like every sailor from anywhere in Greece who is stationed outside Khania, he had a wallet bulging with snapshots of the *pentozali* being danced at Bouzounieri's, of first shipmates and of last girlfriends made and lost before the longed-for homecoming to mountain villages like Komitades. Cretans are very proud of their village origins, and in the cities will ask the foreigner anxiously, 'Do you know *my* village?'

Komitades, at any rate, was worth knowing, for besides its marvellous site it has a small Byzantine church dating from AD 1313 containing a good ikon of a red and gold Resurrection and fragments of frescoes similar in design and colour to the more complete ones at Kritsa, which would make Komitades's frescoes as old as the church itself.

Many caves open along the roadside to Frangokastello, some of them still used for cooking and storage. One is famous in Cretan history as the Cave of Daskaloyiannis – John the Clerk, a popular Cretan hero. A Sfakian shepherd copied down the story of the Clerk's life as told by a wandering bard sixteen years after Daskaloyiannis's cruel death. This is the ballad known as *The Song of Daskaloyiannis*. Not only did the Clerk own many ships, but he spoke several languages and had contacts with the Russians who were then fighting the Turks. When Daskaloyiannis led the rebellion of 1770, he expected the Russian fleet to come and help the Cretan cause. But the Turks eventually captured him. According to the ballad, the Clerk was tortured in Iraklion's fortress and then skinned alive in the main square without uttering a cry. The cave bearing his name is where the Sfakian freedom fighters set up their own mint during the uprising.

Today the Sfakians have different enemies to fight. Yet the most oppressive of these is not new – poverty. The people do not escape from poverty, as in history they did from other oppressors, by going to other Greek islands or the mainland, but by emigrating to the USA or Germany. But because they are Cretans and love their villages in the stark mountains, the emigrants often return, so that in almost every settlement on the island there is at least one 'Greek-American'. There was such a man in the next village en route to Frangokastello and I was reminded of a poem by Louis MacNeice who also loved rural Greece:

> Did not these whitewashed rooms among wine-gourds, goat-skins,
>   ikons
> Include a letter or two with a foreign postmark
> From Cleveland and Detroit, diners and luncheonettes,
> From wholesale grocers, coffee jobbers, gobetweens,
> Who proved there was a horizon when they crossed it
> Yet still are sons and uncles. Hermes came from Olympus,
> Tipster and god of the market; these across the Atlantic,
> Tides invading the tideless.

HUBERT BUTLER
1900–1991

'When I was a boy of fourteen,' wrote Hubert Butler, 'I decided I was
going to live in the place where my father, grandfather and great
grandfather had lived before me.' Born in County Kilkenny, he
returned to live there in 1941 – following an Oxford education,
working with the Irish County Libraries, teaching English in
Alexandria and Leningrad, and a period of three years in Yugoslavia
on a scholarship from the London School of Slavonic Studies. This
essay, from *Escape from the Anthill* (1985), is the fruit of the latter
experience. Of its setting he wrote: 'When one went south and
penetrated to Montenegro, one seemed to pass from our cruel,
complicated century to an earlier one, just as cruel, where each man
was responsible to his neighbours for his crimes and where organised
twentieth-century barbarity had not yet emerged.' Following his
return to his roots, Butler revived the Kilkenny Archaeological Society
and, with Lord Dunboyne, founded the Butler Society. He wrote
extensively, and in the 1950s was review editor of the Dublin-based
magazine *The Bell*.

THE LAST IZMERENJE

For three days the rain had fallen steadily. When we arrived in
Kotor, the top of Lovcen was invisible, and festoons of moist cloud
swam across the mountains behind us. Nonetheless, there was a
band to meet the boat and a great crowd, and on an iron mooring
post a youth was arranging salvoes of welcome. Every now and then
there was an enormous bang, and he disappeared in thick white
smoke, for explosions are the Dalmatians' favourite way of celebrating
great occasions, and today was a feast day in both the Catholic and
Greek Churches. It was Easter Day for the Orthodox, while for the

Catholics it was the feast of St Hosanna, a nun whose mummified body lies below an altar in one of the Kotor churches.

I pushed my way through the crowd, and asked the first likely person I met where the monastery of Grbalj was, and what time the 'izmerenje' was to be. Nobody knew, though I had heard in Belgrade about it three hundred miles away, while here it was only half-an-hour's drive by car. It was not till I had searched the town for information that I found, at last, that I was a day too early. I was rather relieved; perhaps the next day the rain-clouds would have lifted.

In the afternoon, with two others, I made a half-hearted attempt to drive to Cetinje, but soon after we had passed the old Austrian customs house, at the frontier of Dalmatia and Montenegro, we were in dense fog and the whole panorama of Kotor Bay, which must be one of the loveliest in the world, had disappeared, and we were shivering with cold and damp. We went back; and that evening, when I was having tea in one of the old houses at Dobrota, I was told the story of the Montenegrin blood feud by a lady who had studied law and had attended the trial of Stevo Orlovich in an official capacity.

The Orlovichs and the Bauks were two families living some fifteen miles from Kotor, not in Montenegro itself, but observing the old Montenegrin customs. Two years ago the Orlovichs had made enquiries and learnt that Stjepo Bauk, whose father was dead, would let his sister accept a proposal from Stevo Orlovich. Stevo, thereupon, set out with a group of his relations to make a formal offer, carrying firearms, as was the custom, so as to celebrate the betrothal with the usual explosions. When they reached the Bauks' house, they were told that the offer was refused.

It appeared that an old uncle of the Bauks had been greatly insulted that his permission had not been asked. He had made a row, and Stjepo had given in to him. Stevo Orlovich was outraged and indignant, and whipping out his gun he fired at Stjepo Bauk and hit him in the leg. Bauk fired back and injured Orlovich – there was a scuffle and the Orlovichs took to their heels. A few days later, Stjepo Bauk's leg had to be amputated, and he died. The case was tried in the courts, and Stevo Orlovich was sentenced to three years' imprisonment.

But the Bauks were not in the least pacified by this; they held to the old Montenegrin tradition that blood should be avenged by blood, and the Orlovichs continued to feel uneasy. Near Podgorica, in Montenegro, just such a murder had taken place in 1930, and since then thirty murders have followed it in alternate families, the last one six months ago. It has been impossible for the courts to collect satisfactory evidence; though the relations of the victim in most cases knew the murderer, they would scorn to hand him over to justice. Revenge is a private, not a public, responsibility. But there was a way out, and this the Orlovichs took.

Some ten months ago, when Stevo Orlovich had had the rest of his sentence remitted for good behaviour, twenty-four 'good men' of the Orlovichs called on the Bauks, and asked them to agree to the izmerenje ceremony. The Bauks refused. Five months later, the Orlovichs appealed again, and this time they were granted a day's armistice for every member of the deputation, that is to say, twenty-four. After that they came a third time, and at last the Bauks granted their request. It would be the first izmerenje celebrated in the neighbourhood for more than a generation, and it was this ceremony that I had come to Kotor to see.

'Of course,' my friend said, 'it won't be nearly as elaborate an affair as it used to be. In the old days the murderer had to crawl on his hands and knees and beg forgiveness; and then he must give a gun to the head of the other family as a token. And then there were the babies at the breast. Seven women of the murderer's family had to come with their seven babies in cradles, and ask the head of the family of the murdered man to be the "kum" or godfather, and he was obliged to accept.

'That shows what size the families were,' she added. 'Today, in all Dobrota, you couldn't find seven babies at the breast, far less in one family.'

The birds were singing next morning at six o'clock, and the fog seemed to have lifted completely from Lovcen. It looked as if the day was to be fine. I was told to be ready on the quay at 7 am, and was to share a car with the two judges who had sentenced Orlovich, two local correspondents of a Belgrade paper, and one of the hundred guests invited by Orlovich. This guest was so confident that the ceremony would wait for him that we were an hour late in starting. To get to the monastery of Grbalj you must climb up the slope of Lovcen out of the Boka, and then down again towards Budva on the open sea. Most of the district is a 'polje' or flat space between the mountains, and relatively fertile; the peasant houses are placed for the most part on the rocky, barren slopes, where nothing grows except scrub or wild pomegranates and stunted oak; their farms lie below them in the polje, full of vines, fig-trees, beans and potatoes, market crops that they can sell in Kotor.

The people of Grbalj were always an enterprising community from the time of the great medieval Tsar of Serbia, Dushan; they had their own laws, and the Venetians, when they occupied the Boka and its surroundings, respected the Grbalj Statute, which was only abolished when Dalmatia was seized by Austria after the Napoleonic wars.

We soon saw the monastery perched on a hill on the left – an unexpectedly small, insignificant building, its courtyard black with moving people. The larger half was completely new.

'The old building was raided and burnt by the Montenegrins themselves during the war,' the judge told me. 'They say the Austrians were using it as a store for ammunition. It was rebuilt, and they opened it again last year. There are some twelfth-century frescoes in the end of the chapel, but they're badly damaged by damp, as it was roofless for so long.'

Behind us, a mile or two away, but plainly visible as it lay open on the rocky face of the mountain over against the monastery, was the cluster of houses where the Bauks and the Orlovichs lived. They were large red-tiled farmhouses two or three storeys high, with big windows and several annexes. The Bauks' house was the bigger of the two.

'The Bauks have a dozen families scattered over the place,' said the judge, 'but the Orlovichs only have two, so I don't know how they'll pay for the dinner; you see, they must bring a hundred of their supporters and the Bauks must bring a hundred of theirs: the Bauks will be the hosts, but the Orlovichs must pay for it all. It may run them into a couple of thousand dinars [about £8]. If either side brings more or less than a hundred, it's a gross insult, and they'll have to start the whole business over again.'

The hundred Orlovich guests were already there when we arrived; outside the wall of the churchyard a group of women and neighbours, whom neither side had invited, were leaning watching. The women, in Montenegrin fashion, had their thick black hair wound across their foreheads in heavy plaits, a black lace veil fell from behind to their shoulders.

There were two long tables stretched out in the courtyard covered with brown paper, but the Orlovichs were most of them sitting upon the wall. The six 'good men' who headed the Orlovich deputation were in the vestry when we arrived, drinking Turkish coffee. One was a fat, pleasant-looking priest in a grey soutane from a neighbouring parish. Two seemed prosperous town relations in smart overcoats, clean-shaven, with gold teeth and Homburg hats; two were well-to-do farmers in full Montenegrin dress, round caps with red crowns embroidered in gold and the black bands that all Montenegrins wear in mourning for the battle of Kossovo, when the Serbians were defeated by the Turks in 1399. They had red waistcoats with heavy gold embroidery, orange sashes and blue breeches with thick white woollen stockings and string shoes. The other ninety-four Orlovichs had compromised about their clothes; they nearly all had the caps and some had either the breeches or the waistcoat, but they mostly had an ordinary Sunday coat on top of it. They all had black moustaches, and held either a heavy stick or an umbrella in their hands. I saw one or two men who had both.

One of the journalists from Kotor beckoned me into the church, and introduced me to the priest and a small dark man with terrified eyes who stood beside him.

'That's the murderer,' he told me. 'You are the murderer, Stevo Orlovich, aren't you?' he asked to make certain.

'Yes' – and we shook hands.

We shook hands with his brother, too, an older, solid-looking man. He, too, had received a bullet wound in the leg as he was running away from the Bauks' house. Stevo Orlovich shrank away behind the chapel walls as soon as he could; he was very slightly built, and had black bristly hair and a small Charlie Chaplin moustache; he wore a neat but worn black suit, with a fountain pen clipped in the breast pocket. He was evidently in an agony of shame and embarrassment about the ceremony he was going to have to go through. But he was sufficiently collected to make it clear that he wasn't pleased to see us.

All at once a boy began to toll the three small bells of the chapel, and five or six people went in to hear the priest celebrate the short Easter Mass according to the Greek rite. I saw the correspondent of the Belgrade *Politika* standing beside them leading the responses in a booming voice.

'Christ is risen!'

'Lord, have mercy on us!'

The priest was swinging a censer vigorously, and the whole courtyard was filled with sound and the smell of incense.

It lasted a quarter of an hour. When I came out of the church one of the Orlovichs who was sitting on the seat, cried out, 'Hello, boy!' and I went and sat down beside him. He had been at the copper mines at Butte, Montana, and said that at least ten others present had been there, too. I complimented him on his gorgeous embroidered waistcoat, but he said it was nothing to what they used to have. Times were bad . . . .

'Montenegrin mans should do like Irishmans,' he said, 'raise hell, holler!'

Evidently, a good deal of information about Ireland had filtered via Butte, Montana, to Grbalj, because he had a muttered conversation with his neighbour about de Valera and the Lord Mayor who had died after a seventy day hunger-strike.

'I was telling him about the Liberty Irish State,' he said.

The six good men walked out of the churchyard and he said: 'You see that bunch? They go fetch the otha bunch!'

But the six Orlovichs returned alone and another hour passed before down the mountain slope the procession of the Bauks, a long black line like a school crocodile, issued slowly from behind a little wood. They were a long way off still. From the terrace of the priest's house I watched them going down a small lane through an olive grove into the main road, crossing the wooden bridge over a very swift stream then climbing up the hill towards the monastery.

A man came out of the monastery with a big basket of bread and he was followed surprisingly by a sailor with some paper table napkins. Carafes of rakkia were planted at intervals along the table. . . . The Orlovichs got up and walked leisurely towards one side of the churchyard, they formed themselves in a long row, fifty abreast, two deep. In the back row towards the end I saw the murderer flatten himself against the wall. He was fingering his fountain pen nervously. His brother was beside him.

The little priest in the grey soutane came bustling out of the church.

'Take off your hats,' he said, and we all did so.

Then the Bauks came in, headed by two handsome elderly priests, with their hats still firmly on, facing a hundred with bare heads. It was like Sir Roger de Coverley.

There was a long silence and then one of the Bauk 'good men', a professor from Kotor, came out into the middle and in a loud voice read the sentence. This is a slightly abbreviated version of what he read:

In the name of Christ the Saviour Who is eternal peace between men.

Today, when the Ascension is near at hand, in the year of Our Lord 1937 in the monastery of the Blessed Virgin of Grbalj good men have met together and pleaded with the families of Bauk and Orlovich to lay aside their blood feud which arose in the month of February 1935.

In the name of God from Whom all true justice proceeds and after long cognition, they pronounced this sentence which shall be executed on the third day of Easter, 1937, in the monastery of the Blessed Virgin of Grbalj.

Seeing that God's justice fell upon the wounds of Stjepo Bauk, the son of Vuk and Stevo Orlovich, the son of Lazo, who remained alive after wounds received, and seeing that Mirko Bauk valiantly forgave the murder of his brother Stjepo and reconciled himself through God and St John with the Orlovichs, we declare this sentence:

1   That the brothers Orlovich wait with a hundred of their people on the Bauks with a hundred of theirs.

2   That the Orlovichs humbly, according to custom (but not carrying firearms), shall approach the Bauks who shall embrace them in this order.
    Mirko Bauk, the son of Vuk, shall kiss Stevo Orlovich, the son of Lazo.
    Vaso Bauk, the son of Rado, shall kiss Ilya Orlovich, the son of Lazo.

3   That at the first baptism of a child of theirs the Orlovichs shall ask Bauk to be godfather and he shall accept.

4   That from this reconciliation everlasting friendship and mutual respect for their mutual honour in word and deed shall proceed and that this blood feud shall be ended for all time.

Each family must receive a copy of this sentence and one must be preserved in the archives of the monastery where this reconciliation was made.

Drawn up by the undersigned: [Here follow the signatures of the six good men of the Bauks and the six good men of the Orlovichs.]

The professor stepped back into the Bauk ranks and put the sentence back into his leather portfolio.

Then one of the Orlovich good men cried out in a voice breaking with emotion:

'Steven Orlovich!'

The murderer folded his arms across his breast and bending down from the waist he darted forward from the wall. He was like someone in a trance. He did not see where he was going and butted his bowed head into a man in front. It was a second before he had disentangled himself from the overcoat and was heading once more for the Bauks. Mirko Bauk, a fat young man with fair hair and moustache, all in black except for the red crown of his Montenegrin cap, stepped out and raised him up.

'Forgive me!' said Orlovich.

'I forgive you my brother's blood,' Bauk answered and they kissed each other on both cheeks. I heard people sobbing behind me. Then Vaso Bauk, who was small and puny, embraced Ilya Orlovich and finally all the hundred Bauks stepped forward and shook hands and greeted the hundred Orlovichs. Then they all took their seats at the table, the Orlovichs sitting at one table, the Bauks at another. Stevo Orlovich did not appear but stayed in the monastery with his brother.

I and the four men from Kotor were preparing to go home but the Bauk professor pressed us to stay.

'The Orlovichs would like to ask you,' he said, 'but they have to be so humble today – it isn't the custom – so we invite you.'

A table was brought out from the vestry and a red table cloth and we sat by ourselves in the other side of the courtyard.

Before we started to feed, the Bauk priest got up and began an Easter hymn . . . and once more the journalist's big voice filled the courtyard.

At lot of forks arrived and a platter heaped with boiled beef. Someone else explained to me that when the monastery had been rededicated last year, there had been six hundred guests and each had a knife for himself and also a tumbler; but today it was different – it was custom. So there were no tumblers and we pushed round from mouth to mouth, first a big bottle of rakkia, then a big flask of an excellent red wine.

'Please you thank you, Mister!' the journalist with the big voice said every time he gave the flask a shove in my direction.

He then muttered very rapidly into my ear a couple of verses of a poem beginning:

My 'ome iz zy ocean
My 'arth iz ze ship!'

The meal was quite good and the platters were constantly replenished by the sailor and two men running backward and forward with white napkins held in their teeth. After the beef came boiled ham. Except at our table nobody talked very much. There seemed to be no fraternisation between the Bauks and the Orlovichs. First came forgiveness, a little later, perhaps, friendship would follow.

They must have had an extraordinary capacity for keeping the practical and the emotional side of their lives distant for on the slope of the hill their two houses seemed only a few hundred yards apart. Their sheep must graze the same mountains, they must use the same tracks. How had they managed to pass two years so close without lending things and without borrowing things?

There could be no doubt, anyway, that the quarrel had at last been settled. The sentences of the law courts usually leave bitterness and dissatisfaction behind but the ceremony at Grbalj, so impressive and deeply moving, aimed at something far higher. Did it achieve it? I thought so, but couldn't be sure. Did Mirko perhaps look a bit too self-righteous? Does one ever feel very friendly towards people who force on one too abject an apology or towards one's relations who watch it? I think Stevo may go to Butte, Montana.

Most European law is based on compensation and punishment, justice is important, but it is also impersonal. Montenegrin custom on the other hand takes into account forgiveness which English justice ignores, and because of that, when 'izmerenje' passes away, as pass it must, an important element of justice will have gone with it.

The journalist borrowed the copy of the sentence from the monastery archives.

'Meet me in the Café at Kotor,' he said to me, 'and I'll let you have a read of it.'

And we crammed in eleven of us, for some of the Orlovich friends came too, into the car . . . . There was some angry tooting behind us and a lemon-coloured sports car thrust past, containing the professor and two of the Bauk 'good men'.

A moment later we were on the main highway to Cetinje, negotiating the hair-pin bends of that incredible road. Every now and then we passed policemen with fixed bayonets and we dodged a charabanc full of German tourists. Below us at Kotor a yacht lay at anchor by the quays, a procession of soldiers was marching through the streets which were green with acacia trees. The grimness of the mountains lay behind us and we were in the twentieth century again.

'It's beautiful,' I said to one of the judges.

'Yes,' he replied, 'but you should have seen it when the King and Mrs Simpson were here. The evening they arrived all the bay from Tivat to Kotor was illuminated – bonfires and petrol. It was wonderful. One of the bonfires set alight to some dry grass where there were some young trees. Not much damage done, but it made a wonderful blaze!'

By the time our car had drawn up at the Town Kafana, the izmerenje at Grbalj was like something that happened in a dream. Will there ever be another one in Montenegro? I can hardly believe it. The 'good men' in the Homburg hats were getting self-conscious about it and I am convinced I heard the murderer and his brother grumbling about the journalists behind the chapel wall. I was glad he didn't know that someone had suggested bringing a film apparatus. Nowadays, too, one can always interrupt blood feuds by going to Butte, Montana.

WILLIAM FRANCIS BUTLER
1838–1911

Born in County Tipperary, Butler saw service with the British army in
many African campaigns, including the Sudan, where he fought under
Wolseley. A born soldier, he thirsted for action and at one stage
during his curious mission to North America considered throwing in
his lot with the French. In 1869 he was kicking his heels in Ireland
when news arrived of an insurrection in the Red River Settlement in
Manitoba, Canada, which had been founded in 1812 by an eccentric
Scottish peer, Lord Selkirk. Butler immediately volunteered his
services and was successful in resolving what he described as 'this
petty provincial quarrel', which involved a French Canadian
demagogue, who was exploiting the fears of the local Indians that they
would lose their lands to the all-powerful Hudson's Bay Company.
Butler's subsequent travels took him to the far west and his account of
his adventures, *The Great Lone Land* (1889), from which this extract is
taken, ran into many editions.

REVOLT AT RED RIVER

The steamer 'International' made only a short delay at the frontier
post of Pembina, but it was long enough to impress the on-looker
with a sense of dirt and debauchery, which seemed to pervade the
place. Some of the leading citizens came forth with hands stuck so
deep in breeches' pockets, that the shoulders seemed to have formed
an offensive and defensive alliance with the arms, never again to
permit the hands to emerge into daylight unless it should be in the
vicinity of the ankles.

Upon inquiring for the post-office, I was referred to the postmaster
himself, who, in his capacity of leading citizen, was standing by.
Asking if there were any letters lying at his office for me, I was

answered in a very curt negative, the postmaster retiring immediately up the steep bank towards the collection of huts which calls itself Pembina. The boat soon cast off her moorings and steamed on into British territory. We were at length within the limits of the Red River Settlement, in the land of M. Louis Riel, President, Dictator, Ogre, Saviour of Society, and New Napoleon, as he was variously named by friends and foes in the little tea-cup of Red River whose tempest had cast him suddenly from dregs to surface. 'I wasn't so sure that they wouldn't have searched the boat for you,' said the captain from his wheel-house on the roof-deck, soon after we had passed the Hudson Bay Company's post, whereat M. Riel's frontier guard was supposed to hold its head-quarters. 'Now, darn me, if them whelps had stopped the boat, but I'd have jist rounded her back to Pembina and tied up under the American post yonder, and claimed protection as an American citizen.' As the act of tying up under the American post would in no way have forwarded my movements, however consolatory it might have proved to the wounded feelings of the captain, I was glad that we had been permitted to proceed without molestation. But I had in my possession a document which I looked upon as an 'open sesame' in case of obstruction from any of the underlings of the Provisional Government.

This document had been handed to me by an eminent ecclesiastic whom I met on the evening preceding my departure at St Paul, and who, upon hearing that it was my intention to proceed to the Red River, had handed me, unsolicited, a very useful notification.

So far, then, I had got within the outer circle of this so jealously protected settlement. The guard, whose presence had so often been the theme of Manitoban journals, the picquet line which extended from Pembina Mountain to Lake of the Woods (150 miles), was nowhere visible, and I began to think that the whole thing was only a myth, and that the Red River revolt was as unsubstantial as the Spectre of the Brocken. But just then, as I stood on the high roof of the 'International' from whence a wide view was obtained, I saw across the level prairie outside the huts of Pembina the figures of two horsemen riding at a rapid pace towards the north. They were on the road to Fort Garry.

The long July day passed slowly away, and evening began to darken over the level land, to find us still steaming down the widening reaches of the Red River.

But the day had shown symptoms sufficient to convince me that there was some reality after all in the stories of detention and resistance, so frequently mentioned; more than once had the figures of the two horsemen been visible from the roof-deck of the steamer, still keeping the Fort Garry trail, and still forcing their horses at a gallop.

The windings of the river enabled these men to keep ahead of the boat, a feat which, from their pace and manner, seemed the object they had in view. But there were other indications of difficulty lying ahead: an individual connected with the working of our boat had been informed by persons at Pembina that my expected arrival had been notified to Mr President Riel and the members of his triumvirate, as I would learn to my cost upon arrival at Fort Garry.

That there was mischief ahead appeared probable enough, and it was with no pleasant feelings that when darkness came I mentally surveyed the situation, and bethought me of some plan by which to baffle those who sought my detention.

In an hour's time the boat would reach Fort Garry. I was a stranger in a strange land, knowing not a feature in the locality, and with only an imperfect map for my guidance. Going down to my cabin, I spread out the map before me. I saw the names of places familiar in imagination – the winding river, the junction of the Assineboine and the Red River, and close to it Fort Garry and the village of Winnipeg; then, twenty miles farther to the north, the Lower Fort Garry and the Scotch and English Settlement. My object was to reach this lower fort; but in that lay all the difficulty. The map showed plainly enough the place in which safety lay; but it showed no means by which it could be reached, and left me, as before, to my own resources. These were not large.

My baggage was small and compact, but weighty; for it had in it much shot and sporting gear for prospective swamp and prairie work at wild duck and sharp-tailed grouse. I carried arms available against man and beast – a Colt's six-shooter and a fourteen-shot repeating carbine, both light, good, and trusty; excellent weapons when things came to a certain point, but useless before that point is reached.

Now, amidst perplexing prospects and doubtful expedients, one course appeared plainly prominent; and that was – that there should be no capture by Riel. The baggage and the sporting gear might go, but, for the rest, I was bound to carry myself and my arms, together with my papers and a dog, to the Lower Fort and English Settlement. Having decided on this course, I had not much time to lose in putting it into execution. I packed my things, loaded my arms, put some extra ammunition into pocket, handed over my personal effects into the safe custody of the captain, and awaited whatever might turn up.

When these preparations were completed, I had still an hour to spare. There happened to be on board the same boat as passenger a gentleman whose English proclivities had marked him during the late disturbances at Red River as a dangerous opponent to M. Riel, and who consequently had forfeited no small portion of his liberty and his chattels. The last two days had made me acquainted with his history and opinions, and, knowing that he could supply the want I was most in need of – a horse – I told him the plan I had formed for evading M. Riel, in case his minions should attempt my capture. This was to pass quickly from the steamboat on its reaching the landing-place and to hold my way across the country in the direction of the Lower Fort, which I hoped to reach before daylight. If stopped, there was but one course to pursue – to announce name and profession, and trust to the Colt and fourteen-shooter for the rest. My new acquaintance, however, advised a change of programme, suggested by his knowledge of the locality.

At the point of junction of the Assineboine and Red Rivers the steamer, he said, would touch the north shore. The spot was only a couple of hundred yards distant from Fort Garry, but it was sufficient in the darkness to conceal any movement at that point; we would both leave the boat and, passing by the flank of the fort, gain the village of Winnipeg before the steamer would reach her landing-place; he would seek his home and, if possible, send a horse to meet me at the first wooden bridge upon the road to the Lower Fort. All this was simple enough, and supplied me with that knowledge of the ground which I required.

It was now eleven o'clock pm, dark but fine. With my carbine concealed under a large coat, I took my station near the bows of the boat, watching my companion's movements. Suddenly the steam was shut off, and the boat began to round from the Red River into the narrow Assineboine. A short distance in front appeared lights and figures moving to and fro along the shore – the lights were those of

Fort Garry, the figures those of Riel, O'Donoghue, and Lepine, with a strong body of guards.

A second more, and the boat gently touched the soft mud of the north shore. My friend jumped off to the beach: dragging the pointer by chain and collar after me, I, too, sprang to the shore just as the boat began to recede from it. As I did so, I saw my companion rushing up a very steep and lofty bank. Much impeded by the arms and dog, I followed him up the ascent and reached the top. Around stretched a dead black level plain, on the left the fort, and figures were dimly visible about 200 yards away. There was not much time to take in all this, for my companion, whispering me to follow him closely, commenced to move quickly along an irregular path which led from the river bank. In a short time we had reached the vicinity of a few straggling houses whose white walls showed distinctly through the darkness; this, he told me, was Winnipeg. Here was his residence, and here we were to separate. Giving me a few hurried directions for further guidance, he pointed to the road before me as a starting-point, and then vanished into the gloom. For a moment I stood at the entrance of the little village half-irresolute what to do. One or two houses showed lights in single windows, behind gleamed the lights of the steamer which had now reached the place of landing. I commenced to walk quickly through the silent houses.

As I emerged from the farther side of the village I saw, standing on the centre of the road, a solitary figure. Approaching nearer to him, I found that he occupied a narrow wooden bridge which opened out upon the prairie. To pause or hesitate would only be to excite suspicion in the mind of this man, sentinel or guard, as he might be. So, at a sharp pace, I advanced towards him. He never moved; and without word or sign I passed him at arm's length. But here the dog, which I had unfastened when parting from my companion, strayed away, and, being loth to lose him, I stopped at the farther end of the bridge to call him back. This was evidently the bridge of which my companion had spoken, as the place where I was to await the horse he would send me.

The trysting-place seemed to be but ill-chosen – close to the village, and already in possession of a sentinel, it would not do. 'If the horse comes,' thought I, 'he will be too late; if he does not come, there can be no use in waiting,' so, giving a last whistle for the dog (which I never saw again), I turned and held my way into the dark level plain lying mistily spread around me. For more than an hour I walked hard along a black-clay track bordered on both sides by prairie. I saw no one, and heard nothing save the barking of some stray dogs away to my right.

During this time the moon, now at its last quarter, rose above trees to the east, and enabled me better to discern the general features of the country through which I was passing. Another hour passed, and still I held on my way. I had said to myself that for three hours I must keep up the same rapid stride without pause or halt. In the meantime I was calculating for emergencies. If followed on horseback, I must become aware of the fact while yet my enemies were some distance away. The black capote flung on the road would have arrested their attention, the enclosed fields on the right of the track would afford me concealment, a few shots from the fourteen-shooter fired in the direction of the party, already partly dismounted deliberating over the mysterious capote, would have occasioned a violent demoralisation, probably causing a rapid retreat upon Fort Garry, darkness would have multiplied numbers, and a fourteen-shooter by day or night is a weapon of very equalising tendencies.

When the three hours had elapsed I looked anxiously around for water, as I was thirsty in the extreme.

A creek soon gave me the drink I thirsted for, and, once more refreshed, I kept on my lonely way beneath the waning moon. At the time when I was searching for water along the bottom of the Middle Creek my pursuers were close at hand – probably not five minutes distant – but in those things it is the minutes which make all the difference one way or the other.

We must now go back and join the pursuit, just to see what the followers of M. Riel were about.

Sometime during the afternoon preceding the arrival of the steamer at Fort Garry, news had come down by mounted express from Pembina, that a stranger was about to make his entrance into Red River.

Who he might be was not clearly discernible; some said he was an officer in Her Majesty's Service, and others, that he was somebody connected with the disturbances of the preceding winter who was attempting to revisit the settlement.

Whoever he was, it was unanimously decreed that he should be captured; and a call was made by M. Riel for 'men not afraid to fight' who would proceed up the river to meet the steamer. Upon after-reflection, however, it was resolved to await the arrival of the boat, and, by capturing captain, crew, and passengers, secure the person of the mysterious stranger.

Accordingly, when the 'International' reached the landing-place beneath the walls of Fort Garry a strange scene was enacted.

Messrs Riel, Lepine, and O'Donoghue, surrounded by a body-guard of half-breeds and a few American adventurers, appeared upon the landing-place. A select detachment, I presume, of the 'men not afraid to fight' boarded the boat and commenced to ransack her from stem to stern. While the confusion was at its height, and doors, &c., were being broken open, it became known to some of the searchers that two persons had left the boat only a few minutes previously. The rage of the petty Napoleon became excessive, he sacréed and stamped and swore, he ordered pursuit on foot and on horseback; and altogether conducted himself after the manner of rum-drunkenness and despotism based upon ignorance and 'straight drinks'.

All sorts of persons were made prisoners upon the spot. My poor companion was seized in his house twenty minutes after he had reached it, and, being hurried to the boat, was threatened with instant hanging. Where had the stranger gone to? and who was he? He had asserted himself to belong to Her Majesty's Service, and he had gone to the Lower Fort.

'After him!' screamed the President; 'bring him in dead or alive.'

So some half-dozen men, half-breeds and American filibusters, started out in pursuit. It was averred that the man who left the boat was of colossal proportions, that he carried arms of novel and terrible construction, and, more mysterious still, that he was closely followed by a gigantic dog.

People shuddered as they listened to this part of the story – a dog of gigantic size! What a picture, this immense man and that immense dog stalking through the gloom-wrapped prairie, goodness knows where! Was it to be wondered at, that the pursuit, vigorously though it commenced, should have waned faint as it reached the dusky prairie and left behind the neighbourhood and the habitations of men? The party, under the leadership of Lepine the 'Adjutant-general', was seen at one period of its progress besides the moments of starting and return.

Just previous to daybreak it halted at a house known by the suggestive title of 'Whisky Tom's', eight miles from the village of Winnipeg; whether it ever got farther on its way remains a mystery, but I am inclined to think that the many attractions of Mr Tom's residence, as evinced by the prefix to his name, must have proved a powerful obstacle to such thirsty souls.

Daylight breaks early in the month of July, and I had been but little more than three hours on the march when the first sign of dawn began to glimmer above the treetops of the Red River. When the light became strong enough to afford a clear view of the country, I found that I was walking along a road or track of very black soil with poplar groves at intervals on each side.

Through openings in these poplar groves I beheld a row of houses built apparently along the bank of the river, and soon the steeple of a church and a comfortable-looking glebe became visible about a quarter of a mile to the right. Calculating by my watch, I concluded that I must be some sixteen miles distant from Fort Garry, and therefore not more than four miles from the Lower Fort. However, as it was now quite light, I thought I could not do better than approach the comfortable-looking glebe with a double view towards refreshment and information. I reached the gate and, having run the gauntlet of an evily-intentioned dog, pulled a bell at the door.

Now it had never occurred to me that my outward appearance savoured not a little of the bandit – a poet has written about 'the dark Suliote, in his shaggy capote', &c., conveying the idea of a very ferocious-looking fellow – but I believe that my appearance fully realised the description, as far as outward semblance was concerned; so, evidently, thought the worthy clergyman when, cautiously approaching his hall-door, he beheld through the glass window the person whose reiterated ringing had summoned him hastily from his early slumbers. Half opening his door, he inquired my business.

'How far,' asked I, 'to the Lower Fort?'

'About four miles.'

'Any conveyance thither?'

'None whatever.'

He was about to close the door in my face, when I inquired his country, and he replied, –

'I am English.'

'And I am an English officer, arrived last night in the Red River, and now making my way to the Lower Fort.'

Had my appearance been ten times more disreputable than it was – had I carried a mitrailleuse instead of a fourteen-shooter, I would have been still received with open arms after that piece of information was given and received. The door opened very wide and the worthy clergyman's hand shut very close. Then suddenly there became apparent many facilities for reaching the Lower Fort not before visible, nor was the hour deemed too early to preclude all thoughts of refreshment.

It was some time before my host could exactly realise the state of affairs, but when he did, his horse and buggy were soon in readiness, and driving along the narrow road which here led almost uninterruptedly through little clumps and thickets of poplars, we reached the Lower Fort Garry not very long after the sun had begun his morning work of making gold the forest summits. I had run the gauntlet of the lower settlement; I was between the Expedition and its destination, and it was time to lie down and rest.

Up to this time no intimation had reached the Lower Fort of pursuit by the myrmidons of M. Riel. But soon there came intelligence. A farmer carrying corn to the mill in the fort had been stopped by a party of men some seven miles away, and questioned as to his having seen a stranger; others had also seen the mounted scouts. And so while I slept the sleep of the tired my worthy host was receiving all manner of information regarding the movements of the marauders who were in quest of his sleeping guest.

I may have been asleep for some two hours, when I became aware of a hand laid on my shoulder and a voice whispering something into my ear. Rousing myself from a very deep sleep, I beheld the Hudson Bay officer in charge of the fort standing by the bed repeating words which failed at first to carry any meaning along with them.

'The French are after you,' he reiterated.

'The French' – where was I, in France?

I had been so sound asleep, that it took some seconds to gather up the different threads of thought where I had left them off a few hours before, and 'the French' was at that time altogether a new name in my ears for the Red River natives. 'The French are after you!' altogether it was not an agreeable prospect to open my eyes upon, tired, exhausted, and sleepy as I was. But, under the circumstances, breakfast seemed the best preparation for the siege, assault, and general battery which, according to all the rules of war, ought to have followed the announcement of the Gallic Nationality being in full pursuit of me.

Seated at breakfast, and doing full justice to a very excellent mutton chop and cup of Hudson Bay Company Souchong (and where does there exist such tea, out of China?), I heard a digest of the pursuit from the lips of my host. The French had visited him in his fort once before with evil intentions, and they might come again, so he proposed that we should drive down to the Indian Settlement, where the ever-faithful Ojibbeways would, if necessary, roll back the tide of Gallic pursuit, giving the pursuers a reception in which Pahaouza-tau-ka, or 'The Great Scalp-taker', would play a prominent part.

Breakfast over, a drive of eight miles brought us to the mission of the Indian Settlement presided over by Archdeacon Cowley.

Here, along the last few miles of the Red River ere it seeks, through many channels, the waters of Lake Winnipeg, dwell the remnants of the tribes whose fathers in times gone by claimed the broad lands of the Red River; now clothing themselves, after the fashion of the white man, in garments and in religion, and learning a few of his ways and dealings, but still with many wistful hankerings towards the older era of the paint and feathers, of the medicine bag and the dream omen.

Poor red man of the great North-west, I am at last in your land! Long as I have been hearing of you and your wild doings, it is only here that I have reached you on the confines of the far-stretching Winnipeg. It is no easy task to find you now, for one has to travel far into the lone spaces of the Continent before the smoke of your wigwam or of your tepie blurs the evening air.

MAURICE COLLIS
1889–1973

A Dubliner educated at Rugby and Oxford, Maurice Collis was greatly
influenced by the Irish nationalist movement and literary revival and
tried his hand at writing Yeatsian verse. In 1911, however, he joined
the Indian civil service, being posted to Burma where he spent in all
some twenty-five years and rose to be District Magistrate of Rangoon
in 1928. His expressed sympathy with Burmese nationalism
threatened his further promotion and in 1934 he retired to devote
himself to writing. His first book, a study of the traveller and
adventurer Samuel White, was followed by some thirty novels,
biographies, historical works, and travel books, from one of which,
Into Hidden Burma (1953), the following is extracted. His book on
Cortés and Montezuma (1954) was a bestseller and was translated into
six languages. At the age of sixty-eight, Collis took up painting,
holding one-man exhibitions in London and becoming founder
member of the International Association of Art Critics. He contributed
art criticism to national newspapers and other media and wrote a
study of L.S. Lowry.

THE ASTROLOGER

It was with a delightful sense of regained freedom that I took the
noon train for Mandalay on February 24, 1920. Since I had first been
there in 1913 I had always considered it the most delightful official
headquarters in Burma because of its historical associations, the
beauty of the old royal city, and its proximity to the Shan highlands.
As senior magistrate there, or *Myo Wun* as it was called in Burmese, I
should have to try what cases the deputy commissioner transferred
to me and help him by signing papers of a routine nature. The office
hours would not be long, for I always disposed of my cases very

rapidly and, as I believed in trusting my clerks, did not bother and
tire them by unnecessarily checking their entries in the registers. So I
should have ample leisure for writing. I would, too, renew my
acquaintance with the ancient monuments of the place, spend time in
the great bazaar where perhaps I might pick up some works of art,
talk to the people, who had easier and more amusing manners than
in any other town in Burma, and walk by the moat side at sunset to
watch the transmutation of colours, as the light slowly ebbed away.

The train got in at 7 am and in the dry fresh air of the Upper Burma
cold weather I drove in a gharry, that ramshackle form of cab drawn
by a pony of twelve hands, to the government resthouse inside the
old royal city. I had brought with me only my clothes and books; the
rest of my belongings, with the pictures and objects of art I had by
now collected, were stored in Rangoon, to be picked up when I
passed *en route* to Myaungmya.

It was a complete change of scene. Service in Burma had that
characteristic. Two days before I had been an assistant in a Rangoon
office; I was now senior magistrate of the old capital of Burma. In
Rangoon I had belonged to an intellectual set; in Mandalay there was
nothing of that kind. After office I could play tennis at the club or
explore a town which, though it appeared to be no more than a
huddle of wooden houses between the moat of the royal city and the
river Irrawaddy, had its strange corners and unexpected mysteries.

Of my work in Mandalay, where I stayed for only seven weeks, I
remember little. But one trifling case sticks in my mind. A certain
princess brought a complaint against a man for publicly abusing her.
With the fall of the dynasty in 1885 and the dispersal of the court,
many of its inmates continued to live in Mandalay and the government
granted small pensions to women with the title of *minthami* or princess.
The princess in question was the daughter of such a lady of the court,
and custom allowed her to use the title. Her pension was something
very small, about thirty pounds a year. Nevertheless, though poor
and the descendant of a fallen house, she still thought of herself as a
princess. Living in one of the simple wooden houses of a side street
near the moat, in sight of the red royal walls, inside which her
mother had once resided, she was treated by her neighbours with a
little more than ordinary consideration. When, therefore, a small
shopkeeper shouted filthy language at her in the presence of passers-
by, because one of her hens had entered his compound, she was

more humiliated than a mere commoner would have been. The usual penalty in a case of abuse bad enough to lead to a breach of the peace was a fine of ten rupees, about thirteen shillings. I imposed, however, one of thirty rupees and ordered that it be paid in compensation to the complainant, a discretion which the law permitted. In making this order I remarked that, though everyone was talking of democracy, there remained distinctions and that for a princess to be publicly abused was more hurtful to her than it would be, say, for a bazaar girl.

This astonished everyone in court. Thirty-five years before, the British had exiled the King and Queen, shut up the palace and turned out its inhabitants; the princes and princesses, though granted a small maintenance, were never received by authority nor recognised in any way. For a British magistrate, sitting as the *Myo Wun* of the old capital, to go out of his way to give a minor princess face, seemed very odd. But it immensely pleased the population. The country people of metropolitan Burma had not recovered from the shock their minds had sustained at the fall of the dynasty. In their dramas they had an imaginary world into which they could retreat and hear the king's voice as he addressed his ministers, a scene repeated over and over again, which they never grew tired of watching. Kings, queens and princesses, real no longer, had become ghosts of a former glory. But here was a real magistrate treating a live princess with special consideration. It made the British seem less cold.

The princess herself had expected nothing more than a verdict in her favour. Now suddenly she found herself being respectfully congratulated. Early next morning, still in my dressing gown, I was writing verses in my room, when I saw a woman enter the veranda, accompanied by an attendant carrying flowers. It was the princess. She approached and, as I rose to receive her, threw herself at my feet in the ceremonial prostration known as the *shiko*. I begged her to get up, but she would not do so, until she had completed the prescribed movements. When at last she raised herself from the floor, she gave me a bunch of roses. It is not easy for a foreigner to carry off such a situation, particularly when speaking Burmese, a language rich in appropriate polite phrases, not in common use. But she expected nothing, only wanted to thank me, and saying: 'I will never forget,' signed to her maid and went off lightly to her house by the moat.

This little episode gave me in a flash better understanding of Burmese thought and ways than all the hours I might have spent poring over official papers could ever have done.

There was another class of person resident in Mandalay which had also been connected with the old court. The kings of Burma had maintained a corps of astrologers, and most of these men were still alive, living in a quarter together somewhere in the network of wooden houses. I was brought in touch with them through knowing Charles Duroiselle and his wife.

Duroiselle, a Frenchman, was superintendent of the archaeological survey. Archaeology was directed by the government of India. Burma was covered with old sites waiting to be dug, but very little money was allowed for his purpose. My Rangoon friends had written about me to Duroiselle. Accordingly, I took an early opportunity to call at his office and found a typical French colonial savant, rather dry and meticulous. Wretchedly underpaid and engaged on work which the government of Burma thought of minor importance, his manner with me was guarded at first. He was married to a Eurasian wife, a stout half-educated woman of good heart, and this had prevented him from moving in club circles, even if he could have afforded the drink bills. It was hardly likely that the Senior Magistrate, a Civilian, would treat him with more than correctness. But when he saw that I was humbly interested in what he was doing, he thawed and showed me the twelfth-century glazed plaques of Jataka scenes which he had recently excavated at Pagan. The sight of these nearly drove me mad, I so wanted to possess one. Seeing my state he altogether melted and gave me an inscribed votive tablet from Hmawza, the eighth-century Pyu site near Prome, which I had seen when staying at Christmas with Swithinbank. This I carried away in my hand, glancing at it continually, feeling, smelling and even tasting it. The acquaintance was thus well started. After that I was often at his office and was even invited to his house, where I met his Eurasian wife.

Unaccustomed to civilities from officials of standing, Mrs Duroiselle wanted to repay me for mine and, after telling me one day about the late King's astrologers, said that if I cared to have my horoscope cast by one of them, she could arrange it. Nothing could have pleased me better than this chance of exploring a byway of Oriental life. It seemed that a man called Krishna was the best astrologer, and was now employed by the Shan Sawbwas. As the name shows, he was not Burmese; from time immemorial the court of Burma had recruited most of its astrologers from India and some of the present survivors were Manipuri Brahmins. Krishna's fee was seven and sixpence; if I supplied the year, month, day and hour of my birth, he would, for that sum, calculate my celestial map and draw the deductions.

I gave Mrs Duroiselle the money and the particulars and in due course I received from Krishna through her what is called in Burmese a *zada*. It consisted of an oblong of yellow palm leaf, tough and resilient, folded over a core, to which it was bound, both back and front being covered with letters and figures. These, I was told, were scratched with a steel point, and made visible by rubbing ink over the whole surface and immediately wiping it off, when ink remained only in the scratches. On one side was the statement of the time of my birth and the resultant position in the constellations, English and Burmese time being correlated, and on the other was the map itself, a central circle divided into twelve parts with three concentric outer circles divided into sixteen segments, with their appropriate figures. Adjoining were thirty tables, all containing five figures and a name, and the drawing of a *pyathat*, a tiered roof of five stories. The remaining space was filled with no less than 1,058 small squares, a single number in each. The reader will demur that for seven and sixpence I could not have got the manual labour involved in scratching the 1,058 squares, let alone the calculations involved. I can only reply that I have the *zada* before me as I write and that with some trouble and strain to the eyes I have just counted the squares.

Accompanying this curious document (whose craftsmanship is so high that it merits to be called a work of art) was a letter in Burmese containing Krishna's deductions, both general and particular. My name was not mentioned, as Mrs Duroiselle had not given it to him. The sense of the general deductions was that the horoscope was a fortunate one. The owner would become a high official with jurisdiction over land and water; would have a reputation for learning and surpass those with whom he was now associated as an equal. It would be to his own independent efforts rather than to help or patronage that he would owe his advance. In particular it was predicted of the immediate future that he would have a rise in position beginning from April 20, a decline in September, and a recovery from December 1920 to June 1921, when he would return to his native place.

I did not go to see Krishna nor ask him to explain how he had arrived at his conclusions. There seemed no use in putting such a question, because I could not have followed his reply, which would have been framed in Burmese astrological technicalities. Nor did I think of asking whether I was to surpass my then equals as a man of learning or as an official.

One other episode of my stay in Mandalay is worth recalling. This was my visit to the Arakan pagoda. This building, rather a shrine than a pagoda, houses the colossal image of Buddha which was carried away from Arakan in 1784, when the Burmese King Bodawpaya conquered that country. Supposed to have been a likeness of the Buddha made in his lifetime, it was for centuries the palladium of Arakan and, when installed in Mandalay, became Burma's most sacred image. The shrine lies on the southern outskirts of Mandalay and is entered through a long colonnade, on each side of which are bazaar stalls, where you may buy, among other things, food, gold leaf, candles and incense.

When I came out to Burma in 1912, the Burmese did not mind Europeans entering sacred precincts with their shoes on, though they themselves always took them off, as we take off our hats on entering church. After the war of 1914–18 some monks, responding to the first articulate protests against the continuance of an autocratic foreign government, wanted to give the British a rap and had the idea of preaching against their wearing shoes in pagodas. In consequence, pagoda trustees in the principal places had by 1920 begun to put up notices prohibiting shoes. It was foreseen that the British would refuse to take off their shoes, as to do so would render them ridiculous, and so they would have to give up visiting pagodas. The new rule caused some ill feeling in British circles because strolling on pagoda platforms, particularly the Shwedagon's at Rangoon, where there were curious objects to be seen, had always been a favourite pastime. However, there was nothing to be done, as the trustees had the legal right to put up the notices.

In the Mandalay of March 1920 the shoe question, as it came to be called, had not yet reached this state of definition. I had barely heard of it, and though the notice 'foot wearing prohibited' was already up outside the Arakan pagoda, I did not think it would be enforced against me. I had never received anything but politeness from the Burmese; they would not be rude to me, the *Myo Wun*, a man who was known for his goodwill. Nevertheless, confronted by the notice, I inquired from those with me, who included one of the pagoda's trustees, whether there was any objection to my keeping my shoes on. He assured me it would be all right, and I entered the colonnade leading to the shrine where sat the great Buddha, followed by my conductors.

Almost at once I had the uncomfortable feeling that the stallholders had taken note of my shoes and were disturbed at the sight of them. About halfway up a young man appeared from the side and blocked the way, saying something about my shoes. He was clearly irritated and ready to flare into a temper. On the trustee, however, whispering 'the *Myo Wun*', he subsided and stepped aside, though with the look of a person who thought one was behaving badly. We went on and were soon in front of the great image, where it sat beneath the supporting pillars of the central *pyathat* of seven roofs. It had been so plastered with gold leaf by worshippers that its antique beauty was covered up. Rows of candles burnt at the base and incense rose from burning sticks into a ceiling of mosaic. The half light, the strong scent of the incense, monks passing, the sound of gongs, distilled a sense of devotion more intense than I had ever noticed at a Buddhist shrine before, where in general all is gently devout. My conductors were fallen on their knees; I alone remained standing, a conspicuous figure with my shoes on. It suddenly struck me that I was committing a rudeness, and I wished I had not come. The people showed no incivility but were cool and distant. I grew more uncomfortable and felt like an outsider, or worse, like an oppressor who was taking advantage of his office. My escort, however, did not seem aware of this. Having made their bow to the Buddha, they took me on a tour of the precincts, showed me the tank full of huge ancient turtles, a courtyard jumbled with stone inscriptions which Bodawpaya had collected from monastic sites, not for historical but for revenue reasons, and in another courtyard six large bronzes of men and elephants, part of the loot captured by the Burmese from the Siamese in 1564, which in 1599 had been carried away by the Arakanese and in 1784 recaptured by the Burmese. These bronzes, which are among the most curious antiques in Burma, so absorbed me that I forgot my earlier discomfiture.

How excited I should have been, had I known that four years later I would visit the hill in Arakan on which this great image of the

Buddha had originally rested, and that what I heard there would
enable me twenty-two years later to write a book called *The Land of
the Great Image*!

JOHN CORRY
c. 1770–?

Born in County Louth, John Corry was a prolific writer of both
national and local histories as well as of a number of novels, including
The Suicide (1805), and lives of prominent contemporaries and near-
contemporaries, such as William Cowper and George Washington. His
Satirical View of London, from which this passage is taken, was
published in 1801 and ran into many editions. Apart from the satire, it
also comprehended solid tourist information such as 'RATES OF
CHAIRMEN. For any distance not exceeding one mile, 1s. One mile and
a half, 1s 6d; and every half mile afterwards 6d . . . .' It was followed in
1820 by *The English Metropolis*. Corry's *Poems* were published in 1797.
The date of his death is unknown, but it probably occurred in London
some time after 1825.

THE NATIVES OF LONDON

With respect to those tradesmen, artists, and mechanics who inhabit
the city, they are in general a self-opinionated people. Accustomed to
behold the magnificence of the public buildings, and the abundance
of merchandise which fills the shops and warehouses, they, by an
absurd association of ideas, consider themselves connected with this
grandeur and opulence, and hold every foreigner in contempt.

Their pride, however, seldom originates in a consciousness of
personal merit; in that respect it must be acknowledged they are
unassuming. They form a much more judicious estimate of the value
of things; and are proud of their riches, the opulence of their relatives,
comparatively brisk trade, and other accidental circumstances. Their
knowledge is very limited, insomuch that they would prefer a good
dinner, or even a pot of porter and a clean pipe, to the circle of the
sciences.

The intellectual attainments of the citizens in general are either premature or very limited. A boy in London too soon becomes acquainted with amusements, popular opinions, and that general, but superficial knowledge of the world, which is a kind of twilight of intellect. Self-love is productive of pride; the stripling is a man in idea, while he is only a boy in stature. He imagines he has attained the pinnacle of knowledge, and there he stops. Hence his intellectual progress is arrested by vanity, and he attains the age of maturity, but remains an infant in real knowledge.

It must be confessed, however, that the shopkeepers of the metropolis are distinguished by an air of gentility, and are remarkably clean in their person and dress, as far as their business will permit.

In consequence of their too general neglect of learning, many citizens remain in a state of ignorance, which, notwithstanding their expertness in trade, renders them liable to be duped by quack doctors and impostors of every description. Indeed, their self-love is highly gratified by these gentlemen-like foreigners, who come smiling and bowing to impose upon their credulity. They imagine that these strangers are drawn hither by the fame of the capital, and come to admire its inhabitants.

Their mental attainments are generally confined to a knowledge of trade, and a calculation of money; and they really consider themselves as the greatest people in the world. A citizen of London! enviable pre-eminence! This alone confers an imaginary dignity on every rank of citizens, from the sooty sweep-chimney to the gambling stock-jobber.

NATIVES OF ENGLAND, WHO COME FROM DIFFERENT PROVINCES TO RESIDE IN LONDON

These form a very considerable part of this great community; they are in general healthy, active, industrious men, whose assistance in the more laborious avocations is highly conducive to the ease and comfort of the citizens.

A great number of them are shopkeepers, whose probity requires no eulogium. Mechanics form another division, and almost the whole weight of the drudgery of London rests on stout young men from the country, who are allured to town by the expectation of higher wages than the farmers can afford to give. These adventurers find ample scope for the exercise of their corporeal and mental powers in the metropolis, into which they incessantly flow like streams into a reservoir.

They are distinguishable by the peculiarity of their provincial dialect, so different from the language of the cockney; while their florid countenances, and muscular forms, sufficiently evince that they are not natives of a city.

That *good sense* which has ever been the characteristic of the English nation, is the most conspicuous trait of these honest men, whose activity contributes so much to the prosperity of London. A firmness which sometimes borders on obstinacy marks the unsophisticated countryman, who is more sincere, though less polished, than the luxurious citizen.

Goldsmith has distinctly characterised this description of Englishmen in the following lines:

A thoughtful band,
By forms unfashion'd, fresh from Nature's hand!
Fierce in their native hardiness of soul,
True to imagin'd right – above controul.
While e'en the peasant boasts those rights to scan,
And learns to venerate himself as man.

WELCHMEN

Most of the Welch residents in London have imperceptibly adopted the manners of their English neighbours, yet their characteristic sincerity is still perceptible to the reflecting observer.

Honest in their dealings, proud of their ancestry, and inflated with an imaginary superiority which they feel as Ancient Britons, they are too apt to have a contemptuous opinion of the rest of mankind; but they are generally distinguished by that simple dignity of conduct which is ever the companion of integrity.

SCOTCHMEN

The principal motive of a North Briton's visit to London is a desire to profit by his industry and learning. Frugal, temperate, and religious, his natural sagacity is preserved amid the enervating allurements of the town; hence he pursues his avocations with steadiness, and appropriates the fruits of his industry with the strictest economy. His success is facilitated by that national partiality for which Scotchmen are remarkable.

With respect to their merit as authors, Scotchmen have often distinguished themselves as historians, critics, moralists, divines, and physicians.

The natives of Scotland now resident in this metropolis may be divided into four classes: nobility and gentry; merchants and tradesmen; literary adventurers; and labourers: all of whom we shall describe indiscriminately under the general heads.

The Scotch nation has for many ages been remarkable for a steady adherence to Christianity. Their writers have indeed rather represented truth with the solemn air of a recluse, than the more animated demeanour of a smiling grace, but the people have, nevertheless, proved their attachment to her dictates, even to martyrdom!

IRISHMEN

No people of any nation now resident in London present such a curious diversity of character as the Irish.

We shall first classify and delineate those Irishmen most remarkable for their foibles, and conclude with the most estimable.

Among the other qualifications of young Irishmen who migrate to this city their eloquence is the most remarkable. From their constitutional vivacity they are generally possessed of such a superabundance of animal spirits, that their loquacity is astonishing. In almost every tavern or coffee-house you may meet with one or more of these orators, whose wit and fluency are exerted for the amusement of the company.

Whatever be the topic – philosophy, politics, or the news of the day – the Irish orator speaks with impressive energy; and this communicative disposition is, doubtless, sometimes pleasing and sometimes tiresome to his auditory.

Our most sensible poet observes, that

Words are like leaves, and where they most abound
Much fruit of sense beneath, is rarely found.

This is applicable to the Irish orator; but the true cause of his volubility, is the sprightliness of his imagination. This is also the reason why lively Irishmen so often commit blunders, as they generally speak without much reflection or arrangement of ideas. Were we to account physically for this *flux of sounds*, it might be asserted that it is necessary both for the health of the individual and the peace of society, that a volatile Irishman should be privileged to talk as much as he thinks proper – whether sense, nonsense, or as is too often the case, an intermixture of both. For it is probable that those vivid animal spirits, which when volatised fly off from the tip of the tongue, would be taking another course, agitate the limbs, and discharge themselves in kicks and cuffs, to the great annoyance of the community? This hypothesis deserves the attention of the faculty; and if duly investigated by a Scotch or German medical writer, might form a valuable treatise of four or five hundred pages in quarto!

The foible of the Irish nobility and gentry resident in London is a passion for luxurious pleasures; and the virtues which they possess in an eminent degree are candour and generosity. These amiable traits of mind are indeed conspicuous among every class of the Irish nation; even their enemies confess the truth of the assertion. But undoubtedly their candour too often degenerates into insolence, and their generosity becomes profusion. Could they pursue the golden mean equally remote from extremes, they possess the social qualities of the heart, which conduce, in an eminent degree, to the happiness of society.

GENERAL COMPARISON OF THE ENGLISH, SCOTCH, AND IRISH NOW RESIDENT IN LONDON

Though black and white, blend, soften, and unite
A thousand ways; are there no black and white?

POPE

It is amusing to develop the distinguishing traits of the natives of these three kingdoms, now united in one mighty empire.

The *love* of the Englishman, though often intense, is commonly influenced by some secondary consideration; such as riches, or the benefit of a respectable connection. The North Briton loves a *bonny lassie* dearly, and his affection is not diminished by wealth: whilst the Hibernian, though often reproached as a fortune-hunter, generally loves his mistress for her beauty and accomplishments.

The *friendship* of the Englishman is cordial and consistent; the Scotchman is also a sincere friend: but the friendship of the Irishman, though more fervid, is like the blaze of a taper, too often liable to be extinguished by the first gust of his anger.

In *religion* the Englishman is as systematic as in the regulation of his business; the Scotchman is still more strict in performing the duties of his faith; and the Irishman, who loves God and his neighbour as well as either, is but seldom solicitous to appear religious.

In *literature* as in commerce, the Englishman has a large capital, which he improves to the greatest advantage. The Scotchman, who derives part of his intellectual wealth from others as it were by inheritance, applies the rich bequest of Homer, Virgil, and other illustrious ancients, to his own use with propriety; but he rather lives on the interest than increases the stock. On the contrary, the Irishman inherits but little from the ancients. His literary wealth consists in the rich, but unrefined ore of his own genius, with which he adventures to almost every part of the globe, and is often unsuccessful, though sometime his bullion is coined into current money.

For solid learning, sound philosophy, and the happiest flights of the epic and the dramatic muse, the English are superior to any other nation. The Scotch literati, with less claim to originality, successfully pursue the useful study of divinity, history, and criticism; while the Irish, without either the extensive knowledge of the former, or the discriminating sagacity of the latter, excel in genuine wit, ironical humour, and that pathos of sensibility which melts the heart. In support of this assertion, England has produced a Newton, a Milton, and a Shakespeare; Scotland can boast of a Blair, a Robertson, and a Beattie; and Ireland, as a proof of the justice of her pretensions, can bring forward a Swift, a Goldsmith, and a Sterne.

With respect to *pride*, the Englishman glories in the superiority of his country in wealth, trade, and civilisation; and his opinion is confirmed by the appearance of merchants from all nations in London. The ambition of the North Briton is cherished by his learning and the antiquity of his family; and the pride of the Irishman is generally confined to his own endowments, the beauty of his mistress or wife, or the accomplishments of his friend.

Both the Scotch and Irish residents in London seem pretty unanimous in their preference of the productions of their respective countries to those of England. From their eulogiums it should appear, that the oatcakes of the former were, like the heavenly manna, delicious to every palate; and the potatoes of the latter, at least equal in flavour to pine-apples!

LORD DUFFERIN
1826–1902

'Rarely, if ever, has a more interesting visitor set foot on the historic
soil of Iceland than this Irish nobleman, thirty years old, Irish of the
Irish, and beau-ideal of the aristocracy, full of irresistible charm and
fascination', wrote Jon Stefansson in his introduction to the Everyman
edition of *Letters from High Latitudes*, first published in 1857. Born
Frederick Blackwood in Florence, the 1st Marquess of Dufferin and
Ava spent ten years after graduating from Oxford managing his Irish
estates in Clandeboye, County Down. A distinguished career in the
British diplomatic service took him to the governor-generalship of
Canada and the viceroyalty of India, as well as to several
ambassadorial postings. A keen sailor, his account of his northern
voyage took the form of letters to his mother, distinguished in her own
right as author of the poem 'I'm sitting on the stile, Mary'. Dufferin
was wrong in dismissing the early Irish colonisation of Iceland as
evidenced by relics 'supposed to have been left by Irish fishermen'.
He died at Clandeboye.

LETTERS FROM HIGH LATITUDES

STORNAWAY, ISLAND OF LEWIS, HEBRIDES,
JUNE 9, 1856

We reached these Islands of the West the day before yesterday, after
a fine run from Oban.

I had intended taking Staffa and Iona on my way, but it came on so
thick with heavy weather from the south-west, that to have landed
on either island would have been out of the question. So we bore up
under Mull at one in the morning, tore through the Sound at daylight,
rounded Ardnamurchan under a double-reefed mainsail at two pm,

and shot into the Sound of Skye the same evening, leaving the hills of Moidart (one of whose *seven men* was an ancestor of your own), and the jaws of the hospitable Loch Hourn, reddening in the stormy sunset.

At Kylakin we were obliged to bring up for the night; but getting under weigh again at daylight, we took a fair wind with us along the east coast of Skye, past Raasa and Rona, and so across the Minch to Stornaway.

Stornaway is a little fishing-town with a beautiful harbour, from out of which was sailing, as we entered, a fleet of herring-boats, their brown sails gleaming like gold against the dark angry water, as they fluttered out to sea, unmindful of the leaden clouds banked up along the west, and all the symptoms of an approaching gale. The next morning it was upon us; but, brought up as we were under the lee of a high rock, the tempest tore harmlessly over our heads, and left us at liberty to make the final preparations for departure.

Fitz, whose talents for discerning where the vegetables, fowls, and pretty ladies of a place were to be found I had already had occasion to admire, went ashore to forage, while I remained on board to superintend the fixing of our sacred figure-head, executed in bronze by Marochetti, and brought along with me by rail, still warm from the furnace.

For the performance of this solemnity, I luckily possessed a functionary equal to the occasion, in the shape of the second cook. Originally a guardsman, he had beaten his sword into a chisel, and become a carpenter; subsequently, conceiving a passion for the sea, he turned his attention to the mysteries of the kitchen, and now sails with me in the alternate exercise of his two last professions. This individual, thus happily combining the chivalry inherent in the profession of arms with the skill of the craftsman and the refinement of the artist – to whose person, moreover, a paper cap, white vestments, and the sacrificial knife at his girdle, gave something of a sacerdotal character – I did not consider unfit to raise the ship's guardian image to its appointed place, and after two hours' reverential handiwork, I had the satisfaction of seeing the well-known lovely face, with its golden hair, and smile that might charm all malice from the elements, beaming like a happy omen above our bows.

Shortly afterwards, Fitz came alongside, after a most successful foray among the fish-wives. He was sitting in the stern-sheets, up to

his knees in vegetables, with seven elderly hens beside him, and a
dissipated looking cock under his arm, with regard to whose
qualifications its late proprietor had volunteered the most satisfactory
assurances. I am also bound to mention, that protruding from his
coat-pocket were certain sheets of music, with the name of Alice,
Louisa, written thereon in a remarkably pretty hand, which led me to
believe that the Doctor had not entirely confined his energies to the
acquisition of hens and vegetables. The rest of the day was spent in
packing away our newly purchased stores, and making the ship as
tidy as circumstances would admit. I am afraid, however, many a
smart yachtsman would have been scandalised at our decks, lumbered
up with hen-coops, sacks of coal, and other necessaries, which, like
the Queen of Spain's legs, not only ought never to be seen, but must
not be supposed even to exist, on board a tip-top craft.

By the evening, the gale, which had been blowing all day, had
increased to a perfect hurricane. At nine o'clock we let go a second
anchor; and I confess, as we sat comfortably round the fire in the
bright cheerful little cabin, and listened to the wind whistling and
shrieking through the cordage, that none of us were sorry to find
ourselves in port on such a night, instead of tossing on the wild
Atlantic, though we little knew that even then the destroying angel
was busy with the fleet of fishing-boats which had put to sea so
gallantly on the evening of our arrival. By morning the neck of the
gale was broken, and the sun shone brightly on the white rollers as
they chased each other to the shore; but a Queen's ship was steaming
into the bay, with sad news of ruin out to seaward, towing behind
her boats, water-logged, or bottom upward, while a silent crowd of
women on the quay were waiting to learn on what homes among
them the bolt had fallen.

About twelve o'clock the Glasgow packet came in, and a few
minutes afterwards I had the honour of receiving on my quarter-
deck a gentleman who seemed a cross between the German student
and swell commercial gent. On his head he wore a queer kind of
smoking cap, with the peak cocked over his left ear; then came a
green shooting jacket, and flashy silk tartan waistcoat, set off by a
gold chain, hung about in innumerable festoons, while light trousers
and knotty Wellington boots completed his costume, and made the
wearer look as little like a seaman as need be. It appeared, nevertheless,
that the individual in question was Mr Ebenezer Wyse, my new

sailing-master; so I accepted Captain C.'s strong recommendation as a set-off against the silk tartan; explained to the new comer the position he was to occupy on board, and gave orders for sailing in an hour. The multitudinous chain, moreover, so lavishly displayed, turned out to be an ornament of which Mr Wyse might well be proud; and the following history of its acquisition reconciled me more than anything else to my Master's unnautical appearance.

Some time ago there was a great demand in Australia for small river steamers, which certain Scotch companies undertook to supply. The difficulty, however, was to get such fragile tea-kettles across the ocean; five started one after another in murderous succession, and each came to grief before it got halfway to the equator; the sixth alone remained with which to try a last experiment; should she arrive, her price would more than compensate the pecuniary loss already sustained, though it could not bring to life the hands sacrificed in the mad speculation; by this time, however, even the proverbial recklessness of the seamen of the port was daunted, and the hearts of two crews had already failed them at the last moment of starting, when my friend of the chain volunteered to take the command. At the outset of his voyage everything went well; a fair wind (her machinery was stowed away, and she sailed under canvas) carried the little craft in an incredible short time a thousand miles to the southward of the Cape, when one day, as she was running before the gale, the man at the wheel, startled at a sea which he thought was going to poop her, let go the helm, the vessel broached to, and tons of water tumbled in on the top of the deck. As soon as the confusion of the moment had subsided, it became evident that the shock had broken some of the iron plates, and that the ship was in a fair way of foundering. So frightened were the crew that, after consultation with each other, they determined to take to the boats, and all hands came aft, to know whether there was anything the skipper would wish to carry off with him. Comprehending the madness of attempting to reach land in open boats at a distance of a thousand miles from any shore, Wyse pretended to go into the cabin to get his compass, chronometer, etc., but returning immediately with a revolver in each hand, swore he would shoot the first man who attempted to touch the boats. This timely exhibition of spirit saved their lives; soon after the weather moderated; by undergirding the ship with chains, St Paul fashion, the leaks were partially stopped, the steamer reached her destination, and was sold for £7000 a few days after her arrival. In token of their gratitude for the good service he had done them, the Company presented Mr Wyse on his return with a gold watch, and the chain he wears so gloriously outside the silk tartan waistcoat.

And now good-bye. I hear the click click of the chain as they heave the anchor; I am rather tired and exhausted with all the worry of the last two months, and shall be heartily glad to get to sea, where fresh air will set me up again, I hope, in a few days. My next letter will be from Iceland; and, please God, before I see English land again, I hope to have many a story to tell you of the islands that are washed by the chill waters of the Arctic Sea.

REYKJAVIK, ICELAND,
JUNE 21, 1856

We have landed in Thule! When, at parting, you moaned so at the thoughts of not being able to hear of our safe arrival, I knew there would be an opportunity of writing to you almost immediately after reaching Iceland; but I said nothing about it at the time, lest something should delay this letter, and you be left to imagine all kinds of doleful reasons for its non-appearance. We anchored in Reykjavik harbour this afternoon (Saturday). H.M.S. *Coquette* sails for England on Monday; so that within a week you will get this.

For the last ten days we have been leading the life of the 'Flying Dutchman'. Never do I remember to have had such a dusting: foul winds, gales, and calms – or rather breathing spaces, which the gale took occasionally to muster up fresh energies for a blow – with a heavy head sea, that prevented our sailing even when we got a slant. On the afternoon of the day we quitted Stornaway, I got a notion how it was going to be; the sun went angrily down behind a bank of solid grey cloud, and by the time we were up with the Butt of Lewis, the whole sky was in tatters, and the mercury nowhere, with a heavy swell from the north-west.

As, two years before, I had spent a week in trying to beat through the Roost of Sumburgh under double-reefed trysails, I was at home in the weather; and, guessing we were in for it, sent down the topmasts, stowed the boats in board, handed the foresail, rove the ridge-ropes, and reefed all down. By midnight it blew a gale, which continued without intermission until the day we sighted Iceland;

sometimes increasing to a hurricane, but broken now and then by sudden lulls, which used to leave us for a couple of hours at a time tumbling about on the top of the great Atlantic rollers – or Spanish waves, as they are called – until I thought the ship would roll the masts out of her. Why they should be called Spanish waves no one seems to know; but I had always heard the seas were heavier here than in any other part of the world, and certainly they did not belie their character. The little ship behaved beautifully, and many a vessel twice her size would have been less comfortable. Indeed, few people can have any notion of the cosiness of a yacht's cabin under such circumstances. After having remained for several hours on deck, in the presence of the tempest – peering through the darkness at those black liquid walls of water, mounting above you in ceaseless agitation, or tumbling over in cataracts of gleaming foam, the wind roaring through the rigging, timbers creaking as if the ship would break its heart, the spray and rain beating in your face, everything around in tumult – suddenly to descend into the quiet of a snug, well-lighted, little cabin, with the firelight dancing on the white rosebud chintz, the well-furnished book-shelves, and all the innumerable knick-knacks that decorate its walls, little Edith's portrait looking so serene, everything about you as bright and fresh as a lady's boudoir in May Fair, the certainty of being a good three hundred miles from any troublesome shore, all combine to inspire a feeling of comfort and security difficult to describe.

These pleasures, indeed, for the first days of our voyage, the Icelander had pretty much to himself. I was laid up with a severe bout of illness I had long felt coming on, and Fitz was sea-sick. I must say, however, I never saw any one behave with more pluck and resolution; and when we return, the first thing you do must be to thank him for his kindness to me on that occasion. Though himself almost prostrate, he looked after me as indefatigably as if he had already found his sea legs; and, sitting down on the cabin floor, with a basin on one side of him, and a pestle and mortar on the other, used to manufacture my pills, between the paroxysms of his malady, with a decorous pertinacity that could not be too much admired.

Strangely enough, too, his state of unhappiness lasted a few days longer than the eight-and-forty hours which are generally sufficient to set people on their feet again. I tried to console him by representing what an occasion it was for observing the phenomena of sea-sickness from a scientific point of view; and I must say he set to work most conscientiously to discover some remedy. Brandy, prussic-acid, opium, champagne, ginger, mutton-chops, and tumblers of salt water, were successively exhibited; but, I regret to say, after a few minutes, each in turn *re*-exhibited itself with monotonous punctuality. Indeed, at one time we thought he would never get over it; and the following conversation, which I overheard one morning between him and my servant, did not brighten his hopes of recovery.

This person's name is Wilson, and of all men I ever met he is the most desponding. Whatever is to be done, he is sure to see a lion in the path. Life in his eyes is a perpetual filling of leaky buckets, and a rolling of stones up hill. He is amazed when the bucket holds water, or the stone perches on the summit. He professes but a limited belief in his star, and success with him is almost a disappointment. His countenance corresponds with the prevailing character of his thoughts; always hopelessly chapfallen, his voice is as of the tomb. He brushes my clothes, lays the cloth, opens the champagne, with the air of one advancing to his execution. I have never seen him smile but once, when he came to report to me that a sea had nearly swept his colleague, the steward, overboard. The son of a gardener at Chiswick, he first took to horticulture; then emigrated as a settler to the Cape, where he acquired his present complexion, which is of a grass-green; and finally served as a steward on board an Australian steam-packet.

Thinking to draw consolation from his professional experiences, I heard Fitz's voice, now very weak, say in a tone of coaxing cheerfulness –

'Well, Wilson, I suppose this kind of thing does not last long?'

The Voice, as of the tomb – 'I don't know, Sir.'

Fitz – 'But you must have often seen passengers sick.'

The Voice – 'Often, Sir; *very* sick.'

Fitz – 'Well, and on an average, how soon did they recover?'

The Voice – 'Some of them didn't recover, Sir.'

Fitz – 'Well, but those that did?'

The Voice – 'I know'd a clergyman and his wife as were ill all the voyage; five months, Sir.'

Fitz – (Quite silent).

The Voice, now become sepulchral – 'They sometimes dies, Sir.'

Fitz – 'Ugh!'

Before the end of the voyage, however, this Job's comforter himself fell ill, and the Doctor amply revenged himself by prescribing for him.

Shortly after this a very melancholy occurrence took place. I had observed for some days past, as we proceeded north, and the nights became shorter, that the cock we shipped at Stornaway had become quite bewildered on the subject of that meteorological phenomenon called the Dawn of Day. In fact, I doubt whether he ever slept for more than five minutes at a stretch, without waking up in a state of nervous agitation, lest it should be cock-crow. At last, when night ceased altogether, his constitution could no longer stand the shock. He crowed once or twice sarcastically, then went melancholy mad: finally, taking a calenture, he cackled lowly (probably of green fields), and leaping overboard, drowned himself. The mysterious manner in which every day a fresh member of his harem used to disappear, may also have preyed upon his spirits.

At last, on the morning of the eighth day, we began to look out for land. The weather had greatly improved during the night; and, for the first time since leaving the Hebrides, the sun had got the better of the clouds, and driven them in confusion before his face. The sea, losing its dead leaden colour, had become quite crisp and burnished, darkling into a deep sapphire blue against the horizon; beyond which, at about nine o'clock, there suddenly shot up towards the zenith a pale, gold aureole, such as precedes the appearance of the good fairy at a pantomime farce; then, gradually lifting its huge back above the water, rose a silver pyramid of snow, which I knew must be the cone of an ice mountain, miles away in the interior of the island. From the moment we got hold of the land, our cruise, as you may suppose, doubled in interest. Unfortunately, however, the fair morning did not keep its promise; about one o'clock, the glittering mountain vanished in mist; the sky again became like an inverted pewter cup, and we had to return for two more days to our old practice of threshing to windward. So provoked was I at this relapse of the weather, that, perceiving a whale blowing *convenient*, I could not help suggesting to Sigurdr, son of Jonas, that it was an occasion for observing the traditions of his family; but he excused himself on the plea of their having become obsolete.

The mountain we had seen in the morning was the south-east extremity of the island, the very landfall made by one of its first discoverers.[1] This gentleman not having a compass (he lived about AD 864), nor knowing exactly where the land lay, took on board with him, at starting, three consecrated ravens, as an MP would take three well-trained pointers to his moor. Having sailed a certain distance, he let loose one, which flew back; by this he judged he had not got halfway. Proceeding onwards, he loosed the second, which, after circling in the air for some minutes in apparent uncertainty, also made off home, as though it still remained a nice point which were the shorter course toward terra firma. But the third, on obtaining his liberty a few days later, flew forward, and by following the direction in which he had disappeared, Rabna Floki, or Floki of the Ravens, as he came to be called, triumphantly made the land.

The real colonists did not arrive till some years later, for I do not much believe a story they tell of Christian relics, supposed to have been left by Irish fishermen, found on the Westmann islands. A Scandinavian king, named Harold Haarfager (a contemporary of our own King Alfred's), having murdered, burnt, and otherwise exterminated all his brother kings who at that time grew as thick as blackberries in Norway, first consolidated their dominions into one realm, as Edgar did the Heptarchy, and then proceeded to invade the Udal rights of the landholders. Some of them, animated with that love of liberty innate in the race of the noble Northmen, rather than submit to his oppressions, determined to look for a new home amid the desolate regions of the icy sea. Freighting a dragon-shaped galley – the *Mayflower* of the period – with their wives and children, and all the household monuments that were dear to them, they saw the blue peaks of their dear Norway hills sink down into the sea behind, and manfully set their faces towards the west, where – some vague report had whispered – a new land might be found. Arrived in sight of Iceland, the leader of the expedition threw the sacred pillars belonging to his former dwelling into the water, in order that the gods might determine the site of his new home: carried by the tide, no one could

---

1 There is in Strabo an account of a voyage made by a citizen of the Greek colony of Marseilles, in the time of Alexander the Great, through the Pillars of Hercules, along the coasts of France and Spain, up the English Channel, and so across the North Sea, past an island he calls Thule; his further progress, he asserted, was hindered by a barrier of a peculiar nature, neither earth, air, nor sky, but a compound of all three, forming a thick, viscid substance which it was impossible to penetrate. Now, whether this same Thule was one of the Shetland Islands, and the impassable substance merely a fog, or Iceland, and the barricade beyond, a wall of ice, it is impossible to say. Probably Pythias did not get beyond the Shetlands.

say in what direction, they were at last discovered, at the end of three years, in a sheltered bay on the west side of the island, and Ingolf[2] came and abode there, and the place became in the course of years Reykjavik, the capital of the country.

Sigurdr having scouted the idea of acting Iphigenia, there was nothing for it but manfully to beat over the remaining hundred and fifty miles, which still separated us from Cape Reikianess. After going for two days hard at it, and sighting the Westmann islands, we ran plump into a fog, and lay to. In a few hours, however, it cleared up into a lovely sunny day, with a warm summer breeze just rippling up the water. Before us lay the long wished-for Cape, with the Meal-sack – a queer stump of basalt, that flops up out of the sea, fifteen miles south-west of Cape Reikianess, its flat top white with guano, like the mouth of a bag of flour – five miles on our port bow; and seldom have I remembered a pleasanter four-and-twenty hours than those spent stealing up along the gnarled and crumpled lava flat that forms the western coast of Guldbrand Syssel. Such fishing, shooting, looking through telescopes, and talking of what was to be done on our arrival! Like Antæus, Sigurdr seemed twice the man he was before, at sight of his native land; and the Doctor grew nearly lunatic when, after stalking a solent goose asleep on the water, the bird flew away at the moment the schooner hove within shot.

The panorama of the bay of Faxa Fiord is magnificent, with a width of fifty miles from horn to horn, the one running down into a rocky ridge of pumice, the other towering to the height of five thousand feet in a pyramid of eternal snow, while round the intervening semicircle crowd the peaks of a hundred noble mountains. As you approach the shore, you are very much reminded of the west coast of Scotland, except that everything is more *intense*, the atmosphere clearer, the light more vivid, the air more bracing, the hills steeper, loftier, more tormented, as the French say, and more gaunt; while between their base and the sea stretches a dirty greenish slope, patched with houses which, themselves both roof and walls, are of a mouldy green, as if some long-since inhabited country had been fished up out of the bottom of the sea.

The effects of light and shadow are the purest I ever saw, the contrasts of colour most astonishing – one square front of a mountain

2 It was in consequence of a domestic feud that Ingolf himself was forced to emigrate.

jutting out in a blaze of gold against the flank of another, dyed of the darkest purple, while up against the azure sky beyond rise peaks of glittering snow and ice. The snow, however, beyond, serving as an ornamental fringe to the distance, plays but a very poor part at this season of the year in Iceland. While I write, the thermometer is above 70°. Last night we remained playing at chess on deck till bedtime, without thinking of calling for coats, and my people live in their shirt sleeves, and – astonishment at the climate.

And now, good-bye. I cannot tell you how I am enjoying myself, body and soul. Already I feel much stronger, and before I return I trust to have laid in a stock of health sufficient to last the family for several generations.

DESMOND FENNELL
1929–

Born in Belfast and educated in Dublin, where he graduated with a
degree in Modern History from University College, Desmond Fennell
travelled widely as a young man in Europe, the USA, the USSR and the
East. 'By Irish standards I am a city man,' he wrote, 'but in the world I
set out to see I was quickly made to understand that I was essentially a
peasant and came of a nation of peasants.' Editor from 1964 to 1968 of
an international review of theology, philosophy and politics based in
Freiburg and Dublin, he then moved to the Conamara Gaeltacht (Irish-
speaking region) where he helped to launch the first Gaeltacht
political movement and wrote and broadcast extensively in Irish. He
has been subsequently a university lecturer, journalist, author and
broadcaster, with a particular interest in the effect of nationalism in
Ireland and the wider world. This evocation of rural Japan is from his
1959 travel book, *Mainly in Wonder*.

WEEKEND IN BOSO

It was the rainy season in June and the meteorologists ran almost no
risk at all in predicting a rainy weekend. But there are times when
you just must get out of Tokyo. Nakata-san thought I was mad, but
he was Japanese and would never say so directly. I told him I was
Irish and loved rain. I knew he wanted to practise his English and I
was glad he was coming for he was a good interpreter.

The Boso peninsula stretches for nearly a hundred miles south-
east of Tokyo and we were heading for Shirahama, a small fishing
town, at the tip of it. We took a train on the Sunday morning and got
to a straggling place called Tateyama about noon. That's a market
town and seaside resort ten miles from Shirahama. There was a bus
waiting and we left the town along a bumpy road. There were some

71

girls on the bus dressed smartly in city fashion – they were probably working in towns. But all the old women wore the blue kimonos with white patterns which you see on peasant women all over Japan. Some young men too wore dapper city clothes.

In Shirahama we wandered down the main street looking for a place to eat. At the end of a lane we saw a house that was evidently a sort of worshipping place. There were a few tombstones in front. We walked over to it and looked through the glass of the sliding door. There was a shrine with a Shinto mirror in the centre – the mirror is a symbol of God – and there were beads hanging over it and many vases of gaudy artificial lotus flowers around. The lotus and beads were Buddhist so this was evidently a combined Shinto-Buddhist shrine. At the other end of the long room we could see tatami mats spread out and three or four old women were sitting around a brazier. One of them saw us and came to the door. Would we come in and have a rest? Nakata-san asked could we have tea and they said yes.

So we went and bought some buns and things at a shop. We sat on the tatami mats and the old women made a big kettle of green tea and cut up a dishful of cucumber slices, which they served us with soya sauce. One of the old women lived in that house, the rest had come there to chat. There was a photograph displayed on the wall of a group of the local men around the fire-pump which the village had acquired three years before. One of the women had spent forty years in Tokyo and knew it well. She was very intelligent and the others looked up to her. When we asked questions about life in Shirahama and so on, they said, '*She* can answer, we don't know.' She knew the kabuki theatres of Tokyo well.

The local girls in Shirahama, she said, preferred Western dress to Japanese. They get married about twenty-one or twenty-two. Usually they have their husbands chosen for them. She thought a foreigner – she meant a Westerner – made a good husband for a Japanese girl. They were very kind to their wives, she said. A few village girls had gathered in the door of the house by now and she asked me which I'd like to marry. I asked her which she thought the prettiest and I was surprised that our choices coincided.

The village had three temples, she said, all of the Zen Buddhist sect. Where we were was apparently just a 'place of worship' in that general sense that Far Easterners find natural. Times, she said, were much better now than when she was young. There were plenty of jobs going today – she meant in the towns and in far-away Tokyo. We had still to find an inn so we thanked the old ladies and bowed to them and went off to look for one.

The biggest inn in Shirahama was full of film people on location. We settled with a smaller one for bed and breakfast, at 500 Yen or ten shillings. I left Nakata-san there to take his bath and a nap and I went towards the lighthouse. It was raining, of course. The waves were breaking perfunctorily along the line of rocks, and the straw shacks of the *amahs* or diving women stood here and there. They leave their clothes in these shacks and when they come out of the water they sit around big fires inside and warm themselves.

Not far from the lighthouse was an isolated shop-cum-restaurant for the summer season and four or five people inside were looking intently at me. I smiled under their gaze and a mad young man opened the door and called out to me to come in. I went in and sat down. The mad fellow introduced himself as Takahashi. He said he was with the film people from Shintoho Studios on location. They were doing a film called *The Trembling of the Amah*. The other people were the shopkeeper and his family. They showed me a magazine that had featured photos of the local diving women and I discovered a drawing of W.B. Yeats amidst the jungle of Japanese writing and six lines of his poetry printed in English –

Wine comes in at the mouth
And love comes in at the eye;
That's all we shall know for truth
Before we grow old and die.
I lift the glass to my mouth,
I look at you, and I sigh.

I could understand the Japanese liking that – sensitive, melancholy hedonists that they are.

Takahashi-san asked me to look him up in his hotel that night and he shook hands extravagantly and vowed eternal friendship.

I went down to the rocks and saw a group of almost naked boys diving in the water close to the shore and hunting fish with spears. There was a boat a bit offshore and many *amahs* lying on the water around it with their little round baskets bobbing. Every now and again their heels would show for a second and they were gone. A couple of minutes later they'd reappear beside their baskets. Some *amahs* in other parts dive for pearls, but these were after a kind of conical shellfish that clings to the sea-bottom. The rain was driving and the wind sent the sea swelling on to the rocks. The bodies of the diving women floated there and they were one and the same thing with the elements. It was a wedding of long standing, an intimate and primeval embrace.

It began to rain very heavily on the way back to the town and I took shelter in a shop. There was a man and his wife and a fat smiling girl. When they asked in Japanese where I was from, I said Ireland, but that meant nothing to them. I made signs with my hands and said 'Near England'. As soon as the girl heard 'England' she smiled at her mother and said 'Gentleman!' She was a village girl and probably knew two or three English words, no more. But here in this Japanese back-of-beyond the news and the concept of England had penetrated, inseparably linked with the idea of a 'gentleman'. I was impressed.

Some *amahs* began to arrive from the sea, carrying their baskets, on their way home. There had been an *amah* in the shop already when I arrived – tall and lean, her face bronzed and healthy. You could always recognise them. Her husband was away on a long sailing voyage, she said. I took a snap of one of the *amahs*, a young woman, carrying her basket and walked with her towards the town until she turned off towards her home.

Back at the inn I had my bath. They had a pretty bathroom with an artificial stream and rocks and so on and an old man scrubbed my back for me. Nakata-san had got a bit of a chill, taking a nap after his hot bath. We went and had a good rice meal in a shop near the lighthouse and took a look at a Shinto shrine nearby. One of its *torii* or ceremonial gates was at the very edge of the water, to greet the fishermen as they landed. There were votive cloths with writing on them in the shrine itself – they had been put there by the fisher people.

We went to visit my *amah*, the one I had taken a photo of. There was a narrow room at one end of the house and the end wall of that room slid back. She was sitting on the tatami mat near this opening and a little boy lay sleeping against her bare breasts. Children are weaned very late in Japan. Her father-in-law was lying on the tatami behind her wearing one of those loose house kimonos that they call *yukatas.* She told us she went diving most days from April to September. On a good day she would get 1,500 Yen worth – about thirty shillings – of the shellfish. On a bad day, 300 Yen worth. Her father-in-law had a sightseeing boat. In the off-season he fished for sardines. The tourist season in Shirahama was late July and August. Many of the shops and little restaurants closed during the winter. Her husband was away with the deep-sea fishing fleet.

Her mother-in-law arrived back then, a smiling, stout woman. She asked us had we had our evening rice. The girl said she would be diving in the morning at nine o'clock – we would see her if we came down. Her name was Nami, which means 'Wave'.

We went to the hotel where the film people were staying and looked up Takahashi-san. I think he had been drinking *sake* or beer. He gave us a great welcome and brought along a couple of his friends. We sat in the ballroom and had beer. He told us that he played gangster and tough parts in films, did stunts and the like. He kept telling us in Japanese and broken English that he was a No. 1 actor in the Shintoho studios. He pointed to one of his friends and said he was a No. 7. A third chap said very humbly that he was a No. 10. He was new to the studio. An effeminate type, just out of a Tokyo university – the very opposite of Takahashi-san. Takahashi-san talked loudly of his exploits in *kendo* or Japanese fencing, told how good he was at judo and how magnificently he swam. We must come and see him at the studio in Tokyo, he said, and he kept shaking hands with me vigorously. Film people – actors, producers and the director – kept passing through the room, dressed in the strange clothes that film people wear. Someone brought Takahashi-san a guitar. He played extremely well and he promised to sing something if *I* did. So on that condition I sang *Kelly the Boy from Kilann*. Then the Japanese sang *Sakura* or 'Cherry-blossom', which is their most popular song.

We left Takahashi-san still in boisterous mood and made a detour along the sea-front before heading for bed. Coming back down the street Nakata-san was looking for fruit – the shops were still open, though it was after ten. Suddenly Takahashi-san appeared out of one of the fruit shops and hailed us in. He was sitting with the shopkeeper's family in back and it was clear that he had got to know them well. The shopkeeper was there and his wife, a tall, strong, handsome woman, and a plump, pale girl – as evidently *not* an *amah* as her mother evidently *had* been one – and the girl's sickly-looking brother.

We asked the people for fruit and passed it around and Takahashi-san called for tea. He began to relate his film exploits in detail. He showed the cuts on his foot where a rock had caught him in a dive and the big woman nodded in professional appreciation. He showed his crushed little finger and told us the ranks he had reached in kendo and judo. A couple of girls had drawn near and were standing listening from the shop outside. He told how he had arrived in a clap of thunder as Superman and – quite seriously – how he could reach America faster than jet planes. He had a charmed life, he said, luck had always been with him – except in love, he said sadly, except in love.

Soon after, we got up to go and he insisted on paying for the fruit. As we passed out he made a joking remark to one of the girls who had been listening. She answered saucily and he slapped her bottom. She slapped him back on the bare arm and I saw her tremble as she touched the sinewy limb. I wondered for a moment at his unsuccess in love. And then it became suddenly clearer, and I saw him as an odd man out, a bashful boaster, one of the world's sad harlequins.

We went to the inn and found that our beds had been spread and the square green tent of the mosquito net hung above them. The serving girl who had shown us in that afternoon came and asked did we want anything and we said a little tea. We'd have got to sleep then if it hadn't been for her.

When we arrived at the inn for the first time that day, she and the hostess had knelt in the doorway to greet us, as the custom is in Japan. She had taken our shoes from us and served us tea in our room. She had been wearing a skirt and blouse then and when she brought the tea she stopped to chat a little. Now it was near eleven at night and she stood in the door of our room in a lovely red and white kimono, that she had put on for the evening. She had made herself up a bit and looked very pretty. She was about twenty-one. I sat under the green mosquito net and drank the green tea she had brought. Nakata-san stood outside the net.

She told us she was from the fishing village of Mera, a few miles away. Her father was dead, she said. She spoke impulsively and very expressively. 'What's your big ambition in life?' I asked her. 'To find a wonderful husband!' she said, and her face was ecstatic. 'Mightn't you like to have a hotel of your own, like this one?' 'Yes,' she said, but with her husband. She had only had this job a few months, she said. Before that she had been telephone operator in a geisha house in Tokyo. She had wanted to become a geisha, but her big sister, who was married and lived in Yokohama, wouldn't let her. Then her mother became very ill and she had come home to Mera to look after her. The hotel job was handy, because she was always near home. 'But you wanted to be a geisha,' I said. 'That's very different from marrying.' 'I know,' she said, 'I used to want that, but not now. Now I want a man. I don't care whether he's from Tokyo or whether he's a farmer or a fisherman. I just want a wonderful man!'

She said she didn't like the hotel job much. It wasn't a very suitable job for a young girl. Often a group of men would come and take a room together and she'd have to serve them when they'd stay up late drinking. They sometimes said rude things to her, talked about her being a little girl still and knowing nothing. If she were married, it would be different, she said. What did she think of a Westerner as a husband for a Japanese girl? If he meant it in earnest and wasn't just playing, he'd be fine, she said. She said good night and we went to sleep. I awoke after midnight and the house was still astir. It was hot and there were a lot of mosquitoes, but they were outside the net.

I awoke again at six and went out walking. The first light of early morning, that false light that doesn't last, was lying on the rice fields. I walked away from Shirahama towards a farming village. Clear water was gushing through the channels between the rice fields. 'Water the life of the rice', it sang, 'and rice the life of man'. Women were washing clothes and chattering at a washing trough in the fields. A woman passed me weighed down under a heavy load she was carrying on a ladder-like frame. Then I passed an old woman walking with no burden, but her back was bent almost parallel with the ground from a lifetime of carrying. Children putting on their clothes stared at me through a window. Over the gateways to the farmhouses hung tufts of splayed rope, one of the sacred symbols of Shinto.

I went past the houses through the rice fields to the foot of the wooded hills. There was a Shinto shrine there and I sat on a hewn stone at the entrance. There was movement in the rice fields, the first early workers walking to their patches, some already bending their backs. Soon, the converging streams of schoolchildren came, picking their way along the narrow banks between the paddies. Hundreds of frogs croaked. A couple of little girls came out of the house and looked at me, the new god or devil, sitting at the entrance to their shrine. They went away and shortly afterwards some more little girls and boys peeked out from the wings, so to speak, and then walked timidly across the stage trying not to look at me.

Now and again a woman came from the fields, went up the steps to the shrine, clapped her hands to attract God's attention and prayed with bowed head before the wooden grill in the shrine door.

I went and looked inside. Through the grill I could see an empty room with one of the large slit chests for throwing in money offerings. There was another grill behind and, beyond it, some indistinguishable objects. Perhaps the women knew what was there.

I left the shrine and a man washing himself at a fountain near his house looked up at me. I walked towards the school and skirted it to avoid a stampede. I met some older boys arriving and they were very dignified and looked very deliberately not at me. When they had passed, they turned around and stared after me.

I walked back to the inn and found Nakata-san up. The serving girl was folding up the mattresses and bed clothes. Her face was drawn and sleepless. We left the inn and walked towards the rocks. We saw a group of five men – obviously city men – tramping about and wearing only loose kimonos – *yukatas* they call them – and very obvious and unbeautiful underwear. One sat to get his photo taken and his flannel drawers were certainly the most impressive part of the picture. Nakata-san, who lived a lot in the world of proverbs, told me of one that said, 'Whoever has shame on an outing is a fool.'

We went back to the town and started walking towards Chikura, a big fishing town about ten miles away, there we were going to get the train back to Tokyo. The coastal scenery on our right was gentle, and to our left, towards the land, crags rose steeply. They were partly wooded and reminded me of the Rhine. Rice fields lay between these crags and the sea. Now and again we passed a little stone statue set in a niche along the highway and clothed in a red robe. That was a *jizo* or local guardian – or, as some call him, the Wayside God. We passed through fishing villages with dozens of fine sturdy boats. I looked into some houses. The paper of the sliding screens was often soiled and torn, which was not a sign that these people were slovenly, but that they hadn't much money. A tripod generally stood in the living-room over a charcoal fire and there was a kettle on it for making green tea. But the cooking kitchen was always separate, or even outside in a small outhouse. In some houses there were incongruous pieces of Western furniture – a dressing-table or the like.

After a few hours' walk we reached a village, where we decided to take a bus. It was at the bus-stop that we met Horii-san. He had soon told us his name, but the very first thing he told us was that he was a student at Waseda, one of the two best universities in Tokyo. He knew by the look of us that we were from Tokyo. His home was in Chikura and he had been home for the weekend. He had a pleasant, husky voice, unusual for a Japanese. The bus came and Horii-san took us in hand. We wanted fried fish for lunch? We would get it. In Chikura we got out at a hotel where he straightway ordered it. He telephoned for a taxi and it took us to his house.

His house had a shop in front and he helped himself to cigarettes. The place was by itself, down towards the sea and was quite an extensive establishment. Dwelling-house, outhouses – one he laughingly called the 'summer villa' – it had a broad floor spread with tatami. 'You can come here in the summer – pay 60 Yen a day. Some of my friends come – on their way to better places. They like helping around the house.' He had already told us that his father owned two ocean trawlers. We found his mother in an outhouse sorting onions, an old wizened woman. She uncovered her head and bowed to us. We met his grandfather walking about the garden – a healthy, wiry-looking old sailor. He said 'You wouldn't believe I'm eighty-six, would you?' I said no, not for a minute. He laughed with great satisfaction. As we walked away he asked Nakata-san how old I was.

From a height we could see the sea and the rocks. They had a sizeable Shinto shrine on their land, complete with *torii*. His father, Horii-san told us, was away now off the northern island with one of his boats and his crew of thirty. The town sent out about five hundred men on motor-trawlers. We got into the taxi again and went on a tour of the port. There were lots of boats from other parts and men at work everywhere – on the boats, the nets, in the fish warehouses. Several people waved to Horii-san and looked at me. The last street we came down was the town's Ginza – every Japanese town has its Ginza named after the great Ginza avenue in Tokyo.

Horii-san dismissed the taxi at the hotel without paying anything. We were shown to an upstairs room with a couple of scroll paintings, some pieces of Buddhist sculpture and a finely-carved transom. The open window gave us a view of the landscape garden and the countryside. Horii-san told us his father and uncle were Waseda graduates, the only ones in Chikura. Two of his brothers, including the eldest, were in the fishing with his father. He himself was in a quandary. Should he come back here when he had finished in Tokyo and enjoy the prestige of a Waseda graduate in a small town? Even more than that – because of his family's position and the importance of Chikura, he could be one of the bosses, as he put it – the dispensers of influence – in Chiba Prefecture. (Chikura is a town of Chiba Prefecture, which stretches for a hundred miles to the north of it.) Or should he stake his chances on Tokyo, where he would be much less at first, but could get farther in the end?

Life in Chikura was limited, he said. That was true. There were no regular dances, only now and again at the big festivals, a dance in the schoolhouse – and old Japanese dances on the beach. Boys and girls didn't really come together and most of them had their marriages arranged for them. There was no big café or the like and nothing like Sunday church-going, which was such a useful social get-together for country-people in the Western world. In Chikura, even the bars were small. And of course, there was gossip.

He laughed and said, 'Sometimes gossip has its advantages. Already it's all around the town that I have an American visitor and have been showing him the town from the car. That gives me a lot of face.'

So many young people were leaving the town now to work in Tokyo. Why, in the Tokyo department store, near where he lodged, there were about thirty Chikura girls and he had to be careful not to go there with a girl, or the word would be all round Chikura next day. Of course, they expected him to come back and marry a Chikura girl, but he would much prefer to marry one from Tokyo.

We had finished our lunch and our beer. We paid for it and Horii-san called the genii of the taxi and took us to the station. He was going the ninety-odd miles to Tokyo himself that night on a fish-lorry. He told us where we could find him there.

It was about four in the afternoon. We got on the train that would leave us in Tokyo at nightfall, when the great city of eight and a half millions puts on its neon, bares its phosphorescent fangs, and calls once again the heady tune that has the boys and girls of Chikura dancing. Not only of Chikura. There were many Chikuras in the old Japan.

ROBERT GIBBINGS
1889–1958

The son of a canon of Cork's Church of Ireland cathedral, Robert
Gibbings studied medicine for two years at the city's University
College before turning to art and continuing his education at the Slade
School, London. After war service with the Royal Munster Fusiliers, he
took up engraving, becoming a founder member of the Society of
Wood Engravers in Britain. From 1924 to 1933 he was proprietor of the
Golden Cockerel Press, which specialised in fine limited editions,
many illustrated by himself. From 1936 to 1942 he taught book design
at the University of Reading. With *Sweet Thames Run Softly* (1940), an
account of a river journey by punt, he embarked upon a highly
successful series of eight travel books, illustrated with his own
engravings and ranging from the South Seas to Europe and his native
Cork, a series that combined his eclectic talents as writer, engraver,
book designer and naturalist. He died at Oxford in January 1958. This
extract is from *Over the Reefs* (1948).

THE IRISH OF THE PACIFIC

I found little comfort in Apia until I found 'Tina's'. Then I found
luxury; a large room for a study, with a bedroom adjoining, and both
of them opening on to a balcony from which I could look across the
harbour to the town and its encircling hills. Frank, the only other
lodger in the house, was working for an examination and was also in
love, 'either of them enough to keep a man quiet'.

'You won't be disturbed. I'll see to that,' said Tina; and she did.

Instead of being a headquarters, the house very soon became a
home. Whether I got back early or late from an expedition there was
always a welcome. 'Come in, come in! Did you have a good trip? I
made a lemon pie for lunch, I thought you'd be back, but I saved a
piece for your dinner. And I've got you a bottle – on lease-lend from

Frank. I said, Frank, that man's coming back today, I must have something for him. Are you hot now? Do you want a shower before your tea? Mind the paint in the bathroom, it's wet. There was a man in here asking for you, a Major somebody – said he met you in Fiji. I said you were a busy man, couldn't see anybody. And that girl in the store, she came round wanting you to make a picture of her. I said you go along get your photo taken, Mr Gibbings got no time for that, he's working hard on his book. I've taken the chair out of Frank's room for you; he doesn't need it. You can have another pillow from his bed, too, if you like – he won't miss it.'

Although Tina was strict with casual callers, established friends had no difficulty in finding me. Usually I had warning of their approach from Tina's conversation shouted to them as they mounted the stairs. 'Mind yourself on the back balcony; Frank's got Nancy's bicycle up there. She left it on the road where the truck would go over it.' Or: 'Have you got any eggs at Mulifanua? I must have some. Mr Gibbings likes them for his sandwiches.' Or: 'Why didn't you come in the daylight? I could have shown you my new banana plants.'

One day Captain Matheson of the schooner *Tagua* came to see me. They were sailing for the Tokelau Islands next day, he said, and there was a spare bunk on board. Would I care to come? The doctor would be coming too, on a tour of inspection, and there was a chap called Deasy, a trader, who wanted to have a look around. We would have a day or two at each of the three islands while they were putting stores ashore and taking copra on board. He suggested that I should bring with me any old shirts that I could spare, or a few lengths of cotton or some bars of soap, to trade for mats – 'the best mats in the Islands,' he said.

So the following afternoon I was on board the schooner, and we were heading north for the Tokelaus, three hundred miles away. Nothing to do but sit in the shade of the mainsail, watch the sea go by, and listen to the chief engineer or Sparks, the radio operator, or Deasy, spinning yarns and arguing.

Deasy, who comes from Donegal, has been in the Islands for twenty years. 'Disi,' the natives call him. His fair skin has never got used to the tropical sun and is constantly peeling, and his shock of red hair has never got used to discipline and is always in revolt. He is lean and active, ever ready to turn his hand to anything, but restless, never able to stay long in one place.

'I'm a rolling stone,' he said, 'and I'm gathering little moss; I'm not even getting a polish.'

'You're Irish and you're just like the Samoans. You don't care much for hard work, you'd rather sit about and talk,' said the chief engineer. He and Deasy were old friends.

'And may I ask,' said Deasy, 'why you're sweating your soul out in the engine-room day after day? Isn't it only to earn enough to retire on and do damn all ever after?'

'The Samoans are the Irish of the Pacific. They're always agin the Government,' said the chief.

Deasy stretched his hands above his head as if to claw down chunks of atmosphere. 'Isn't every country in the world agin a government that isn't its own? Isn't every patriot a rebel to the other side?'

'Let's talk about love,' said Sparks.

'In the Cook Islands,' said the doctor, 'there's a curfew at nine o'clock every night. Any one found out of doors after that is fined. It isn't so very long since any young couple walking together after dusk had to carry a lighted torch between them, just to show they weren't holding hands. Yes, and if a man was seen to cry over a dead woman that wasn't an immediate relation of his he was hauled off to the court and fined.'

The three islands of the Tokelau group, Fakaofu, Nukunono, and Atafu, to which we were sailing, suffered grievously from slave-raiders during the latter half of the nineteenth century. Between the years 1850 and 1870, and in particular during the period from 1862 to 1864, the islands were raided by ships from South America, 'black-birding' for the guano islands and sugar plantations of Peru. The population was almost exterminated. A native teacher, resident at that time on Atafu, wrote: 'This is my letter. Our country is destroyed. All our people have been carried away in a foreign ship. They were deceived by offers of trading. The captain told them to take off to the ship coco-nuts and fowls to sell, and he brought forth some cloth and a shirt and trousers, and said to the men, bring your coco-nuts and fowls to buy these things. Then I said, come on shore and purchase. The captain replied, I don't wish to purchase ashore; it will be better to buy aboard . . . All the people of this island are carried off. They have taken the chief, Oli, who was in Samoa, and thirty-four other men. All that now remain here are women and children, and six male adults. Sir, it is most piteous to witness the grief of these women and children. They are weeping night and day; they do not eat, there is none left to provide food for them, or to climb the coco-nut trees. They will perish with hunger.'

At about the same time two hundred and forty-seven men, women, and children were kidnapped from Fakaofu, of whom only one ever returned; 'many of the women far advanced in pregnancy, others with children at the breast.' Only eighty inhabitants out of several hundred were left on Nukunono. It was a widespread traffic. From Nukulaelae in the Ellice group, five hundred miles to the west, they captured nearly three hundred out of a population of about four hundred. Not one ever returned. From Penrhyn, eight hundred miles to the east, they took close on a thousand, most of whom died away from home. From Pukapuka they took about a hundred, of whom only one saw home again. Easter Island, four thousand miles to the south-east, and others not so far away, Niue, Manihiki, Mangaia, all suffered in the same way.

But the only things that we hoped to take from the islands were spiders, rats, and mats. The doctor wanted all the spiders he could collect for a museum in New Zealand; he wanted to inspect the rats for fleas, which are carriers of plague, for the sake of the islanders; and we both wanted mats for the sake of our floors. Meanwhile, having arrived, we had to get ashore.

The Tokelau canoes are very much bigger than the craft one sees in Samoa, many of them being up to forty feet in length – in the olden times still longer. Nevertheless, they do not inspire any great confidence. The bottom of the hull is composed of sections of a hollowed tree which meet, end to end, without morticing, and are held together with lashings of sennit. The sides are a built-up patchwork of many irregular scraps of wood shaped to fit each other, and, like the sections of the keel sewn together with sennit – a technique evolved owing to the scarcity of large trees on the atolls. One's emotions are mixed when, a mile from the shore, with only a few inches of freeboard and a thousand fathoms of water below, one watches fountains of water pouring through the holes only partly filled by the stitching. But the Tokelau bailer is shaped to fit the inside curve of the canoe, and the flood of events is to some extent controlled.

The reef is wide, and successive lines of waves surge in obliquely. If, now, they are charging from the right, a moment later there will be a broadside from the left. Only by constant quick changes of direction were we able to reach calm water and wade towards the glare of the white sand, forgetting the glare of the sea.

Fakaofu is an atoll of sixty islets surrounding a lagoon, triangular in shape, about seven miles in length and five at its greatest width. The average height of the land above sea level is not more than a dozen feet. The whole population, of close on six hundred, lives in an overcrowded condition on one islet – so overcrowded that piers have been built into the lagoon to give further ground space for houses. Many of the other islets would be equally suitable for habitation, but there is rivalry between Protestant and Catholic congregations, and each needs all its adherents close at hand. They still remember that one of their high chiefs was killed in a war between champions of the two creeds.

But the village is a model of town planning, with roads and paths carefully laid out and edged with stone. Even the chickens have their appointed roosts. Though free to roam during the day, each one returns at night to its own perch, set up over a rectangle of sand and edged with stones like the road.

No sooner were we ashore than it seemed to the crowd of inquisitive children who had surrounded us that the doctor was showing signs of lunacy. Pointing to the sky, he appeared to be offering cigarettes to any child who would go there. His audience was bewildered. At first they thought he was being playful for their benefit, and crowded round him; but, with further and more excited gesticulations on his part, they thought he was mad, and edged away. Just then the policeman appeared in sight. 'Come quickly,' shouted the doctor, 'come quickly! Tell them I want that spider. There it is – hanging from that breadfruit leaf, about two feet down.'

The children burst out laughing. The chiefs who had gathered to watch became solemn, as if anxious. This was the official who had come to inspect their health. But a boy went up the tree, and with a long wand entangled the web and brought the spider to earth.

'Tell them,' said the doctor, 'that I'll give a cigarette for every spider they bring me.'

The children were incredulous.

'And tell them,' he added, 'that I'll give two cigarettes for every rat they bring me.' This was too much even for the composure of the chiefs. They, too, burst out laughing. 'I want to see what fleas they are carrying,' said the doctor. That was funnier still. And because I had come ashore with the doctor, and because I seemed to understand what he was doing, I was classed as a potential lunatic. I couldn't move without being followed by a crowd of hopeful children. If I stopped to look at one of the long poles, forked at the end, with which they twist the breadfruit from the upper branches of the trees; or if I paused beside a house to look at the clusters of empty coco-nuts strung on sennit with which they draw water from their wells; or if I watched an old woman husking coco-nuts on an iron spike stuck in the ground; or a young man boring a hole in a piece of timber with the point of a spiral shell to make a patch for his canoe, my action was fraught with possibility. I might at any moment do something sensational. They found it hard to understand why I should be interested in a few balls carved out of a solid piece of wood. It was to them the obvious way of making and storing cricket balls. When a new one was wanted it was only a matter of cutting it from those that hung ready made in the house. That the doctor, too, should want to take away such commonplace things as fish-hooks and paddles, not to mention the wooden buckets with water-tight lids in which fishermen carry their food when at sea, was altogether astonishing.

THOMAS COLLEY GRATTAN
1792–1864

Intended for the law, Thomas Grattan, born in Dublin, the son of a
Kildare landowner, opted for the Louth Militia. Failing in a military
career, he decided to emigrate to South America, but met en route to
France an Irish girl whom he married and settled with in the Bordeaux
region. He moved to Paris where he embarked upon a literary career
and became the friend of Thomas Moore, Washington Irving,
Lamartine and others, and a regular contributor to the *Edinburgh*
Review. His own journal, the *Paris Monthly Review of British and*
Continental Literature, survived only a few issues and in 1828 he moved
to Brussels, where his house was destroyed in the 1830 revolution. He
lived thereafter in Antwerp and Heidelberg, producing among other
works a successful history of the Netherlands. In 1839, through the
influence of King Leopold I, whose respect he had earned, Grattan,
now again living in Brussels, was appointed British Consul to the State
of Massachusetts. He lived in London from 1846, continuing to write,
and his prolific output included fiction and travel. *Tales of a Walking*
Gentleman (1823), from which this extract is taken, combines
both genres.

ONE MAN AND HIS DOG

Travelling, as I always do, without guide or compass, it is no merit
of mine if I sometimes light on pleasing scenes, or mix with interesting
people. I have traversed France from frontier to frontier; cut across
the highways, and struck into the open country; passed by where
curiosity is generally arrested; loitered in spots unknown to Fame or
Fashion; always yielding to the impulse of feeling or the whim of
fancy. Chance has so often led me into scenes of soft adventure, that
I ask no other pilot; but had I made the most nicely-balanced choice,

I could not have better suited my taste than in that district called Le Périgord, and the country bordering upon it.

Sauntering along the course of the river Dordogne, I had left far behind me the mountains of Auvergne; but I occasionally stopped to observe the autumnal sunbeams playing round their distant peaks. I dwelt on the recollection of the wondrous scenes they exhibit, and marvelled that so few of our travellers had explored their secret charms – until I recollected that they were inaccessible to the approach of four-wheeled carriages. They gradually melted from my sight, and new and different beauties turned my thoughts aside.

I had seen the Dordogne in the heart of those rugged hills – born in volcanic sources, nursed on beds of lava, and swathed with basaltic hands – a riotous little stream, hurrying on its passage with the waywardness of a noisy child. A little further I had fancied it to glide along in the quiet and smiling loveliness of female youth, through groups of gentle acclivities, of wild yet verdant aspect. Now, I paced its widely-separated banks, and marked it swelling into full-grown beauty, rolling its course with conscious dignity along congenial plains; while tufts of stately trees, converted by my imagination into enamoured lovers, wooed their liquid mistress with bent and graceful branches, which wafted salutation, or sipped her passing sweets. A little more, thought I, and this proud beauty sinks into that sea, where all rivers are finally lost! – and I was just getting into a train of deep analogies, when I was roused by the flapping wings of a covey of partridges behind me. I turned, and saw my dog fixed steadily at a point at some distance. I cocked my gun, but the game had escaped me. Ranger came slowly forward with a surly and reproving look, such as many a musing sportsman has observed, when the faithful follower, who has done so well his duty, would tell you that you have neglected yours.

In all my rambling I am accompanied by my dog; not that I despise the companionship of man – far from it. But where can we find a friend so like ourselves, with thoughts and feelings so moulded into ours, that he will think and talk, stand still, move forward, eat, drink, and sleep in perfect unison with us? This strict coincidence exists not between men; and without this, such a course as mine is better run alone. Pursuits there are, and pleasures, it is true, which two minds sufficiently congenial may soothingly follow together. Hours, nay, days entire, of social fellowship have fallen to my lot; and I look forward with hope to a renewal of such intercourse, when ripened thought shall have mellowed the young fruit of earlier associations. But to wander for months in foreign scenes; to mix with strange society, yet be not a stranger in it; to give the mind up to that reflective abandonment which likes to revel uncontrolled, you must have no companion but your dog. With him you have no ceremony to constrain you; and he, poor thing, is ready for your every mood. If you are gay, he frisks and capers; if sad, he trudges slowly on, and thinks, or seems to think, as deeply as yourself. When you eat, he has always a ready appetite; when out of the reach of food, he murmurs not. Lie down to sleep, he is your guardian; rise up when you will, you will find him freshly at your call. A gun is the natural accompaniment of a connexion like this. It gives both employment and amusement to man and beast. It is a passport for the woods and mountains; an excuse for idleness; a remedy against painful thought; and removes the mendicant and vagabond air from a poor fellow who journeys with a wallet and a staff. In France one runs but little risk of stoppage or impediment. I do not speak of the environs of cities, of fortified towns, or military posts. These naturally bring with them a train of ills – suspicion, petty tyranny, and insult. But in the happier portions of the kingdom, where rustic occupation takes place of warlike possession; where the fields are paced by the husbandman, not trodden down by the soldier, a traveller may feel himself at home. A straggling gendarme sometimes asks to see his licence, but a foreign face is nearly always a sufficient protection. As I, however, was furnished with both, I walked unmolested – a privileged man. Never yet did surly keeper drive me from a preserve; and often has the honest proprietor of some rural spot invited me, in passing, to kill his game, and share his dinner too.

But to return. – The birds were wild, and flew high in the direction of the rising ground which lay to my left. I marked them into a thick copse, behind which rose a young plantation. Thither I bent my steps, and Ranger soon led me to the prey. I got a couple of shots, and brought down my birds. The remainder of the covey rose wildly round me, and scattering over the plantation, I quite lost their trace.

The day was young and warm. I walked towards a projection which commanded a charming view, and afforded at the same time shelter from the sun. Arrived at this little point, I flung myself under the shade of an acacia, my gun beside me, and Ranger not far off. It was one of the sweetest moments of my life. I seemed throned on the very summit of repose. Far beneath me spread the fertile plain of Bergerac, bounded on each side by chains of hills, and divided into nearly equal parts by the broad and placid river. The richly-wooded landscape was sprinkled with cottages, and showed here and there the tall chimneys of a château, rising among the foliage; or the smoke from some humbler habitation, hid in a mass of chestnut trees, whose leaves protect the peasant from the heat, and whose fruit is his chief nourishment. Three or four small towns lay in sight; the one from which I had last started just visible in the distance.

It was vintage time, and numerous groups of grape-gatherers were scattered in the valleys, as happy as they were busy; for their joyous songs and bursts of merriment rose up from all sides on the pure and gentle breeze. A party of sportsmen ranged through the low grounds by the river, and an occasional shot came sharply on the highly rarefied air. The bark of an ill-trained dog, and the shout of the country people, when a partridge or a hare escaped their pursuers, were borne to my ear with a distinctness as perfect as if each group were close beside me. Many deeply-laden boats were floating down the river, gaily and unobstructed; the helmsmen unemployed, and the drowsy passengers carelessly leaning over the sides. One solitary barge, managed by a single boatman, was working its way against the current. Ungarnished by canvass or streamer, it formed a striking contrast to those which passed so rapidly by. The very breeze was hostile, and seemed to sport in the fluttering sails of the others, like those light and worthless parasites who fan the minions of good fortune. They swept in quick succession round a point that hid them from my view. Others came on, and were alike soon lost to me; but the single boat, working against both wind and tide, appeared, though ever moving, ever to stand still. I felt, that if I chose to indulge in similes, I had a parallel at hand: but I felt this without asperity or discontent, and seemed at the moment to rise above ill fate.

BEATRICE GRIMSHAW
c. 1880–1953

Brought up in Belfast, Caen and London, Beatrice Grimshaw was a no-nonsense Ulsterwoman who, with the might of the British Empire behind her, found no difficulty in quelling obstreperous natives with a glance. She was, nevertheless, a dedicated and unrelentingly inquisitive traveller who, at a time when lone women explorers were far from common, was a genuine pioneer. She was the first white woman to reach remote areas of Borneo and New Guinea, including the Sepik River valley, and her books, most of which are concerned with the South Pacific, seriously examine the complex issues raised by colonisation. *From Fiji to the Cannibal Islands* (1917), from which this extract is taken, records her travels in the Fiji Islands and the New Hebrides in 1905.

NIGHT ON THE WAINIKORO

Northward of Viti Levu ('Great Fiji'), where I had been travelling, lies Vanua Levu ('Great Land'), the second largest island of the group. It is over one hundred miles long, and thirty miles across. On the map, it looked interesting and easy; so I took a steamer up to Lambasa, the principal port, intending to see something of the island.

Six weeks afterwards, I came back, having travelled about a hundred and eighty miles in the interior; spent the best part of a month, in different slices of time, waiting for steamers; and learned, once for all, what being 'off the road' really meant. Viti Levu was a mere summer's day picnic compared to Vanua Levu. Stanley (I cannot get rid of the comparison) would have liked Vanua Levu. He would have enjoyed the total absence of bridges, the fine profusion of swamps and gullies, the days when the men had to keep their knives always ready to hack a path through choking lianas, the

91

mornings when it rained horribly, and one had to go on, and get
soaked; the evenings when one had to put up in a house without any
doors, each open doorway serving as a sort of opera-box for a score
or two of greatly excited and interested natives, looking on eagerly at
the performance inside. He would have liked to eat ancient biscuits
soaked through with rain, and thoughtfully wrapped up by one of
the men in a spare sulu, *only* half soiled – he would have enjoyed
rough-washed clothes, cleaned by himself in a river with a scrap of
toilet soap – the acquirement of a permanently scarlet nose would
not have grieved him as it grieved me, and I am quite sure that he
wouldn't have got surly and unamiable every time it was necessary
to dirty his clothes with wet red clay.

I do not apologise for writing about the mere personal impressions
of this trip, because many books of travel have taught me that the
modesty which omits them is mistaken. Most people like to know
how a traveller in out-of-the-way regions feels and thinks; without
such details, the account becomes a mere dose of undiluted geography.

There were some small risks in the Vanua Levu journey, but no
genuine perils; many little hardships, but no starvation, fever, thirst,
dangerous heat or cold. The only real difficulty was the responsibility,
which, hour after hour, and day after day, lay somewhat heavily on
my unaccustomed mind, new to uncivilised travel. I wanted to see
and understand the resources of the country for myself, and to this
end, it was necessary to select the best tracks, from data furnished by
a mass of incoherent native statements, badly translated – to decide
where to go, in a country where each rare white settler knew his own
neighbourhood, and very little beyond – to keep my horse from
breaking his legs, or getting drowned, every hour in the day, prevent
my men from running away, and keep myself in good condition on a
diet of tinned meat, dry biscuit, and milkless tea. All these were tasks
that called for a good deal of energy, trifling though they might
appear to those real explorers whose feats I was faintly copying, as
Early Victorian ladies used to copy fine steel engravings in pale
niggling pencil-work. Yet I enjoyed the trouble, enjoyed even the
inconveniences, after a fashion, since they were richly paid for, in the
pure gold coin that Nature mints for sailors, campers, and gipsy
wanderers alone. Some need, so exceedingly deep down in the roots
of humanity that one cannot even define or name it, seems to be
satisfied by wanderings such as these. It is a need not felt by all

(though lying latent in very many who never suspect its existence, until sudden changes of circumstances call it out), and those who do not experience it find it hard to understand. Yet it is one of the strongest forces in the world – hunger, love, the lust of battle, alone can rank with it in power over humanity. The 'Song of the Road' – the 'Call of the Wild' – and other names coined by an analytical generation for this unknown force, leave the kernel of the matter untouched. But those who know what it is to *come home* to Earth, understand the meaning of the call, although at the very coming, she lays a cold finger on their lips for welcome, and says, 'You shall know, you shall enjoy, but you shall never tell. . . .'

. . . After the monotony of Society in Suva – after the days under galvanised iron roofs, and the chatter about infinite nothings, and the long-tailed frocks worn in shaded, scented drawing-rooms – came the out-of-doors again; 'boot-and-saddle' once more (it hurt my sense of the dramatic unities to think that I didn't wear boots, but shoes), and again the rough, half-known country of the kindly brown man. Lambasa is the only oasis of civilisation on Vanua Levu, and even it consists merely of a Colonial Sugar Refining Company estate, with what Goldsmith would have called 'all its busy train' of Indian and Solomon Island labourers, and white managers, overseers, clerks and mechanics. There is a store or two, also a Government Armed Native Constabulary Station, and outside, the wilderness. No roads, no towns save some Fijian villages, no white men, except stray specimens at intervals of several days' ride; no regular mails, no stores, save a little shanty or two at very wide intervals, kept by Indians or Chinese. Even the native villages are far apart; you may journey twenty miles without seeing one, whereas in Viti Levu there is always food and shelter within ten miles at farthest.

Nor are the people of Vanua Levu like the people of Viti Levu. Farther away from civilisation, and less under the influence of their own chiefs, they are rougher and wilder in every way than the natives of the greater island. In Viti Levu, any native I might chance to meet on the road at once removed his head-band, and laid down his bundle from his shoulder (both acts of respect), whereas in Vanua Levu, parties of Fijians travelling along the bush tracks would stare boldly and rudely, swagger past with their head-bands in place, and even keep their bundles of food on their shoulders while passing –

which, in a Fijian, is simply an act of deliberate rudeness and defiance.
Nor did my men remonstrate with them for their discourtesy. A
Fijian, at best, is only outwardly submissive to the white race. He is a
craven at heart, and therefore easily kept down by the British rule;
but loyalty to an employer is not one of his virtues. Attack from these
natives was a thing barely within the bounds of possibility, so I did
not fear it; but I knew that if any trouble had occurred, my three big
Fijians would simply have run away to avoid being concerned in it,
and left me to see it out by myself.

Hearing that there was a good deal of excellent native land available
at Wainikoro, some twenty-two miles from Vuo, where I landed, I
secured a horse, and engaged a couple of carriers to accompany
myself and Gideon, my special interpreter and servant, whom I had
brought on from Viti Levu. The horse belonged to the local Buli, and
had every vice that a native horse can have. He shied, in a manner
that I can only classify as virulent, deleterious and disconnective; he
bit like a rat at bay; he kicked at me one-leggedly, like a misogynistic
ostrich; he was thick in the wind, didn't like hills, was afraid of
slippery places, and endeavoured (apparently as a matter of principle)
to wipe me off against every cocoanut-tree he met. Such as he was,
however, he was the only means of travel available, so I engaged him
for a few weeks, and trusted to time and care to improve his manners.
The men named him 'Somo-somo,' and always addressed him by his
title. I asked what it meant, and they told me, 'Fiji flower, plenty
good flower' – which led me to infer that either their knowledge of
horses was small, or their charity large; for if Somo-somo was the
flower of Fijian horseflesh, it did not say much for the remaining
steeds of the colony.

The Flower did not like my side-saddle, first of all; secondly, he
entered a protest against that unexpected outrage, my riding-habit;
and thirdly, he objected very strongly, in gross and in detail, to
myself. These prejudices having been overcome in some degree, and
a start made from the hospitable house where I had been entertained
on my arrival, we got on our way to Wainikoro.

The chiefs of Vanua Levu would not allow their men to go away
for more than a few days, so (as a Buli, or chief, has power over all the
men in his district, and none of them can leave it without his
permission) I had several different sets of carriers during my
journeyings, instead of keeping the same men right through, as in

Vanua Levu. This was not so good a plan, as the men were making less money, and were therefore much more prone to desert me, and to lag carelessly behind, over country where they could easily have beaten my horse. On the way to Wainikoro, I saw little of them, except at meals. There was no question in Vanua Levu of the demoralising Capuan luxury that I had experienced on the Singatoka. Villages were far apart, and poor, and though the contents of my purse obtained sufficient food for all, there was no superfluity.

Half the day's journey to Wainikoro lay through 'The Company's' fields of bright green sugar-cane. Afterwards, we came into woods beautiful as all the Fijian forests are, and most pleasantly cool. The track was about a couple of feet wide in most places, and so steep that a good deal of walking had to be done. Gideon was in his element, with a new audience for his boastings and braggings about me. I caught odd fragments of conversation, as we journeyed on, that told me my social status was increasing. In Viti Levu, I had merely been an intimate friend of King Edward's. Here I was an 'Andi', or princess, according to Gideon: I had bags full of gold, and a hundred boxes of clothes in Suva – he had carried them up from the steamer himself. I was such a great lady that I lived on tinned meat and biscuit every day, and constantly had tea with sugar in it, and I was splendidly generous, as befitted such a personage; for every now and then I would give as much as sixpence to buy tobacco for the men (Fijian tobacco, of which one gets a good handful for that sum), and I often gave away whole quarter-pounds of sugar, just to eat as they liked. I had a revolver that would kill twenty men at a mile away, and I had fought all through the Boer War (in which struggle the Fijians took the warmest interest), shot hundreds of Boers, and cut their heads off afterwards. . . . With these and other fictions did my henchman entertain the gaping carriers, who evidently swallowed every word, and, in consequence, respected their informant all the more, in that he was privileged to be the servant of such a celebrity.

I was not sorry that the men stayed out of sight a good part of the day, for I could enjoy the beauty of the scenery better when quite alone, and it certainly was very lovely. Once the track broke suddenly out of a grove of feathery ironwoods into the staring sun, and dipped downwards towards a wide green plain bordered by brown and purple hills, with just one line of distant mountain peaks rearing their blue battlements on the horizon. . . . Only a range of mountains, covered with reeds and forest here and there, rough and uninteresting, no doubt, when one reached it, with ups and downs and gullies and thickets just like the ground about my feet, and yet. . . . And yet, if I could write all that those distant summits said to me, as they lay sleeping in the still yellow light of the waning afternoon – all that the eternal hills, far away and blue and utterly out of reach, have said to countless souls since the beginning of time – I should speak with the tongues of men and angels, and tell what human lips have never told, and never will.

I turned the horse down into the valley, and soon the woods shut in the path again. But for long after, as I rode through the quiet forest, with no company but the murmuring hill-river at my side, two lines from some half-forgotten poet kept chanting in my mind sadly, as befitted the lonely land and the waning day:

> . . . The heights of heaven
> Where I shall never win.

Sunset was near, and sunset, in these latitudes, means dark. I waited for the men, and told them they must hurry. It was well that I did so, for we came soon to a place where the track disappeared in a bog, and 'Somo-somo' had to be coaxed and driven over the narrowest part, where it was quite safe for him to cross, although he could not be induced to see the matter in that light at first. After ten minutes' dragging and yelling and beating, he was compelled to make the attempt, and landed safely on the opposite side, not without a flounder or two that made me glad I had the sense to dismount. Then one of the carriers opened a window into that strange storehouse of contradictions and oddities, Fijian character, and showed me the queerest curiosity it had yet furnished – a specimen of Fijian sense of humour. He had watched the horse being got over with a perfectly grave countenance, but as soon as it was fairly across and I was mounting again, he went to the side of the track, carefully picked out a soft piece of grass, laid aside his load, and, flinging himself down on the ground, began to roll and kick and screech with a mad, violent, almost terrifying laughter, that surpassed any effort in that direction I could have imagined in my wildest dreams. That any human being could laugh like that, and not kill himself, was in itself a most astonishing thing. He choked, he crowed, he howled, he let out wild, eldritch yells that woke all the echoes of the black, sinister valley along which we were travelling; he lay on his face and kicked, he lay on his back and writhed, he gave himself over body and soul to a very devil of laughter. And, at intervals, he screeched, in a voice half choked with cackling: 'The horse wouldn't go over. It wouldn't go over.'

It took some time before I realised that I was merely witnessing a Fijian struck with amusement, not a man dying in a fit. When I did realise it, I called him a commoner of the fourth degree (which is Fijian vituperation), and told him to get up and come on. But I have never yet been able to make out where the fun came in.

Having brought no watch on this journey, I had been trying to learn to tell the time by the sun. It sounds simple enough, until one attempts it; and then one discovers that even in tropical latitudes the sun is not exactly in the centre of the sky at noon; also, that it seems to travel much faster at the beginning and end of its journey than in the middle. After a good many days' practice I found myself able (judging by the sunset, which was about six o'clock) to tell the time within half an hour or so; but I never got any nearer. As for the natives, they have extremely little knowledge of time in any case, and are never troubled at the prospect of being benighted on the road. That again, is 'the white man's burden,' not any business of theirs.

We did get benighted on this occasion, and extremely unpleasant it was, trying to bring Somo-somo safely over the various bad and boggy bits in the dusk. Dark had fallen by the time we reached the Wainikoro River, which I knew to be near the town – and behold, there was not a sign of a human being, and no boat!

A lovelier spot I had never seen, even in beautiful Fiji. There was no moon, but the wonderful tropic starlight burned in the purple sky with such a clear radiance of its own that the wide glassy river, edged with feathered reeds, the splendid palms, lifting their dark coronets eighty feet up among the stars, the orange-trees on the further side, dropping their juicy globes now and then into the waveless mirror below with a dull, dead-ripe splash, all were plainly visible. It was like a daylight scene viewed through a piece of deep violet glass. The stillness was intense: the palm-trees on the banks stood motionless as ebony-coloured plumes on a catafalque; the black river moved by without a ripple. A spot where one could have dreamed and wondered for hours; where fauns and dryads, in the magic starlight. . . .

'Sa senga na kakana, saka' ('We have no food, sir').

A Fijian has no poetry in his soul – especially if he has also nothing inside the most vital part of his mortal machinery. My poetical musings were scattered at once, and I came down to the plain prose of night, hunger, an impassable river, and the men wanting their supper.

We had only a few biscuits left – the tinned meat was unavailable until we reached a town, as none of the men happened to have a knife. (I don't think Speke or Livingstone would have forgotten the tin-opener, as I did.) I gave out the biscuits, reserving rather less for myself, in the dark, as I knew my hunger was more easily satisfied than theirs; but the men seemed to guess what I was doing, and gave back part of their share determinedly. A Fijian woman would have had to manage with the scraps they left; a white woman was as good as a man to them, and men must share equally.

We could do nothing but wait for a native to pass; so the men made a fire to keep the mosquitoes off; walked up the cocoanut-palms like flies, and threw down half a dozen green cocoanuts, husked them on a sharp stick stuck in the ground, opened them, and handed them about. Then they lay down round the fire to eat and drink, while I walked about the bank, waiting for a native.

It seemed as if no one was likely to come; but after half an hour or so, I heard a crackling in the woods on the far side. The noble savages ought to have heard it before I did; but they never noticed it, being intent on sucking cocoanuts, and when I called attention to it, they said it was probably a pig. When the dark form of a native, very slightly clad, appeared like a slim shadow on the opposite bank, I called the men up again, and pointed across. 'That is not a pig,' I said. They laughed; and one more delusion about the 'noble savage' vanished from my mind. If he couldn't tell the time by the sun, never knew when it was going to rain, and did not know a man's footstep from a pig's, it seemed to me that he was not fit for his part, and ought to be hissed off the stage.

Gideon, at my direction, yelled to the man, and asked if there was a boat or a canoe. No, there was neither. They had a canoe, but it was away up the river, and wouldn't be back till tomorrow. The men laughed – they always did when we came to a deadlock – and sat down at once to smoke. I hustled them up again, and told them to unsaddle Somo-somo, and lash a few sticks together to put my luggage on. We should have to swim for it.

They did as they were told, and I went down to the river's edge to reconnoitre. I tasted the water – it was brackish. Now, if there is danger of sharks high up in the Fijian rivers, there is very much more close to an estuary. I did not like it.

'Ask that man if there are any sharks,' I told Gideon.

'No shark stop!' he replied confidently. As neither he nor the carriers had ever been within twenty miles of the river, and as Fijians are absolutely reckless about sharks, I did not set much value on his remarks, but called over to the native on the far side, in rather bad Fijian:

'Sa senga na ngeo?' ('Are there any sharks?').

Instead of the loud, comforting 'Seng'ai, saka' ('None, sir') which I hoped for, came a complicated reply I could not translate. Gideon's version was: 'He say sometime shark he stop, sometime no stop.'

This was not good enough. Despite the astonishment of the native, and the amused scorn of the men, I declared I would not swim; that they must get the canoe; that I was a fearfully revengeful person, and would assuredly kill somebody if the Wainikoro people didn't go and capture that boat, and bring it along alive or dead – and other things to the same effect. The men's amusement at my fear of sharks broke up into fright, and they yelled to the native to get the canoe – get anything – for this was a terrible *marama* (lady), and there was no knowing what she would do unless pacified.

There is no power on earth like that of ill-temper – real or manufactured. In an hour's time, the canoe appeared, and Gideon hastily packed my goods and myself on board. Across the Wainikoro we went, followed by the small, meek, dripping head of Somo-somo just above the water, and in another half-hour I was installed in the usual native house, with the usual gaping crowd at the doors, and the usual fowl and yam preparing. Fowl is the one thing that a Fijian eats off a plate, instead of a leaf. He does not care to lose any of the precious water it was boiled in, so he always serves the murdered bird on a tin plate, which in many cases belongs to the village at large, and is sent about from house to house, whenever a feast is in progress. There was the usual fuss about hunting up the village plate while the food was preparing, and at last it was brought triumphantly in. Next morning, as I left, I saw it being hurried to the native teacher's house, by which I concluded that godly men from another village were expected, and entertainment was being prepared for them. Yam and ndalo are the common food of the people, fowl and pig being rare luxuries, except among the chiefs. In these days, the British Government keeps some curb on the exactions and tyrannies of the native rulers, and they cannot treat the 'kaisi,' or commonalty, as high-handedly as of old. Yet, even so, the lower classes live plainly and poorly, while the chiefs annex everything that takes their fancy, in the way of food, order the 'kaisi' about like dogs, and compel them, as a matter of course, to work for their superiors without pay. In Vanua Levu, which is nearly all wild unbroken country, with very few white residents, I saw Fiji in the rough, and it did not seem to me that the lot of the 'kaisi' was at all a happy one. Thirty or forty years ago, their chiefs could slay them at pleasure. Now they must respect life, at least; but the 'kaisi' is not allowed to have a soul of his own. He cannot leave his village without the chief's permission; he must work without pay as much as his superior desires, building houses or boats, or cultivating the communal patches of yam and ndalo. Ambition is impossible to him – born a 'kaisi,' he must remain one, and cannot hope for improvement in his lot. Something of this is reflected in his ways of living, and even his expression of face. In the other Pacific groups I have visited, a village at dusk is bright and merry, sounding with music and laughter, and full of lights. In Fiji, the towns are dark and silent at night; there is little singing, and the amusements are of a quiet kind, card-playing and yanggona-drinking being the chief. The Samoan, the Tongan, the Tahitian, or Cook Islander lives for pleasure and amusement – picnics, travelling parties, continual dances and songs, games of every kind enlivening his day and night. Chiefs, in these other groups, are less oppressive, and the communal system, with its care for the tribe, and harshness to the individual, is much less strictly carried out. But in Fiji, the 'kaisi' has not much heart to invent games and amusements. He can be a jolly fellow enough in his own way; he is exceedingly good-natured, readily pleased, and delighted with a joke. Still, at bottom, he has a spring of darkness and melancholy that is ever ready to rise and overflow the surface sunniness. His fathers lived lives of gloom and terror, always under the shadow of the war-club and the braining-stone, and within sound of the terrible 'lali,' or death-drum. When a chief died, the 'kaisi' were slain in dozens, and thrown into his grave, because – 'a chief must have grass to line his tomb, so that he may lie soft.' When a war-canoe was launched, it went down to the sea over hundreds of writhing human bodies, whose life-blood stained its keel, and whose death-yells sped it on its way. Living men were placed in the holes that received the supporting pillars of every chiefly mansion; human bodies, frequently alive, were daily forced into the red-hot cooking-ovens that supplied the meals of the chief. What wonder that the shadow of these hideous days – which can yet be remembered by the older men – should still rest upon the younger generation!

MAURICE N. HENNESSY
1906–

As a young man Maurice Hennessy joined the strict order of the
Discalced Carmelites and received a formidable classical education in
Roscrea and Dublin. Having questioned his vocation, however, he
found himself at the age of twenty-four 'out in the world utterly ill-
prepared for so many of the experiences ahead'. These were to include
a brief spell as a policeman in South Africa and longer periods as
lecturer, colonial official and British soldier in Africa and Burma and,
later, United Nations correspondent, journalist, teacher and author in
the United States, where he was African affairs consultant to the
American University in Washington DC. Africa remains, in his own
words, 'my country still', and his books about that continent include
Congo (1961) and *Africa Under My Heart* (1965), from which this extract
is taken. A Corkman, Maurice Hennessy now divides his time
between Ireland and the USA.

'HENNESSY'S BUSTARDS'

In 1940 there was little in the African bush that suggested either
luxury or comfort. But the bush had its compensations, and for me
they far exceeded any of the discomforts I had to suffer. It was not
beautiful but I have never recaptured the calm and peace that I felt
very deeply in the quiet, pleasant, orchard bush of Nigeria. Admittedly
there were ants, sweat flies, tarantulas, and a host of other creepy,
crawly things in abundance, but I got used to them.

I am not quite sure what I really expected on my first visit. The
battalion was to have its first taste of bush training so I was sent
ahead to make the necessary preparations. On arrival at the roadhead
my small party set off on foot into the selected area. With a machete
we chopped off the bark of a tree on the road and wrote on it the
compass bearing on which we were moving. This was essential

because one of the easiest things in the world is to lose oneself in thick orchard bush since one is far away from anything suggestive of modern civilisation.

As we walked along listening to the hum of insects and the bird calls, Amadu told me about the honey bird and urged me to listen carefully. As our party moved along the very narrow and barely discernible path, I heard the whistle of a bird; it was a short, sharp, but not unpleasant sound. He explained that this was the honey bird, which followed people in the hope that they would remove the honey from the various beehives to be seen in the treetops. The African actually uses the honey bird for determining where the honey is to be found.

On the first evening I wanted a bath; water was scarce although we had set up camp at a place where it was supposedly available. However, as it was the dry season, there was not much, but Amadu did manage to put a few inches of water in the small canvas bath in which I squatted. I asked him if there was any possibility of getting some more and his remark, 'More be coming, Baturi,' was something of a puzzle since there did not seem to be any more around. Lost in reverie and contemplating the eerie quiet of my surroundings, I was startled into semi-shock as a shower of water descended on me suddenly. Opening my eyes, I saw an African woman walking away from me with a bearing that would have done justice to a queen. She had gone about three yards before it happened the second time, and then a third. Altogether, I saw five women walk away with scarcely a glance, carrying empty gasoline cans on their heads, having dumped their contents over me. They appeared to be as unconscious of my nakedness as I was surprised by their presence. I noticed a strange gleam in Amadu's eyes – the kind of glint that always intrigued me for I never really knew what he was thinking. I am quite convinced that he had little regard for the rather strange reticence and idiosyncrasies he attributed to all white people.

There was much to be done to prepare for the arrival of the whole unit. The local chief supervised a number of men who came to build grass huts which they erected with incredible speed. These 'rumfas' were our homes for months on end, and although they were simple and crude they were perfectly comfortable. Light at night was a problem, but in those days we used a couple of kerosene bush lamps which probably did not help our eyesight but at least enabled us to read. The pleasure of reading was enhanced enormously because of the difficulty involved.

Throughout Nigeria, and indeed in most parts of Africa, the cotton tree grows from eighty to a hundred feet. Apparently its wood is utterly useless; one of my colleagues in the forestry department who had spent some thirty years in the country before I went there remarked: 'It is even too useless to burn.' My full enjoyment of the bush was hindered by the existence of these tall, worthless trees that seemed to spring up out of nowhere. Their roots were all too shallow, and the trees attracted lightning readily during the terrifying electrical storms which were an intimate part of Africa. During my first thunderstorm, preceded as it was by sharp gusts of wind and rain, one of them fell, crushing three of the bush houses as if they were made of matchsticks. Two years later I witnessed similar havoc in another storm; on this occasion the twelve soldiers who were in one of the huts were all killed.

Some twelve miles away was the village of Kufana commonly known as 'Starko' because its married women went absolutely naked. I remember one Sunday morning visiting the small grass Christian church which was run by American missionaries. It seemed such a completely incongruous sight to see naked women and almost nude men singing Christian hymns in that small edifice. Yet, for the first time, I felt that the missionaries were really endeavouring here to fit Christianity into the culture of the people. The particular tribe which inhabited this village was one to whom nudity was a sacred custom. The wise missionaries, believing that its abolition would serve no useful purpose, especially as it was a very significant factor in the daily lives of the people, compromised with conventional Christianity and with excellent results. One of these same missionaries provided me with another somewhat unique experience, which I will always remember. I had to leave our own camp and go to a nearby village to find a suitable artillery range for the brigade. During the night I stayed in an old disused guesthouse, and I decided to sleep on the inside instead of outside. This I did on the advice of Amadu who also insisted that I keep the door closed. I never realised why. It might have been that he had had some previous experience of the area. In the middle of the night I heard a loud banging on the door. Scrambling from under my mosquito net, I groped in the dark to open the door.

I was greeted abruptly by a sharp American feminine voice saying: 'I am a missionary. Do you mind if I spend the night here?'

I was almost nude, so I promptly lumbered back under my mosquito net and sheet. Then came her second remark: 'There is no need for a light. I have my own here.' In the shadowy darkness I could see a figure pushing a bicycle into the hut. In complete silence the visitor went to bed. I was amazed that she was able to make up her bed with the light from a hand flashlight. When I awoke in the morning she was gone and I have often wondered what she looked like.

The battalion arrived and the months sped by in the bush, training, training, training. Marches, drills, more exercises, and wet and uncomfortable night operations all became part of the daily grind. Strangely enough I endured them without feeling too sorry for myself. Somehow the peace and quiet out there and the removal from the world of brigadiers breathing down one's neck, from tiresome general inspections, and from the countless irritations that man inflicts on man were compensation enough. I had found the Africa I loved, the Africa I had dreamed about. I felt completely at home. Even now I still think of those days when I learned that there is no softer pillow when one is utterly weary than a hard rock. I remember how a few sips of water were nectar after a long march in a temperature of over a hundred degrees and how lying down on a camp bed after an exhausting day could be enhanced by the African night.

There was another aspect of living in the bush: it was the strange comradeship which it seemed to create between the Africans and ourselves. There were no barriers; there was, in fact, a strong sense of companionship which, as the months went by, grew into real warmth. This does not mean that there were not occasions when I felt there was a wide gap between ourselves and the Africans. But while the Africans were learning much from us, we learned much from them, although possibly some of the knowledge we assimilated we could very well have done without.

There was one strange African attitude I had never been able to understand. Although our soldiers were well disciplined and responded to the strong ceremonial sense that military parades engender, there were occasions when they became absolutely impossible to control. No matter how solemn the parade, no matter how splendidly they were turned out in their red Zouave jackets, any kind of wild animal running across the parade ground meant that immediately the whole parade disintegrated in order to give chase. No matter how senior the officers were, this was one attack they could never stop! Even for bewildered officers watching the chase there was much excitement, for the Africans' speed of movement was such that they were nearly always successful in capturing the animal. It was an amazing spectacle to see troops appearing from nowhere on such occasions. They came from the most unexpected directions.

Every time I saw it happen I remembered an incident from my school days. A field mouse had strayed into the corridor of the building and its appearance coincided with the end of a class period. As the students saw the wretched little animal they all gave chase. A near riot ensued until the college president could make himself heard over the melee. He bellowed: 'I hold all the hunting rights in this school.' The instinct for the chase is close to the surface in all of us; it is a little more so in Africans.

The subject of hunting reminds me of an odd experience I had at this time. Nigeria is noted for some very large birds which are as edible as they are good looking. Such a one is the great bustard, which is somewhat larger than a turkey and has rather dark, brownish-grey feathers. One officer in the unit was an expert at shooting bustards, and whenever he brought the birds to the cook it usually meant an excellent meal for the officers – something different from the dread monotony of bully beef, scrawny chicken, and the kind of beef that had been killed a few hours before it was cooked. I was a little envious of my fellow officer's success and decided that I would try my hand at it. Very early one morning I had to leave on a visit to a company some distance away and I consulted the bustard expert before my departure. He informed me that the particular road over which I would travel was quite well known for bustard and that after dawn they can usually be seen pecking at some juicy morsel they find buried in the laterite dust on the roads.

I set off in a staff car with my orderly and Amadu and a couple of guns. After a few miles I saw a tall and stately bird stalking across the road; I managed to get close enough for a shot. The bird fell into the bush with a noise like a small airplane falling. The orderly rushed off to retrieve it, brought it back, and threw it into the rear of the car. I examined my prize and after some hesitation decided that it was a bustard. A little farther on I was fortunate enough to see a flock of guinea fowl and brought down four of them with two barrels. They, too, were tossed into the car, and together with the bustard made quite a mound of feathers.

About five miles farther down the road I could scarcely believe my eyes when I saw my second tall, stately bird. This one, too, was an easy target – almost too easy, in fact, for when I threw it on top of all the other birds in the back seat I felt a niggling doubt. However, upon meeting the company commander, who was a veteran of many years in Africa, I asked him if the birds were really bustards and he said, 'Indeed they are.'

'The cook will be delighted,' I answered happily and with not a little relief that my doubts had been so foolish.

When I returned to camp I presented my prize to the cook who, like most cooks – even African ones – tended to be temperamental. To my horror he looked at the birds and then registered utter disgust. 'They not be bustard,' he said glumly, 'them be snakebird.' I had never heard of a snakebird and my first reaction was to suspect some kind of game. I had the feeling that he wanted me to say, 'Well, then, get rid of them,' which he could easily do by selling them in the village.

At that moment, however, I had a visitor. He was the police superintendent of the district who had just stopped by on a routine check. I decided to query him about the birds to see if I had made a mistake, after all. He took one look at them and said, 'They are not bustards and they will cost you eighty pounds.' (In those days that was $400.) His serious expression as he delivered the verdict revealed the truth instantly: I had shot protected birds. Indeed, I had broken the law, for I had shot two of the rarest of birds – the secretary bird. It happened to be one of the most protected birds in the world since it is the enemy of the more lethal snakes and many undesirable animals.

I never did pay the eighty pounds, but that leniency was due to the special kindness of the police superintendent. However, as events turned out, the pounds would have been a cheap penalty; what was very much worse was having my leg pulled mercilessly for at least a year afterward. The three battalions in the district dubbed the unfortunate secretary birds as 'Hennessy's bustards' which, in typical army fashion, was duly twisted.

Every officer in the African Army, by the very nature of things in the bush, had much more responsibility for any domestic problems affecting the men in his company than his British counterpart. Each Saturday morning in every unit in West Africa a period of time was set aside as the 'complaints hour'. At that time men could come and discuss with their officers any personal affairs or domestic difficulties. Many of the officers were, in fact, recruited colonial officials in whom the soldiers had considerable confidence. For those it was one of the busiest hours of the week which placed heavy burdens on them; for the rest of us it was a most instructive time. Though the problems of the soldiers sometimes seemed simple, their solution was always vital to the morale of the individual concerned. For example, a soldier might be worried about sending a letter to someone; the officer had to find a letter writer for him and then had to make sure that the latter wrote what he was supposed to write! Sometimes there was a need to satisfy an angry father because the balance of the dowry for a newly-married daughter had not been sent. Often it was offering advice to a soldier on the matter of the bride price for a new wife.

I found it all a great human experience; it brought home clearly the universal truth that people in all parts of the world share common problems. The Africans had become my people and like most of the officers I tried my best to smooth their somewhat stormy paths, although there were times when it was difficult to know what to do or advise.

One day an angry soldier came into my office and said: 'My wife's belly done spoil. This be third time. I no want her.' This posed quite a problem. Would it be advisable to write to his local chief and find out about the matter? Or would it be better to follow the book and try to persuade him to hold on a bit longer? One had to keep reminding oneself that these men were quite sensitive and easily offended. I could easily have followed the Mohammedan rule; that way the difficulties were few. The law laid down that a wife who actually became pregnant but who did not carry a baby the full period could be put aside, but the law did not permit the dowry to be returned to the husband. Sometimes a soldier wanted to divorce his wife because they had been married three or four years and there were no children. The problem here was how to tell a soldier (particularly an African Mohammedan) that maybe the fault was all on his side and that he, too, might be impotent. Usually this was an impossible task; one had just to sit by and allow the law to take its course.

The complaints were, indeed, varied and many. One day an African corporal came to see me, and his request for an interview had certain unusual qualities about it. He had refused to discuss his particular problem with his company commander, and the latter was rather hesitant about sending him to the adjutant without knowing the facts. However, he felt there was a certain validity about the request and spoke to me about it. In due course, the corporal arrived and informed me that his wife, for whom he had paid fourteen pounds ($70 then), was living with one of my European sergeants. My first reaction was complete admiration for the corporal's delicate handling of the situation since he apparently did not want the European sergeant, who was in his own company, to be taken to task. My second reaction was to see that he had justice.

I sent for the sergeant and asked him in the presence of the corporal if the latter's accusation was correct. He confirmed that it was. I turned to the African and asked him whether he would be satisfied if he collected the full dowry payment which he had made for his wife. He agreed that this would be quite fair. Having dismissed the corporal, I then informed the sergeant (and not very gently) that I would pay the fourteen pounds to the corporal out of the battalion fund but that I would arrange for it to be deducted from his pay. I pointed out to him that if he wished to break up an African family, he had no alternative but to abide by the African law which governed such actions.

A bully by nature, the sergeant asked to see the brigadier immediately; he questioned the justice of my punishment and intended to go to the top in his efforts to have it revoked. I told him that by all means he could see the brigadier and I advised him to put his request in writing. In the meantime I also checked his record and warned him that a report of his own service record and the full story of the incident with the corporal's wife would accompany his request to the brigadier. Of course, he never followed through on his threat to see the brigadier. He paid the fourteen pounds unwillingly, and at the first opportunity I got rid of him. I did not send him away because he had fallen by the wayside but because he considered the complaint of an African corporal of no concern to him.

Since we were stationed in so remote a spot, it was considered necessary to organise various games of mutual interest. As we discovered later on it was really *not* a necessity, for if there is one thing that an African can do better than anyone else it is entertain himself. In Katchia, especially, was I to learn that the art of conversation still thrived in the African continent. Africans love to talk. This talk consists of telling stories far from the truth; in fact, the individual who can tell the biggest whopper and never bat an eyelid while doing so is the favourite of all listeners. No one commands as much respect in Africa as the nomad who can sit at food in the evening and tell tall tales far beyond the imagination of the men who wrote the tall tales of this country.

On one occasion the Africans decided to put on a show for the Europeans. Apart from the usual dancing and singing, we were treated to an incredible display of mimicry and wrestling. With a few pieces of sacking some of the entertainers dressed themselves up as monkeys. Their antics not only caused hilarity, the like of which we had not enjoyed for months, but they impressed upon us the amazing powers of observation the Africans possessed. They were able to imitate monkey actions in the tiniest details. Had Alexander Pope been a member of the audience he would have summed it up: 'What oft was seen but ne'er so well expressed.'

After the monkey show came a display of wrestling by men of the Dakokerry tribe. That the rules of wrestling governing the contest, and the methods came down from the Grecian era there is no doubt. Should anyone ever feel inclined to make a study of African wrestling in relation to the Greek sport, he ought to find it an all-absorbing academic harvest.

AIDAN HIGGINS
1927–

Aidan Higgins was born in Celbridge, County Kildare, in an eighteenth-century house that was later to serve as the location for his first novel, *Langrishe Go Down*, which won the James Tait Black Memorial Award and was shortlisted for the Booker Prize. While working on his second novel, he spent some years in southern Spain, although his travels had begun following his education at Clongowes (where James Joyce was a former pupil), first in Britain and later in Africa, where he toured with a marionette company. After his period in Spain, he lived in Germany and London before returning to Ireland. Essentially an autobiographical writer, Higgins's travel is reflected both in his fiction and his shorter prose. 'Autumn in Cómpeta' was written in 1976 and was collected in *Ronda Gorge and Other Precipices* (1989).

AUTUMN IN CÓMPETA

The natives of these parts have a pithy saying to the effect that 'nothing dead lasts long'. Headgear, as various as the owners, is worn as if hats had just been invented, clamped or stitched to the head and removed most reluctantly, the abstracted hand passed over the scorched scalp and headgear replaced with an anguished expression as if something long-pondered had at last been resolved. Then air is expelled from the mouth – 'Ouff!', a husky fifenote. The hats might be narrow-brim, well-worn straw, sweated-into grey Homburg, elegant Anthony Eden, dusty black beret with a little knob at the crown. Their gossiping is liberally enlivened with '¡Cojónes!', the male term for emergent life.

Insects rise; all is calm; a breeze blows from the right hand, the olive trees shiver, exposing their silvery undersides. Now a mule is led past by an old man with head lowered, a small dog standing on the saddle like a circus act. I hear the robin in the valley, a repeated series of high fidgety twitterings.

The wind whines in the fence about the ugly new barracks-like edifice of red brick. To the rear of this awkward structure, as you go by San Antonio, I heard the wind whine and took it to be the demented droning of hens shut up for the night and rallying themselves for sleep on their perch. But it was only five o'clock on a late October afternoon, far too early for fowl to be shut up. The wind went gustily as a vibraphone through the wire fence as I passed down into the valley full of birds.

Below the finest little mosque in all Christendom, converted centuries ago into a Catholic church and now a chapel of rest for corpses from Canillas *en route* to the *cementerio*, stood an ugly new factory for the manufacture of sanitary towels or disposable knickers, which afforded labour to the local girls.

I heard the plangent sound of a guitar near the round threshing-stone where they still worked the grain in the old way, throwing it into the air to winnow it. Along the road there the *novios* conducted their courtship in the old style, walking out together as in Straffan and Naas and Clane in the summers of long ago, on the by-roads free of motorised traffic. It reminded me of a past which now hardly seems to belong to me, this by-road slow-linking courtship, and the drone of hens, a valley of birds, perpetual summer. Mere tokens, signs of oncoming senility and nothing more. Token symptoms of insanity making a strong effort to be reasonable. Sufficient to say that hereabouts all nature is in gentle riot.

Coming from a day of walking in the hills I had heard a male voice singing from a high place and thought I saw a figure working on the mosque but when I came below the mosque the singing human figure had become part of the electrical installation. There, on the other side where the swallows fly below the path, the land seems to induce song. Finding themselves on high places the men have an urge to sing and in those hours when the light is going fast their songs most resemble the evening prayer-songs of their old conquerors calling out of their minarets, all turned to the east. As sometimes too, when very drunk, the involuntary cries are wrung from them. A tilted condition suited to Canillas and Cómpeta, hill villages put together at angles of forty-five degrees, and thus a uniquely tilted drunkenness, and they call out in great distress, this double syllable of anguish, a cry wrung from the mouths of men who should not drink at all, let alone drink to excess, and ulcers at fifty. Again the distressed cry from the mouths of their conquerors who in the eight long centuries of occupation had kept their own religion and become assimilated into España, particularly in the province closest to their own land and most resembling it. Become in fact another race. Not of España but a mixture of the two races, become a third mixed race called *los Moros*. Two great trading races come to live as one, when the time for trading for both had ended.

'*¡AAAAaaaiii! ¡¡AAAaaaaiiiiie!!*', the tortured drunk cries out from the high bedroom window, just a slit in the outer wall, presumably holding onto the bed-rail within, his eyes closed. How mortally ashamed of myself am I! How mortified that I am I, and so drunken in Cómpeta!

The ones who did not drink stayed on to build aqueducts for the dry impoverished land and by an ingenious system of ways and means brought water and vegetation into dried-out valleys and even raised up their own dreamlike architecture within the conquered towns and cities, a nomad dream of palms and palaces and cool secret places fit for rendezvous. But above all watercourses and fountains, the most persistent nomad dream: flowing water.

And the other, the other half, the body of the land that nothing could transform, and the people on it whom no conqueror could change, no matter how long the conquest? It and they sank into poverty together, into a prolonged dream out of which not even General Franco himself could wake them, but rather plunged them deeper, further from their own nature.

Near the old Arab cemetery – as strange as an English cemetery in India, even to long-dead English names on gravestones – Trull and the semi-demented painter and whilom remittance man Carsten had observed three silent dark citizens, in that port of pick-pockets, drug-pushers, perverts and outstretched palms. Observed them seated side by side on a public bench, swaying gently this way and then that as the wind turned; the breeze passed through their beards again, they turned with it, saying nothing but smiling to themselves, hooded in their desert clothes. They smiled because they felt *other than themselves*, part of the breeze that blew through the palm trees, part of another race. They were curious to be alive, smiling to themselves as they swayed on the bench near or in the cemetery there.

Conrad wrote that curiosity is one of the forms of self-revelation. Duplication of vision: I see an image with multiple forms in the light, trembling in the glare of Arab day. On yet another occasion, not unfree of incident, Trull and I had spent a day in Tangier. He limping around with an ingrowing toenail and far from cordial. We were pestered by pickpockets and an itinerant trader of woollen caps whom we could not shake off. Wherever we went he was sure to be there before us, or just coming in the door after us, or walking by outside and hailing us, a fellow who claimed to be Charlie Chaplin. The woollen caps were made in the interior.

After being silently molested on the sea-front by a pickpocket we took a meal among Berbers in a sort of lean-to in the main square. An ancient Berber leaning across was civil enough to inform the crusty Trull that salt was bad for him. Or so we understood from his dumbshow and grimaces. Trull poured out a liberal handful into his soup and over his meat, and bending down applied himself to his meal, causing the ancient Berber to withdraw into his djellaba in the most frosty manner imaginable.

We found a bar with wide windows overlooking the passing parade and ordered vodka and fresh orange juice. The drinks well iced were hardly set before us than in came Charlie Chaplin, delighted to see us again, calling out 'Tchollie! Tchollie!'

I saw nothing of Chaplin in him, looking for the tramp. But presently, talking to another customer, he drew out a piece of material, cocked his head, sketched a gesture, and there stood the stout white-haired rubicund father of half a dozen children, the Chaplin of *Limelight* with the old talent gone. Enough of Tangier. We flew back, were delayed, ran up a huge drinks bill on Iberia. I feared for my life with a mad Moorish taxi driver, then a low fellow who drove like one possessed from the airport to the town, its lights shuddering in the distance.

But now I am walking in the valley, or sitting on the bridge, smoking a Goya, where the road bends by the Mass Path there. Rounding a corner I came upon a local youth up to his chest in what appeared to be a grave, and still digging. His transistor played Irish traditional music, strange to hear there, and I was back again on Camus Bay in a little cemetery by the crooked seashore and it was raining as usual. Or was I with the countess in a miserable bar overlooking a seaweed factory and a drenched fish-dock with parked cars and from the radio behind the bar a female voice sang soothingly, 'I'd love to see old Ireland free once more.' And then a rendering of 'The Wexford Men of '98'. And then the name of the bar came back to me: Kilkieran's on a bay of the same name.

Now I saw with failing eyesight what I took to be a goatherd effortlessly transforming himself into several divided beings. The intent here was in no way clear to me. I was sitting on one of those blocks of cemented brick that guard the bend, then I saw him above me, over the road, on a ridge in the company of half a dozen goats, a roan ram and buff ewes to be pedantic. He seemed to be addressing them. Sounds carry far in that acoustic valley. I heard the rough voice going on amiably, confidentially. They talk to dogs here, and to the earth, so why not to goats. Perhaps he was whiling away the time telling them the old stories?

The oldest and best stories in the world, the ones that do not change. Of the snakes that venture down from the mountains in hot weather and swim in the aqueducts or even crawl into the gardens by the sea to drape themselves in the oleander. Or even venture into the house, out of curiosity, or for the cool, and drape themselves around the toilet seat, for coolness that takes some beating. And very unsettling for the person at stool or for a woman looking down at what are supposed to be water-pipes and sees a snake, as has indeed happened to me. Or of the one who gets into a lady's handbag.

Or tales of the foxes who steal the grapes and rob from the *basuras*, the trash barrels, hunting not singly but in groups. And the meaning of their mournful nocturnal cries. Or, nearer home, of the known potency of Cómpeta wine, stored in great barrels in cool places. To my way of thinking a cross between bad sherry and worse Montilla, and certain death to the liver when not taken in moderation, which is the way it is generally taken. Or of strong coffee with goat's milk laced with Cognac, good on cold nights. Or taken with *churros*. Better still on cold mornings, with a shot of anise, a shock to the system, a pecker-up, a stirrer of the blood sluggish at that hour. All these without exception good things.

Or of the taste of *callos*, which we call tripe, or *pulpo*, which is octopus with its eight suckered arms around the mouth. Or of all the good things that dwell in the sea. And of the force of *cerdo* (pork), for pig is everywhere and in everything, their death-shrieks heard one night of every week. So tenacious of a life that never seemed so good, now that it is ending. *Adios* to the carefree hours in the piggery, always good. *Cerdo* cooked with the *vino terreno* and teeth of *ajo* (garlic), for garlic certainly goes with everything.

And the goats, who had certainly heard these stories before, and many times, or stories very like them – being spared only the stories of the pungency of *cabra* itself, good as a main dish, fine as a cheese, excellent fine as *tapas*, titbits given free in bars with orders of drink – stories of slaughtered kids, not to put too fine a point upon it. Good as milk, which is said to inhibit potency. But this is surely incorrect, for the milk in the Bar Perico near the church was always goat's-milk, and Luis Perico himself was the father of eleven sons and daughters.

The same stories told in exactly the same words, the blurred dreamlike words of the old story, for any deviation would be wrong. The same stories told over and over. And told to the goats before them, back to the great dreamlike herds of their forebears on the plains, in the time of the black and blue men brought over by General Franco to put the fear of God into the whole province. Men with black and blue faces and cut-throat propensities, in the endless centuries of the occupation. And before that in the time of the seagoing Phoenicians, who had brought rabbits into Andalucía and tin to Málaga.

It was doubtless with yarns like these that the herdsman was boring the udders off the ewes. Or with others as similar or as long-winded, a pleasant way of passing the time. Or perhaps again stories of the lewdness of all foreign women, whose morals were by definition habitually loose. When carnal tendencies take hold of them then Satan himself must be allowed to work his way. Or of the lustful ways of abbesses, having their way with abbots and bishops, gardeners too, in the cool privacy of the cells, lips if not anus gleaming with glycerine and eyes ablaze with unquenchable lust. Or of all the good growing things of the earth, never limp, no good in bed but splendid up against a wall.

I hear the nanny-goats sniggering in the private evasive way by which these contemplative beasts express their not so dumb amusement, the ram hee-heeing away like old Cornok himself into its shaggy beard.

Now the scraggy leaves of the cane plantation fidget in the breeze as it pours through their rows. Depressed as old coats on hangers stand the stems, turning up their curled leaves. The sugar bushes, some call them.

A small cloud appears over the ridge, brief as a puff of smoke from a steam-engine, appearing in the evening of this cloudless blue day. On the path below, the trampled form of a frog with outstretched arms is imprinted in the dust, with a few spent cartridges for company. The hunting season has started and the guns are going in the hills. Then the cloud has evaporated and the herdsman appears to be now addressing himself to an unseen friend, for I seem to hear other rough tones answering. The goats cavort on the slopes, enjoy the play of air, as the evening breeze comes up the steep narrow valley full of so many varieties of birds.

Now again all is calm on the slope, the human voices silent. The tattered appendages droop and rustle, as if despised, aware of their poverty, just old useless coats, as the wind, gathering force, rushes through them, setting them all to fidgeting and trembling. And the two owls who have been calling to each other have settled on one branch on a tree over the *barranca*. In two hours it will be dark. Are they even owls? Their sharp cries octaves above hooting.

It's a boy whom the herdsman addresses, perhaps his grandson. The goats are browsing, the herdsman wrapped in his mantle, the boy staring down at the road where nothing moves, least of all me.

And presently the boy has disappeared and the herdsman is standing hurling stones and abuse at his flock who scatter, some escaping to higher ledges and others jumping down. I hear the rough voice choking. But in a little while they come together again and he seems to be frolicking with them.

Now seated, a long confabulation ensues between the one seated on a rock and another unseen one. I hear distinctly 'Dos cognac'. But now the herdsman addresses himself only to a low silent form, perhaps not even human. . . .

When attempting the language it is foolish to speak slowly or attempt clear articulation, for that way will get you nowhere. First the gutturals must be mastered, no easy job, since the language abounds in gutturals. As you move higher into the hills it becomes harder to follow, closer to true Arab, the words running together. In the north they speak another language: Basque. Another race

altogether, stolid, unimaginative, hard-working; a people whose chief
gifts to España have been bankers and industrialists, latterly terrorists
in the cause of independence. Their language is inherited from the
Stone Age, now slowly dying out because unsuited to modern times,
and so difficult that no one can learn it.

With Cómpeta *español* a general picture is preferable; the submerged
constructions surfacing and sending the rest out towards what may
not be total comprehension but at least partial and, moreover,
sounding as though delivered in an idiom generally acceptable in the
village. A fish held in the palm of the hand first thing in the morning
is thought to bring luck.

To them, and more so to their children's ears, English sounds a
feeble and indeed ridiculous tongue, a trance-speech of caste.
'*Weeeshywashy!*', the children call out in mockery on hearing English
spoken.

The married women retire at sunset and are up at cockcrow. They
laugh a lot, shrug their shoulders and laugh off misfortune. All are
watchful observers, the habit deepening with age, particularly among
the males, who seem to be observing themselves rather than you,
attentive to some inner process, their cane chairs tilted against the
wall of the church or arranged in a half-circle outside the Mirror Bar:
the Old Hats, Trull calls them, being a bit of an old hat himself. They
have a complicated expression for these long murmurous discussions,
their retelling of the day's events, for which the synonym might be
the-last-shout-on-the-stairs. Their language well reflects the charming
and uncomplicated nature of the people themselves. God's name is
in everything they say, as in Connemara or Bavaria. Hissed
imprecations are a sign of exasperated sensibility and nothing more.
They are past masters of the contrapuntal serpent hiss. Abstract
thought is unknown to them and when they hear it attempted they
become embarrassed. Hence perhaps the need for nights of loud
convivial shouting in the bars, with which the village is liberally
supplied, after a day spent labouring on the land. Overcoats are
never worn, not even in the severest winters, but umbrellas carried.

Empty the head of preconceived notions and fill the mouth full of
syllables and then spew them out with little or no regard for accuracy
or even sense. In this you will gain a reputation for speaking their
mountain lingo 'very well', even though no single word has been
understood. It is the sounds that matter and the intent behind the

sounds, generally hammered home with the hand, a vein in the forehead throbbing. While no strangers to the ecstatic vision, up there at 550 metres, it's considered the height of bad manners to refer to this. The word for savings bank is identical to the word for coffin. They are a happy people.

PAMELA HINKSON
1900–1982

Daughter of a Mayo Resident Magistrate and the writer Kathleen
Tynan, Pamela Hinkson was educated privately in Ireland, Germany
and France. She travelled widely as a journalist in Europe and
America, contributing to the *Observer*, the *New Statesman* and the
Manchester Guardian. Her book *The Ladies' Road* (1932) sold 100,000
copies in the paperback edition. Pamela Hinkson's visit to India as a
guest of the viceroy in the late 1930s inspired her *Indian Harvest* (1941),
from which the following chapter is taken. 'India,' she concluded,
'whether one loves it or hates it, or – more likely – does both in turn, is
unforgettable.' During World War II she made a lecture tour of the
United States for the British Ministry of Information and also worked
at the Shamrock Club for Irish servicemen in London. After the war
she lectured in Germany and returned to live in Ireland in 1959.
Pamela Hinkson's books include *The Golden Rose* (1944) and
The Lonely Bride (1951).

A MISSION AT AGRA

At a cocktail party in Delhi, a General's wife, down from Dehra Dun
for a day or two – with a soft speech that revealed her at once as a
countrywoman of mine – asked me if I wanted to go to Agra. For she
had a friend who must see the Taj Mahal before she went home and
was looking for a companion for the expedition. The next day I met
the friend at lunch, and a few days later we set out for Agra together.
It was a fortunate chance that sent me such a perfect companion for
that visit to Agra, for we found ourselves of like mind and sympathies.

I acknowledge that but for G—— I should not have done my
sightseeing so thoroughly. We saw the Taj with the sun setting on it,
and rose in the dark to see it by moonlight and then to wait and

watch the sun rising on it. At that hour we had the gardens to ourselves, with all the mystery and magic of the moon illuminating those fairy-like walls. The formal pools of water below, in which in the daylight another Taj is reflected, were gleaming strips of silver. Below the marble terraces the Jumna river took its silver, winding way to Delhi. The moon faded and the sun came over the dark cypress trees to take the world from it, gilding and warming the beauty that had been snowy white and cold under the moon. The sun came slowly as if it hesitated, not with sudden flooding light but with a first, delicate touch of one lovely tower before it took the whole into its radiance. It was still night when we arrived, and chilly, and the figures that came running on bare feet to let us in were ghostly and sad in their fluttering white garments – inadequate for the cold nights of Northern India, even with woollen rugs thrown over them. We sat on a seat in the garden wrapped in our warmest coats, watching the changing light on the Taj. The evening before there had been other sightseers – obvious sightseers, wearing topis as visitors to India wear them, so that they are unmistakable as visitors. But now the moonlight shone on the Taj, and the rising sun lit it slowly for us alone.

We saw it in the day-time, with the guide's voice in our ears: 'Twenty thousand workmen.' And – how many lakhs of rupees to make this tomb, which took twenty years to build, for the mortal remains of one woman? And for the upkeep of which the tribute of thirty villages was assigned by Shahjahan.

'Indian jasmine flowers,' the voice murmured. 'Indian stone. Cornelian, lapis lazuli, agate, bloodstone. Italian work.'

The white marble had been brought from Jaipur, the red sandstone of the gateway and the Mosque and the Mausoleum of the Maids of Honour that stand either side of the gate from Fatehpur Sikri. They sent to Baghdad for cornelians, to Badakshan for rubies, to Panna for diamonds, and to Tibet for turquoise. And from Baghdad, Turkey and Persia the artists came to use these materials.

Standing outside the marble screen, pierced to the most delicate lacework, that surrounds the two tombs of Mumtaz and Shahjahan, which lie side by side, we were given sprigs of jasmine flowers – withered and smelling too sweet and a little sickly. Rupees were taken from us – for the flowers, or as an offering to a Mahomedan saint who would answer our prayers if we made them. Outside in the sunlight one of the keepers of the Taj was dusting the beautiful inlaying and carving of a doorway with an enormous feather duster on a long stick, such as housemaids use on a smaller scale in England.

If Shahjahan had had his way there would have been a second Taj for his own tomb. He laid the foundation stone of that before he was made a captive in his old age by his son, Aurangzeb, and spent the last days of his life looking from the Jasmine Tower of Agra Fort, across the waters to the Jumna, to the Taj. That is the most beautiful of all the views of Mumtaz' Tomb. When he died Aurangzeb thought, reasonably, that to build a second Taj for his father would be waste of money. So he buried Shahjahan beside the wife he had loved.

I had a different mission to fulfil at Agra. Just before I sailed I had met an Irish lady of my acquaintance in the street. She had said: 'If you go to Agra will you visit the grave of my only brother, who died there? My sister and I have never seen it.' I had said yes, but had forgotten to ask the name of that brother. His sisters were both married and widows. So I had sent a wire from Delhi, and the reply reached me at Agra: 'Captain ——, Royal Irish Regiment.' The name of that regiment stirred many childhood's associations for me.

We drove out to the British Cemetery to look for the grave in the late afternoon. We searched in that flooding gold evening light up and down the rows of gravestones. It was, we realised almost at once, like looking for a needle in a haystack. A *mali* came to help us, but he spoke almost no English, and we no Hindustani. 'Church of England?' he asked, seeking for a clue. Some of the later graves were segregated according to religion. 'Roman Catholic?'

'Roman Catholic.'

He led us to that section of the graveyard. But the search was in vain. Although later I discovered that I had passed the grave and the cross marking it for which I sought without discovering it in that first search. We wandered about looking for it while the gold light deepened and all the quiet graveyard lay drenched in it. Outside lay the dusty road and the parched polo ground. The dust was in the graveyard, for all the care with which it was tended. And suddenly the dust became India, and I felt overwhelmingly the loneliness of these graves dug in that dust, and the homesickness of those who lay there. It is something that perhaps no one can imagine who has not walked through such a cemetery at Indian evening, reading the names on the stones. The usual terrible percentage of children – and of young wives and mothers. One, a little dim in its lettering, stood over the bones of a man from 'Sligo, Ireland,' who had been buried there sixty years ago. How green and cool and exquisite, Sligo in Ireland appeared to me, standing beside that grave! An aching nostalgia – as though someone else's feelings had entered mine – came in a wave over me as I stood looking at that name.

We gave it up temporarily. There must be a parish priest who would have the records and could help me. We inquired and were directed to Father Francesco. His house was beside the church. But he was an old man now and went to bed early, so we must not be too late.

G—— still insisted on accompanying me, being both interested and sympathetic. We took a taxi. The driver's face brightened when we gave the address.

'The Father,' he said. Presumably he was a Mahomedan. But there was something in his voice as he spoke of 'the Father'. I understood when I had met Father Francesco.

We drove in the dusk up to his low, simple bungalow beside the church. When we got out of the car three or four enormous dogs leapt from the shadows, barking. They were – or had been – pi dogs, undistinguishable mongrels. But – how different from their brothers and sisters, from whom I had learnt to turn away my eyes! These were fat and well cared for, with luxuriant silky coats, the picture of well-being and happiness. When we spoke to them they leapt on us affectionately and confidently, wagging their tails and licking our hands.

A servant followed them, a dim white figure in the dusk.

'Father Francesco?' He was out, but would be back in ten minutes. Would we come in and wait? 'Ten minutes,' the man repeated, smiling, as he led us into the house.

I knew that 'ten minutes,' having heard it before. It was the specified time that I had been given so often in India when waiting for someone to return. It might mean an hour – two hours. We were offered something to drink – tea? Water? We refused both, having just had tea at the hotel.

But we could hardly have waited a full ten minutes in Father Francesco's bare little room, with the crucifix and a few religious pictures on the walls, books on the table, when the dogs, who had accompanied us in, cocked their ears. They rushed to the door and out of it before our slower hearing had caught the step outside. I saw Father Francesco as he came, framed in the open doorway, the light from the room streaming out on to the picture he made. Wearing a brown habit, a tall old man with a long white beard, he might have stepped out of an Italian picture. As he came the dogs leapt on him joyously and he fondled and pushed them away at once.

We introduced ourselves, explaining our business, and we shook hands. Father Francesco thought for a moment, repeating the name. He could not remember. (How many people had he buried in his life? I wondered.) He shook his head and went into another room and came back with an enormous book – the Burial Book. He put it on the table, and as he sat down before it the dogs leapt on him again. One was across his knees, adoring him, another standing up on his shoulder, another fighting for his hand. They were big dogs and they had no manners, obviously, only so much love that they must burst with it if they did not pour it out. Perhaps they had had that love, unspent, torturing them, before the fortunate day when they came to Father Francesco.

'You are like Saint Francis,' I said as he sat there, the dogs devouring him with love.

He pushed one off his knees affectionately. 'Ah,' he said, looking up at me suddenly. 'What would I do without them? I am alone, you see.'

He turned to business then before I could say anything more. I looked over his shoulder at the records written in that immense book. I was not sure of the date of the death – only of the name. After turning the pages for a few minutes, back into the last century, Father Francesco found a clue and gave it to me, remembering suddenly: 'Wait! There was an Irish regiment here in 1911.'

While we had looked in the 'nineties, even the 'eighties, I had had a glimpse of what lay behind the records. Causes of death included: cholera, heat-stroke, gunshot wounds, suicide. I had not then imagined the loneliness and homesickness that I had felt in the graveyard, when the dust had become India, with all the menace of India in it. These things had been left behind there by those who had experienced them fully.

We traced the grave at last – not from the book but from a gift to the church which the two devoted sisters had presented. Father Francesco, remembering, got to his feet and went out, we following him.

'Jean Baptiste!' he called in the darkness that had come quickly while we talked, and Jean Baptiste, the Indian boy with the French Christian name given to him on his conversion, came running. He opened the door of the sacristy, which was locked for the night, and we went in and found what we wanted. Now Father Francesco remembered everything. He blessed that grave every year on All Souls' Day. I would tell the ladies? And that their gift was used and highly valued. He would send someone tomorrow morning to take me to the grave.

We went back into the house. Father Francesco closed up the book and talked to us for a few minutes across it. I explained that I was Irish, my friend English. And he? What part of Italy did he come from?

Florence, he said. And something in our expressions as he said the name told him before we spoke of it that we both knew Florence.

'Ah. You have been there?' Just for a moment something of longing stirred in his peaceful face.

'How long have you been in India?' I asked.

'Forty-five years.'

'Without going home?'

He smiled his answer.

'Do you ever go home – your order?'

He shook his head and lifted his hand towards the ceiling, indicating Heaven above it.

'My home is up there.'

'Is it lonely sometimes?' I asked, remembering what he had said about the dogs.

He shook his head. 'I have my dogs.' He fondled the head of one of them. 'And . . . one sows a little seed and one watches it grow.'

He looked up again. So near did that Home of his seem, so near and intimate and simple, that I almost felt he might leave us at any moment and go to it!

'He – He does it all,' he said, as though he spoke of a Friend Whose ways he knew well.

He asked me how long I had been in India and about my impression of the country. I said, among other things, that on the whole I found it sad and the people so, and was oppressed at times by the appalling poverty.

He smiled, shaking his head.

'They are much happier than you think,' he said, speaking slowly, with only a faint foreign accent defining the words more clearly. 'Their needs are very small. They can build a house for themselves in two days. . . . And live on very little.'

I wanted to stay and wring from him, if I could, some of what he had learnt in his forty-five years in India, with no leave home to break or disturb it. What he could have told me, since he told me so much in a few minutes! But he was old and liked to go to bed early, I remembered, and it was getting late. So I stood up reluctantly. He came to the door with us. And as he stood there saying goodbye he asked us what we had thought of the Taj – for of course we had come to see that, else why would we have been visitors in Agra?

I said exactly what I was feeling – that I had seen too many tombs in India, and wanted now not to see another tomb for a long time. I felt – for all the beauty – the sickliness of this glorification of the body in death, and the sickliness remained with me with the remembrance of the over-sweet, withering jasmine flowers that we had been given by Mumtaz' tomb. I had thought there again, with relief, of the Christian kings who had been laid humbly on a bed of ashes when their time came to die.

Answering Father Francesco, I said something of this. I was sure that he would agree with me when I spoke of being sickened by this glorification of the mortal body in death. I thought he would agree warmly and that he would say, perhaps, that only for the glory of God should such a beautiful building be raised, such exquisite work provided to ornament it. I was sure that that would be the thought of Father Francesco, who had spent forty-five years in India for the love of God, and would go to Heaven some day – quite soon, probably – without ever seeing his beloved Florence again, although the mention of it could still stir him, as his face had shown; and who was content in his loneliness because he had sown a little seed and watched it grow in those forty-five years.

Instead he looked at me with gentle eyes over his great white beard.

'Oh, I don't know,' he said slowly, with that faint accent cutting his words more clearly. 'I think, if he loved her as much as all that, he was quite right to do it.'

All the tolerance and wisdom and compassion of the ages was in that slow speech of the man who had given up everything – the celibate, looking from his long peace of renunciation on the human love and passion – with its ecstasy and pain – of men and women.

Only after I had returned from India and had written this, did I read a description of the tomb raised about the bones of St Francis Xavier at Goa, which, the writer declared proudly, could be compared to that built for Mumtaz-i-Mahal at Agra! I read it a little sadly, remembering how my mind had rested, among the tombs, on the thought of the simplicity of Christian death. After all human nature, Eastern or Western – Indian or Portuguese – is not always so different in its expression of veneration.

DENIS JOHNSTON
1901–1984

Denis Johnston's first and best-known play – *The Old Lady Says 'No!'* – owed its title to its rejection by Lady Gregory, then a director of Dublin's Abbey Theatre. Subsequently produced in 1928 by Edwards and Mac Liammóir at the Gate, it was followed by the more conventional *The Moon in the Yellow River*. Born in Dublin of a father who was to become a Supreme Court judge, Denis Johnston was himself called to the Bar but, following the moderate success of his plays, became a scriptwriter and television drama producer in Belfast and London. During World War II he was a BBC war correspondent, reporting with daring and originality from North Africa, Italy, the Balkans and Germany. His book *Nine Rivers from Jordan* (1953), from which this chapter is taken, records his wartime experiences, including his periodic return to neutral Ireland; it is subtitled *The chronicle of a journey and a search*. In 1950 he embarked on a new career as a teacher in several American universities.

THE THRONE OF CHARLEMAGNE
NOVEMBER 1944

There is snow over Verdun, where, ankle deep in slush, 12th Army Group Headquarters is housed in an old Cavalry Barracks. A bitter wind whistles over the battlefields of an earlier war, as a Military Policeman holds us up and makes us take down the hood of our jeep.

– General Patton's orders.

– But General Patton has nothing to do with me.

– I should worry. These are his rear areas, and if General Patton says, No jeep covers, that means No jeep covers.

I suggested putting it up again as soon as we were round the next corner, but our driver and his buddy were in a hurry to get back for a dance that evening. So we sat and shivered through Longwy, and over the open frontier into yet another country – Belgium.

First it was Peraea and the Land of the Ammonites. Then I crossed the Jordan and passed through the Wilderness of Judaea. By Edom and the Desert of Sinai I had reached the Delta of the Lower Nile – traversed Marmarica and Cyrene and came to the Island of the Knights of St John.

Then over the Middle Sea, by the coasts of Sicily and Calabria, to where I had landed in Apulia, still journeying onwards in search of something that might perhaps have been more discernible if only I had been certain what it was. Through Samnium and Campania, through Latium and Etruria I had continued my search. Umbria knew me, and Picena. Until now by way of Burgundy and the country of Lothaire, I had entered Brabant, and before me lay the lair of the beast, deep in the dark forests of Mitteleuropa.

The milestones of this journey are like the footsteps of the race. In some odd and rather mystical way they seem to parallel the course of life itself, from childhood to maturity – a journey, maybe, in search of its own meaning.

In the heat of youth we live in a world peopled by giants and pygmies – an exciting and chivalrous affair, full of gaiety and despair. The earth is wide and empty, lit here and there by camp fires, and resounding with songs and revolver shots. It is a universe of heroes and villains, where empires are staked on the spin of a coin. It has a loneliness that can be most profound; but it also has an exhilaration that one never finds again.

This is the beginning of our journey, and it is like the beginning of life too.

Then you grow up a little. You enter a land of chaffering and intrigue, where early romantic values fade away, giving way to cynicism and a series of question marks. In place of the sweat and the fiery dust, there is mud and rain, and long days and slow-moving nights of profitless discomfort. The heroes and the villains are no more. There is nobody now, except Competents and Incompetents – and most of them rogues. The struggle becomes far more profound, and a new note of bitterness creeps in. Death becomes a reality and is no longer a romantic myth.

Yet there are compensations: and although you look back on desert days with some nostalgia, it is unlikely that you would go back even if you had the chance.

In middle age, too, you begin to think about religion, if you are at all inclined that way. You are past the time when, to lay claim to a personality of your own, it is necessary to be *der Geist des Wiederspruchs* – the Spirit that Denies. The accumulated wisdom and experience of the human race ceases to be a thing to be contradicted on principle, and you find that you have become strong enough to separate the kernel from the husk. Even to one who is neither frustrated nor afraid of Hell, Religion turns out to have a meaning. What it is, I am not certain yet; and I shall take nobody's verdict until I have found out for myself.

Maybe that is what I am looking for – here in snowclad old age – in and out of these overheated hotels, with the blizzard beating on the windows, and a well-balanced diet of transatlantic vitamins.

Mir ist es winterlich im Liebe.

We have nearly gone full circle now, for these Ardennes are whiter than my temples, and after some years' delay, my steel helmet, painted to match the sandhills of El Imayid, is in camouflage again – or would be if I had not lost it long ago. Full circle, and nearly home.

Colour of hair – Black?

Yes, I have the makings of a gnarled old man now – more careful and yet more indifferent, slower moving but farther moving, dashing about far less but covering much more ground. And although I no longer have any of that old urge to be shelled, I am, I believe, far more genuinely nonchalant about my personal fate than ever before. I would like to be luckier than my Mother, and die a violent death. (I hope her grave is being looked after.) Yes – a violent death would be a happy ending.

But not just yet. There are still several things that I have to do.

As a Correspondent most of my personal aims have been achieved. I have seen the turn of the tide, and have helped to set a pace that has long outstripped me. There is no argument now as to where our proper place is. Vaughan has recorded over Berlin, and Guy Byam has jumped in Normandy. Stan Maxted has been through Arnhem, and Matthews has interviewed Tito. Indeed, the difficulty now is to be given the opportunity to attempt these things. Everybody is chasing glory, and the hotels are crammed with War Correspondents of all sexes.

It seems that I have been relegated to our allies, the Americans, while the others fight amongst themselves for what they imagine to be the centre of the stage – the British Second Army. I can see from the way they handle the news, that my employers are not in the slightest interested in the American Armies or anything that happens outside the North Belgian area.

But, they are wrong again – dear old smarties – and I have once again got just what I would have chosen.

If the Egyptians and the Arabs were to people my Homeric period, and the British and the children of Machiavelli were to be my companions in middle age, how appropriate it is that this Third Movement should be conducted by the New World . . . a crowded, fast moving world – cruel yet warm-hearted, with the Big Time Stuff as its watchword.

From now on it is going to be the Americans' war. And now that I am alone amongst Americans and no longer floundering in an area of divided control, I am beginning to notice the qualities that I once knew, and sadly missed in Italy. More important still, I can see that – in the words of one of their songs – they are Going My Way, and will help me to carry out the remaining items of a private programme. I have, for instance, not yet visited Eckartsberga, or found the Dove that will tell me I am home.

How lucky I am not to be expected to entertain the British public every evening from Eindhoven, as all my colleagues wish to do.

US First Army Press Camp is in a hotel behind the Bubble Baths in Spa. At the reception desk sits an uninterested youth smoking a cigar and reading an illustrated paper. Beside him, a small portable wireless plays a popular tune. He does not know anything about my arrival and cares less. In the Drivers' Waiting Room – occupying the best part of the main lounge – a mass of adolescents are shouting each other down over another radio, and they look with some distaste on this new arrival who has ventured to intrude with an enquiry about morning transportation into Aachen.

My arrival in a new campaigning area has put me back where I started from in the matter of transport. My beloved jeep is still in

Rome, and it seems my employers imagine that I will be content to ride with other Correspondents in PR jeeps, towing my recording equipment behind me in an open trailer. This arrangement is intended to free the BBC vehicles (of which there are now great numbers) for the use of the Mammoth Circus at Eindhoven – except for a few that are required by Engineers in Paris and Brussels for other purposes. But they can think again. I know a thing worth two of that.

However, there are some excellent changes. Silken-voiced PROs no longer regard us as 'guests', and relegate us to the garrets and the cellars, while they reserve the best accommodation for themselves. The Press is considered a legitimate part of the Americans' war. I have a good-humoured and companionable recording engineer called Laurie Heyhurst – a bright and obliging youth with a cupboard full of bottles, and a lamentable thirst for any sort of danger. A vast network of coffee stalls and evening movies make life more tolerable in spite of the weather. And we have, of course, Americans in their thousands, with their own set of habits, tricks, enthusiasms, and peculiar little ways.

As every Briton's ideal is to have an Assistant, so most Americans like to invent Administrative Machinery. With the boundless energy that makes them shout and act tough, they are never satisfied simply with doing whatever has to be done. They love to organise it. Take the Piazza Garibaldi in Naples where there used to be some traffic congestion. They organised that all right. In fact, they tied it into such knots that a couple of British Redcaps, without whistles of course, had to go down and straighten it out. Then there is this matter of indoctrination. Driving into a ruined town, where most of the roads were impassable, I drew up beside a GI who was on duty in the central square.

– Say, fella, I asked, which is the way out of this town?

– Couldn't rightly say. Ain't been here more'n a day or two myself.

– Well, is there an Information Post or an MP anywhere around?

– Couldn't say for sure.

– You couldn't say. Well, maybe there's an officer or a CP where I could ask a few questions?

– Reckon there must be somewheres.

– Look, bud, what are you doing here yourself?

– I'm on guard.

– Over what?

– Well, I guess the Sergeant didn't say what. I just gotta stick around and see everything's OK.

– Suppose the Sergeant never comes back, what will you do? Where will you go?

– He'll come back. I've got his mail.

– OK, bud. You win.

I told this story to some of my pals as an illustration of what was on my mind about the American Army, and one of them said:

– Ah, but you don't see the point of that. That was really Security. He wasn't going to give away valuable information to any Tom, Dick or Harry who happened to turn up and ask him questions. He's been indoctrinated.

In the Field Post Office at Spa there are two men. One stops and sends back all my outgoing mail because it has an American stamp on it when it is not going to America. As soon as I remedy this, the other steps in and sends it back because it has not got an American stamp on it. I have no sooner cleared the matter up to nobody's satisfaction, when a new man arrives and stops it all over again, because it is addressed to Eire – a neutral country – and he has here on his file a lengthy brochure headed 'Mail to Neutral Countries' that has been framed to regulate the correspondence of GIs with characters in Switzerland and Spain. From Paris another official carries on a long wrangle with both Betty and myself, saying that I should not endorse my envelopes with 'APO240' as heretofore instructed, but with 'APO878b', and that Betty should write to me under the same veil of secrecy. But when we comply, her letters are promptly returned, marked 'Address unknown. Return to Sender'.

However, Betty and I soon manage to find a way of writing to each other in spite of these difficulties. I enclosed my letters in the Paris Press Bag, where somebody usually handed them over to the British; while she wrote to me:

c/o British Liberation Armies
Brussels

where some good angel would chew over the name on the envelope and say:

– That's the BBC man. Didn't I hear him on the air from the Yanks? Send it up to Public Relations, Spa.

Of course, both practices were illegal, but you have to be illegal when dealing with American machinery. And nobody thinks any the worse of you when you are found out; because they are all being illegal themselves in some way or another.

But perhaps my most characteristic experience was in connection with a steel helmet. To avoid the nuisance of being continually harassed in General Patton's rear areas for not wearing a helmet, I made up my mind to obtain one of these pieces of headgear, and presented myself at a Sales Store hoping to buy one.

Oh no. I couldn't buy a helmet. Helmets were Issue, and were not for sale. So much the better, I replied. Then please issue me one. But oh no, they don't Issue anything at a Sales Stores. Everything here is for sale. Then where do they issue Helmets? They really didn't know. Check.

– Look here, I said to the attendant, let's get down to fundamentals. You have a helmet yourself?

– Sure.

– Well, where did you get it?

– I got it back in the States.

– Check. Well, let's suppose you lost your helmet in the mêlée of a great battle. What would you do then?

– But I didn't lose it. I'd get into trouble if I lost it.

– My friend lost his helmet once, an interested onlooker interposed.

– Good. What did he do to get another?

– He went to his Supply Sergeant.

– Now we're really getting somewhere. Where is the nearest Supply Sergeant?

– Right across there in the other building.

– Thanks, pal, that's all I want to know.

In the Supply Sergeants' Store I found two extremely unattractive characters brooding over shelf-loads of precious objects – flashlamps, shot-guns, goloshes, cakes of soap, insect powder, blankets, jeep-cushions, mufflers, and HELMETS by the dozen . . .

– Please, can I have a helmet?

– We ain't got no helmets.

– Well (pointing), might I have one of those things over there, off that shelf?

His face assumed a malevolent expression.

– What happened to your own helmet?

– I never had one. (This was not strictly true, but I felt that to enter into a description of the Libyan Campaign would be beyond my powers of endurance.)

– Then why do you want one now?

– To please General Patton. He says I ought to have one.

This was definitely too much. They didn't care a damn about General Patton. If General Patton wanted me to have a helmet, let him give me one himself. And anyway those ones there were only the outsides of helmets. They were no good without the insides, and they wouldn't have insides till next week.

Checkmate.

I went away to think this over. I was definitely getting nowhere by these methods. Obviously, the difficulty was one that could be met only by the method of the Indirect Approach. So I studied my Liddell Hart for the rest of the week, and presently turned up before another but very similar Supply Sergeant.

– What's on your mind? he asked.

– I want a flashlamp.

– Oh, so you want a flashlamp?

– Yes, that's what I want.

– And who might you be?

– I am a War Correspondent. A *British* War Correspondent.

The enormity of this took his breath away. When he had fully recovered, he started to work on me. These flashlamps, he said, had not been brought four thousand miles through storm and peril just to be given away to War Correspondents – least of all to Limeys. Who did I think I was, expecting to be issued with valuable equipment like a flashlamp? How were his GIs going to get about at nights, maybe to and from the movies, if he was to issue all these good American flashlamps to anybody who liked to walk in here and just ask for one? Why didn't I have a flashlamp of my own? Didn't they make them in England?

– I am really very sorry, I said, as soon as he had spent himself. You see, I thought this was a Supply Store, where I could get any equipment that I needed.

– Sure, it's a Supply Store. Who said you can't get equipment? That's what we're here for, if it's necessary. But what's necessary about a flashlamp? That's a luxury. And, brother, you'll get no luxuries out of me at the expense of our GIs.

I hung my head. I saw it all now. I should never have come here with such a request. It would have been quite different if I had been in a jam about something that wasn't a luxury? But a flashlamp – oh dear!

– You've said it. There's a war on. We're here to do business. Not to hand out luxuries.

– Of course. It'd be quite different if I was going up forward and hadn't got something like – say, a steel helmet?

– Sure it would be different. That would be reasonable. But not flashlamps!

– Good. Then *give me a helmet*!

I got it. Indeed, before many moons had passed I had a flashlamp too. It only requires time and a little application.

So, over the frontier and into the Rhineland. Our first contact with hostile civilians was in the town of Eupen. This is one of those places that belonged to Germany before the first war and was taken by Belgium in 1919, and then was taken back again by Hitler in 1940, and is now being liberated for the third time – very reluctantly, if the stony stares are any guide. Maybe too much liberation dulls the taste.

Behind the Dragons' Teeth of the Siegfried Line lie enemy pillboxes, half buried in soil. This seems to have been the simplest way to deal with them. A Tankdozer approaches, and scoops a great heap of earth over them, and then passes on, leaving the occupants buried, until a convenient moment arrives to dig them out.

But it is Aachen that is the really thought-provoking sight. An entire city wrecked from end to end – the few remaining inhabitants creeping out from their cellars to scrounge for God-knows-what on which to live.

Aachen had been frantically defended from street to street and from house to house – like Ortona and Cassino, but on a larger scale. In a newspaper is the photograph of four small boys, from eight to eleven years, who took part in its defence, and are now the object of much controversy. Are they Franc Tireurs, to be properly executed as civilians in arms? Or members of the Home Guard? Or four extremely brave little boys who were doing their best to protect their homes, and who, if they were British or Americans, in the same circumstances would be remembered as heroes? The consensus of opinion is that they are little gangsters who will have to be taught a lesson. It just goes to show the influence of Hitlerism on youth. So they have been lined up and photographed, before being marched off to some unknown destination.

In the Hurtgen Forest, both sides are bogged down in a savage stalemate, and the shells are bursting in the branches of the trees, thus causing twice as much human destruction. From a slag heap overlooking Eschweiler I pick up another of those pamphlets.

The war is not over yet – it says. Another Christmas in the field. And for what? For the Poles, for the Bolshies and for Tito.

Maybe this Christmas. But I would not mind betting it will be the last Christmas when such a question will arise. Nothing can save them now – not the six SS Panzer Divisions that we know are lurking in the shrubbery – not the Endwaffe – this mysterious final weapon, that we know both sides are racing to acquire – not these flying bombs that roar over our heads day and night on their way to Liège, to Antwerp and to England. All they can do now is to infuriate the people at home beyond the bounds of reason, and make the Peace a terrible one.

As an instalment of which we now have a 'No Fraternisation' Order, lest the fighting men should be tempted to show any of their normal good feeling.

God, what a world we live in! What an unfortunate, maladjusted species we are! For it is all inevitable. We must go on into Germany and they must try to keep us out to save their own poor bloody lives. And then somebody will discover the Endwaffe, and after that, I suppose it may be expected that the Human Race will no longer be capable of coping with the problems that its own ingenuity creates.

I suppose God is tired of us. Or maybe we are just tired of ourselves?

Through the industrial suburbs and slagheaps we work our way in the wake of the slowly moving battle – Laurie Heyhurst, a French Correspondent called Nivelle, and myself. Through rain and snow and continual blizzards, until at last we enter a dreary factory town called Eschweiler that has been in the centre of the battlefield for a considerable time. This, for the Americans, is 'Thanksgiving Day' – though what anybody has got to be thankful for it is difficult to see.

I am going through a mass of junk and old files in the ruins of the Police Barracks to see if I can find anything of interest, muttering a fragment of a nursery rhyme in which the name of one of my companions is immortalised.

> *Le Chien de Jean Nivelle,*
> *S'en va quand on l'appelle.*

There is the usual hole in the roof, and the stairs are wet and slippery with rain. My hands are full of papers, and I have some fancy police insignia that I feel would be appreciated by my son, if I could ever get them to him. Suddenly my feet slip from under me, and I find that I have no hands to save myself.

At the bottom of the stairs I pick myself up, less hurt than might be imagined. But back in Spa that evening, it becomes increasingly evident that the point of my elbow is broken off. . . .

WILLIAM KELLY

c. 1813–1872

Born in County Sligo, the son of a flax merchant, William Kelly was
bred to the law but in 1849 left Ireland for America and the Californian
goldfields, subsequently recording his experiences in a book published
in 1852. On his return to Europe, his curiosity was aroused by
rumours circulating as to the wealth of the Australian goldfields and
he set off with his brother for Melbourne, arriving in April 1853. For
the next four years he travelled extensively in Victoria, embarking on a
succession of business ventures which failed to make his fortune but
which enabled him to gather material for a witty and informed
account of antipodean mores which was published in two volumes in
1859 under the title *Life in Victoria*. This extract, from volume two,
offers a first-hand account of Australia's first and so far only
revolution, led by Irishman Peter Lalor. Kelly was later attracted to the
goldfields of British Columbia before marrying and settling in France,
where he died.

THE DIGGERS' REVOLT

I would be sadly wanting in pleasurable and grateful reminiscences
if I omitted noticing the introduction of ice at this time, for which the
colony stands indebted to the enterprise of a Boston house represented
in Melbourne – a speculation, by the way, which most handsomely
reimbursed the projectors. Ice is a domestic luxury which of late
years has come to be understood even in the colder parallels of
latitude, but to be thoroughly appreciated, to be enjoyed with
worshipful thanksgiving, and hailed as one of Nature's most delicious
benefactions, it must be used in the tropics, or in those bordering
regions of the earth which burst into jungle and all sorts of rank
vegetation, as if from the sweltering perspiration from man and

beast which saturates the soil. When returning home from my rambles in California, the Sandwich Islands, and Central America, I well remember what an ice-worshipper I became during our few days' stay at the beautiful island of St Thomas's. How constant I was in my attendance at the cool, shaded, marble-slabbed shrine, where that delicious soluble crystal was ministered in an endless variety of fascinating forms, courting silent reverence in a 'lemon cream,' creating audible worship in a sherry-cobbler, and frequently superinducing fanaticism under the guise of 'raspberry-punch'. But it was not until I came to Victoria, and got half baked in the dry, roasting, hot winds of the country, that I became fully indoctrinated in the virtues of ice. Believe me, the transition from breathing high toast Australian dust to sucking the frigid essence of a brandy-spider through a straw, is something which must be experienced before it can be at all understood.

It was 'a right-down sight' to witness the fevered crowds that besieged the bars of the Criterion and the Union as soon as the three monosyllables, 'Ice! Ice! Ice!' in titanic letters, figured over their portals. During the famine year in Ireland, when gaunt hunger griped the bowels of the people in its torturing grasp, I never saw suffering groups in a soup-kitchen half so importunate as those whom I saw clamouring for their drinks at the above dispensaries. Nor did I ever observe poor creatures, weakly from inanition, in the outskirts of a starving crowd, more perfect impersonations of wistful wretchedness than some of the exhausted sponges who were watching in the background for a gap to the counters. A paraphrase of the barber's sign would have suited admirably for those houses that were fortunate enough to obtain some splinters from this marvellous magnet:

Let those now drink who never drank before,
And those who always drank, now drink the more;

though, in fact, no such exhortation seemed in the least necessary, for everybody drank freely, and many incessantly. Unrestrained by the slightest qualms of fastidiousness, although the precious riches which were mumbled in the foul mouths of the front rank were thrown (before their eyes), with their drainage, into the ice-tub from which their successors were helped with a bare hand, it never created a murmur; not did I hear a remonstrance, though I frequently saw sodden straws, lukewarm from the clammy lips of one man, coolly stuck into the sherry-cobbler of him that came after. But thirst is admitted to be the most despotic of appetites, and when a poor fellow gets into its clutches, adieu to all squeamishness. Perhaps the knowledge that the supply of the first season was a short one, helped, with the usual perversity of human nature, to beget and sustain the inordinate demand; for we all know that desire increases with restriction, and that the same article which in its abundance is neglected or despised, in its scarcity is craved for and sought after with avidity. However, scarcity is not likely again to prevail in the Victorian ice market, for the original purveyors, at the first experiment, found the public appetite so genuine, that they made arrangements which, since then and for the future, will prevent anything like dearth in that Arctic commodity. And now that rapid communication with the interior is ensured by means of well-organised lines of fast coaches, ice is quite an ordinary article of consumption in the very remote settlements. Even Beechworth, the capital of the Ovens district, at a distance of two hundred miles from the capital, is every summer fully supplied with the crystallised surface-water of Wenham Lake.

Parliament continued to sit through October and the principal part of November in a regular and methodical manner, and as there was no subject of public importance brought under its consideration, the debates were never relieved from their humdrum, dead-level monotony by any corruscations of that wit or oratory which, like other of the long-hidden treasures of the colony, may lie entombed in the brains of Victorian statesmen, buried beneath a thick craniological formation, the blue trap of Professor M'Coy, and equally difficult of penetration. Far otherwise, it is to be regretted, were the deliberations of the digging community at Ballarat, where the digger-hunting was in the zenith of its glory, and the temper of the people at a white heat. The receipts of gold in the treasury were seriously affected by this state of things, for the diggers only worked fretfully, by fits and starts, unable to settle down to continuous labour while their minds were so agitated.

Public meetings were of daily occurrence, where extreme counsels were vehemently urged, especially by Scotch and American agitators, but the calmer and more rational exhortation of some influential parties induced them to have recourse to all the resources of moral remonstrance before resorting to physical force. And such, I believe, would have been their tactics, only for the wanton aggravation of those in power, who, not content with following up the persecutions of the license-tax with the utmost rigour, most improperly and unconstitutionally determined on dispersing all assemblages of the people for whatever purpose convened. This illegal determination was enforced in the most arbitrary and offensive way, charging crowds of people, peaceably assembled to discuss their grievances and the proper mode of seeking their redress, as if they were armed rebels levying war against the Queen. Such insane and unjustifiable conduct had the effect which any one but a quarter-deck despot might have easily foreseen. The masses became incensed to the last degree, to the uttermost edge of forbearance, advancing from moral remonstrance to passive resistance, only separated by the narrowest of Rubicons from open insurrection.

A final resolution was come to at a monster meeting on the Bakery Hill, where all diggers who possessed licenses came voluntarily forward and threw them within a circle – a ceremony which continued until the last was laid upon the heap, which was then set on fire, and as the flames arose a simultaneous and unanimous vow ascended to heaven with all the solemn sincerity of a religious ritual, pledging the entire congregation 'never again to take out a license, be the consequences what they might'. By this move it was calculated the Government would be checkmated, as they could not arrest the entire community, and if they did, there was no prison sufficiently large to confine them. This, in reality, was a state of things quietly and adroitly brought about by the well-disposed citizens of Ballarat, who calculated to a certainty that when affairs arrived at such a crisis the Government would seize it with avidity as a pretext for abandoning or gradually backing out of its infatuated policy. But its jaundiced vision was not to be cleared; Sir Charles was not a man to revoke his decrees. He nailed his colours to the mast, determined to abide the consequences – a brave, perhaps a commendable, resolve in a sailor, but a silly, short-sighted policy for a statesman.

When things came to this pass, the intervention of moral-force men was repudiated. Their homilies were scouted, and men who had arms began looking them up, while those who were without them set out in search of a supply. Still the diggers determined not to be the aggressors, but to be prepared for any extremity. The Scotch and American instigators were now in their glory at the near prospect of collision. The fiery cross was ready for telegraphic despatch, and the Californian Rangers were primed and loaded, both ready and anxious for the fray. The next move on the board was a concerted agreement to allow the authorities peaceable ingress and egress over the field, but to rescue any prisoners they arrested. This led to several scuffles, but to no general mêlée, until a policeman, with a hold of a digger, was seized and thrown bodily into a hole. Then the police, horse and foot, charged in different directions, hoping to split up and disperse the people, but, failing in their manoeuvres, and receiving some injuries in the conflict, a mounted trooper was despatched to the camp for the military, who, after a lapse, came down at double-quick with fixed bayonets. Prior to their arrival at the scene of tumult, the crowd had separated into detached groups to take ulterior counsel as to ultimate measures. Nothing, however, deserving the character of organisation was chalked out. No concerted movement was agreed upon. There was all the raw material for a formidable revolt, but there was no master-mind to marshal it into effective shape, no elected leader to stand at the head of the array. The mouse that emerged from this convulsive parturition was the erection of a flaunty flag – the Southern Cross – for a few hours on Bakery Hill, whence it was removed on a Wednesday evening to the Eureka, and became recognised as the rallying-point for the discontented and the designing. At this rendezvous, under the stimulating counsels of American declaimers, who expatiated flippantly on the glories of republicanism, extreme measures were at length decided on, and all men who volunteered to join in the mad movement for achieving independence from the British yoke were enjoined to come armed and prepared for immediate action. This injunction was the final resolution of the Thursday evening, but when the following morning had lengthened sluggishly out towards noon, it became painfully palpable that, as the critical moment drew nigh, the muster-roll, instead of swelling, became perceptibly defective. Even the braggart, fire-eating instigators absented themselves from head-quarters. The Gallic tone or the Yankee twang no longer led in the chorus of revolt; the accents prevailing amongst the deluded mob, who still continued to rally beneath the standard of the southern hemisphere, was the Irish brogue and the German accent, and from each of these races a commander was chosen. The choice of the former fell upon a young

man, who inherited from his honest and patriotic sire, Pat Lalor,[1] a
hatred of oppression and a genuine love of independence, but his
early lessons in the art of acquiring civil liberty were not tinged with
blood or tinctured with crime. The rudiments of his political education
initiated him into the conviction, which he carried with him from his
native country, 'that freedom, at the cost of human blood, was not to
be regarded as a blessed possession'; and, true to his parental
inculcations, as also, I believe, to his natural instincts, he used all the
influence he could wield, from the very modest position he assumed
in the movement, in inducing his fellow-colonists to abstain from
any physical opposition to the constituted authorities, until every
legal and constitutional resource was perfectly exhausted; but seeing
that his countrymen, both committed and determined, were blindly
bent on rushing to their doom in utter ignorance and confusion, he
acquiesced in their selection, while he deplored the folly and
hopelessness of their cause. He placed his head beneath the axe
rather in sympathy than expectation, for he never looked forward to
any result but that which ensued. He showed his brethren that his
blood as well as his counsel were at their service in any emergency.
Mr Vern was the man chosen by the Germans. Of his antecedents I
know nothing, but of his conduct in his capacity of commander of the
German legion I have heard several of his countrymen talk in terms
of denunciation, and never an individual indulge in any eulogistic
observation.

Peter Lalor was, however, more regarded as commander-in-chief,
and his earliest order was to fortify their position by means of a
stockade, which was erected in a rude and hasty manner with slabs
and hurdles. A smith's forge was erected inside, for the purpose of
making and repairing hostile weapons, casting bullets, and cooking
victuals; and on Saturday morning, as the defections from the camp
became more serious, mustering parties were despatched into the
various districts, to coax, and, if necessary, coerce the attendance of
recruits, as well as to collect all idle arms. This manœuvre, however,
not only failed, but proved disastrous, for a sort of panic seized the
great majority of the diggers, numbers of whom deserted their tents
and claims, secreting themselves in the Bush, or retreating to Creswick

---

1   Peter Lalor, surnamed 'honest Pat,' was chosen as the representative of his native county in the
Imperial Parliament by the popular voice, and was greatly respected in 'the House' for his
independence and sound sense.

Creek, where their dismay is said to have disbanded a formidable array of a thousand well-armed men who were about marching to the camp.

This sad state of affairs soon became known at the Government camp by means of scouts, who were privily distributed through all the disaffected districts, and brought about an entire change in the military dispositions there. Previously the confident impression was that the whole body of diggers were to act on the offensive, and invest the Government quarters *en masse*, and, in consequence, the soldiers and police, under the command of General Nicol, entrenched themselves as strongly as possible, never venturing beyond the precincts of their encampment, and always ready to stand to their arms at an instant's notice. But, so soon as the intelligence of the popular wavering and apprehension reached them, General Nicol resolved to bring matters to an immediate issue by marching on the stockade, to force it if possible in a bloodless way, but, under any circumstances, to gain possession of it, and break up the rebel nucleus at any cost, for, independent of the highly demoralising effect produced by its continued existence, the public loss by the general idleness was calculated at tens of thousands of pounds a day.

On Saturday evening, instead of ten, or at least five thousand men-at-arms, which was confidently calculated on, the malcontents barely numbered two hundred; and so far from the appearance of allies arriving, the entire neighbourhood around the stockade became literally deserted. Still, the hope of succour was not entirely abandoned; every distant noise was interpreted into the approach of a Scotch reinforcement, or the advance of the Californian Rangers. However, when evening merged into night, Lalor, after sounding the disposition of the handful of true and desperate men around him, and finding them still fixed in their purpose, despatched a few trusty men to reconnoitre about the camp, and about an hour before dawn they returned with the intelligence that the military and police were under arms marching down to attack the stockade. Lalor then hurriedly reviewed his scanty, ill-assorted band, and issued a positive order 'not to fire except in return, or until the troops attempted forcing their entrenchments'; but as soon as they were discerned in the grey light advancing in close column, and before they had come within range, a ruffian, who was subsequently discovered to have been a Government spy, discharged his powder-loaded musket in the direction of the troops, who, as if it was a preconcerted signal, jumped into a double-quick with Captain Wise at their head; but they halted suddenly as they approached the rebel entrenchments, and discharged a deliberate volley, under which several fell mortally wounded. This was returned by a prompt discharge from the other side, which unfortunately took effect on Captain Wise, when in the act of scaling the stockade, and calling on his men to follow him to the capture of the flag; two soldiers also received deadly wounds, but a flanking fire from the police, and a renewed round from the soldiers, carried death and dismay amongst the misguided revolutionists, who had not time to reload before they were charged and routed at the point of the bayonet. Fourteen diggers were found dead around the flagstaff, and a large number of wounded were carried off, Mr Lalor amongst them, wanting his left arm; one hundred and fifty prisoners were also captured in and around the stockade, an within half an hour from the discharge of the signal-shot the Ballarat rising was at an end.

ARTHUR LEARED
1822–1879

'A record of what was seen of a Court and its surroundings, in which
pomp and barbarism are strangely blended': thus Dr Arthur Leared, a
Wexford man, of his account of *A Visit to the Court of Morocco* (1879),
from which this passage is extracted. He had joined a delegation from
the Embassy of Portugal in Tangier which was proceeding to Fez to
congratulate the Sultan on the occasion of his accession to the throne,
but the latter opted to receive them in Mequinez (now Meknès), here
described. Arthur Leared, who was accompanied by his wife, acted as
physician to the expedition – and to a number of chance 'patients'
encountered en route. He was an inveterate traveller and, in his
professional capacity, the inventor of the double stethoscope; he also
wrote a medical treatise in Icelandic, having visited that country
several times. This account of Morocco was based on a paper read in
1878 at the Dublin meeting of the British Association for the
Advancement of Science.

GUESTS OF THE SULTAN

The guest house of the Sultan, to which we were conducted, situated
in a blind street near the great Mosque, El Kebir Cubith Sook, was in
fair repair for a Moorish building. The open-air central tiled space or
patio, in which was a fountain that constantly played, was 35 feet
square. A lofty room ten feet wide opened on each side into the patio.
These rooms had no windows, and the weather being hot, the large
arched doorways were only closed by curtains. On the floor above,
rooms, the counterparts of those below, opened on to a wide wooden
balcony. It was, in fact, an eight-roomed house, having attached to it
some small dark rooms for kitchen, bath rooms, &c. The stone stairs
resembled those found in mediæval castles, in their narrowness and

steepness. The rooms were simply whitewashed, and without decoration, except that the lower part of the sides of the doorways was covered with tiles arranged in patterns. We had iron bedsteads, and some rooms, in addition to the divan or sofa, boasted of a chair. It was curious to observe pieces of English carpets usurping the places of the more appropriate and more handsome Moorish rugs.

As there are no milestones in Morocco, and no surveys have been made, I took pains to ascertain the distance travelled. Taking the walking pace of a mule at four miles an hour, and carefully allowing for stoppages, I arrived at the conclusion that Mequinez is 157 miles from Tangier by the road we travelled. Such was our slow progress, that eighteen days were consumed in accomplishing the journey.

Mequinez is a more modern-looking city than Fez, with wider streets. It is the sacerdotal city of the empire, and contains many large mosques and seminaries. Its high walls, with towers at about two hundred paces' distance from each other, and huge gates, some of them very handsome, gave it somewhat of a defiant aspect. The walls were made of a compound of lime and sun-dried clay, disfigured, as all such walls are in Morocco, by a number of square holes, which might be taken for loopholes for musketry. These holes are caused by the insertion of pieces of timber in building the wall, by a process to be afterwards described. The filling of these holes falls out after a time, and nesting places for birds are thus formed. Owing to this, an amazing number of hawks, jays, and pigeons, all appearing to live on perfectly friendly terms, were flushed when one went round the walls. The outside circuit of the walls seemed about five miles, and the number of inhabitants was set down by an intelligent Moor at 25,000. It was evidently formerly much larger, as so far from there being any appearance of tension from want of building room, there were many gardens and ruins within the walls. And, although we traversed the city in all directions, I saw only one house in course of erection, and that was in the Mellagh, or Jews' quarter.

In the eyes of the Moors, Mequinez, and all that belongs to it, are regarded as perfection. The mere mention of the place causes them at times to lift one shoulder in an expressive way, accompanying the act with what may be called a whistle in a whisper, as who would say, 'Ah, I believe you; that *is* the place.' The women of the city are regarded as the handsomest in Morocco, and the term 'Mequinesia' applied to any woman is looked on as a great compliment. The

political power, trade, and vastness of Fez, are duly lauded, but
Mequinez is the seat of learning, which means of theology. A great
number of the inhabitants are connected with the court, or else with
the army.

The second day after our arrival, we went by invitation to dine at
the house of the Vizier, or Prime Minister, Sid Moosa Ben Hamed, an
elderly, acute, pleasant-faced man, of very courteous manners. We
were entertained in a room opening on to a fine garden, with fountains
and terraces kept in good order. Our host, with some of his friends,
did the honours well, without partaking of the feast. A Lord Mayor's
dinner could hardly compete with this in number and variety of
dishes. The meat and poultry dishes for our small party numbered
thirty, the salads twelve, and the sweetmeats thirty-two; but there
was no dessert, and of course no wine. The ladies were admitted
afterwards into the harem, where they saw a crowd of fifty or sixty
women, varying from twelve or thirteen to fifty years of age; two of
the great man's wives were as fat as the fattest creatures ever seen at
a cattle show. The children were reported as beyond counting.

Our ladies had several other opportunities of knowing all about
this harem. The entrance was always guarded by black slaves,
creatures hardly to be called men. The Sid's legal wives were always
courteous and pleasant. Each had her own department in
housekeeping, such as cooking, washing, cleaning, &c., and they
evidently possessed extensive powers over the other women. All the
women were polite, although inquisitive; their questions were
confined to the very few subjects suggested by their limited experience
of life. Ornaments, dress (this was also very practically examined
into), health, babies, and husbands, formed the chief points of
discussion. The smallness of our ladies' waists, compared with their
own, made them laugh immoderately. The sight of Europeans was
an event in their monotonous lives. It is believed that, with the
exception of two daughters of Sir J.D. Hay, no English, probably no
European women, had been seen at Mequinez in recent times.

Four days after our arrival, the grand event of the journey, our
public reception by the Sultan, took place. At eight o'clock in the
morning we rode, through a gateway of noble proportions, into a
large quadrangular enclosure of the palace, surrounded by high
walls. From that we passed into a similar enclosure, and finally into a
third, about three acres in extent. Soldiers standing closely together

lined the walls of these great spaces. Having dismounted from our horses, we were arranged by the M'Chouar, or master of the ceremonies, opposite to a large gateway. The Ambassador, Senhor Bomtempo, and Mr Butler, were in official uniforms. Just behind us five mules stood in a row, laden with the presents from the monarch of Portugal to his Moorish brother.

Presently there was a blast of trumpets, and the great wooden gate was suddenly thrown open, and from it issued five magnificent led horses, gaily caparisoned, and bearing themselves as if conscious of the dignity of the occasion.

But the step from the sublime downwards is often abrupt. Next came forth a one-horse chaise driven by a man on foot, there being no driving seat. The horse was harnessed a long way from the little yellow vehicle. Where this could have originally come from, it would be difficult to say. One must suppose that as no one drives a carriage in Morocco, it was intended to typify the might and grandeur of its august owner, whom it immediately preceded.

The Sultan now made his appearance, mounted on a splendid grey horse. A man with a bright spear gleaming in the sunlight walked at each side of his charger. Behind the spearman on the right walked an attendant bearing a large red umbrella with a golden knob on the top of its long handle, with which his Sharifian Majesty's face was carefully shaded. Two other attendants, with white silk handkerchiefs in their hands, seemed to be assiduously dusting both horse and rider, but the meaning of this was that the troublesome flies were no respecters of persons.

At the instant the Sultan came in view, every soldier present bowed almost to the ground, and shouted at the top of his voice, 'Allah bark amar Sidna' ('The blessing of God fill our Lord'). Twice was this shouting and bowing repeated. The effect was really grand; turn where one would, hundreds of dusky faces were seen bending downwards in trained obedience, while the blended clamour of many thousand throats almost persuaded one that the object of so much devotion must be more than mortal. Anything more impressive it would not be easy to find.

We now approached close, and stood face to face with His Majesty, or more correctly speaking, with his horse. The Ambassador then read an address and handed it to the Sultan, who handed it to his Prime Minister, standing with other high officials in close attendance.

Some complimentary words were now exchanged through the medium of Mr Butler, and then the Ambassador presented us each in turn to the Sultan. Mr Murdoch, although present unofficially, received a special recognition. His name was well known to His Majesty as one of the principal merchants trading in his dominions. The reception did not occupy more than a quarter of an hour. When it was over, His Majesty, attended by his spearmen, his umbrella-bearer, and his fly-flappers, rode leisurely away through a different gate from that by which he entered. And now came the clang of Moorish music, and the uproar of five fieldpieces rapidly discharged, while the report of each was tripled by echoes from the surrounding walls. Moreover, the soldiers, no longer under restraint, added to the noise and confusion. It was a very chaos of disorder.

The ladies, mounted on their mules, witnessed the reception at a distance of about twenty yards, and it was observed that the royal eyes frequently wandered in their direction.

The Sultan, Hassan Ben Mohammed, seemed to be about forty years of age. He was tall, and of good presence. His complexion was pale and his features expressive. He gave the impression of energy and mental power. He was dressed in the usual white haic, with light blue underclothing. The horse-trappings were green-coloured, and embroidered with gold.

After the reception, we were taken to see various things connected with the royal establishment. We saw the Sultan's horses, to the number of between thirty and forty, tethered in a large yard exposed to the rays of the burning sun. Many of them were splendid animals, showing much breeding, and some were decidedly vicious. All the horses in Morocco are stallions, but the stranger must not expect to find amongst them a preponderance of fine animals. The Barb horse has a good reputation; but the truth is, most of the Moorish horses are poor mongrels, small and ill-shaped, but hardy and serviceable. Those of the right sort are highly valued, and consequently by no means easy to obtain.

We passed through two of the royal gardens, which, except in extent, differed little from others we had seen. They were orchards rather than gardens, in which were apple and pear, plum, peach, and cherry, orange, lemon, citron, pomegranate, almond, and other trees, besides vines, and a few common flowers. As the ground was well irrigated, all these grew in great luxuriance. Fairly-well-kept walks divided the grounds, and some of them led up to summer houses, decorated with tiles and arabesque ceiling decorations. In one of the summer houses was a velvet-covered French sofa.

We were also shown a large park-like enclosure, in which a number of ostriches were confined, and where they bred – an ostrich farm, in fact. The birds were very shy, and they had for companions, gazelles as wild as themselves, and also camels and horses.

Our reception by the Sultan, as might be supposed, caused us to be honoured by invitations from high officials. Sid Abdallah Ben Hamed, Governor of Fez, Sid Moosa's brother, entertained us handsomely. Our host was a small man about seventy years of age, showing more negro blood than his brother, to whom he was said to be greatly inferior in ability. He received us in an octagon room measuring about twenty-five feet from side to side, with a lofty green-painted ceiling, and green-and-white tiled floor spread with rich carpets. One side of this apartment opened by a door into a long narrow room, while the counterpart of this door and room were placed exactly opposite. On the floor of one of these outer rooms were squatted fourteen fat and sleek ulemas of the highest rank; gentlemen who combined the somewhat incongruous professions of law and divinity. Amongst them were some fine faces; that of a personage, whose post corresponded with that of our Lord Chief Justice, was particularly striking. But truth to say, what with the heat, the monotony of the music intended to entertain us, and of looking at wretched Franks feeding – all this combined intellect of the land was soon unconscious of our presence. In a word, the magnates fell asleep! In the opposite room, a number of merchants, chiefly from Fez, were congregated. Invitations had evidently been given to all these notables by our host, to come and see the Christians then on view.

This time we had napkins, plated forks, and German painted tumblers, but the only thing provided to put into the latter was tepid water. All the time of dinner – about an hour – we had to endure the noise of four singers and players on a kind of fiddle and tambourine. The viands and sweetmeats were much the same as at the Prime Minister's.

We also dined at the Grand Chamberlain's, Hadge Mahomed Ben Aish, a burly, big-featured, but good-natured looking man. He entertained us in a room opening on to a really nice garden, laid out with tiled walks, tanks, and a fountain. Our dinner service was the old willow pattern; the forks, the old steel ones. The apartment was handsomely decorated in the Moorish style, but spoiled by articles from Europe. There were great bunches of tawdry artificial flowers under tall glass shades on shelves at each end of the room; two moderate-sized mirrors in gold frames, and, most objectionable of all, four clocks, two smaller French ones, and two larger, all ticking away. In another room were two other clocks. Our host's passion for clocks was very remarkable.

The commandant of the soldiers who accompanied us from Tangier, Kaîd Mehedi, lived at Mequinez, and his invitation could not be refused. Here there was no taint of Europe. He gave us baked mutton, fowls, and kuscussoo, which we consumed in true Moorish style, without knife or fork, using only the right hand, an awkward proceeding for a novice, but in accordance with etiquette. The upper room in which we dined looked into a small patio below, and here the gimberi and tom-tom players were placed, and also a dancer and clever contortionist. One of his performances was very curious: while standing he bent his body backwards so as to pick with his eyelids a pin out of a handkerchief on the ground. A whole crowd of veiled women and children looked down on these performances from the roof of the house. One wondered where they could have come from, but it soon appeared that the inmates of neighbouring harems had, according to custom, climbed from their own roofs, attracted by the chance of a little excitement in the dull routine of their lives.

ANITA LESLIE
1914–

Daughter of Sir Shane Leslie of Glaslough, County Monaghan –
himself a prolific writer – Anita Leslie's own books range over travel,
biography, autobiography and social history. Educated privately,
during Word War II she served as an ambulance driver in South
Africa, Syria, Italy and France, transferring to the French army, with
whom she entered Berlin. She was awarded the Croix de Guerre. Her
memoirs, *Train to Nowhere* (1946), were widely considered to be the
best war book by a woman. Her other works include a biography of
Winston Churchill's American grandfather, *The Fabulous Mr Leonard
Jerome*, a bestseller when published in 1954, and a social history of
Edwardians in Love. In 1951 she sailed a small boat, the *Galway Blazer*,
with her British husband and very young baby through the Caribbean,
recording the journey in *Love in a Nutshell*. This extract opens in
Nelson's Dockyard, English Harbour, Antigua.

GUADELOUPE

Calm mornings dawned, a week of them in succession, when we
rose to swim in unrippled water that reflected the fierce scarlet
sunrise and found it too hot to walk until dusk. Just before sunset we
would row to the landing-stage opposite the dockyard and climb up
past Clarence House (a small Georgian house built for William IV
when he was the fat Duke of Clarence, a naval captain here). The
road led steadily up to a large ruined building that was once the
commander-in-chief's house. Here, where a bunch of little Negroes
watched their herds of shiny-black, browsing goats, Nelson used to
woo Mrs Mudie in her husband's absence. The road then ascended to
the heights of Fort Charlotte, where from an old stone gun platform
beside its cannon half-buried in purple fire-weed, we could sit with a
view of miles of jagged coast and jade-green bays, while the trade

winds which had swept across the Atlantic cooled the sweat off our brows.

Gradually I was beginning to understand wind! In Galway I had learnt to hide from it, building walls and shelters against the prevailing westerlies which Bill called 'wonderful air blown right across the Atlantic'. And here we were again sniffing breezes which had swept from another continent, only now it came from the east instead of the west. 'Can't one ever get to where there is no wind?' I puzzled, 'to its base, so to speak?' Bill tried to draw an Atlantic wind chart in the dry red earth. 'It never stops. It has no base. It blows round in circles. . . .' I wondered why the spinning earth did not straighten out the winds so they all blew one way, but I'd learnt not to put such questions because Bill would be sure to answer them – very technically – with pencil and diagrams.

Far below Fort Charlotte, where the bored British redcoats must have idled away their days scanning the sea for French raiders, lay a wide valley. Here long before Nelson's day the Governor had a house. A narrow arm of the sea stretches up the valley and one dark night in 1640 a party of raiding Carib Indians came up this creek by canoe. They launched a surprise attack on the Governor's house, captured his wife and carried her off by sea to their mountain stronghold in Guadeloupe. Their fighting tactics and seamanship must have been very expert to paddle in dugouts across forty miles of rough Atlantic rollers, find their objective and triumphantly paddle back.

It was some months before a return raid could be fitted out by the English – I could not find out the exact time lag, which in the circumstances is interesting – but a force was eventually dispatched to Guadeloupe and the Governor's wife was recaptured, only to reveal she had been living happily with the handsome Carib chief who she preferred to her worthy Governor! One can imagine the resultant scenes between husband and wife! It ended in angry scandal and the Governor's lady was banished to Ding-a-Dong Nook, an inaccessible bay on the other side of English Harbour. There she lived for years with heaven knows what memories or regrets. A ghostly bell tolls in the valley and the legend of her wild romance will linger on. One half-hopes that her chieftain may sometimes on dark nights have paddled his canoe to see her, but the European concept of love is so completely a result of the trained intellect that one doubts if an Indian who came to raid would return to woo.

Owing to the violent current the forty-mile channel between Antigua and Guadeloupe always has a big swell, but on the days when English Harbour lay like a mirror, with the yachts doubled in detailed reflection, up on Fort Charlotte we could see the rollers only slightly crested with white. Bill, with his face to the sky, judged the force of abating winds by the slowed pace of the great clouds that chased in endlessly from the east. In February he reckoned even Tarka Dick could go sailing and the faint outline of Guadeloupe beckoned with increased allure.

We spent several days preparing for departure. The stowage of pots of cold cream and honey so they would not crash about when the ship keeled over I had reduced to a fine art. The most violent roll never produced a jingle. But now, as well as our possessions, there was a most precious bundle to be secured in comfort for an eight-hour sail. Tarka Dick was fully weaned and we planned to leave him tucked in his basket, which in turn would be wedged in the bunk with cushions, and not to remove him during the entire trip, for the danger in sailing with a small baby lay in dropping him when a wave hit the ship. Before leaving for new lands we obtained our Bill of Health from the harbour master, and this is a document for a scrap-book, for it includes an official Crew List with brief descriptions, and the third member of our complement is solemnly registered 'height 2 ft.'.

When the local inhabitants of English Harbour heard of our intended departure they produced a touching series of farewell presents. Theodore with our last load of washing brought a red bead starfish for baby, and Nurse, knowing we loved vegetables, rowed out with the biggest egg-plant in the world. 'I'd never get tired of that little face,' she sighed wistfully as he sat in his nightgown waving both arms up and down.

We got up at five next morning, just before dawn had broken. Hardly a ripple stirred the harbour. It was *the* perfect day. While I made tea, Bill untied the sails and sweated at the anchor chain. 'You see what I meant about the importance of a boat I could manage single-handed, don't you?' he called down.

'But you aren't single-handed –'

'No, but my mathematics are so good I could calculate in advance that when one-third of the crew is preparing bottles for another third, all work has to be done by –'

'Don't dramatise yourself,' my lips opened to say, but after helping to hoist Dinghy aboard and watching the sheer gut-twisting labour of weighing anchor, I remained silent.

Meanwhile, Tarka Dick lay in a cushioned basket well wedged into the bunk with a strong fish net spread over the whole which would prevent him falling out in the most violent lurch.

He had chortled gleefully at the early morning activity, pre-supposing a day of more than extra pleasure, but by seven, when the mainsail went up and we moved slowly out of the harbour – past *Palmosa* and *Mollihawk*, past the waving Nicolsons and Nurse Blackwell and Guy Cole – he had tangled his toes in the fish net, decided it was a dull game, and finding he could not sit up, began to roar blue murder, so that his voice drowned our friends' shouts of good luck. English Harbour takes some time to tack out of and I thought he would die of fury before we reached the open sea. But the moment we slipped outside the entrance the swell rocked him to sleep. The trade winds caught us hard so that the little ship strained and bounded away from Antigua, her bow smashing through wide sapphire troughs of Atlantic breakers while the silver bodies of flying fish streaked arrow-like on every side. With mizzen and jib and mainsail pulling hard in a reaching wind the boat was at her shivering best, and at seven knots we knew the height of sailing bliss, as with lee rail submerged, *Galway Blazer* reached her highest possible speed and spray embellished her hull with new jewelled wings.

I spent eight hours glued to the compass, for concentration on steering which makes some people sick has the opposite effect on me, and with *two* men aboard to whom sea-sickness was unknown it would have been unbearably humiliating to succumb. I looked at Bill revelling in the wind's violence and heard occasional sleepy chortles from Tarka when the buffeting sea roused him from sleep. Their laughter would be unendurable.

Naturally I did not *want* Bill or the baby to be sick, but there was something very aggravating about having to take such care when I was the person who had the idea of a sailing boat in the first place.

Determination to remain out in the cockpit all day and to concentrate on steering the course preserved me from all but the fear of disaster. Bill scrambled about the heaving deck, altering sails and maintaining his balance on one toe while exhorting me to steer slightly more to windward or continuing my technical training by shouting in my ear questions such as: 'If I fell overboard now what would you do?'

'Turn into the wind or jibe?'

My terrorised mind slowed to crawling pace by the pounding waves and fear of nausea would frantically try to calculate how to jibe in one's tracks. We passed one ship, a trading schooner coming up from the south.

'Who gives way?' shouted Bill.

'We do.'

'Why?'

'Because the wind is coming from over there.'

'Say it properly.'

'*They* are on the starboard tack.'

And so I learnt.

Mont Serrat, a mountain-top of an island to the west, gleaming like pink crystal in the afternoon sun, moved slowly northwards as Antigua's cliffs faded from view. Once, in a rough patch, when my eyes had begun to ache ominously, a shoal of dolphins danced around the boat. They leapt in pairs like circus horses and teams of big silvery bodies shot through the waves on each side, suddenly arching in the air and then diving underneath us. 'If it's calm you can hear them breathe,' yelled Bill in my ear, and their pointed faces looked so friendly that I forgot about feeling seasick and hung out of the cockpit watching them till the sails began to flap violently and we were almost in irons and off our course, and it was all my fault.

Only when sailing can the mind leap to quite such intense extremes, from such rapture to the depths of pusillanimous misery. A heavy swell with little wind drives even those who are immune to sickness to despair, making them swear that never will they set to sea again, but within a few minutes unbearable hell turns to heaven and smiles show on every face. Morbid thoughts, grey-green gloom, longings for death change almost instantaneously to a sensation of excitement and speed. The sea is no longer the enemy, but foam-capped and lovely. Rainbow-tinted spray flies around and you know the elation of tearing through your own bejewelled paradise, free of all mankind.

Once we were half-way across the channel both current and wind diminished. Towards sunset, when the waves turned from blue to amethyst, we were in the lee of Guadeloupe. From the sea we looked up at sinister forest-covered mountains that soared straight up some

5,000 feet. The vegetation looked the opposite of Antigua's, where there are no high hills to catch rain, and therefore no big trees or rivers. It might have been a different continent instead of a sister island, and I imagined the last of the Carib Indians retreating into those inaccessible heights, postponing their own extinction in majestic solitude. Brutality entwined with the romance of Caribbean history throws a lingering sadness over all these lovely islands, and the dark cloud-capped mountains do seem to brood around Mont Soufriere from whose crater smoke and flames still issue forth as if the island breathed and moaned with anger.

If the story of the West Indies was less nauseating perhaps these mountains might elate, but though (unlike the gentle Arawak Indians whom the Spaniards tortured and exterminated) these Caribs were fierce warriors, their slow extinction after a long-drawn-out struggle still casts a gloom over the savage peaks. After them came gold-lusting white men and unhappy Negro slaves. All that one can sincerely say when studying the history of the early discoverers of America is how much better if such loathsome people had stayed home!

Before sunset we crept in towards the sombre heights and anchored in Des Hayes Bay, a cove of sandy beaches which according to the chart appeared to be the only good shelter on the entire east coast of Guadeloupe. A village of small cube-like wooden shacks lies on the strand, and as approaching nearer we saw a pretty white church with a red belfry, banana groves and scampering children on the sand, I visualised the luscious fruits we would at last be able to buy. The wind died as we crept slowly towards the shore, and it was easy to take the sails down and drop anchor about 200 yards from a broken wooden pier. 'Let's be quick to get the wind-sail up,' said Bill, 'before a horde of French officials come out to stifle us in the cabin.' This canvas wind-sail hung down into the opened forehatch and kept a breeze blowing through the cabin in the hottest weather. Bill had modelled it on one in his submarine and it proved most effective.

Des Hayes Bay was not a port of entry, but we imagined yachts must often call here because of the good anchorage. We were flying our yellow quarantine flag, so formalities of some sort were to be expected before we could be allowed ashore, but a friend in Antigua had assured us that Monsieur the head of the Gendarmes in Des Hayes Bay was a gentleman delighting in the dispensation of special permissions, and one who especially liked the British because they had liberated him from a Nazi camp. All he required was lively conversation and a box of candy for his wife, 'to prove the evening had been spent with respectable people'. So having our Bill of Health and a bar of nut-milk to hand, we waited casually for the arrival of this monsieur and his minions.

But no boat to put out. 'Just as well. We'll have a night's sleep in peace,' said Bill. But I could not understand it and still expected natives to paddle forth in canoes or on logs carrying succulent fruit or even garlands of flowers, for the luxuriant vegetation stretching right down the mountain-sides gave promise of paradise. Dark fell without a voice hailing us and the local lack of curiosity seemed rather annoying. If *I* had been a native of Des Hayes Bay when a beautiful sailing boat anchored two cables from shore how interested *I* should have been!

Morning found us rocked gently by a breeze from the sea. We were too sheltered in this western bay for the trades to touch us, but we watched them ceaselessly crowning the mountains with mist. It was always raining up there. You could see the clouds getting stuck on the peaks and pouring themselves out in silvery showers, a few drops of which might reach us down on the sunlit shore. Bill threw little Dinghy overboard by a new technique he had invented, to spare himself my help. It made an unorthodox splash, but proved successful, and instead of having to lift her back on the hatch by strength of arm he rigged out one of the twin jib-booms and hoisted her. Simple labour-saving gadgets mean even more in a short-handed boat than in a servantless house.

As no one had paid the slightest attention to us, Bill now decided to row ashore with our passports, Bill of Health and a large bundle of baby washing. 'Tell them I was an ambulance driver in the French Army and everything will be easy,' I called after him, and set to getting the cabin in order. An hour later Bill returned; he was hot and cross. 'They don't care if Jeanne d'Arc is aboard,' he said, 'and the gendarme who loves the British has gone to some other post. His successor loves no one and says he is unable to give a *permission de circuler*. However, a vague telephone call has been put through to a prefect in Basseterre and he may have an answer tomorrow, for the moment he just lolls in an office with a cigarette stub hanging from the corner of his mouth and we are supposed to sit here like lepers under our yellow flag.'

Only one hopeful incident had occurred. This was when a scruffy individual in an unbelievable uniform heard Bill desired to hire a car of some sort to drive along the coast. Brightening up considerably he murmured in Bill's ear something about his nephew owning a taxi. The machinations of this person might prove of avail. Otherwise our plight evoked no interest. Having been forbidden to circulate, Bill immediately proceeded to do so in search of a laundress. Inquiries finally led him to a rush hut.

'*Où est Madame?*'

'*Pas là,*' insisted a small squint-eyed boy, but the sweating skipper of *Galway Blazer* pushed past and found the washerwoman asleep beside an ash-heap. After terse bargaining he had left the laundry and returned to the boat.

'Well, let's take a day's rest and do nothing,' I suggested amiably. So we just swam and cooked and tidied up as one always has to when a boat has been at sea. Next day *Monsieur le Gendarme* actually had himself rowed out to speak to us. We tried to help him on board, but he clung pathetically to the ropes and explained he was 'not very strong at getting into boats'. Telephonic communication with Basseterre had been established. The authorities wanted to know why we had not arrived at a port of entry. 'But we have come all the way from Antigua. We have no engine and we have a baby on board.' Tarka Dick peeking out of the hatch gave a wide smile. '*Il est gracieux, le petit!*' exclaimed the gendarme, but he could give us no definite advice or suggestion.

We made our own decision about our rights ashore. Even if the permission never arrived and our request had been relegated to the bottom file of some worn-out, liver-racked, gone-to-pieces-in-the-tropics petty official, nothing was going to prevent us refilling water cans and getting diapers washed. We did not like to leave Tarka Dick alone on board, for the anchor might drag, so he came in with us to visit *Monsieur le Maire*.

The picturesque little village smelt appalling, but the huts had neat interiors all opening on to the one main street. We saw they had polished wood floors and tables spread with white cloths, greatly at variance with the filthy yards outside. *Monsieur le Maire*, an enormously fat, jovial man, sat in an open office attending to heaven knows what with maximum noise and good humour. His *café au lait* clerks and underlings lolled in other open-air offices and a crowd of small children romping in and out of the *Mairie* collected in a silent row to stare at the ash-blond baby in my arms. These natives looked extraordinarily different from the Antiguans in whom childish joy of life was always visible. Here they seemed quiet and devoid of animal spirits. They were much lighter of skin and the injection of white blood seemed to have devitalised. The small boys, instead of racing around clutching big sun hats, stood solemnly before us, all in black berets like the boys in any French town, while the older Negroes behaved as if they were the most cynical and *désillusionné* of Frenchmen. Their manners were wearily polite and they spoke a pretty musical French, but beyond courteous replies lay a sense of disenchantment. Only *Monsieur le Maire* received us with jollity; if it lay within his power to circulate us he would, but answers from Basseterre twenty miles away took a long time.

'Tomorrow? After tomorrow?'

'Perhaps.'

If the reply arrived within twenty-four hours he would row out to let us know. If not, we would hoist Dinghy aboard and sail south without our taxi ride.

This settled we strolled off to buy cheese at the corner café whence the handsome proprietor (son of the mayor) directed us to one Monsieur Ambrose, reputed to sell fruits. We found this gentleman sitting on the ill-smelling beach holding a bunch of bananas and a fish net. *Non*, he said with finality, all the fruits were *fini* long ago, and as far as that goes so was he.

He resembled a dark bronze version of the moustachioed French workman who clatters around every port in sabots. After scrutinising us at length his face lit up with a slow, rather engaging smile, the smile of a grand duke viewing the quaint. 'Oh, so you are the little family from the little boat, eh? *Très pittoresque.* Tonight, *perhaps*, I bring you cabbages and carrots.' Having extracted as much promise as possible Bill trudged off with a two-gallon water-can to fill up-river. It was very hot, so I wandered along the beach to the stream's mouth where women were washing clothes. One of them, asking if I would like to bathe the baby, led me upstream, past a tangle of banana trees and some unamused black pigs asleep in the mud. Bill had already followed the path in search of clear water for the ship. Now he was lugging the can back, and we both gazed longingly at the mountain torrent which tumbled down from the uninhabited rain-catching peaks.

I had never carried Tarka Dick so far before and he seemed to have gained a lot of weight on the boat, in fact my little gilt-skinned son made my aching arm feel as if he were modelled in solid gold. We decided to abandon the water-can with monsieur the café proprietor and to circulate ourselves by ourselves up-stream – and the devil take all lazy *prefects* and permissions that do not arrive. Bill carried baby easily on his shoulder and we followed the river up its course, splashing through pools and climbing over boulders.

Within ten minutes of the baking hot, garbage-smelling shanty-town we were sporting ourselves in a mountain torrent in a paradise lovely beyond words. Far overhead the jungle trees entwined their dark green leaves and a hundred kinds of exotic ferns and bushes tumbled down to the bank, while dappled sunlight filtered through into the racing river which danced over great stones. You could creep under a waterfall or lie full length in cool brown pools full of inch-long spotted trout. Tarka Dick had the splash of his life trying to catch sunlight in the frothing water and was then set on a warm stone to dry. Bill had not known the delight of fresh water for months. Neither Gibraltar nor the Canaries have enough for baths, and Antigua is notoriously dry, so that to plunge and plunge again without even having to turn off a tap was unbelievable. For potential plague-carriers we had a very good time. The joys of a mountain torrent are superb at any time, but on a very hot day after long arguments with petty officials they must be felt to be believed.

We rowed back to our boat intoxicated with cascading water and soft gold-mottled light.

No answer ever came from Basseterre regarding our situation, but Monsieur Ambrose, evidently amused by what he called *les pittoresques*, rowed out as he had promised with cabbages and carrots; with these and a few gatherings from the trees which dripped bananas along the shore we had to be content. Next day at dawn we set sail in the off-shore breeze. Moving along the coast of Guadeloupe we could make out ravines choking with luxuriant vegetation and imagine the sweet rivers of each; houses and hamlets lay engardened along the coast road and above them rose the flowering lonely mountains. There can be no more enchanting way of viewing a new land than to glide slowly along its shore in a sailing boat – or so I thought until the wind dropped. The sounds and smell of engine-driven transport are vile, and as long as you are not being battered to pieces at sea or completely becalmed about a mile from your destination the peace of sailing is unequalled. There is time to see what a coast really looks like.

We were creeping along in the late afternoon when a stoutly built yacht with a pink mainsail came into sight from the south. As she approached we saw the blue ensign and hailed her. She turned out to be *Moonraker* of Fowey, a well-known Cornish fishing boat which had been refitted by Dr Pye of London and sailed across the Atlantic. There were two men and a woman aboard – the same crew as *Galway Blazer*'s – only all grown-ups; Dr Pye called out: 'You must go to Iles des Saintes – Basseterre has bad anchorage,' and with a 'see you in Bermuda,' we sailed on our diverse ways. Tarka Dick went off to sleep with a bottle and the wind dropped. Although one was bound to be sheltered along the lee of each island I had not realised how completely all breeze could die on the wide water. We sat with sails flapping helplessly and wondered if we should reach Basseterre that night.

Bill hoisted the genoa to catch any faint tease of wind that rustled by. We drifted slowly past a tiny inlet which *The Pilot* mentioned as a refuge for ships in time of hurricane. We ought to have stopped trying and anchored calmly here for the night, but a flicker of breeze lured us on towards Basseterre only a couple of miles down the coast, and we were anxious to get ashore where a bank could be found to cash a traveller's cheque and stock up with the luscious fruits with which legend accredits these islands. So far we had seen only bananas – mostly green.

Basseterre crept into view and eagerly we scanned its waterfront of odd-looking wood houses and narrow streets. After half an hour with binoculars I almost felt I'd lived there, and a rather unalluring smell reached us even half a mile off. 'I say, isn't it Sunday?' It was. The banks would be shut and the market closed. So we decided to skip Basseterre and make for Les Saintes, just as the wind decided to disappear for the night. Sailing is curiously soporific, pancaked between sun and sea, half-drugged with salt air and staggering around clutching at handrails, I became more than usually numbskulled. The effort required to change Tarka Dick into his night attire and give him supper seemed enormous. Although there was not a breath of wind the heaving of the boat in the ocean swell meant I had to brace myself continuously to avoid being tumbled over. Even Bill said, 'Perhaps there *are* times when it would be useful to have an engine.' But it was safer not to carry fuel with a baby on board.

'Is it always like this at sea? Either being becalmed or in a gale? Is there no continuous gliding?'

Bill laughed.

'It's a special kind of hell. That's why people are so mad about it.'

I braced my head as firmly as possible against the deckhead to make Tarka's final bottle while burning my fingers in the scalding water and spilling as little sieved carrot as possible on to his clean nightie.

The sun dropped down, a huge golden penny that made a pedestal for himself to sit on during a thirty-second sink into the molten-grey sea and then our sails came down for the night. We hoped to awake in almost the same spot and slept fitfully amidst the boat rattles and rustles and splashing waves, for a night spent drifting at sea is extraordinarily full of noise. By morning the current had drawn us back six miles and we were some way to the north of the cove where wiser people might have spent a comfortable night. Every bit of canvas went up to catch the brief morning breeze, but by noon we were becalmed once more with the genoa flapping like a ridiculous petticoat, and Basseterre just about where it had been that time yesterday. The breathlessness seemed unbelievable. We had so much canvas up that I felt it ought to be possible to lie back in the cockpit huffing and puffing, and blow her along with one's own breath. 'The maddening thing is,' said Bill, 'I can see white horses half a mile away where the island ends and the trade winds begin.'

'Can't we paddle her along with oars?'

'Just too far –'

Slowly, very slowly, an inch at a time it seemed, we crept forward, and towards evening we were out of the island's shelter. But even in the channel the trades were blowing lightly. They carried us along towards the group of tiny islands that lay only seven miles south of Guadeloupe, but darkness raced us.

The sun turned again into a golden penny and set exactly as he had done yesterday. We were still a half-hour's tack to windward from the Saintes and with a baby aboard we could not risk entering by dark, so we prepared to spend a second night at sea, rocked, we hoped, in the small shelter of the eastern rocks. The current drove always westward so we could but be carried out into the Caribbean towards Jamaica, a thousand miles away. Tarka Dick, delighted at the sloshing waves that play with a drifting boat, crowed in his sleep all night. When at four in the morning Bill hurried on deck for the tenth time it was to find we had drifted at least ten miles off our course. Guadeloupe looked very small on the horizon when dawn crept up, but a breeze came to our rescue and we tacked rather angrily back to windward while the sky lightened behind the group of rocky mountain tips which are the famous Iles des Saintes.

HANNAH LYNCH
1862–1904

The Ladies' Land League was founded in the United States in 1880 by Fanny Parnell, sister of the leader of the Irish Party in the British House of Commons. It was extended to Ireland in the following year by another sister, Anna. The League, like its male counterpart, was active in the land war, supporting evicted tenants and encouraging the withholding of rents. Hannah Lynch was one of the young ladies recruited by Anna Parnell to staff the office in Dublin, where she worked on the production of *United Ireland*, organ of the National Land League. When the paper was suppressed, she took the materials to Paris, where she was to settle and die, and supervised its printing there. Her books include both travel and fiction; the best-known of the latter were *The Prince of the Glades* and *Clare Monroe*. This example of her extensive travel writing is from *French Life in Town and Country* (1901).

PEASANT AND ARTISAN

From earliest youth I had been accustomed to the trim and pleasing aspect of the French peasant, and I was long enough living in Paris without ever having had occasion to examine this class more closely than a walk in the country permits. I chanced to summer one year in the Saintonge, and friends made me acquainted there with an excellent miller and his wife who dwelt upon their lands. I published in the *Speaker* something about these delightful people afterwards, and I cannot do better than quote from that forgotten source: 'In the Saintonge, as elsewhere, the local mood is ruled by politics, and private friendship gives way to public rivalry. I learnt all about these feuds from my friend the miller of La Pellouaille. Intellect was not his strong point, but there was a cheerful cynicism about him to lend

flavour to his commonplaces. While others affected the heroic or
patriotic, he was content to accommodate himself to circumstances.
In reply to my query – which party he belonged to – he said, with a
humorous smile, "*Dame*, I go with the strongest, naturally," which
did not prevent him from giving his own sly hit at the Government. I
give his views for what they are worth – neither brilliant nor original,
but expressed with a certain geniality of tone and temper that kept
him from bucolic dullness. If the Republic kept France out of mischief
for the next twenty years, and carried her into fair prosperity, he
believed, by that time, neither Bonapartist nor Legitimist would be
remembered. For the moment the land was in a state of ferment, and
he thought it a pity such excessive use should be made of those big
words, Liberty, Equality, and Fraternity. These three Republican
assurances he qualified as mere *blagues*; and told me of a jocose
tobacconist who wrote them on the signboard of his shop, with an
empty tobacco-pouch suspended from each, the pouches in France
being called *blagues*. But the miller's wife was certainly his pleasanter
half. It was a delight to look upon a creature so human and wholesome
and resourceful. She was a large, handsome woman, with a smile as
fresh as new milk, and hazel eyes as clear as daylight, beaming with
goodwill, with vitality, and interest in her fellows. The kine browsing
in the fields were not more mild. Such a woman has you right at
nature's heart – big and broad and bountiful. She is peasant in the
best sense, proud of her spotless cap and apron, free and independent
in her carriage, with shoulders that know no cringing stoop, and
voice that cannot whine.'

   This good creature took me rambling through the woods, she
picking the nuts, and I devouring them; and I found her talk ever
sensible and entertaining. Thanks to the natural good manners and
intelligence of the French people, there is far less difference than in
England between the uneducated and educated classes. My friends
of the mill honoured me once with an invitation to dinner. The sky
was menacing, and, as I entered the long park avenue whence the
mill was visible, I saw the miller and his son anxiously scanning the
heavens and the green-roofed aisle of walnut and sycamore by which
I came. They hailed me with vigorous welcome, and, as I rested in
their beautifully clean kitchen, with broad and generous fireplace,
where the wood crackled pleasantly, and shone upon polished brass
dogs and gleaming bronze pots, with the high French bed in the deep

recess, the miller's wife mixed me some *cassis* and water. A more excellent dinner I have never eaten than that cooked, without fuss, or haste, or delay, by the miller's wife. In a twinkling, as it seemed to me, she had savoury tomato-soup on the table; and while she laid the cloth, the miller sat in front of the capacious mouth of flames, and saw that the browning chicken was kept moist with grease. I told them the story of Alfred and the cakes, and the miller's wife cried: 'She struck a king – a peasant, just like myself!' *'Dame,'* laughed the miller, 'it doesn't make much difference, when it is a woman, whether she be queen or peasant!' And I thought the remark one that an English peasant would have been incapable of making. He would have been incapable of such a point of view.

The French peasant has not the charm of the Irish peasant – the women, above all, lack the lovely complexion and beautiful eyes of the Irish – and he has less of the grand air. He is much more the son of the soil, and less of the gentleman. The writer, wishing to be true to life, could never make such enchanting 'copy' out of him as Jane Barlow made of the Irish peasant in her delightful 'Idylls.' There is too little poetry about him, and he is too evenly balanced and cool-headed to offer us many of the adorable surprises of humour. I have heard it said, by French persons who live in the country, that Zola comes nearer to truth and reality in his presentment of the peasant than George Sand in her exquisite pastorals, or M. René Bazin in such a tender and lovely story as 'La Terre qui Meurt.' But Balzac himself did not weave us tales of romance and delicate feeling when he touched upon the theme; and so it is very likely the fellow is more of a brute than he seems to be in casual intercourse, without, however, sinking to the loathsome depths of the realism of 'La Terre.' I, when I recall him to mind, own that I ever see him a dignified, well-mannered figure in blue blouse, generally clean, sometimes incredibly patched by his thrifty wife, frugal, sober, hard-worked, not too garrulous, and yet not resentful of easy speech, nor suspicious of the stranger who accosts him with courtesy. I find him in all things, as he presents himself to the eye and offers himself for observation, the superior of his British brother Hodge, neither so gross nor so unintelligent, with a look in his eye much resembling humour. He has his demands upon life, too, which are not those of the clownish brute, the inarticulate rustic. Not for nothing was the Revolution made, since by it has he learnt that he has his own share in the joys of civilisation, and that if he work hard enough, his sons may aspire to such a measure of education as a harsher lot denied him. When business brings him into a little town or a great city, his eye alights on beautiful objects placed there as much for him as for the owners of seigneurial dwellings. Flowers, trim parks, legends in stone, splendid cathedrals, every gracious blending of line and colour combine to train his eye in beauty and refine his nature. He need thread these quaint and lovely streets with no slouching step, for he, and such as he, are too conscious of their stable efforts in the general work of order and national prosperity. He need touch his forelock to no great lord for permission to breathe the free air of heaven, for does not he, too, possess his bit of land, his little dwelling, from which none can oust him? And, on feast-days and Sundays, are there not always public museums at hand for his instruction and entertainment? No country in the world takes such care to provide museums for the people throughout all the provinces as France. Every year the State purchases pictures at the annual exhibitions of Paris, to add to these provincial collections; and in every little town you pass through you are personally urged by some native to visit the Musée. This fact may have something to do with the astonishing intellectual superiority of the French peasant over Hodge beyond the Channel. For the fact remains that you can talk to the blue-bloused son of the soil, and hope to learn something from him, when the absence of loquacity and ideas and manners in Hodge will leave you discouraged and in despair. The French peasant loves so many things that educate and refine: flowers and pictures and military bands, spectacles of all kinds, and independence.

His standard is by no means an exalted one. His frugality is practised in the interest of his old age. His honesty is chiefly, I suspect, a shrewd protection against the probable dishonesty of others, for the simple law of comradeship demands that you shall treat fairly the man who treats you fairly. And his religion does not go down as deep as the fellow's soul, or whatever may serve him as such. It is with him merely a material influence, since it furnishes a serviceable plank for getting safely across the perilous abyss into a better world, and enables him to be decently baptised, married, and buried as a member of a Christian community. All other phases of religion, its emotions, exactions, penalties, and devices he leaves to the foolish womenfolk. Indeed, this seems to be the conviction of the average male Catholic the world over, if I may except Ireland, the one Catholic country in which I have found men to take their religion seriously, and the little Celtic corner of France, where the blue-eyed Bretons so closely resemble them. When I have visited at a French country-house in the shooting season, I have never known a male guest to attend mass, the explanation given being that *la chasse* had begun before the hour of mass. But if a woman stayed away from mass she would create a scandal. In Spain I have seen acquaintances of mine, while their womenfolk knelt and prayed with fervour, stand throughout the Sunday service with a bored and perfunctory air, only looking towards the altar and the priest at the moment of the elevation of the Host in a casually respectful way, as an officer might salute the passage of a military chief, and seemingly relieved to be able to examine again the faces and dresses of the women about them. Children barely in their teens, young lads going to school, carefully imitate this attitude of merely tolerant recognition of religious form, and their elders never dream of encouraging them to use a Prayer-book, or kneel, or show any sign that the weekly mass is to them more than the bored attendance at an official ceremony.

What is a moral influence with them? High above religion is their sturdy passion for independence. It is this passion that enables them to scrape, and serve, and suffer privation with dignity and patience. However meagre their resources may be, they are content with their lot, provided the roof they sleep beneath is their own, the land they till their own, the goat, the pig, the poultry theirs to do what they will with. This is no mean standard, and it works miracles in France. Would they were by nature and instinct kinder to their beasts; but this, too, is not a Catholic characteristic. I am assured that the Bretons and Provençals are the worse offenders. However, they do not sink so low in cruelty to animals as the purely Latin races, like the callous Spaniards and the Italians, and even in France the condition of animals is considerably ameliorated, though horses and donkeys are still often maltreated, and geese are killed in the cruellest fashion, their prolonged agonies in peasant esteem lending flavour to the cooked flesh.

What should, however, be a source of perennial admiration is the extraordinary absence in the class of anything approaching snobbishness. The eternal simplicity and unpretentiousness of the race are my constant wonder and delight. You will see a man in blue blouse, his wife in spotless cap and coloured kerchief, the man in appearance and fashion of speech and manners a gentleman, the woman educated, with her *brevet supérieur*, not destitute of music or art, working and living like peasants, because they are working their own land, and receiving on lines of perfect equality their humbler neighbours, without any thought of giving themselves the vulgar airs so common in my own land and in England. When they take their well-earned holiday at the seaside or among mountain waters, you will rarely find them seeking to pass for other than they are, or talking loudly of their advantages of fortune or station. Their natural dignity is such that they are content to abide by it and be judged accordingly. This class of the French race may be described as the least vulgar, the least boastful of the world. With these cleanly and self-respecting toilers no insane aping of the idler, no cheap imitation of the bourgeois in dress, no awful spectacle of girls with hideous feathers, and hats the grossest assertion of ill-placed ambition. Finery of any kind is recognised as the advertisement of something worse than bad taste, of the bonnet gone clean over the mill and morals gone after it. The peasant woman's vanity is to dress as her mother dressed before her, her pride is to belong to her land and her people. And it is because of this wholesome vanity and this noble pride that France is France, and the land is such a pleasant one to travel over.

F.L. M'CLINTOCK
1819–1907

In 1845 the Franklin Expedition, which had been endeavouring to
prove the feasibility of a North West Passage, disappeared without
trace. A series of search parties failed to locate any evidence of its fate,
but information gleaned by some of them led Lady Franklin to
commission the 170-ton yacht *Fox*, under the command of Captain
M'Clintock, a Dundalk man who had joined the British navy in 1831
and who had already made several voyages to the Arctic. He sailed in
1857 and, in May 1859, found documents and other relics of the
Franklin Expedition on the west coast of King William's Land. On his
return, he published a highly popular account of his voyage and was
knighted for his services and given the freedom of the City of London,
where he died. M'Clintock Channel in Canada is named after him.
King William's Island lies off the northern coast of Canada's
Northwest Territories between Longitude 95° and 100°W.

THE EMPTY CAIRN

A few miles beyond Cape Herschel the land becomes very low;
many islets and shingle-ridges lie far off the coast; and as we advanced,
we met with hummocks of unusually heavy ice, showing plainly that
we were now travelling upon a far more exposed part of the coast-
line. We were approaching a spot where a revelation of intense
interest was awaiting me.

About 12 miles from Cape Herschel I found a small cairn built by
Hobson's party, and containing a note for me. He had reached this,
his extreme point, six days previously, without having seen anything
of the wreck, or of natives, but he had found a record[1] – THE RECORD

---

1 The stains upon the record – as represented in the facsimile – were caused by the rusting of the tin
cylinder in which it was contained: the original record, together with all the relics brought home in
the 'Fox' have been deposited in the Museum of the United Service Institution, Whitehall Yard.

so ardently sought for of the Franklin Expedition – at Point Victory, on the N.W. coast of King William's Land.

That record is indeed a sad and touching relic of our lost friends, and, to simplify its contents, I will point out separately the double story it so briefly tells. In the first place, the record paper was one of the printed forms usually supplied to discovery ships for the purpose of being enclosed in bottles and thrown overboard at sea, in order to ascertain the set of the currents, blanks being left for the date and position; any person finding one of these records is requested to forward it to the Secretary of the Admiralty, with a note of time and place; and this request is printed upon it in six different languages. Upon it was written as follows:

28th of May, 1847. { H.M. ships 'Erebus' and 'Terror' wintered in the ice in lat. 70° 05′ N., long. 98° 23′ W.

Having wintered in 1846–7 at Beechey Island, in lat. 74° 43′ 28″ N., long. 91° 39′ 15″ W., after having ascended Wellington Channel to lat. 77°, and returned by the west side of Cornwallis Island.

Sir John Franklin commanding the expedition.

All well.

Party consisting of 2 officers and 6 men left the ships on Monday, 24th May, 1847.

GM. GORE, Lieut.
CHAS. F. DES VŒUX, Mate.

There is an error in the above document, namely, that the 'Erebus' and 'Terror' wintered at Beechey Island in 1846–7, – the correct dates should have been 1845–6; a glance at the date at the top and bottom of the record proves this, but in all other respects the tale is told in as few words as possible of their wonderful success up to that date, May, 1847.

We now know that, after the last intelligence of Sir John Franklin was received (bearing date 26th July, 1845) from the whalers in Melville Bay, his Expedition passed on to Lancaster Sound, and entered Wellington Channel, of which the southern entrance had been discovered by Sir Edward Parry in 1819. The 'Erebus' and 'Terror' sailed up that strait for one hundred and fifty miles, and reached in the autumn of 1845 the same latitude as was attained seven years subsequently by H.M.S. 'Assistance' and 'Pioneer'. Whether Franklin intended to pursue this northern course, and was only stopped by ice in that latitude of 77° north, or purposely relinquished a route which seemed to lead away from the known seas off the coast of America, must be a matter of conjecture; but the document assures us of one thing, that Sir John Franklin's Expedition, having accomplished this examination, returned southward from latitude 77° north, which is at the head of Wellington Channel, and re-entered Barrow's Strait by a new channel between Bathurst and Cornwallis Islands.

Seldom has such an amount of success been accorded to an arctic navigator in a single season, and when the 'Erebus' and 'Terror' were secured at Beechey Island for the coming winter of 1845–6, the results of their first year's labour must have been most cheering. These results were the exploration of Wellington and Queen's Channel, and the addition to our charts of the extensive lands on either hand. In 1846 they proceeded to the south-west, and eventually reached within twelve miles of the north extreme of King William's Land, when their progress was arrested by the approaching winter of 1846–7. That winter appears to have passed without any serious loss of life; and when in the spring Lieutenant Gore leaves with a party for some especial purpose, and very probably to connect the unknown coast-line of King William's Land between Point Victory and Cape Herschel, those on board the 'Erebus' and 'Terror' were 'all well,' and the gallant Franklin still commanded.

But, alas! round the margin of the paper upon which in 1847 those words of hope and promise were written, the following words had subsequently been faintly traced:

April 25, 1848. – H.M. ships 'Terror' and 'Erebus' were deserted on the 22nd April, 5 leagues N.N.W. of this, having been beset since 12th September, 1846. The officers and crews, consisting of 105 souls, under the command of Captain F.R.M. Crozier, landed here in lat. 69° 37' 42" N., long. 98° 41' W. Sir John Franklin died on the 11th June, 1847; and the total loss by deaths in the expedition has been to this date 9 officers and 15 men.

(Signed)   (Signed)
F.R.M. CROZIER,   JAMES FITZJAMES,
Captain and Senior Officer.   Captain H.M.S. 'Erebus'
and start (on) tomorrow, 26th. for
Back's Fish River.

With the exception of the signatures, and the note stating when and where they were going, which was added by Captain Crozier, the whole record was written by Captain Fitzjames.

There is some additional marginal information relative to the transfer of the document to its present position: I insert it here by itself, having omitted it in its proper place in order to simplify the more interesting part of the record.

This paper was found by Lt. Irving under the cairn supposed to have been built by Sir James Ross in 1831, 4 miles to the northward, where it had been deposited by the late Commander Gore in June, 1847. Sir James Ross' pillar has not, however, been found, and the paper has been transferred to this position, which is that in which Sir James Ross' pillar was erected.

This little word *late* shows us that poor Graham Gore was one of those who had passed away within the twelvemonth.

In the short space of twelve months how mournful had become the history of Franklin's expedition; how changed from the cheerful 'All well' of Graham Gore! The spring of 1847 found them within 90 miles of the known sea off the coast of America; and to men who had already in two seasons sailed over 500 miles of previously unexplored waters, how confident must they then have felt that that forthcoming navigable season of 1847 would see their ships pass over so short an intervening space! It was ruled otherwise. Within a month after Lieutenant Gore placed the record on Point Victory, the much-loved leader of the expedition, Sir John Franklin, was dead; and the following spring found Captain Crozier, upon whom the command had devolved, at King William's Land, endeavouring to save his starving men, 105 souls in all, from a terrible death by retreating to the Hudson Bay territories up the Back or Great Fish River.

So sad a tale was never told in fewer words. There is something deeply touching in their extreme simplicity, and they show in the strongest manner that both the leaders of this retreating party were actuated by the loftiest sense of duty, and met with calmness and decision the fearful alternative of a last bold struggle for life, rather than perish without effort on board their ships; for we well know that the 'Erebus' and 'Terror' were only provisioned up to July, 1848.

Lieutenant Hobson's note also told me that he had experienced extremely bad weather – constant gales and fogs – and thought he might have passed the wreck without seeing her; he hoped to be more successful upon his return journey.

Encouraged by this important news, we exerted our utmost vigilance in order that no trace should escape us.

Our provisions were running very short, therefore the three remaining puppies were of necessity shot, and their sledge used for fuel. We were also enabled to lengthen our journeys, as we had very smooth ice to travel over, the off-lying islets keeping the rough pack from pressing in upon the shore.

Upon the 29th of May we reached the western extreme of King William's Island, in lat. 69° 08' N., and long 100° 08' W. I named it after Captain Crozier of the 'Terror', the gallant leader of that 'Forlorn Hope' of which we had just now obtained tidings. The coast we marched along was extremely low – a mere series of ridges of limestone shingle, almost destitute of fossils. The only tracks of animals seen were those of a bear and a few foxes – the only living creatures a few willow-grouse. Traces even of the wandering Esquimaux became much less frequent after leaving Cape Herschel. Here were found only a few circles of stones, the sites of tenting-places, but so moss-grown as to be of great age. The prospect to sea was not less forbidding – a rugged surface of crushed-up pack, including much heavy ice. In these shallow and perpetually ice-packed channels, seals are but seldom found; and it is highly probable that all animal life in them is as scarce as upon the land.

From Cape Crozier the coast-line was found to turn sharply away to the eastward; and early in the morning of the 30th May we encamped alongside a large boat – another painful relic which Hobson had found and examined a few days before, as his note left here informed me; but he had failed to discover record, journal, pocket-book, or memorandum of any description.

A vast quantity of tattered clothing was lying in her, and this we first examined. Not a single article bore the name of its former owner. The boat was cleared out and carefully swept that nothing might escape us. The snow was then removed from about her, but nothing whatever was found.

This boat measured 28 feet long, and 7 feet 3 inches wide; she was built with a view to lightness and light draught of water, and evidently equipped with the utmost care for the ascent of the Great Fish River; she had neither oars nor rudder, paddles supplying their place; and as a large remnant of light canvas, commonly known as No. 8, was found, and also a small block for reeving a sheet through, I suppose she had been provided with a sail. A sloping canvas roof or rain-awning had also formed part of her equipment. She was fitted with a weather-cloth 9 inches high, battened down all round the gunwale, and supported by 24 iron stanchions, so placed as to serve likewise for rowing thowells. There was a deep-sea sounding line, fifty fathoms long, near her, as well as an ice-grapnel; this line must have been intended for river work as a track line. She had been originally 'carvel' built; but for the purpose of reducing weight, very thin fir planks had been substituted for her seven upper strakes, and put on 'clincher' fashion.

The only markings about the boat were those cut in upon her stem; besides giving her length, they indicated that she was built by contract, numbered 61, and received into Woolwich Dockyard in April, 184–; the fourth figure to the right hand was lost, as the stem had been reduced as much as possible in order to lessen her weight; from this cause part of the Roman numerals indicating her length were also lost.

The weight of the boat alone was about 700 or 800 lbs. only, but she was mounted upon a sledge of unusual weight and strength. It was constructed of two oak planks 23 feet 4 inches in length, 8 inches in width, and with an average thickness of 2½ inches. These planks formed the sides or runners of the sledge; they were connected by five cross-bars of oak, each 4 feet long, and 4 inches by 3½ inches thick, and bolted down to the runners; the underneath parts of the latter were shod with iron. Upon the cross-bars five saddles or supporting chocks for the boat were lashed, and the drag-ropes by which the crew moved this massive sledge, and the weights upon it, consisted of 2¾ inch whale-line.

I have calculated the weight of this sledge to be 650 lbs.; it could not have been less, and may have been considerably more. The total weight of boat and sledge may be taken at 1400 lbs., which amounts to a heavy load for seven strong healthy men.

The ground the sledge rested upon was the usual limestone shingle, perfectly flat and probably overflowed at times every summer, as the stones were imbedded in ice.

The boat was partially out of her cradle upon the sledge, and lying in such a position as to lead me to suppose it the effect of a violent north-west gale. She was barely, if at all, above the reach of occasional tides.

One hundred yards from her, upon the land side, lay the stump of a fir-tree 12 feet long, and 16 inches in diameter at 3 feet above the roots. Although the ice had used it roughly during its drift to this shore, and rubbed off every vestige of bark, yet the wood was perfectly sound. It may have been and probably has been lying there for twenty or thirty years, and during such a period would suffer less decay in this region of frost than in one-sixth of the time at home. Within two yards of it I noticed a few scanty tufts of grass.

But all these were after observations; there was in the boat that which transfixed us with awe, viz., portions of two human skeletons! One was that of a slight young person; the other of a large, strongly-made, middle-aged man. The former was found in the bow of the boat, but in too much disturbed a state to enable Hobson to judge whether the sufferer had died there; large and powerful animals, probably wolves, had destroyed much of this skeleton, which may have been that of an officer. Near it we found the fragment of a pair of worked slippers .... The lines were white, with a black margin; the spaces white, red, and yellow. They had originally been 11 inches long, lined with calf-skin with the hair left on, and the edges bound with red silk ribbon. Besides these slippers there were a pair of small strong shooting half-boots.

The other skeleton was in a somewhat more perfect state; it lay across the boat, under the after-thwart, and was enveloped with cloths and furs. This would seem to have been the survivor of the two men whose remains were lying in the boat. Close beside it were found five watches; and there were two double-barrelled guns – one barrel in each loaded and cocked – standing muzzle upwards against the boat's side. It may be imagined with what deep interest these sad relics were scrutinised, and how anxiously every fragment of clothing was turned over in search of pockets and pocket-books, journals, or even names. Five or six small books were found, all of them scriptural or devotional works, except *The Vicar of Wakefield*. One little book, *Christian Melodies*, bore an inscription upon the title-page from the donor to G.G. (Graham Gore?). Another small book, *A Manual of Private Devotion*, by C.J. Blomfield, DD., bore on its title-page,

'G. Back, to Graham Gore. May, 1846.' A small Bible contained numerous marginal notes, and whole passages underlined. Besides these books, the covers of a New Testament and Church of England Prayerbook were found.

Amongst an amazing quantity of clothing there were seven or eight pairs of boots of various kinds – cloth winter boots, sea boots, heavy ankle boots, and strong shoes. I noted that there were silk handkerchiefs – black, white, and figured – towels, soap, sponge, tooth-brush, and hair-combs; macintosh gun-cover, marked outside with paint A 12, and lined with black cloth. Besides these articles we found twine, nails, saws, files, bristles, wax-ends, sail-makers' palms, powder, bullets, shot, cartridges, wads, leather cartridge-case, knives – clasp and dinner ones, needle and thread cases, slow-match, several bayonet scabbards cut down into knife-sheaths, two rolls of sheet-lead, and, in short, a quantity of articles of one description and another truly astonishing in variety, and such as, for the most part, modern sledge-travellers in these regions would consider a mere accumulation of dead weight, of little use, and very likely to break down the strength of the sledge-crews.

The only provisions we could find were tea and chocolate; of the former very little remained, but there were nearly 40 pounds of the latter. These articles alone could never support life in such a climate, and we found neither biscuit nor meat of any kind. A portion of tobacco, and an empty pemmican-tin capable of containing 22 pounds weight, were discovered. The tin was marked with an E; it had probably belonged to the 'Erebus'. None of the fuel originally brought from the ships remained in or about the boat, but there was no lack of it, for a drift-tree was lying on the beach close at hand, and had the party been in need of fuel, they would have used the paddles and bottom-boards of the boat.

In the after-part of the boat we found eleven large spoons, eleven forks, and four tea-spoons, all of silver. Of these twenty-six pieces of plate, eight bore Sir John Franklin's crest, the remainder had the crests or initials of nine different officers, with the exception of a single fork which was not marked; of these nine officers, five belonged to the 'Erebus' – Gore, Le Vesconte, Fairholme, Couch, and Goodsir. Three others belonged to the 'Terror' – Crozier (a teaspoon only), Hornby, and Thomas. I do not know to whom the three articles with an owl engraved on them belonged, nor who was the owner of the unmarked fork, but of the owners of those we can identify, the majority belonged to the 'Erebus'. One of the watches bore the crest of Mr Couch, of the 'Erebus,' and as the pemmican tin also came from that ship, I am inclined to think the boat did also. One of the pocket chronometers found in the boat was marked, 'Parkinson and Frodsham 980,' the other, 'Arnold 2020'; these had been supplied one to each ship.

Sir John Franklin's plate perhaps was issued to the men for their use, as the only means of saving it; and it seems probable that the officers generally did the same, as not a single iron spoon, such as sailors always use, has been found. Of the many men, probably twenty or thirty, who were attached to this boat, it seems most strange that the remains of only two individuals were found, nor were there any graves upon the neighbouring flat land; indeed, bearing in mind the season at which these poor fellows left their ships, it should be remembered that the soil was then frozen hard as rock, and the labour of *quarrying* a grave very great indeed.

I was astonished to find that the sledge was directed to the N.E., exactly for the next point of land for which we ourselves were travelling!

The position of this abandoned boat is about 50 miles – as a sledge would travel – from Point Victory, and therefore 65 miles from the position of the ships; also it is 70 miles from the skeleton of the steward, and 150 miles from Montreal Island: it is moreover in the depth of a wide bay, where, by crossing over 10 or 12 miles of very low land, a great saving of distance would be effected, the route by the coast-line being about 40 miles.

A little reflection led me to satisfy my own mind at least that this boat was *returning to the ships.* In no other way can I account for two men having been left in her, than by supposing the party were unable to drag the boat further, and that these two men, not being able to keep pace with their shipmates, were therefore left by them supplied with such provisions as could be spared, to last them until the return of the others from the ship with a fresh stock.

Whether it was the intention of this boat party to await the result of another season in the ships, or to follow the track of the main body to the Great Fish River, is now a matter of conjecture. It seems more than probable that they fully intended to revisit the boat, not only on account of the two men left in charge of it, but also to obtain the chocolate, the five watches, and many other small articles which would otherwise scarcely have been left in her.

The same reasons which may be assigned for the return of this detachment from the main body (which, it will be remembered, had started under the command of Captain Crozier for the Great Fish River) will also serve to account for the party not having come back to their boat. In both instances they appear to have greatly overrated their strength, and the distance they could travel in a given time.

Taking this view of the case, we can understand why their provisions would not have lasted them for anything like the distance they required to travel; and why they would be obliged to send back to the ships for more, first taking from the detached party all provisions they could possibly spare. Whether all or any of the remainder of this detached party ever reached their ships is uncertain; all we know is, that they did not revisit the boat, otherwise more skeletons would probably have been found in its neighbourhood; the Esquimaux report is, that there was no one alive in the ship when she drifted on shore, and that they found but one human body on board of her.

After leaving the boat we followed an irregular coast-line to the N. and N.W., up to a very prominent cape, which is probably the extreme of land seen from Point Victory by Sir James Ross, and named by him Point Franklin, which name, as a cape, it still retains.

I need hardly say that throughout the whole of my journey along the shores of King William's Land, we all kept a most vigilant look-out for any appearance of the stranded ship spoken of by the natives; but our search for her was utterly fruitless.

MICHEÁL Mac LIAMMÓIR
1899–1978

Until Micheál Ó hAodha published his book *The Importance of Being Micheál* in 1990, it was generally believed that Mac Liammóir was born in Cork and brought up in London, where he certainly appeared with Noel Coward in Beerbohm Tree's *Peter Pan*. In fact he was born Alfred Lee Wilmore in Willesden and had no discoverable links with Ireland until he founded the Dublin Gate Theatre with Hilton Edwards – another Englishman, but an unrepentant one – in 1928. Writer and painter as well as actor, Mac Liammóir was quick to put problems of nationality behind him: his first play, produced in Galway in 1928, was written in Irish. He wrote ten in all, in addition to three one-man shows, including *The Importance of Being Oscar*, with which he travelled the world, as well as books on the theatre, three of which were in Irish. He toured extensively with the Gate Theatre company and included lively accounts of these travels in his books. This excerpt, however, is from *Put Money in Thy Purse* (1952), the diary of the eccentric production of Orson Welles's film of *Othello*, in which Mac Liammóir, a skilful Shakespearean actor, did his best with (as the critic C.A. Lejeune put it) 'an Iago who is only half there as Shakespeare wrote him'. The year is 1949.

THE ROAD TO MOGADOR

CASABLANCA. MAY 19TH

Approach to the town from the air in the dark morning superb; an armful of jewels flung over the black sky and sea. Further inspection on landing revealed series of box-like, half-finished houses, promenades, arcades, dusty palms and a wild salty tang as of *frankincense, leopards* and *pepper* in the air.

No taxis at air-bus terminus. Walter S. had no hotel and had decided to accompany me to Don Cash Shelter (as I thought). Walked through arid new streets, now brightening with dawn, in wake of pock-marked Arab who pushed our bags on a cart. No one seemed to know anything of 'Don Cash', but 'Shelter' produced a gleam of light, and at last we arrived at hotel. Here Nightmare began. Mystery of 'Don Cash' soon cleared up: turned out not to be portion of hotel's title at all but American manager of *Black Rose* film (Tyrone Power cum O.W.) at present in the desert on location. No room had been booked for me, however, until three weeks ahead, said white-robed night porter in Turkish Delight edition of French, as he waved snake-charming fingers at a notice on the wall that read 'Complet'. As for Walter S., continued night porter, nobody ever dreamed of coming to Casablanca without booking a room at least four weeks in advance; the most that could possibly be done either for Walter S. or for Micheál Mac L. would be to let them have, in about an hour's time, a room in which to rest till 9 am, when the room would be occupied by wealthy French gentleman and wife arriving from Agadir. Sudden appearance was made on marble staircase at this point by a Mr Frank Bevis, clad in striped pyjamas and flushed with sleep, who said he was production manager for *Black Rose* and he happened to know that Orson Welles didn't expect me for three weeks. Sympathy with my blank dismay at receiving this news was registered in bluff British Navy fashion, 'Very sorry of course, old man' being keynote of the conversation, with rider to the effect that he, F.B., was driven half dotty trying to fix rooms for actors who either arrived at the wrong time or didn't turn up at all. My riposte to this was that in future I would unhesitatingly belong to the second group. This drove F.B. back to bed, still saying 'Sorry of course, old man.' I then repaired with Walter to landing furnished in Winter Garden fashion with basket-work and glass-topped table, easy chairs and illustrated guides to Morocco (pre-war), and discussed our plight. Myself, meanwhile, numbly ruminated on ignominious tricks of fate, and found I was haunted by refrain of rather sordid little song heard in childhood beginning 'Why did I leave my little backroom in Blooms-bu-ry?' Finished remains of whiskey, its glamour now completely departed, also swallowed some black coffee brought us by Mohamet the Night Porter, and at about 8 retired to recently vacated room suggesting chiropodist's salon and echoing to loud Hammering (can Orson's workmen have failed to track him to Ouarzazate and be filling in time here?). Were not chucked out until noon (Mohamet now replaced by Abdullah, quite indistinguishable, apparently his twin-brother), when we sallied forth bathed and shaved to blinding sunshine and ice-cold wind respectively blazing on and blowing through white and yellow town surging with Arabs, French, Jews, and Spaniards. Walter gave me lunch and we parted regretfully, he to take train for Marrakesh and self to hunt for hotel.

Afternoon spent writing dismal letter to Hilton, on Winter Garden landing. Hotel of repellent aspect (the only one in the town with a free room) discovered at 6 pm in Rue Blaise Pascal. Mystery of my not being wanted as Iago for three weeks (at least) cleared up by telephone calls transferred from Shelter. First communication was from Rita, who is ill after an operation on her teeth in a clinic in Marrakesh. ('Quite ackonising, my dear, my face is really so like a football geschwolen.') Rita said wire from Orson to Ireland postponing dates must have crossed my departure. Second communication was from Orson himself from desert ('Dearest Micheál I'm So Sorry but Miss Mud will provide you with large sums of money, and why don't you visit Fez? Rabat? Marrakesh? Morocco is such a Great country – now you *know* it's great'). Lee Kressel also had a lot to say and confided in a whisper that, from point of view of his own taste, which as I knew was inclined to favour Ritz bar at twilight, life on location in Ouarzazate was a picturesque Hell.

Found myself being difficult and strenuous and saying I was in the mood for Work, not sightseeing, but would be glad of some money. 'Well, why not go to *Rome*,' says Orson, 'and try on your costume, you know I want you to look *good* as Iago and you like Rome'; and his voice, diminishing in weird mechanical fashion, was, after lengthy breakdown of sound, replaced by voice of Lee repeating, 'They cut us off but listen, honey, *Rome*, he wants you to go to *Rome*.' 'Why Rome?' says I. 'Well,' says Lee, 'to try your *costume*, for I know that is what Orson considers essential and it's worrying him very much. You go to *Rome*.'

Opened my mouth once more and yelled that I had already tried on my costume in Rome three times, also wig, and in the midst of great eloquence discovered we were again cut off. Jingled receiver like comic manservant in farce, also shouted to exchange, but no good. Have spent rest of evening in isolation and despair, but will now sally forth to visit town.

MAY 20TH

Twelve hours have finally revealed to me that while loneliness undoubtedly full of interest and profit for the soul if experienced in beautiful wilderness, it is a barren affair in garish modern town which, more than ever on close inspection, resembles toy-town of yellow boxes, many of them plastered with hoardings and regrettably revealing worst excesses of Broadway in Franco-Arab edition. Reminded as I paced about alone last night of Chesterton saying what a grand place Broadway would be if one couldn't read; and finally took refuge in Moorish cabaret where pretty buxom houri waggled hips in *mouvement perpétuel* to the coruscating inanity of modern Arab music. This was provided by beaming male orchestra in European dress; audience, however, also exclusively male, clad in impressive robes and turbans.

Frank Bevis, Prods. Manager for *Black Rose*, rescued me today: lunch and dinner together in gales of laughter at each other's jokes.

A car has been arranged to bear me off to Marrakesh tomorrow to see die Rita.

MARRAKESH. MAY 21ST

Marrakesh of dazzling beauty as of Arabian Nights, all in deep reds and roses and purples, the streets full of bougainvillea and jacaranda trees in blossom under which droves of Arabs wander with linked fingers in robes of white, lilac, violet, and dark crimson. Was told by Rita, whom I visited at tea-time in her clinic, that I must dine in the Place de France, which she assures me is like the ballet of Sheherazade, and I certainly intend to obey her. She was looking very ill, *meine arme süsse Rita*, with face, as described by herself *so wie ein Fussball geschwollen*, her black hair in wild and I thought becoming disarray all over the pillows as she lay prostrate in a room so like a ship's cabin in its pale glistening chastity one almost expected it to roll. Very sad she was at first, too, as she devoured a purée of potatoes followed by creamed rice (surely a depressing diet to one already depressed, and inclined to be like English governess slightingly described by Blanche Ingram in *Jane Eyre*, as 'lachry-mose and low-spirited'), but cheered up at my imitation of Frank Bevis and told me, after a while, all the news.

Mogador. That is chief and, to me, staggering news item. We are to make *Othello* in Mogador, not Rome at all. Or Nice. Or Paris. Or Venice. Just Mogador. That's the latest.

Mogador: not the Parisian theatre noted for musical shows of the kind known as *light*, but a small town on the west coast of Morocco. No hotel, says Rita, lapping up her rice; der Orson will probably take a villa (the difficulty of that may be the sanitation) where you will all be one happy family. (This Family is disinfected throughout with Jeyes' Fluid.) Mogador has a fortress built by the Portuguese (God forgive them) in sixteenth century. Quite perfect, says Rita, but she believes that there is little else. Just a few rocks, some hills – no, not mountains, quite little hills – a palm or two, and possibly an Arab quarter. (Quarter of What, pray, if there's nothing but rocks and a fortress?) There may possibly be, she continues, a funny little *inn* where we can eat kouskous *à l'arabe* and perhaps some fish, and even tea with mint. The sea of course will be *herrlich*, but being also *atlantisch* it will be far too cold to bathe. Even in Summer. Also, she adds, still lapping her rice, the weather is windy and *foggy*. This too comes from the Atlantic, whose waves dash up over the Portuguese fortress all day and all night, and they cause this fog, which will give, she continues, now waving her spoon at me and looking suddenly deeply unattractive, this impression of mystery, of strangeness, this texture, this *Stimmung, was?*, so coveted by der Velles.

'*Ach ja,*' says Rita, handing me her platter (now licked clean and bestowed by my nerveless hands on black japan tray), 'it is not Monte Carlo you are going to. But the film, I am so sure, will be *wundervoll, fantastisch, fantastisch*'; and she lies back exhausted, as well she might.

Fell to pondering on Hilton's holiday planned to be spent with me in Rome or Venice or Nice or Paris or all four, and failed to picture him lost in fog among Quite Little Hills and an Arab or two, but realised this was not correct attitude for serious actor embarking on film career, however belated, and said nothing, but resolved to write self-sacrificing letter insisting on his holidaying alone and leaving self and der Velles to face howling gales, kouskous, and yards of celluloid together.

MAY 22ND

Medina, which is the Arab part of the City as opposed to *Mellah*, which is the Jewish, surpassed all descriptions by Rita or anyone else; an orgy of Islam dyed in ferocious colour, scent and darkness, with sudden flaring lights that reveal multitudes of Arabs and Berbers who buy, sell, beg, dance, sing, juggle, charm snakes, read the Koran, tell tales, perform magical tricks by lantern light, and offer their services as guides, pimps, carriage-drivers, escorts, and purveyors of love.

Dined alone and was invited to drink coffee with pleasant French doctor who sat at the next table; we were afterwards driven by elderly Pandarus of Troy clad in embroidered trousers, a mackintosh, and a vast ragged turban to the *closerie d'amour*, where we were entertained for more than reasonable sums in a series of dazzlingly lighted marble rooms on long puce or sky-blue divans by bevy of unveiled houris smothered in *maquillage* and moles, and dressed, obviously, by Henri Matisse. They all in turn gave us honey cakes and tea with mint, which is revolting, stroked our cheeks, patted our thighs, pinched our biceps, smoked our cigarettes, and finally kissed us very coyly on the nose and cackled at each other in Arabic. This followed in each case by a lot of clinging and pouting and tut-tutting when we got up to go, and in one establishment by some spitting, at which I slapped all the bottoms within reach. This proved a triumphant success. They shrieked and slapped back, and one of them began to throw cushions about and tear off her clothes (in order, I suppose, to defend her virtue with more freedom), and Madame, who was very fat and dressed in what seemed to be a mauve tablecloth with a bead fringe, screeched with joy and threw a box of Turkish Delight at me, which we subsequently all ate together. French doctor was inspired by these activities to do a solo rumba, also triumphant success and soon joined in by the company; and Madame, fanning herself with the lid of the sweet box and jingling her bead fringes, said she had never seen such merry French gentlemen as ourselves before, the French being for the most part, she vowed, her mouth full of Turkish Delight, dull, solemn, and cheese-paring and inclined to forget her own existence. This delicate hint at her faith in her own past charms as in our present generosity did not go unrewarded; Madame got a nice tip, and to express her gratitude flung herself on the floor at our feet with howls of gratitude, then found herself unable to rise, and that was the last we saw of Madame.

Berber dancing boys visited in turn: these, dancing in long white night-shirts with bracelets on their ankles, proved as quiet and docile as if they had been brought up at St Margaret's Hall (which they probably had, or at Schleu equivalent). After the dancing was over, a gentle and very pretty affair concerned chiefly with a soft stamping of bare feet on the floor, and with a fluttering of tiny metallic castanets to the accompaniment of a stringed instrument played by their tutor, a sort of Mussulman Santa Claus, they squatted in the corner to whisper together and drink mint tea, never taking their eyes off us, and Santa Claus, after a brief chat with them, explained in French that they admired our ties and would like them as a souvenir. (Of What, I should like to know? Anyway they didn't get them.)

Everyone friendly, and delight with us expressed by all with the exception of Sir Pandarus of Troy who, sitting morosely on his driver's box, tut-tutting sibilantly whenever we remounted the carriage, said he couldn't understand why we stayed for such a short time at each port of call, adding that we seemed very difficult gentlemen to please and suggesting a visit to other haunts of pleasure where we would undoubtedly find what – surely? – we were seeking. No demands, however complicated, would be found impossible of fulfilment. These offers (in spite of half-formed 'Oh do let's!' which sprang to my eager lips) were severely turned down by doctor and we drove home (Pandarus in condition of bewildered despair), and talked Islamic civilisation (discussion highly speculative as our interest far greater than our knowledge) till small hours.

Today is fantastically hot and spent (stripped to skin in shaded room) partly in writing pamphlet on Irish Theatre (have got through eighteenth century, also Wilde and Shaw and arrived at Yeats) and partly at clinic (fully clad) with Rita, who, true to Orson's promise, gave me lire for journey to Rome. This discussed at all angles. I still think it crazy but agreeable plan to go from Morocco to Rome and back again in order to try on one tunic already tried on, but am now in mellow condition and ready for anything. Die Rita herself will be flying there on 26th and have decided to fly with her. Plane via Paris: surely a long way round, but in addition to being mellow am also getting as used to these whirling journeys as Les Invalides station must be getting used to the spectacle of self arriving at all hours of day and night *en route* for somewhere else.

MAY 23RD

I wandered about in the Souks after dinner and listened to two young girls who stood hand in hand by the roadway, singing for coppers. They were both blind. Their songs, like the *flamenco* songs in Spain and the traditional songs one still hears in Connemara, were set in a mode unconnected with modern European singing, and held me listening there for more than an hour. It seemed as though one heard a kind of whispering of the inmost secrets of two lives addressed to no audience in particular, but to the universe at large; as though the singers were trying to make the air understand the sorrows and ardours, at first simply of two individual girls, and, later on, of a whole people, a whole race. I wished I were a musician, or at least that I could have taken down some of the airs, because they were at once sad and joyful and indescribably stirring. I would like to have known too some of the words they were singing, for when I asked a Moor who spoke a little French what was the subject of the songs he said, after listening for a while: 'They are making up the words and the tunes as they go along. Now the younger one is saying that she has never seen her father or her brothers, and cannot imagine what it would be like to watch the sun coming up in the morning, or the crescent moon on the first night of Ramadan, the feast of the Prophet; and now the older one is saying she wishes to meet a young man as blind as she is herself, for then, though her sister has told her she has no beauty, she could deceive him into thinking her the fairest of all women,' and I was reminded of Synge's *Well of the Saints.*

Yet when he had gone away, and I gave them some more money and begged them to sing again, they tittered and grew shy, and at last began to sing some vacuous air that must be popular in the cabarets, for several people passing by joined in, and a guide, seeing my interest, whispered that they were not *femmes de plaisir* but that if I wished it something might be arranged, and the spell was broken.

CASABLANCA, MAY 26TH

Returned by train and have had recurrence of old miseries of dizziness and lassitude. Sent for doctor and he cured me. Frank B. delightful and kept me amused all the time, also helped me when I got better with difficulties of journey. These very tedious indeed, and involved hours at office of Air France and similar institutions, which increased dizziness. Drove about with Frank and to dispel these symptoms took long walks with him by the sea every evening, these followed by dining at various places. Casablanca, in spite of regrettable resemblance to Toy-Town and general air of Much Ado about

Nothing, is full of good restaurants, La Reine Pédauque I think the best, Frank, however, preferring Le Petit Poucet because, as he says, Petty Pussy is such a *soppy* name, adding that only the French would get away with it, oh yes old boy, I mean, when you come to think of it it *is* the end, I mean *isn't* it?

It's going to be Pédauque tonight, however. Die Rita arrives and is to meet us there: we then fly to Rome via Spain and Les Invalides, leaving poor old Frank behind, and I am still wondering what all this cavorting through the air has to do with the art of the films.

FREDERICK EDWARD MANING
1811–1883

Grandson of a Trinity College professor of oriental languages,
Frederick Maning was born in Dublin and emigrated with his family
to Hobart in 1824. In 1833 he sailed from Tasmania to Hokianga River,
then the chief centre of European settlement in New Zealand, and in
attempting to get ashore was involved in a fracas with a local Maori.
The sequel is described in this passage from *Old New Zealand* (1863).
Maning married a Maori, by whom he had four children, and rose to
be a Justice of the Peace and a judge of the Native Lands court. His
early sympathy for and understanding of the Maoris permeated both
his life and his writing ('Incidents are described in true Maori fashion
with irrelevant detail', as one commentator remarked) but after the
treaty of Waitangi in 1840 he lost a lot of land and his attitude changed
to one of bitterness and intolerance. He turned against his book and
attempted to destroy the original edition, burning on the banks of the
Hokianga all the copies he could collect. Maning died in Britain, but at
his own request was buried in Auckland.

BEEF AGAINST MELONS

Something between a cheer, a scream, and a roar greets our arrival
on the sand. An English voice salutes me with 'Well, you served that
fellow out'. One half of my coat hangs from my right elbow, the other
from my left; a small shred of the collar is still around my neck. My
hat, alas! My hat is gone. I am surrounded by a dense mob of natives,
laughing, shouting, and gesticulating in the most grotesque manner.
Three Englishmen are also in the crowd. They seem greatly amused
at something, and offer repeated welcomes. At this moment up
comes my saltwater acquaintance, elbowing his way through the
crowd. There is a strange, serio-comic expression of anger in his face.

He stoops, makes horrid grimaces, quivering at the same time his left hand and arm about in a most extraordinary manner, and striking the thick part of his left arm with the palm of his right hand.

'*Hu!*' says he, '*hu! hu!*'

'What *can* he mean?' said I.

'He is challenging you to wrestle,' cried one of the Englishmen: 'he wants *utu.*'

'What is *utu?*' said I.

'Payment.'

'I won't pay him.'

'Oh, that's not it; he wants to take it out of you wrestling.'

'Oh, I see. Here's at him. Pull off my coat and boots. I'll wrestle him. His foot is on his own country, and his name is – what?'

'Sir, his name in English means "eater of melons". He is a good wrestler; you must mind.'

'*Water*melons, I suppose; beef against melons for ever. Hurrah! Here's at him.'

Here the natives began to run between us to separate us, but seeing that I was in the humour to 'have it out', and that neither self nor friend were actually out of temper, and no doubt expecting to see the *pakeha* floored, they stood to one side and made a ring. A wrestler soon recognises another, and my friend soon gave me some hints that showed me I had some work before me. I was a youngster in those days, all bone and sinew, full of animal spirits, and as tough as leather. A couple of desperate main strength efforts soon convinced us both that science or endurance must decide the contest. My antagonist was a strapping fellow of about five-and-twenty, tremendously strong, and much heavier than I. I, however, in those days actually could not be fatigued; I did not know the sensation, and could run from morning till night. I therefore trusted to wearing him out, and avoiding his *ta and wiri*. All this time the mob were shouting encouragement to one or other of us. Such a row never was seen. I soon perceived I had a 'party'.

'Well done, *pakeha!*'

'Now for it, Melons!'

'At him again!'

'Take care; the *pakeha* is a *taniwha*; the *pakeha* is a *tino tangata!*'

'Horray!' (from the British element).

'The *pakeha* is down!'

'No, he isn't!' (from English side).

Here I saw my friend's knees beginning to tremble. I made a great effort, administered my favourite remedy, and there lay the 'Eater of Melons' prone upon the sand. I stood a victor; and, like many other conquerors, a very great loser. There I stood, minus hat, coat, and pistols, wet and mauled, and transformed very considerably for the worse since I left the ship. When my antagonist fell, the natives gave a great shout of triumph, and congratulated me in their own way with the greatest goodwill. I could see I had got their good opinion, though I could scarcely understand how. After sitting on the sand some time my friend arose, and with a very graceful movement, and a smile of good nature on his dusty countenance, he held out his hand and said in English, 'How do you do?'

I was much pleased at this. The natives had given me fair play, and my antagonist, though defeated both by sea and land, offered me his hand, and welcomed me to the shore with his whole stock of English – 'How do you do?'

But the row is not half over yet. Here comes the chief in the ship's boat. The other is miles off with its one-man crew still pulling no one knows, or at all cares, where. Someone has been off in a canoe and told the chief that 'Melons' and the 'new *pakeha*' were fighting like mad on the beach. Here he comes, flourishing his *mere pounamu*. He is a tall stout fellow, in the prime of life, black with tattooing, and splendidly dressed, according to the splendour of those days. He has on a very good blue jacket, no shirt or waistcoat, a pair of duck trousers, and a red sash round his waist; no hat or shoes, these being as yet things beyond a chief's ambition. The jacket was the only one in the tribe; and amongst the surrounding company I saw only one other pair of trousers, and it had a large hole at each knee, but this was not considered to detract at all from its value. The chief jumps ashore. He begins his oration, or rather, to 'blow up', all and sundry, the tribe in general, and poor 'Melons' in particular. He is really vexed, and wishes to appear to me more vexed than he really is. He runs, gesticulating and flourishing his *mere*, about ten steps in one direction, in the course of which ten steps he delivers a sentence. He then turns and runs back the same distance, giving vent to his wrath in another sentence, and so back and forward, forward and back, till he has exhausted the subject and tired his legs. The Englishmen were beside me, and gave a running translation of what he said:

'Pretty work this,' he began – 'good work, killing my pakeha; look at him!' (Here a flourish in my direction with the mere.) 'I won't stand this – not at all! not at all! not at all!' (The last sentence took three jumps, a step, and a turn round to keep correct time.) 'Who killed the pakeha? It was Melons. You are a nice man are you not?' (This with a sneer.) 'Killing my pakeha!' (In a voice like thunder, and rushing savagely, mere in hand, at poor Melons, but turning exactly at the end of ten steps and coming back again.) 'It will be heard of all over the country; we shall be called the "pakeha killers". I shall be sick with shame. The pakeha will run away, and take all his taonga along with him. What if you had killed him dead, or broken his bones? – his relations would be coming across the sea for utu.' (Great sensation, and I try to look as though I would say 'Of course they would'.) 'What did I build this pa close to the sea for? Was it not to trade with the pakehas? And here you are killing the second that has come to stop with me.' (Here poor Melons burst out crying like an infant.) 'Where is the hat? – where the koti roa? – where the shoes?' (Boots were shoes in those days.) 'The pakeha is robbed; he is murdered!' (Here a howl from Melons, and I go over and sit_down by him, clap him on the bare back and shake his hand.) 'Look at that – the pakeha does not bear malice. I would kill you if he asked me! You are a bad people, killers of pakehas! Be off with you, the whole of you – away!'

This command was instantly obeyed by all the women, boys, and slaves. Melons also, being in disgrace, disappeared; but I observed that 'the whole of you' did not seem to be understood as including the stout, able-bodied, tattooed part of the population, the strength of the tribe – the warriors, in fact, many of whom counted themselves to be very much about as good as the chief. They were his nearest relations, without whose support he could do nothing, and were entirely beyond his control.

I found afterwards that it was only during actual war that this chief was perfectly absolute, which arose from the confidence the tribe had in him, both as a general and a fighting man, and the obvious necessity that in war implicit obedience be given to one head. I have, however, observed in other tribes that in war they would elect a chief for the occasion – a war chief – and have been surprised to see the obedience they gave him, even when his conduct was very open to criticism. I say with surprise, for the natives are so self-possessed, opinionated, and republican, that the chiefs have at ordinary times but little control over them, except in very rare cases, where the chief happens to possess a singular vigour of character, or some other unusual advantage, to enable him to keep them under.

I will mention here that my first antagonist, 'The Eater of Melons', became a great friend of mine. He was my right-hand man and manager when I set up house on my own account, and did me many friendly services in the course of my acquaintance with him. He came to an unfortunate end some years later. The tribe were getting ready for a war expedition; poor Melons was filling cartridges from a fifty-pound barrel of gunpowder, pouring the gunpowder into the cartridges with his hand, and smoking his pipe at the same time, as I have seen the natives doing fifty times since. A spark fell into the cask, and it is scarcely necessary to say that my poor friend was roasted alive in a second. I have known three other accidents of the same kind from smoking whilst filling cartridges. In one of these accidents three lives were lost and many injured; and I really do believe that the certainty of death will not prevent some of the natives from smoking for more than a given time. I have often seen infants refuse the mother's breast, and cry for the pipe till it was given them; and dying natives often ask for a pipe and die smoking. I can clearly perceive that the young men of the present day are neither so tall, or stout, or strong as men of the same age were when I first came into the country; and I believe that this smoking from their infancy is one of the chief causes of this decrease in strength and stature.

I am landed at last, certainly, but I am tattered and wet, and in a most deplorable plight; so, to make my story short – for I see if I am too particular I shall never come to the end of it – I returned to the ship, put myself to rights, and came on shore next day with all my *taonga*, to the great delight of the chief and tribe. My hospitable entertainer, Mr. . . . . , found room for my possessions in his store, and a room for myself in his house; so now I am fairly housed, we shall see what will come of it.

I have now all New Zealand before me to caper about in, so I shall do as I like and please myself. I shall keep to neither rule, rhyme, nor reason, but just write what comes uppermost to my recollection of the good old days. Many matters which seemed odd enough to me at first have long appeared such mere matters of course that I am likely to pass them over without notice. I shall, however, give some of the more striking features of those delectable days, now, alas, passed and gone! Some short time after this, news came that a grand war expedition which had been absent nearly two years at the south had returned. This party were about a thousand strong, being composed of two parties of about five hundred men each from two different tribes, who had joined their forces for the purpose of the expedition. The tribe with which Mr. . . . and myself were staying had not sent any men on this war party; but, I suppose to keep their hands in, had attacked one of the two tribes who had, and were consequently much weakened by the absence of so many of their best men. It, however, turned out that after a battle, the ferocity of which has seldom been equalled in any country but this, our friends were defeated with dreadful loss, having inflicted almost as great on the enemy. Peace, however, had afterwards been formally made; but nevertheless the news of the return of this expedition was not heard of without causing a sensation almost amounting to consternation. The war-chief of the party who had been attacked by our friends during his absence was now, with all his men, within an easy day's march. His road lay right through our village, and it was much to be doubted that he would keep the peace, being one of the most noted war-chiefs of New Zealand, and he and his men returning from a successful expedition. All now was uproar and confusion: messengers were running like mad in all directions to call in stragglers; the women were carrying fuel and provisions into the *pa* or fortress of the tribe. This *pa* was a very well-built and strong stockade, composed of three lines of strong fence and ditch, very ingeniously and artificially planned; and, indeed, as good a defence as well could be imagined against an enemy armed only with musketry.

All the men were now working like furies, putting this fort to rights, getting it into fighting order, mending the fences, clearing out ditches, knocking down houses inside the place, clearing away brushwood and fern all around the outside within musket-shot. I was in the thick of it, and worked all day lashing the fence – the fence being of course not nailed, but lashed with *toro-toro*, a kind of tough creeping plant like a small rope, which was very strong and well adapted for the purpose. This lashing was about ten or twelve feet from the ground, and a stage had to be erected for the men to stand on. To accomplish this lashing or fastening of the fence well and with expedition required two men, one inside the fence and another outside; all the men therefore worked in pairs, passing the end of the *toro-toro* from one to the other through the fence of large upright stakes and round a crosspiece which went all along the fence, by which means the whole was connected into one strong wall. I worked away like fury, just as if I had been born and bred a member of the community; and moreover, not being in those days very particularly famous for what is called prudence I intended also, circumstances permitting, to fight like fury too, just for the fun of the thing. About a hundred men were employed in this part of the work new-lashing the *pa*. My vis-a-vis in the operation was a respectable old warrior of great experience and approved valour, whose name being turned into English meant, 'The eater of his own relations'. (Be careful not to read *rations*.) This was quite a different sort of diet from 'melons', and he did not bear the name for nothing, as I could tell you if I had time, but I am half mad with haste, lashing the *pa*. I will only say that my comrade was a most bloodthirsty, ferocious athletic savage, and his character was depicted in every line of his tattooed face. About twenty men had been sent out to watch the approach of the dreaded visitors. The repairing of the stockade went on all one day and all one night by torchlight and by the light of huge fires lit in the inside. No one thought of sleep. Dogs barking, men shouting, children crying, women screaming, pigs squealing, muskets firing (to see if they were fit for active service and would go off), and above all, the doleful *tetere* sounding. This was a huge wooden trumpet six feet long, which gave forth a groaning, moaning sound, like the voice of a dying wild bull. Babel, with a dash of pandemonium, will give a faint idea of the uproar.

All preparations had been made at last, and no further tidings of the enemy, as I may call them, I took a complete survey of the fort, my friend the 'Relation Eater' being my companion, and explaining to me the design of the whole. I learned something that day; and I, though pretty well 'up' in the noble science of fortifications, ancient and modern, was obliged to confess to myself that a savage who could neither read nor write – who had never heard of Cohorn or Vauban – and who was moreover avowedly a gobbler up of his own relations, could teach me certain practical 'dodges' in the defensive art quite well worth knowing.

A long shed of palm leaves had been built at a safe and convenient distance from the fort. This was for the accommodation of the expected visitors, supposing they came in peaceful guise. A whole herd of pigs were also collected and tied to stakes driven into the ground in the rear of the fort. These were intended to feast the coming guests, according to their behaviour.

Towards evening a messenger from a neighbouring friendly tribe arrived to say that next day, about noon, the strangers might be expected; and also that the peace which had been concluded with their tribe during their absence had been ratified and accepted by them. This was satisfactory intelligence; but, nevertheless, no precaution must be neglected. To be thrown off guard would invite attack, and ensure destruction; everything must be in order; gun cleaning, flint fixing, cartridge making, was going on in all directions; and the outpost at the edge of the forest was not called in. All was active preparation.

The path by which these doubtful friends were coming led through a dense forest and came out on the clear plain about half a mile from the *pa*, which plain continued and extended in every direction around the fortress to about the same distance, so that none could approach unperceived. The outpost of twenty men were stationed at about a couple of hundred yards from the point where the path emerged from the wood; and as the ground sloped considerably from the forest to the fort, the whole intervening space was clearly visible.

Another night of alarm and sleepless expectation, the melancholy moan of the *tetere* still continuing to hint any lurking enemy that we were all wide awake; or rather, I should say, to assure him most positively of it, for who could sleep with that diabolical din in his ears? Morning came, and an early breakfast was cooked and devoured hurriedly. Then groups of the younger men might be seen here and there fully armed, and 'getting up steam' by dancing the war dance, in anticipation of the grand dance of the whole warrior force of the tribe, which, as a matter of course, must be performed in honour of the visitors when they arrived. In honour, but quite as much in intimidation, or an endeavour at it, though no one said so. Noon arrived at last. Anxious glances are turning from all quarters towards the wood, from which a path is plainly seen winding down the sloping group towards the *pa*. The outpost is on the alert. Straggling scouts are out in every direction. All is expectation. Now there is a movement at the outpost. They suddenly spread in an open line, ten yards between each man. One man comes at full speed running towards the *pa*, jumping and bounding over every impediment. Now something moves in the border of the forest – it is a mass of black heads. Now the men are plainly visible. The whole *taua* has emerged upon the plain. 'Here they come! Here they come!' is heard in all directions. Then men of the outpost cross the line of march in pretended resistance; they present their guns, make horrid grimaces, dance about like mad baboons, and then fall back with headlong speed to the next advantageous position for making a stand. The *taua*, however, comes on steadily; they are formed in a solid oblong mass. The chief at the left of the column leads them on. The men are all equipped for immediate action – that is to say, quite naked except their arms and cartridge boxes, which are a warrior's clothes. No one can possibly tell what this peaceful meeting may end in, so all are ready for action at a second's notice. The *taua* still comes steadily on. As I have said, the men are all stripped for action, but I also notice that the appearance of nakedness is completely taken away by the tattooing, the colour of the skin, and the arms and equipments. The men in fact look much better than when dressed in their Maori clothing. Every man, almost without exception, is covered with tattooing from the knees to the waist; the face is also covered with dark spiral lines. Each man has round his middle a belt, to which are fastened two cartridge boxes, one behind and one before; another belt goes over the right shoulder and under the left arm, and from it hangs, on the left side and rather behind, another cartridge box, and under the waist-belt is thrust behind, at the small of the back, the short-handled tomahawk for close fight and to finish the wounded. Each cartridge box contains eighteen rounds, and every man has a musket. Altogether this *taua* is better and more uniformly armed and equipped than ordinary; but they have been amongst the first who got *pakehas* to trade with them, and are indeed, in consequence, the terror of New Zealand. On they come, a set of tall, athletic heavy-made men; they would, I am sure, in the aggregate weigh some tons heavier than the same number of men taken at random from the streets of our manufacturing towns. They are now half-way across the plain; they keep their formation, a solid oblong, admirably as they advance, but they do not keep step; this causes a very singular appearance when distant. Instead of the regular marching step of civilised soldiers, which may be observed at any distance, this mass seems to progress towards you with the creeping motion of some great reptile, and when coming down a sloping ground this effect is quite remarkable.

The mimic opposition is now discontinued; the outpost rushes in at full speed, the men firing their guns in the air as they run. *Takini; takini!* is the cry, and out spring three young men, the best runners of our tribe, to perform the ceremony of the *taki*. They hold in their hands some reeds to represent darts or *kokiri*. At this moment a tremendous fire of *ball* cartridge opens from the fort; the balls whistle in every direction, over and around the advancing party, who steadily and gravely come on, not seeming to know that a gun has been fired, though they perfectly well understood that this salute is also a hint of full preparation for any unexpected turn things may take. Now, from the whole female population arises the shrill '*Haere mai! Haere mai!*' Mats are waving, guns firing, dogs barking; the chief roaring to 'fall in', and form for the war dance. He appears half-mad with excitement, anxiety, and something very like apprehension of a sudden onslaught from his friends. In the midst of this horrible uproar off dart three runners. They are not unexpected. Three young men of the *taura* are seen to tighten their waist-belts and hand their muskets to their comrades. On go the three young men from the fort. They approach the front of the advancing column; they dance and caper about like mad monkeys, twisting their faces about in the most extraordinary manner, showing the whites of their eyes, and lolling out their tongues. At last, after several feints, they boldly advance within twenty yards of the supposed enemy, and send the reed darts flying full in their faces; then they turn and fly as if for life. Instantly, from the stranger ranks, three young men dart forth in eager pursuit; and behind them comes the solid column, rushing on at full speed. Run now, O 'Sounding Sea' (*Tai Haruru*), for the 'Black Cloud' (*Kapua Mangu*), the swiftest of the Rarawa, is at your back; run now, for the honour of your tribe and your own name, run! run! It was an exciting scene. The two famous runners came on at a tremendous pace, the dark mass of armed men following close behind at full speed, keeping their formation admirably, the ground shaking under them as they rushed on. On come the two runners (the others are left behind and disregarded). The pursuer gains upon his man; but they are fast nearing the goal, where, according to Maori custom, the chase must end. Run 'Sounding Sea'! Another effort! Your tribe are near in full array, and armed for the war dance; their friendly ranks are your refuge; run! run! On came the headlong race. When within about thirty yards of the place where our tribe was now formed in a solid oblong, each man kneeling on one knee, with musket held in both hands, butt to the ground, and somewhat sloped to the front, the pursuing native caught at the shoulder of our man, touched it, but could do no more. Here he must stop; to go farther would not be 'correct'. He will, however, boast everywhere that he has touched the shoulder of the famous 'Sounding Sea'. Our man has not, however, been caught, which would have been a bad omen. At this moment the charging column come thundering up to where their man is standing; instantly they all kneel upon one knee, holding their guns sloped before their faces in the manner already described. The elite of the two tribes are now opposite to each other, all armed, all kneeling, and formed in two solid oblong masses, the narrow end of the oblong to the front. Only thirty yards divide them; the front ranks do not gaze on each other; both parties turn their eyes towards the ground, and with heads bent downwards, and a little to one side, appear to listen. All is silence; you might have heard a pin drop. The uproar has turned to a calm; the men are kneeling statues; the chiefs have disappeared – they are in the centre of their tribes. The *pakeha* is beginning to wonder what will be the end of all this and also to speculate on the efficacy of the buckshot with which his gun is loaded, and wishes it was ball. Two minutes have elapsed in this solemn silence, the more remarkable as being the first quiet two minutes for the last two days and nights. Suddenly from the extreme rear of the strangers' column is heard a scream – a horrid yell. A savage of herculean stature, comes, *mere* in hand, rushing madly to the front. He seems hunted by all the furies. Bedlam never produced so horrid a visage. Thrice, as he advances, he gives that horrid cry, and thrice the armed tribe give answer with a long-drawn gasping sigh. He is at the front; he jumps into the air, shaking his stone weapon; the whites only of his eyes are visible, giving a most hideous appearance to his face; he shouts the first words of the war song, and instantly his tribe spring from the ground. It would be hard to describe the scene that followed. The roaring chorus of the war song; the horrid grimaces; the eyes all white; the tongues hanging out; the furious yet measured and uniform gesticulation, jumping, and stamping. I felt the ground plainly trembling. At last the war dance ended; and then my tribe (I find I am already beginning to get

Maorified) starting from the ground like a single man, endeavoured to out-do even their amiable friends' exhibition. They end; then the newcomers perform another demon dance; then my tribe give another. Silence again prevails, and all sit down. Immediately a man from the new arrivals comes to the front of his own party; he runs to and fro; he speaks for his tribe; these are his words: 'Peace is made! peace is made; peace is firm! peace is secure! peace! peace! peace!'

JOHN MITCHEL
1815–1875

Mitchel is the solitary representative in this collection of what might be termed the involuntary traveller: his visit to Tasmania (then Van Diemen's Land) in the early 1850s was in his capacity – as he states on the title page of his *Jail Journal* (1854), from which this passage is taken – as 'prisoner in the hands of the English'. The son of an Ulster Presbyterian minister, Mitchel studied law at Trinity College Dublin and became involved in the nationalist movement in reaction to the miseries of the Great Famine of the 1840s. He founded the *United Irishman*, and his advocacy in its pages of armed insurrection led to his conviction for treason-felony, a crime specially invented for his benefit, in 1848. He was transported first to Bermuda and from there, via South Africa, to Van Diemen's Land, from which he escaped in 1853 to the United States, where he championed the southern cause in the Civil War. He died in Newry, County Down.

REUNION AT LAKE SOREL

April 13th, 1850. – The village of Bothwell, where John Martin and myself are now privileged, by 'ticket-of-leave,' to live or to vegetate, contains about sixty or seventy houses; has a church where clergymen of the Church of England and of Scotland perform service, one in the morning and the other in the evening of Sunday; has four large public-houses, or hotels, establishments which are much better supported on the voluntary system, and have much larger congregations, than the church; has a post-office, and several carpenters' and blacksmiths' shops, for the accommodation of the settlers who live in the district; and a police-office and police-barrack, with the police magistrate of the district predominating there.

It is situated in a valley about three or four miles in width, and twice that in length, at an elevation of 1,000 feet above the sea; and is surrounded by rough wooded mountains, rising perhaps 1,000 feet higher. Through the valley, from north to south, runs the little river Clyde, turning two mills. Two miles below Bothwell, the Clyde makes a leap of forty-five feet into a profound cauldron between high rocks, and thence enters a narrow gorge between lofty and rocky banks, where it rushes along with great rapidity, and about sixteen miles lower down passes another village with a Lanarkshire name, 'Hamilton,' from whence it still continues a southern course, till it enters the large river Derwent, which collects the drainage of all the high central region of the island. This particular valley of the Clyde was settled principally by Scotch colonists, which accounts for the Lanarkshire names.

Hamilton, however, is a police-district by itself, and lies out of the bounds of our dungeon. Northward the district of Bothwell extends twenty-four miles to the shores of Lake Crescent and Lake Sorel; and the farther shores of the lakes bound the territories of Meagher and O'Doherty. Eastward the district of Bothwell is defined by the course of the Jordan, a stream still smaller than the Clyde, which I crossed on my way hither a few days ago, without knowing it : for it is always dry except in winter. Westward we reach the large river Shannon, which runs through a lonely wilderness of forest and mountain, between lofty banks, and after joining with the Ouse, a still more western river, loses itself in the same Derwent. Beyond those rivers lies the almost unexplored region of the island, utterly barren and inhospitable, spreading in a great plateau, at an elevation of nearly 4,000 feet, to the Western Sea.

We climbed today one of the minor hills, and from the summit commanded a vast view of endless mountains, covered with wood, closed to the south-west by a great range already covered with snow, though it is still warm autumnal weather here.

The trees are almost all of one or other of the gum species; lofty and vast, but not umbrageous, for the foliage is meagre, and but ill clothes the huge limbs. In some of the huge valleys, however, there is more richness of foliage and along the river's bank the gum-trees are chiefly of the sort called black gum, which makes a grand leafy head, almost as massive as the European beech or sycamore. On the slopes of some of the hills are great thickets of mimosa, called by the colonists the wattle-gum, a most graceful evergreen tree, but stripped at this season of its splendid gold-hued blossoms. The air is laden with the fragrance of these gum-trees, and illuminated by the flight

of parrots of most glowing and radiant plumage, that go flashing
through the arches of the forest like winged gems.

I grow stronger every day. And whether it be the elastic and balmy
air of these mountain-woods that sends the tide of life coursing
somewhat warmer through my veins – or unwonted converse of an
old friend that revives the personal identity I had nearly lost – or the
mere treading once more upon the firm flowery surface of our
bounteous Mother Earth, after two years' tossing on the barren,
briny ocean – Mother Earth breathing vital fragrance for ever, for
ever swinging the censer of her perfumes from a thousand flowers;
for ever singing her eternal melodies in whispering tree-tops and
murmuring, tinkling, bubbling streams – certain it is, I feel a kind of
joy. In vain I try to torment myself into a state of chronic savage
indignation : it will not do here. In vain I reflect that 'it is incumbent
on me diligently to remember' (as Mr Gibbon says) how that I am,
after all, in a real cell, hulk, or dungeon, yet – that these ancient
mountains, with the cloud-shadows flying over their far-stretching
woodlands, are but Carthaginian prison walls – that the bright birds,
waving their rainbow wings here before me, are but 'ticket-of-leave'
birds, and enjoy only 'comparative liberty' – in vain – there is in
every soul of man a buoyancy that will not let it sink to utter stark
despair. Well said the Lady Eleanora –

'When the heart is throbbing sorest
There is balsam in the forest
There is balsam in the forest for its pain' –
Said the Lady Eleanora.

Moreover, at my side walks Martin; and pours me out such a
stream of discourse. The slight sketches or partial glimpses I had got
in my seafaring captivity of the history of our most rueful and pitiful
rebellion needed to be filled up: and he has three months' later
history of Ireland than I knew. Three ignominious months!

It seems the three rebels whose dungeon-districts all touch Lake
Sorel are in the habit of meeting almost every week at those lakes,
which is against the rule, to be sure; but authorities connive at it –
thinking probably that no great or immediate harm can accrue to the
British Empire thereby. And Martin is to guide me tomorrow to the
rendezvous; having written immediately on my arrival to the two
others, announcing the day of meeting. Martin has a grey pony;

O'Doherty and Meagher have each a horse; and I, having none yet of my own, am to hire one from a man in the village. This evening I have deluged Martin with talk, as we sat at our wood fire, smoking like two volcanoes. We have lodgings in a neat cottage of the village, our hostess being a woman who conducts the church-singing on Sundays. She is very attentive to us; and to show me she is a person of respectability, she took an early occasion of informing me that she 'came out free'; which, in fact, is the patent of nobility in Van Diemen's Land. Here, a freeman is a king, and the convict-class is regarded just as the negroes must be in South Carolina; which indeed is perfectly right.

I have seen none of the neighbouring gentlemen yet; but John Martin tells me that they have almost all called on him, and shown him kind attentions during the five months he spent here alone. I feel pretty indifferent to society, however, at least yet. But it is agreeable to find that even English and Scotch settlers of good character and rank refuse to regard us as 'felons'. A piece of contumacy indeed against their own government, but a considerable pleasure and advantage to us.

Martin has brought out some books, which, together with my small store, make our lodging look literary. Martin is an old brick; he has listened to me haranguing tonight with commendable attention. So that I trust I have improved his mind.

Tomorrow we start at eight o'clock in the morning for our *re-union* in a certain shepherd's hut on Lake Sorel.

15th. – Lake Sorel. Promontory of the 'Dog's Head,' or Cynoscephaloe. Yesterday morning dawned cold and gloomy; the first morning apparently of their Tasmanian winter. Before we rose it had begun to rain violently; and all the sky was dark. Evidently the day was to be tempestuous; and on the hills round about the valley we could see that it was snow instead of rain that was falling. Our landlady and her husband advised us not to move, as we might be stopped by floods in the high country; and, besides, I was still extremely weak and nervous, though improving rapidly.

We waited till noon; but at noon, as it rained more furiously than ever, we resolved to brave it and mount. We set out north-eastward through the valley, which is perfectly level, sandy, clothed with a short, dry, yellowish grass, and sprinkled with trees. After a ride of four miles we passed a handsome stone house, with very extensive

outbuildings for convict labourers and the tradesmen required on a
sheep-farming estate. It lies nestled at the very root of the great
Quoin hill; and commands a most extensive view over the plain in
front and the distant mountains to the south. This is Denistoun, the
residence of Mr Russell, a Scottish settler, and a good friend of
Martin's; but we rode past without stopping, and through a large
green paddock, surrounded by the stables and workmen's huts.
Immediately on clearing this we found ourselves in the wild bush,
and ascending a gorge of the hill behind. From this point the rain
began to change into snow, and for many miles we rode on through
the blinding tempest, which prevented any special reconnaissance of
the country. I was only sensible that we were continually ascending –
that the track was very obscure, and wound amongst dead trees and
rocks – and that at every mile the forest became more wild, and more
encumbered with naked and fallen trees; until at last I thought the
whole world might be challenged to show a scene of such utter
howling desolation.

Still we rode on, Martin always saying that when we should be
half-way to Lake Sorel, we might turn if we liked. Fifteen miles from
Denistoun we passed a rough log-fence, and saw before us a level
plain extending full two miles, partially adorned with majestic trees,
like some spacious park in Ireland. And, though it was bleak enough
yesterday, with a snow-storm driving and hissing over it, yet it was
easy to see we had got into a country of a different character. In short,
we had finished the long ascent, and we were now on the great
plateau of these two lakes. We galloped over the plain with the snow
beating furiously in our faces, and found ourselves on the bank of a
small river, beyond which seemed to be a tract of very close and
rugged woodland. 'The Clyde again,' said my companion; 'we are
but a quarter of a mile from the point of Lake Crescent, whence it
issues; but you cannot see the lake through the close bush.'

We crossed the river by a rough wooden bridge, made by some of
the settlers for the passage of their flocks when they drive them
down for the winter to the low country; and then for four miles
farther we had a most savage and difficult region to pass, covered
with thick and shaggy bush, and very much encumbered with the
monstrous ruins of ancient trees. No living creature was anywhere
visible; but now and then a few sheep cowering under the lee side
of a honeysuckle tree (for all these regions are parcelled out into

sheep-runs); no sound, but the roaring of the wind, and the groaning and screaming of the trees.

Lake Crescent was now visible on our right; and for three or four miles we had no track, or other guidance on our way save that by keeping the lake in sight, on our right hand, we must strike on the point where the other lake communicates with it by a short stream. And there lay the hut where, I was assured, we should find a human being, a hermit named Cooper, who would be sure to give us a mutton-chop, and enable us to proceed on our way.

I had pretended, up to this time, that I was not fatigued, and could still ride any distance; but the weakness produced by my two years' confinement began now to be visible. My companion encouraged me by the assurance that we were within two miles of Cooper's, and we now got into open ground again, where we could push our horses to a canter. At last we found ourselves on a low tract of land, about half a mile across, having Lake Crescent still to the right, and the great Lake Sorel to the left. This is a magnificent sheet of water, thirty-five miles in circuit measured by the sinuosities of the shore, varied by some bold promontories, one small wooded island, and a fine range of bold hills on its northern side. The water looked black, and had an angry curl; the snow, which had abated somewhat, came down thicker than ever; and at last, to my great contentment, I could see a smoke mounting amongst the trees before us. There, upon the edge of a marsh, and just at the point where a sluggish winding stream leaves Lake Sorel, to carry its surplus waters to Lake Crescent, stood a small hut of round logs, thatched with grass – the first human habitation we had seen since we left Denistoun.

The sound of our horses' hoofs brought out a man of about forty years of age, with a thin, sharp, intelligent face, and hair somewhat reddish, dressed in the blue woollen shirt, which is the invariable uniform of the shepherds and stock-keepers. He welcomed us with great cordiality, and said at once that Mr Meagher and Mr O'Doherty were at Townsend's all day waiting for us. Townsend's is another hut, four miles further on, and situated in the district of Ross, which is usually made the place of meeting, because it is a better house, and has several rooms. On dismounting, however, to sit a little while at Cooper's fire, I found myself too much exhausted to ride any farther; so Cooper took one of our horses, and set off to Townsend's, to ask our friends to come to me, seeing I could not go to them.

'You just keep the fire up, gentlemen,' said Cooper, as he girthed the saddle, 'that I may get the tea and chops ready when I come back, and I'll engage the other gentlemen will be here in an hour or less.' We threw on more wood, and tried to dry our clothes.

It now began to grow dusk, for we had been four hours and a-half on the way; and the evening was fast growing dark, when we heard the gallop of three horses, and a loud laugh, well known to me. We went to the door, and in a minute Meagher and O'Doherty had thrown themselves from their horses; and, as we exchanged greetings – I know not from what impulse, whether from buoyancy of heart, or *bizarre* perversity of feeling – we all *laughed* till the woods rang around; laughed loud and long, and uproariously, till two teal rose, startled from the reeds on the lake-shore, and flew screaming to seek a quieter neighbourhood.

I suspect there was something hollow in that laughter, though at the time it was hearty, vociferous, and spontaneous. But even in laughter the heart is sad; and curses or tears, just then, might have become us better.

Both these exiles looked fresh and vigorous. Kevin O'Doherty I had scarcely ever met before; but he is a fine, erect, noble-looking young man, with a face well bronzed by air and exercise.

After giving the horses each two handfuls of oats, all we had, we turned them out to find shelter and grazing as best they could. Beside the hut is a large enclosure, made by an old post-and-rail fence; and into this, with much compunction, on my part at least, we turned out the poor animals. However, such is the usage that horses are accustomed to here, where they are seldom stabled, even in winter. Indeed, the bush everywhere affords good close shelter for all sorts of animals, under the thickets of 'wattle-gum,' and the dense dark shade of the honeysuckle-tree. Horses also eat the leaves and tender shoots of both these trees, when the ground happens to be covered with snow, which, even at this height among the mountains, is exceedingly rare.

All this time, while we were employed about our horses, Cooper was in the hut broiling mutton-chops, boiling tea in an open tin-can, slung over the fire, and cutting the damper into thick slices – mutton, tea, and damper being the morning refection, and mutton, damper, and tea being the evening meal in the bush. Damper is merely a large flat cake of flour and water, baked in the wood embers on the hearth.

We sat down upon blocks of gum-tree, and Cooper being possessed of but one knife and one fork, we dined primitively; but all were ravenously hungry, and it seems Cooper is notorious in the lake region for the excellency of his chop-cookery.

Our talk was all of Ireland, and of Richmond and Newgate prisons, and of Smith O'Brien; and it soon made us serious enough. I had still very much to learn – though before coming up to Bothwell at all, I had met MacManus at a wayside inn, and he told me all he knew. They have been in Van Diemen's Land just five months; and they inform me that Smith O'Brien has been during that time subjected to most rigorous, capricious, and insolent treatment by the 'Comptroller-General' and his subordinates. His confinement for a while, indeed, was as strict as my own had been in Bermuda; and only the representation of the medical officer, that his health was sinking under it, compelled them to relax the discipline so far that he is now allowed to wander over part of the island at stated times, attended by an armed constable. When he writes to any of the others, or they to him, the letters are all opened by the official people; and so petty has been the system of restriction exercised upon him, that they would not, for a good while, suffer him to receive his usual supply of cigars, sent to him from Hobart Town. To a man all alone, and already goaded and stung by outrage and wrong, even such a small privation as this may be a serious grievance. The 'Comptroller-General,' one Hampton, is specially exasperated against him, because O'Brien could not bring himself to show him some of those external marks of respect which he is in the habit of exacting from the real convicts: and being restrained from using his usual methods of coercion and punishment in our case, scourging, hard labour, and the like, the Comptroller (who is bound somehow to assert his dignity), strives to conquer and torture his haughty captive by hourly mortification in detail. I suppose it is the man's trade; and we must all live; but how much better it had been for that gallant heart, if he had been shot down at Ballingarry, or even hanged before the county-jail at Clonmel.

Our meeting at the Lakes, begun with factitious jollity, soon grew dismal enough; and it was still more saddened as we talked of the factions of Irish refugees in America – factions founded principally on the momentous question, who was the greatest man and most glorious hero, of that most inglorious Irish business of '48; and each imagines he exalts his own favourite 'martyr' by disparaging and pulling down the rest – as if the enemy's Government had not pulled us all down, and ridden roughshod over us. It seems that I have my faction, and Meagher a still stronger one. If our respective partisans could but have seen – as we discussed this question of our own comparative importance – how bitterly and how mournfully we two smiled at one another across the gum-tree fire in that log-hut amongst the forests of the antipodes, perhaps it might have cooled their partisan zeal.

This morning, when we looked out on the snowy waste, we found that all the horses had broken out through the fence into the woods. So we sallied out and spent an hour searching for them all over the rocky country between the two lakes. At last, in a dense part of the forest, we found them cowering under some honeysuckle trees, and nibbling the leaves – a sorry breakfast. Drove them in; and after partaking of Cooper's breakfast, we mounted and rode on to the 'Dog's Head'. This is a fine promontory running about a mile out into the lake, and fringed all round with noble trees. In a snug cove at the northern side of the 'Dog's Head' is a stone house inhabited by the shepherd in charge of a large flock belonging to a Mr Clarke, the owner of all the eastern shores of the lake. The day became beautiful and bright. The snow had all disappeared by twelve o'clock, and the lake lay smooth as a mirror. Opposite to us rise several rough wooded peaks; and all that side of the lake is said to be utterly trackless, and nearly impervious, swarming with 'native devils' and 'native tigers,' two species of hideous beasts of prey about the size of sheep-dogs, which at times make great havoc among the flocks. We have taken the little boat belonging to this station and rowed over to the island, then to another quiet bay where there is a sandy beach, called by the shepherds the 'Diamond Beach,' from beautiful little agates and pieces of yellow quartz found amongst the sands.

18th – Today we reluctantly parted, promising to be at the rendezvous again the week after next; and rode our different ways.

'One of the great travellers of our time', according to her compatriot
William Trevor, Dervla Murphy is the daughter of a former County
Librarian of Waterford, where she was born. She left school at
fourteen, imbued with an abiding ambition both to write and to travel.
The first of many hazardous and adventurous journeys took her, in
1963, to India on a bicycle ('Roz') and resulted in the immediately
successful *Full Tilt* (1965), from which this episode is taken. There
followed travels, with their subsequent accounts, to Nepal, Ethiopia,
India, the Andes and Cameroon, always on a minimalist basis and
latterly in the company of her resilient daughter, Rachel. Dervla
Murphy has also written 'travel of another sort' – on underprivileged
Britain and a book on Northern Ireland, for which she received the
Christopher Ewart-Biggs Memorial Prize in 1978. She lives in Lismore,
County Waterford. The following episode takes place on the road
from Teheran to the Afghan frontier.

GODDAM NUT-CASE

GOOSHEH, 1 APRIL

It's very funny – around here the idea of a woman travelling alone is
so completely outside the experience and beyond the imagination of
everyone that it's universally assumed I'm a man. This convenient
illusion is fostered by the very short haircut I deliberately got in
Teheran, and by a contour-obliterating shirt presented to me at
Adabile by the US Army in the Middle East, who also donated a
wonderful pair of boots – the most comfortable footwear I've ever had
and ideal for tramping these stony roads. The result of the locals' little
error of judgment is that last night and tonight I was shown to my bed
in the gendarmerie dormitory. These beds consist of wooden planks

with padded sleeping-bags laid on them and I have the bed of one of
those on night-patrol. There are no problems involved as 'getting
ready for bed' consists of removing boots, gun and belt and sliding
into a flea-bag so I simply do likewise and that's that! Incidentally,
these barracks are kept spotlessly clean: as much as an accidental
crumb or cigarette ash isn't allowed on the mud floor and everything
is neat and tidy. I bring in my own food and get hot water for coffee
from the lads. I'm now sitting on the edge of my bed writing by a little
oil-lamp while six gendarmes sleep soundly around me.

We left Deh-Namak at 5.30 am when the sun was just up and the
air pleasantly cool. Though the road was much worse than yesterday
we covered eighty-two miles, arriving here at 6.40 pm. I stopped for
lunch at 12.30 pm and slept for an hour in blazing sun; apart from
sunburn (there was no shade available) this is perfectly safe, as in the
wide open spaces between villages there are no men, beasts, insects
or reptiles to molest one, but I suspect I'm in for trouble with sunburnt
arms as I was using my wind-cheater to cover Roz's tyres while I
slept. Actually it is only when stationary that one is aware of the
sun's power, whilst moving there's no sensation of it being 'too hot'.
I believe it'll be the same in Afghanistan, before becoming intolerably
hot in Pakistan and India. (I feel I've earned a few months of perfect
weather!)

Soon after lunch I abandoned the road for over ten miles and
cycled along a dried-up river-bed where the baked mud was firm
and smooth and the boulders en route seemed a mere triviality as
compared with the excruciating, sharp-edged gravel on a road with
an inexorably corrugated surface. When I found the river-bed veering
too much to the south I reluctantly left it and walked over a mile or so
of desert back to the road. The last thirty miles were through another
magnificent mountain range with a very stiff climb up to this village.
I passed the scene of a ghastly smash-up reported a few days ago in
the English-language Teheran paper. A truck and bus were in a
head-on collision on a V-bend – both went into a ravine and fifty-one
were killed. Something similar happens almost every day somewhere
in Persia and the drivers are always blamed. Watching Persian buses
on mountain roads makes me feel quite ill; when I see the dust-cloud
that heralds one I dismount and remove myself to a safe distance.
During ten days in Teheran I witnessed seven bad traffic accidents,
four of them involving the deaths of nine people.

This is a tiny village of some twenty domed mud huts, a tea-house and the barracks. There should be a level road tomorrow as the map shows no passes – but probably we'll have a worse surface each day.

SHAHRUD, 2 APRIL

How right can you be! We only covered sixty-six miles today (5.45 am–6.50 pm) and I had to walk over twenty-five of them, not because of hills, but because no one with any regard for their cycle would ride it over this sort of infernal track. I haven't seen one private car or one lorry since leaving Teheran, though many buses pass, packed with people and overloaded on the roofs with rolls of carpet, bicycles, crates of hens, lambs and kids (alive and kicking – literally!) and diverse bundles containing God knows what. These buses unload for lunch (between 12 and 3) at village eating-houses, which have streams running beside them and a few green trees shading the carpet-covered 'tables' on which everyone sits cross-legged eating their bread and chives and hard-boiled eggs and minced-meat balls and *mast* (the Persian yoghourt). Before the meal all babies present have their napkins changed and these are washed in the stream (as are the chives and everybody's teeth after eating) and spread out to dry before the resumption of the journey. Today I joined one of these parties (obviously a pilgrimage returning from Meshed) and though I was addressed as 'Monsieur' the mere fact that I was from a Christian country provoked hostility. I didn't dare use the camera, though I would have valued a few shots of those fanatical-looking chaps in filthy rags and tatters. Many of them were adolescents, so it's going to take H.I.M a long, long time to tame this lot. The children were terrified of me and wouldn't come for the sweets I offered and the whole atmosphere was so unpleasant that I removed myself sooner than I would have otherwise and took my siesta in the safety of the desert a few miles away.

A phenomenon that intrigues me is the number of Catholic religious oleographs in all these eating-houses and tea-houses – Christ as a baby in the manger or working in the carpenter's shop, the Immaculate Heart of Mary picture, highly coloured, Our Lady of Perpetual Succour, Our Lady of Good Counsel, cheap prints of the Raphael Madonna, and St Joseph. These are in addition, of course, to the Shah, the Empress and baby Prince in various stages of growth, not to mention luscious semi-nude females advertising Pepsi-Cola and aspirin. But how all these Christian pictures got here baffles me; granted the Muslims are devoted to Christ as a Prophet and to Our Lady, but I wouldn't have thought their devotion would go so far.

When I arrived on the outskirts of this town a car overtook me and the driver (manager of a local sugar factory and reader of the daily paper) stopped and said, 'Dervla going to India, yes?' I blushed with becoming modesty at this proof of fame and replied that I was indeed Dervla going to India, so he invited me to spend the night at his home, where I now am, having had a shower and a huge supper. It's quite impossible to retain one's youthful curves in these countries: to refuse food is an insult so one merely unbuttons one's slacks in a surreptitious way and goes on and on eating. Before the meal everyone consumes a vast amount of biscuits, oranges, pastries, figs stuffed with almonds, toffees and bon-bons of all descriptions, pistachio nuts and endless glasses of tea. Then you're expected to welcome with a glad smile a mound of rice you can hardly see over and masses of meat and vegetables.

This is a big town (8,000 population) with electricity, no less! My host's house is full of mod. cons., including a telephone, fridge and washing-machine. But inevitably there's no bath because of the Islamic law about washing in running water – the bathroom is a marble-floored outfit with a shower. (In fact every room in every Persian house is marble- or mud-floored because of the shortage of wood.) My host's wife is away in Teheran on a Now Ruz visit to her family and will be home tomorrow. This is the last day of the Now Ruz festival but my route today was so gloriously desolate that I saw little evidence of the traditional picnicking in the open. The four children here are delightful – two boys, two girls – and are tickled to bits by my arrival, having read about me in the Teheran paper. We were joined for supper by a twenty-year-old nephew of my host, with his sixteen-year-old wife – a made match that was clearly not working very well.

I'm in for torture with sunburn on my right arm – not, I now realise, the result of lying in the sun, but the result of cycling every day due east so that this arm is continuously exposed; and though I don't feel it when cycling it is a fierce sun. There's nothing like carrying six tubes of sunburn lotion across two continents and then forgetting to use it in time!

ABBAS-ABAD, 3 APRIL

We covered eighty-three miles today, but that meant breaking my
'not-after-dark' rule and cycling till 9.30 pm. However, in such
uninhabited country I don't think there's any danger and bright
moonlight showed the way; it was indescribably beautiful on the
huge sand-dunes, which look like mountains. I'm at last getting used
to the uncanny silence of desert landscape and to the odd experience
of seeing things that disappear as you approach them. Also I've
discovered that what looks like a village two miles ahead is actually a
village twenty miles ahead, and I've got acclimatised to fine dust
permeating every crevice of self and kit. In short, I'm broken in!

There was an amusing interlude today when an American engineer
going back by jeep to his work in Afghanistan pulled up to investigate
me and the following conversation took place:

American: 'What the hell are you doing on this goddam road?'

Me: (having taken an instant dislike to him) 'Cycling.'

American: 'I can see that – but what the hell for?'

Me: 'For fun.'

American: 'Are you a nut-case or what? Gimme that bike and I'll
stick it on behind and you get in here and we'll get out of this
goddam frying-pan as fast as we can. This track isn't fit for a camel!'

Me: 'When you're on a cycle instead of in a jeep it doesn't feel like
a frying-pan. Moreover, if you look around you you'll notice that the
landscape compensates for the admittedly deplorable state of the
road. In fact I *enjoy* cycling through this sort of country – but thank
you for the kind offer. Goodbye.'

As I rode on he passed me and yelled: 'You *are* a goddam nut-
case!'

I regard this sort of life, with just Roz and me and the sky and the
earth, as sheer bliss. My one worry at the moment is Roz's complete
disintegration. So far the rear-lamp, the rear mud-guard and half the
front mud-guard have fallen off; the straps tying saddle-bag to saddle
have both broken; the left pannier-bag holder has come apart and the
right pedal has loosened. Everything is being held together by a
system of rope and wire more complicated than you'd believe possible,
but fortunately none of these disabilities is serious. The trouble will
start when wheels or frame crack up. It's astonishing that I haven't
had a puncture since leaving Teheran – a tribute to the extreme care

with which I'm cycling. But obviously my claim that cycling is the best way to *see* a country just isn't valid in this region. I daren't take my eyes off the road for one second and my 'seeing' is confined to the walking intervals and to the frequent stops I make just to look around me.

This village is the most primitive place I've hit so far, with not even a gendarmerie barracks. It's a collection of the usual mud huts, very roughly constructed, and in the tea-house everything is of mud – the 'counter', the seats all around the walls and the steps leading up to an attic where men are smoking opium. I went up there to investigate sleeping accommodation and found five braves all in a trance with their pipes – that's what comes of having no gendarmerie in a place! (My right arm is so stiff tonight that I can't bend it and the pain is *intense* – but better that than frost-bite.) The three men now drinking tea here seem to be neutral towards me: they show no friendliness, but no apparent hostility either. I feel it's just as well I arrived late; the fewer people who know about my presence the better. I'll sleep on one of the long mud seats with Roz tied to me and my knapsack under my head with its straps round my neck – though it's not clear how me being strangled by my own straps will help the situation if someone tries to rob me!

BAGH-JAR, 4 APRIL

I survived last night without incident but despite tiredness slept badly as the sunburn agony woke me every time I moved. We set out at 5.30 am and the whole of today's eighty-five-mile ride was through the Great Salt Desert with flat sand on either side to the horizon and only one town (Salzevar) en route. This seemed an interesting place but was full of Mullahs and turbaned youths who stoned me and cut my sunburned arm five minutes after I'd arrived, so I departed hastily before a riot started. Salzevar is in the heart of the Mullah-dominated country, where the police are afraid of the clergy and simply don't appear if there's trouble, so discretion was most emphatically the better part of valour. I'm now safe with the gendarmerie in a little village, sitting up in my bunk and feeling rotten. My right arm is half the size again of my left and tomorrow all the blisters will burst. I can't think why it's swelled so much; that didn't happen in Spain, where I also had very bad sunburn. Anyway, it's entirely my own fault.

The road was slightly improved today, except where so much sand had blown over it that one couldn't cycle without skidding. I feel quite feverish this evening; possibly it's slight heat-stroke though I didn't feel over-heated to any great degree.

NISHAPUR, 5 APRIL

I woke up feeling much better, though my arm has not burst yet. We only did fifty-five miles today as this is Omar Khayyám's town and I've stopped here to pay homage. Besides, I think I've been pushing myself too hard, so an easy day was not a bad idea.

On leaving Bagh-Jar I had a twelve-mile walk through the mountains on a ghastly road but surrounded by tremendously exciting scenery. Then we suffered more desert until reaching here.

I find the Persian fauna very un-exotic. Bird life round the villages consists of crows, magpies, willy-wagtails, swallows and sparrows. The only unfamiliar birds are little crested chaps rather like thrushes and an occasional fierce, enormous hawk; I've also heard a few night-jars. Animal life is almost nil, though today I saw four roebuck crossing the road. Insect life consists to date of house-flies (very few) and black beetles as in Ireland.

This is a very lovely town; I notice that the towns of Persia tend to be much more attractive than the cities, especially now when the gardens are so beautiful with their smooth lawns, pale green cascades of weeping willow and brilliant beds of carnations, roses, pansies and geraniums. The main streets are always wide and the sun-soaked mud walls look golden under the violet blue of the Persian sky. Almost all the traffic consists of pony-phaeton taxis and innumerable laden donkeys and bicycles. The inevitable *jube* (a channel of water flowing between footpath and road) runs everywhere but on the whole the streets are quite clean and I've come to the conclusion that Persian water is safe if you make it clear you want to *drink* it, not wash with it. Anyway I've been drinking it uninhibitedly with no ill effects.

We arrived here at 3.15 pm and I was immediately captured by a twenty-year-old boy who secured me as his guest for the night against terrific competition from his class-mates; the local students have to pay fifty *reals* for a thirty minutes' English lesson, so an English-speaking guest for the night is considered precious. Three days ago Khayyám's new tomb was opened to the public by the Shah (pity I missed that) and a bevy of youths, laden with dictionaries, grammars and simplified versions of *Jane Eyre*, took me there this afternoon, all bombarding me en route with their particular problems of pronunciation, sentence construction and spelling. The keenness of Persian youths to learn English is positively fanatical but their opportunities remain very limited as few competent teachers are available outside Teheran.

The new tomb represents modern architecture at its grotesque worst; I almost wept to see it over the body of such a man as Omar Khayyám. I also saw the old tomb which is very simple, dignified and appropriate. Why tens of thousands of *reals* had to be spent on this new contraption when the country is swarming with undernourished children I do not know.

The family with whom I'm staying consists of the mother (aged thirty-five), three sons aged twenty, eighteen and twelve, and four girls aged sixteen, fourteen, nine and six. The father works as a draper's assistant in Teheran and the household is obviously very poor. This being Friday (the Muslim Sunday) twelve relatives were rounded up to come and meet me at supper time, but even though the men were close relatives the mother and daughters, including the six-year-old, veiled themselves the moment the visitors appeared. Islam is so rigid around here that *no* man, except father, husband and sons, is allowed to glimpse a woman's face; no wonder the boys can't take their eyes off my poor mug – at least it's a change from mother and sisters!

I ate with the women and was relieved to get lentils instead of rice. We also had a savoury omelet and salad – which I declined, having seen it washed in the *jube* and been warned by everyone to avoid *jube*-washed salad at all costs. There were no chairs or tables or beds in the house and no cutlery – you use the flat pieces of bread to dig your share out of the communal dish. *Mast* with sugar was served as dessert and I found the whole meal very appetising.

Everyone is most concerned about my arm, which certainly looks alarming, though it feels better tonight.

After the meal grandmother and mother took turns smoking the hookah, while one girl played on a timbrel and the rest danced – the traditional Friday evening pastime. I've got to appreciate Arabic music to the point where I have my favourite tunes and I could watch Persian dancing for hours; it's marvellously graceful, particularly in the use of arms and hands. The six-year-old gave a magnificent performance and a two-year-old already had the general idea!

SANG BAST, 6 APRIL

There was quite a change in the landscape today, though none in the road surface. We covered seventy-two miles, some of them between wonderful mountains, and most through what, for this area, is fertile land – i.e. a village, surrounded by little irrigated fields, every twenty miles or so, and in between huge flocks of sheep and goats grazing on some invisible herbage. There are hundreds of tiny lambs and kids with the flocks now and they look absolutely adorable; the lambs have thick fleeces and enormous floppy ears like spaniels, and the kids are very dainty and frisky. I stopped to have lunch with a fierce-looking but actually very amiable shepherd and admired his flocks while eating: we solemnly exchanged bread and salt so are friends forever, according to local custom.

As if Persia wanted to show me what it could do in the way of fauna I saw seven more deer today and one big dog fox of a horrid yellow-grey colour. I also met a tortoise, two scorpions, a hamster and an eagle and along much of the way I was accompanied by lark-song, which made me feel quite homesick.

This village is at the junction of the Teheran–Meshed–Afghanistan road, so I'll be returning to it tomorrow evening after a detour to see the sights of Meshed and to collect my mail. The local gendarmerie are exceptionally nice and sufficiently sophisticated to diagnose my sex so a flea-bag has been put on the office floor for me.

There was a strong east wind against us today – very wearing combined with the atrocious surface. It got quite cloudy too – there might be a nice bit of rain tomorrow, but that's not likely, though last week they did have their first inch for four years in South Persia.

One of the things that most intrigues Persians about me is the fact that I have no brothers and sisters: obviously only children are quite unknown here and they have the greatest sympathy for me. They're certainly a very family-minded people: brothers and sisters show tremendous mutual affection and in times of family trouble do all they can to help each other.

This was the first evening my expired visa was spotted, as a Lieutenant is in charge here; usually there's only an NCO as illiterate as his men. But the Lieutenant is a nice young man who winked and took twenty American cigarettes and said I could be fined over £50 for having American cigarettes in Persia.

SANG BAST, 7 APRIL

We arrived outside the British Council office in Meshed at 7.50 am – ten long minutes to wait for mail! It was a perfect metalled road for the twenty-five miles and I met with no hostility from the locals, who were friendlier than in many other places; but I had to avoid going to the shrine area alone, though I would have given a lot to explore it. Meshed is by far the nicest of the four Persian cities I've seen and it *did* rain this morning so all along the fine wide boulevards, which are lined with birches as big as our oaks, the new green leaves were freshly sparkling. A car was kindly laid on to take me round the city yet it was most frustrating just to glimpse the out-of-bounds beauties of the mosques and shrine and museum and library. That quarter was teeming with Mullahs; I saw three in green turbans, which means they are descended from the Prophet. An American girl who took herself off there two days ago against advice was badly hurt by stones when trying to get colour-shots of the domes and minarets.

One is told of the most blood-curdling tales at each stop. Here the *pièce de résistance* is about three Americans who, when motoring from Meshed to the Afghan frontier, stopped for a picnic and were all shot dead by bandits, who then escaped into Afghanistan but were hunted, by the Afghan police, back into Persia, where they were captured by the Army and publicly hanged in the main square of Teheran. Mr Jones of the British Council said there's no question of me going to Kabul via Mazar-i-Sharif as that area has lots of Communist-inspired trouble. The Russians are really trying hard at the moment to take over the whole of Afghanistan and there's a terrific tug-of-war going on between them and the Americans.

I left the British Council at 2.45 pm after lunch with the Joneses. (Very nice – both lunch and Joneses – and the British Council premises, which used to be the Consulate quarters when Britain had a Consul in Meshed, are really magnificent, with gardens and grounds that seem like Paradise when one comes to them from the desert.) I had decided that Roz would have to go to hospital before tackling Afghanistan so I took her to the city's biggest cycle shop where a few jobs which should have taken half an hour took two and a half hours so that we didn't get out of Meshed till 5.30 pm. This sounds incredible but everyone who has lived here knows it's true: Persians will *not* use a screwdriver – instead they *hammer* every screw into place, and all other repairs and readjustments are done with corresponding brutality. You can't imagine what I suffered, sitting on a stool beside the patient, chain-smoking and drinking my emergency supply of Courvoisier through sheer nerves, while they attacked that unfortunate, long-suffering cycle with hammer and chisel. Eventually we left, having abandoned the back mud-guard. I am now anticipating the worst, as no machine could survive an assault like that without dire repercussions.

CONOR O'BRIEN
1880–1952

'There are not so many adventures offering nowadays that one can afford to miss even a modest one,' said Conor O'Brien of his round-the-world cruise, the first by a yacht under the Irish flag, in 1923–25. An architect by profession, O'Brien had been a member of Sinn Féin and was active in gunrunning for the Irish Volunteers in 1914, later joining the British navy and serving as an officer in World War I. He enjoyed sports, such as mountaineering and sailing, which involved an element of danger, and his original plan when he set out in the 42-foot ketch *Saoirse* was to join a climbing expedition in New Zealand.

Following his return to his point of departure – Dun Laoghaire, County Dublin – on 20 June 1925, he became an inspector of fisheries and stood unsuccessfully for Seanad Éireann (the Irish Senate). During World War II, while living in England, he became a member of the Small Vessels Pool and sailed several craft across the Atlantic from America to assist the Allied cause. He wrote many books on sailing, some for children. This account of a leg of his circumnavigation in *Saoirse* is from *Across 3 Oceans* (1926).

A CLEARANCE FOR DUBLIN

I was not long in scraping acquaintance with the yachtsmen of Melbourne. Early on Sunday morning, my crew being still ashore and I without a boat, I started to drag my anchor and scraped up against most of the yachts in Williamstown. My numerous rescuers, moved no doubt by anxiety for their own boats as much as for mine, offered me a handsome choice of moorings, and every other sort of hospitality. My crew came back, with the necessary bacon and potatoes, and all seemed ready for a start on the morrow.

But I do not get to sea as easily as that. At first dawn I got up, went to shake up the cook, and put my hand on emptiness. So were the other two bunks empty, and the boat was gone. A large trunk, a bag, and a coat or two were in evidence, so at first I supposed that my crew would come back before long, especially as none of them were very well provided with money. I had divided the total cash on board into five parts; one for each of us and one for the ship, and it was only £7 10s. to begin with. Later in the morning I noticed that the bag had collapsed; I looked inside, and found it empty. The trunk was empty. The coats were the kind one usually throws overboard at the end of a passage. The crew had deserted. It was annoying, for I was already a month behind my time, and every day lost was lost out of the middle of the climbing season. I reported to the shipping office as soon as I could communicate with the shore, but that was not very soon. One would expect to see men and boats about early on a Monday morning in a yachting harbour at midsummer, but I expected in vain. One might hope for someone on shore that could read signals, but I had almost given up hope before anything happened. One learns patience in the Antipodes; I was worse marooned at Auckland.

This was now the 4th February; it was only a fortnight's run to New Zealand, and I had no doubt that I could get a crew for that, even if I had to wait a day or two and pay rather fantastic wages. But I had forgotten the Press. To the journalist a plain account of a job quietly and efficiently done is not a story; he wants battle, murder, and sudden death. So one attributed to me a tale of tempest which stamped the writer as a very timid or very inexperienced person; and another represented me as backing every order with a loaded revolver. It was no wonder the decent sort of crews fought shy of me. It is true that my late leading hand stated to an interviewer that he had no complaint of my character, of the ship's seaworthiness, or of the nature of the voyage; but that he was getting twice the wages in Melbourne that he was likely to get in London. But that interview did not appear in the papers that circulated most on the water-front.

I did of course get a certain number of applicants for a berth, mostly people who had never been to sea but who had good reason for getting out of Australia. There was also such a plague of remittance-men looking for free drinks that I grew to distrust anyone wearing good clothes and speaking English. Most of my encounters with these gentry were merely squalid; one was amusing. A soi-distant Lord S. wanted to carry me off to dinner in an opulent-looking motor-car, in which were two other men. Now from references in conversation to mutual acquaintances I had identified Lord S. within a first cousinship or so, and I knew that the seat of the family was S.; but I was not sufficiently up-to-date in the peerage to know whether such a title existed. It was possible, however, so I got into the car and we started for Melbourne. It soon transpired that the owner of the car knew nothing about his passenger, and shortly afterwards Lord S. said he had dropped a five-pound note in the car and could not find it. Then we, growing suspicious, stunned him with cocktails and drove him to the police-station instead of to the hotel. When searched he had not the price of one dinner on him, let alone of four; and next day he was jailed for bilking a taxi-driver. I do not think it was fair of the papers to represent him as a friend of mine without adding that I had delivered to justice a man for whom the police had been looking for six weeks.

But the Melbourne police were at the time inexperienced and handicapped by a wave of crime following the strike and dismissal of their predecessors, and even human life was pretty cheap. I had given a man who was absolutely down and out, but who was a decent honest man when he was sober, a couple of days at rigging work, and paid him for them, intending to sign him on the ship's articles next day. Admittedly he spent his wages unwisely, but he was the kind of man who would always turn up on time if he were alive, so I was rather anxious when he did not. Four days later I was sent for to identify his drowned body. The coroner of course returned an open verdict, without calling as witnesses any of the people who had last seen him. I do not necessarily suggest foul play, but there was nothing to disprove its possibility.

At a later time, when my yacht was in dock in a rather unhealthy neighbourhood, and I was having dinner at Fasoli's, the man who was sitting next to me, and whom I found out to be a police inspector, said: 'If you are going down Dudley Street tonight don't carry that gun in your pocket; carry it in your hand, where they can see it.' For the city is not so bad that robbers dare to use anything noisier than a sandbag; if after a row one is found with a smoking revolver in one's hand it is prima facie evidence of innocence.

A week after I had lost my old crew the Shipping Master found me a new lot. When I signed them on everyone in the Shipping Office was unexpectedly cordial, and, it seemed to me, unnecessarily anxious to get me away to sea. I did not then know why, and duly sailed with three Tasmanians. The weather was fine and the wind light, but southerly, and the rip off Port Phillip Heads, where a 7-knot tide runs over a rocky bottom, was in first-class working order. It laid out two of my hands with sea-sickness, instanter; and the third became nearly as green with fright. I hoped that when we reached the smooth water outside they would distinguish themselves in some other way, but they did not. They did nothing; they could do nothing; when they had stopped being sick they expected me to materialise a cook for them, in the middle of Bass Straits! I did something quite as effective; I found a head wind and a sea which was, if possible, worse than what one gets between Dublin and Caergybi. They talked no more of cooks. After drifting round Bass Straits for a couple of days (I could not get out, for the weather was very thick as well as windy) all three decided they had had enough, and asked me to take them home. I had had more than enough of them and did so. When I went into the Shipping Office to pay them off the atmosphere was despondent. I heard one man say, 'I didn't think he'd get far with that crew,' followed by a low chorus of, 'But why did he bring them back!' Well, I think the Shipping Master might have dropped a rather broader hint to a stranger that manslaughter was indicated. It might have been committed had I known that those Tasmanian devils had walked off with a gold watch and one or two other souvenirs of some intrinsic value. But this is only one side of Melbourne, and I suppose I could be robbed as well in the Commercial Road as in Flinders Street.

Elsewhere I discovered a friendly country, though unfortunately I could not explore it far. (The only night I spent on shore was that on which my man was drowned.) The most interesting people that I met were the owner of the yacht *Seaweed*, a boat of about the same size as mine, which had left Southampton a fortnight and reached Melbourne a month before I did, and his wife; and they had only one man with them; but the same man all the way, which accounted perhaps for their quicker passage, for I lost just a month in Durban, to say nothing of what I lost by light and variable winds going to and coming from that port. The other yachtsmen that I met at Williamstown were extremely helpful, for they were sea-going cruiser-men, and knew what I wanted. At that time two of them were building new yachts, more or less of my size and type; one on the spot, and the other in Hobart. My geographical critic will remark that Hobart is nowhere near Melbourne but at the further end of Tasmania; and so it is, but the Melbourne yachtsmen do not confine themselves to sailing round Port Phillip, which indeed is about the dullest place imaginable, but go all round the Tasmanian coast, and a very beautiful coast it is too. So when one of them criticised my jib sheets, and gave me a pair of chain traces off a dray to replace them (for he was the manager of a brewery), I accepted the criticism and the gift with equal readiness. Everybody gave me things; A. towed me up the river and down again, B. docked me (these are always my first considerations), and so on down the alphabet to the Royal Yacht Club of Victoria; and neither the Pilots nor the Commonwealth nor Victorian Governments, nor the Melbourne Port and Docks Board charged me anything.

And of course the inevitable question was put to me: 'What do you think of Australia?' I did not see Australia, but only Melbourne, and my opinion of it was unpopular. I said that I liked the cable cars because they reminded me of Edinburgh, but that Flinders Street did not remind me of Princes Street; and that considering the amount of money piled up in stone and mortar along Collins Street it was singularly unimpressive. But one might say the same about Adderley Street in Cape Town or Queen Street in Auckland, or, I expect, about the principal street in any colonial city. The chief fault of Melbourne, however, is that it is built in the wrong place. It ought to stretch in a huge semicircle round a continuous quay from St Kilda to Gellibrand Point, and the docks and wharves up the little ditch called the Yarra River should never have been built; even now they have lost much trade to Sandridge and Williamstown. Some day, but not in my lifetime, those two places will join.

But to come back from the city of Melbourne, back, with regret from that delightful Italian restaurant of which the owner is half County Clare and the waitresses wholly County Cork, but which differs from an Irish hotel in that a piano stands in the dining-room and as like as not some operatic star who is visiting the town will give a turn after dinner, to my ship and the chances of my voyage. A very pleasant young man called on me, the second mate of a Finnish training-ship, wanted to sail with me if his captain would let him, for he was in a hurry to get married and his ship was going up the Pacific coast and it was unknown when she would get home. But there was not a chance that his captain would let him go; he could not possibly get out here a substitute with his qualifications of competency, education and language.

I went on board his ship, as I did on the Belgian training-ship in Durban, and as I might have on two other great four-masted barques, one Finnish and one Danish, here in Melbourne, and I saw one of the things they do better in other countries than mine. Here were 50 to 80 boys getting a good general as well as a first-class nautical education, and probably, for all these vessels were carrying full cargoes and making good passages, costing very little either to their parents or to the State. I say they were getting a good general education not because they were learning Greek or Philosophy but because they were learning things generally at first hand, and that is the only good way to learn. It is hard to see things accurately from a mail-steamer or a railway train, blinded, as one generally is, by a mist of conventionality and the distorting mirror of printed books; one wants to drop on things unexpectedly with no preconceived ideas. But one must have a mind capable of assimilating new ideas, and that will not be developed except in surroundings rather more cultured than the half-deck of the average tramp. I say nothing as to the destiny of the finished product of these State-aided training-ships, the junior officer, in view of the overcrowded state of the profession, unless it be a prophecy that no boy who considered the sea as his career would go as apprentice in a privately-owned ship – a good deal to the advantage of every one except the ship-owners; but 60 per cent of those boys will not follow the sea; they went there to see the world and will leave having learned self-reliance and discipline in a way which they could not learn it on shore or in a steamboat.

In the end I secured a crew. First G., a Swedish-American, a soft slow man with a charming smile and an imperturbable temper; a man brought up for the most part in five- and six-masted schooners, no doubt an excellent fellow to work all the gear of his mast with a steam capstan, but altogether too soft and slow for me. He admitted, when we parted at Auckland, that he was no use in so small a vessel and a sore trial to my temper. I was very sorry, for he was an affectionate creature; but what he said was perfectly true. W., the other member of my crew, was a complete contrast; a wiry active man, and a bundle of nerves and complexes. He was of good family and had a good record as an officer, but when he came to me he was eating husks with the swine. He was full of good stories of his adventurous life – except of one episode, which, however, is otherwise recorded as one of the heroic tales of the sea. His temperament was too much like mine for safety, but I was prepared to risk a clash for the sake of having an educated English man to talk to. I killed a fatted calf and wrote a letter home in which I said that all my troubles were over except such as were incidental to a winter passage round the Horn. I am an extremely bad prophet and I misinterpreted what omens there were. I indulged in a sort of trial trip, which was only a Sunday afternoon sail round Hobson's Bay to look at the British Cruiser Squadron, and forgetting that I had three guests on board who were doing all the work I was so much struck by the smartness with which the ship was handled that I prophesied a racing passage. It was too late to go mountaineering in New Zealand, but it would not be too late for the Horn if I got a good start and passed to the southward of Stewart Island. So I got a clearance for Dublin, and sailed.

For a day all went well; then I was stricken down by some sort of poisoning; a distressing malady, which, however, saved the ship. For on the night of the first of April, after passing Goose Island (and who shall say that in such circumstances something foolish is not likely to happen?), I set a course, an obviously imprudent course on such a dark night, for Banks Straits, and went below. But not for long; my malady compelling me I came on deck, went over to the lee rail, and saw a ghastly great pyramid of black rock sticking up well on my lee bow. Fortunately my mate was quick in action, the vessel quick on her helm, the wind off shore, and the water smooth, or the cruise would have ended then and there on Clarke Island. I did not cut any more corners fine that night, and I darkened the ship; for the foolish thing I had done was to leave the gas blazing away in the cabin with the skylight open, so that the helmsman could see nothing; and there was no look-out forward as there should have been in such narrow waters.

As soon as we were clear of the land I decided I was too sick to take any more watches, but the other two were aggressively cheerful and quite prepared to carry on the good work of 150 miles per diem. Unfortunately some one left a fishing line towing astern all night, and at dawn I found that it had hooked and drowned an unfortunate mollymawk, which is a small kind of albatross. Superstition apart, it is an infamous thing to kill an albatross, for they are such friendly birds and one does not have much company in the Southern Ocean; this one of course died an accidental death, but before long retribution descended on the cause of the accident. G. knocked his elbow on a bulkhead, and it swelled up and got sore. We others suffered incidentally, for in a day we were headreaching under short canvas as uncomfortably as might be expected in the Tasman Sea, which is notoriously the roughest bit of water in the world, and all the time getting driven further and further to the northward. However if one can't pass New Zealand on one side, one must go on the other; there is only about 800 miles of it. By the time a fair wind came along the best course was through the middle of it, through Cook Strait; it would have been undesirable on account of the temptations of the seductive harbours that lie on either side of it, were it not that G.'s arm was becoming worse and it might be necessary to go into one of those harbours for a doctor. I was by now all right again.

We did not lose much time over this part of the passage and on the 14th day out I took the morning watch in order to see New Zealand. I was rather anxious about the stage-managing of this; I might have sailed too slowly during the night and seen the land only as a pimple on the horizon, or it might have been less fine, with only a dark mass showing under a bank of cloud; but it turned out all right, the clouds were lying low on the water and high above them the sun was emerging from behind the colossal cone of Mount Egmont, which I had approached within 40 miles.

I think this was the most impressive mountain scenery I ever saw. The parabolic sweep of a volcanic cone is a very beautiful line, but it is commonly rather flat; the andesite of Egmont, however, forms an unusually steep curve, and moreover the less interesting 3,000 feet at the bottom (the whole peak is 8,000 feet) were cut off by the low mists and the curvature of the globe. Various causes make a mountain look big; the stark symmetry of the volcano is one, the complexity of such a system as Snowdon is another, but the most potent is the contrast when one sees them standing on another element, such as the true sea horizon, or a mist lying on a level plain, so that there is a gap of as many miles as one's imagination cares to make it between the foreground and the background. I have admired a great peak 9,000 feet high all day, and, when I got near, it looked positively insignificant beyond icebergs and whales and all the detail of an Antarctic coast-line.

In the course of time I began to see more rather attractive-looking mountains to the southward, and as my mate told me that on that side there was a place somewhat like Glengariff with a hospital (for G. seemed likely to require hospital treatment), I decided to go and see if Picton were really anything like the most beautiful place in the world. It wasn't; at Glengariff trees were (I speak of ten years ago) cut judiciously; in New Zealand they are burned indiscriminately: in the few days that I spent at Picton the aspect of the place was quite considerably changed. It is no good having a long memory for places in this country. Most of the North Island is volcanic, and therefore liable to any sort of transposition of the solider features; the Tarawera eruption changed lakes into mountains, ridges into valleys, and destroyed the famous pink and white terraces which used to draw sightseers from all over the world. (It is proposed to reproduce them in concrete, but that will not guarantee their permanence.) The rest is mud, and visited by torrential rains; it is therefore not uncommon to meet rows of houses sliding down the streets of a town. Hence the houses are built of wood, so that they will float on the mud and may easily be salved. At Rotorua there are both volcanoes and mud; it is so typical they they send tourists there to look at it.

But I had not got to any town yet, and was going slowly enough about getting there. There had been floods up the Wanganui River, and Cook Strait was full of floating logs quite heavy enough to do damage and requiring us to keep a good look-out by day and to heave-to at night.

From a distance the aspect of the rugged promontories that enclose Queen Charlotte Sound is not unlike that of the great headlands of West Cork and Kerry, but as I drifted (for the wind was going down with the sun) alongside the cliffs I noticed a considerable difference. Most conspicuously they were far greener than ours. Cape Jackson does not stick out a very long way into any ocean, but I doubt if any point on the Irish coast has grass growing so low down on it. The seas in this part of the world must be much smaller than ours at home; and this part of the world seems to include everything north of the 40th parallel. I made no comment at the time on the statement in the Sailing Directions that Moonlight Head in Victoria, which faces directly the Southern Ocean, was densely wooded to the water's edge, or the fact which I could observe that it is now completely covered with grass, but I should have remarked it; indeed I did not speculate on the relative severity of the weather here and at home till I saw on Little Barrier Island, which I admit is on an east coast, trees actually growing on a few yards of beach between the ocean and the cliffs; and then I said in my ignorance of the Southern Ocean that there was nothing like the North Atlantic. Certainly the North Island of New Zealand is not like it; the things that sail and steam and motor round the coast here would not be allowed to go out of harbour at home. And just here in Cook Strait they hunt whales in racing motor-launches; exactly how they kill the whales I did not learn, but apparently they do not kill themselves.

The grass, however, on Cape Jackson looked coarse and rank, the earth was raw and there were frequent traces of recent landslips; it is a very new country. A little further on I saw the 'bush,' which, no doubt owing to the fact that it grows on smooth slopes of clay-rock instead of between ridges of hard slate, is denser in appearance than the virgin forest of Cork or Kerry. Further on yet I saw another difference from our scenery. These Sounds were not shaped by glacial action, but by the wear of many streams on the soft rock; they are not cut clean and straight as are our three great bays, nor are they ruled by anything analogous to the Hercynian master-folds; they wander about like any river valley cut in undifferentiated strata, divided by islands and branching into tributary bays. Into one of these we drifted more by the virtue of the tide than of any wind as the moon chased the last light of the sun out of the sky, and into the silence of that black pool surrounded by black mountains let go the anchor.

TADHG Ó CIANÁIN

c. 1575–c. 1625

The event known as 'The Flight of the Earls' marked the final
dissolution of the old Gaelic order and opened the way for the
plantation of Ulster. When Aodh Ó Néill, Earl of Tyrone, Rughraighe
Ó Domhnaill, Earl of Tír Conaill, and Cúchonacht Maguidhir sailed
from Lough Swilly on 4 September 1607, there travelled with them
some ninety men and women, among whom was Tadhg Ó Cianáin, of
a family which for generations had been chroniclers to the
Maguidhirs. As the party made its slow way to Louvain – then, as
now, a centre of Irish learning – and through snowbound Europe to
Rome, Ó Cianáin chronicled the events of the journey, writing
modestly in the third person and beginning his account 'A n-Ainm Dé
(In the name of God) . . . these are some of the adventures and
proceedings of Ó Néill from the time he left Ireland.' The original
manuscript is now in Dublin. This extract, which begins with the
departure from Louvain in 1608, is from a translation by Father Paul
Walsh. Tadhg Ó Cianáin is believed to have died in Rome.

THE PATH TO ROME

LVII. On Thursday, the twenty-eighth of February, 1608, the princes,
with their retinue, set out for Italy, in all thirty-two riding on
horseback. Their ladies had a coach. They left two of Ó Néill's sons,
Seán and Brian, the Baron, the Earl [of Tyrconnell's] son, Aodh, the
son of Cathbharr, Ó Coinne, Seán Ó Hágáin, and others of their
nobles and followers in Flanders with the Colonel.

LVIII. They came that night to a town called Wavre, four leagues
from Louvain, with a troop of the Archduke's cavalry attending and
escorting them. The next day they went six leagues of an ugly, bad
road to Namur. They remained there that night. The governor of the

city came with a large number of noblemen to welcome and receive them with propriety and honour. He sent a company and a half of soldiers to escort them the next day, for fear the enemy might meet them. Because of the unevenness and wetness of the road ahead of them, they left their coach in that city. They put their women on horses. The Colonel and those who accompanied him took leave of them there.

LIX. This is a compact, fine, strong, well-built city, with good, well-made houses, situated in a very beautiful glen. There is a good river directed and divided in many parts through it, with a large number of bridges and a great supply of boats. On a beautiful high hill over the city the King of Spain has a very strong castle, which has command, headship and mastery over the whole town, [manned] with a large body of cavalry and numerous soldiers always.

LX. From there they went eight leagues to Marche. The soldiers of the town came out one league to meet them. They stayed in it that night. That town is small and fortified, and the King [of Spain] has a fort in it with a strong garrison.

LXI. The next day, Sunday the second of March, they went six leagues to a town called Bastogne. They required no escort that day. From there they went six leagues to Arlon, a town belonging to the King [of Spain].

LXII. The next day, Tuesday, they went to a town belonging to the Duke of Lorraine, four leagues distant. They had a convoy with them as far as that. It is there the King [of Spain's] country and that of the Duke of Lorraine meet and separate from each other. There is a very strong fort, built by the Duke, in that town, with many strong guards to protect and defend the frontier of his country against neighbours. Not many are permitted to view or examine that one fortress. The roads from Namur to that place were very bad, rough and wet, and there were many woods and few houses. They went that same day two leagues [further] to a town called Fillieres.

LXIII. The next day they went on seven leagues to a post-town named Malatur. They proceeded that same day through a very pretty town, Conflans. A difficult river, with a very strong current, over which there was a bridge, flowed through it. Father Tomás Strong and Magbhethadh [Ó Néill] were in danger of being drowned in it, for the horse fell under each of them. They were obliged to resort to swimming.

LXIV. They advanced from there five leagues to Pont-a-Mousson, a strong and pretty town belonging to the Duke of Lorraine, in which he has a very good palace.They remained there two nights. They sent people before them to the Duke to announce that they were coming to him. There is a famous river running through the town, on which there is a fine bridge, with a very strong castle with numerous guards on a high hill over it, and from this bridge the town gets its name.

LXV. They proceeded from there three leagues on the left side of the river. They then crossed it in boats. They went to Nancy, the Duke's chief city, a distance of two leagues. Very beautiful and varied was the country through which they journeyed that day, with plenty of vines and wheat, fruitful forests, and many houses. About two leagues from the city, on a beautiful high hill, there is a very strong castle with a large number of guards. It is there the Duke's children are instructed and brought up in their youth. The Duke sent coaches and noblemen a distance from the Court to meet them. When they alighted the Duke's steward came to invite them to the great palace, but they excused themselves for that night because of their journey. After they had heard Mass on the next day the same man came to meet them with good coaches. They then went to the palace. They remained walking and passing the time in an extensive, excellent, beautiful gallery while the Duke was in the church hearing Mass. He came from the church afterwards. He himself was in becoming dress, with some of his noblemen discoursing with him, and his two sons after him. He had a very beautiful guard, and many pages on either side of him. When he came to his hall he sent great lords for them [the Irish]. They went into his presence. He received them with joy and honour, and his children did likewise. They remained for a time discoursing and conversing with one another. Afterwards they sat down to dinner. They were six in number, the Duke and his two sons, Ó Néill, the Earl, and the Baron [of Dungannon]. There were many honourable noblemen waiting on them. He brought them afterwards to his private apartment. There they remained for a time. They then took their leave and retired to their lodgings. There was an Earl, who was head-steward of the Duke, accompanying them. He proclaimed under severe penalty, that no one should accept gold or silver of them while they should be in the city, but that all their expenses during that time should be borne by the Duke.

LXVI. This is a famous and distinguished capital city, one of the strongest, best defended, and most spacious in the countries near it. There is a very deep trench around its wall. There are three gates one behind the other with a large guard. The wall is fourteen yards in thickness without counting the breastworks. On the south side of the city there is a splendid, well-built court in process of erection by the Duke, with two grand palaces artistically situated. There is a great town built around that new court, and joined to the old city. There are two very beautiful churches, a wealthy college, and a good monastery, with a community of Capuchins, built by the Duke in proximity to the new city. In the old city itself there are many fine churches, in one of which there is a fourth part of the body of Saint George, splendidly and reverently enclosed in a shrine of silver with many bright precious stones. The Duke himself has a great beautiful old palace in the city, having an excellent gallery and many splendid spacious apartments. There is a good tennis-court, where the Duke's children and nobles play, near his private room, where he can view and see their sport and games. There is a long stable, with many beautiful, well-shaped horses, which are not large, in the court opposite the palace. There is a *place* where horsemen and noblemen joust and ride, breaking lances on one another's breasts.

LXVII. The next day the princes set out on coaches which the Duke gave them to the church of Saint Nicholas, two leagues' journey from the aforesaid city. One of the hands of Saint Nicholas was shown to them. They advanced from there to a little town called Lunéville, on the bank of the river we have already mentioned. On Tuesday, the eleventh of March, they proceeded from there eight leagues to the town named St Die. The weather and the roads were very good throughout that period. On the next day they crossed the mountain of Saint Martin, over hard, difficult roads covered with ice and snow. They stopped for a short time in a small town where the Duke's country and Germany meet and separate from each other. They left behind them the Duke's territory, with its abundance of vines and wheat and every good fruit, its beautiful rivers, its wide, many-rivered, watery plains, and its tall, fruit-laden woods on the river of Nancy, which is called Meurthe. The Duke has seven mines where salt is manufactured and prepared. He makes one million profit each year by the rent of the seven mines. There is another small city in the country out of which he gets eleven hundred hogsheads of wine for rent every year. Gold and silver are being continually coined for him. It is not every crowned king in Christendom whose rent and profit out of his dominions each year exceeds his. His country is thirty-five leagues in length, and it is as a garden in the very centre of Christendom, giving neither obedience nor submission to any king or prince in the world, but ever steadfast, strong, and unbending in the faith of God's Church.

LXVIII. From that place they went one league to Bonhomme, the German town that was nearest to them. They travelled two leagues across the mountain to a town named Kaysersberg. They passed through a very beautiful valley in which there was a very good river, much vines and good crops, and numerous pretty villages. That night they went three leagues to a remarkable city which is called Colmar, and is very strong, powerful, and extensive. Near to it is the most beautiful, wide, level, and fruitful plain in the greater part of Christendom. Heretics, however, occupy and inhabit it. They remained there that night. The following day they went through a great, trackless, difficult, unfrequented wood to the river which is named Campser, and separates that portion of Germany and part of Burgundy, a country which belongs to the Archduke. The length of the wood was about two leagues. That night they reached a small town called Hotmers, having travelled five leagues in all.

LXIX. On the following day they travelled a league, through the town called Niderharga, to the very famous river Rhine. They moved on to Bâle, a fine, strong, old, remarkable city which is built on it. There is a very good bridge in the centre of the city over the river, and numerous boats afford a means of leaving it and getting to it from Flanders and the country around the river. Those who occupy and inhabit it are heretics. There is a very large church in the middle of the city in which there are images and pictures of Luther and Calvin and many other wicked evil writers. That city is an independent state in itself, and no king in the world claims submission or authority in it. It alone is the main entrance to the land of the Swiss called Helvetia. Afterwards, through fear of conspiracy by the heretics, they left the city. They proceeded two leagues up the river to a small strong town named Liesthal. Its inhabitants were Catholic. It is usual to demand custom in Bâle for the horses of strangers and travellers who cross through the country. The road was even and beautiful, advancing beside the river in a long rich valley. There were two high mountains, with much vines and good crops, on either side of it.

LXX. The following day they went five leagues to the town named Sursee. On the road before them there was a beautiful high mountain with many fir and other trees from which pitch is extracted. They passed that day through two towns with very strong walls, Olten and Zoffingen, on the bank of the Rhine. In each of them custom was taken from them for their horses.

LXXI. The next day, Sunday the sixteenth of March, they crossed the river Rhine by a very long bridge which had a good roof over the whole length of it. They payed custom to the keepers of the bridge. They advanced through a very pretty town named Sempach, and from there to a remarkable city, Lucerne, a distance of two long leagues. The population is Catholic. There is a a papal Nuncio in the city, and it is situated on the Rhine, and has strong walls, numerous, beautiful, well-built houses, and many boats and vessels. There are three bridges over the river. From there they and their horses went in boats across a great lake call Alpnacher-See, which is nine leagues in length and one in breadth. The Alps are all around it. They rowed through the lake till they reached a small town, Flüelen Pourlacu at midnight. They remained there that night.

LXXII. The next day, Saint Patrick's day precisely, the seventeenth of March, they went to another small town named Silenen. From that they advanced through the Alps. Now the mountains were laden and filled with snow and ice, and the roads and paths were narrow and rugged. They reached a high bridge in a very deep glen called the Devil's Bridge. One of Ó Néill's horses, which was carrying some of his money, about one hundred and twenty pounds, fell down the face of the high, frozen, snowy cliff which was in front of the bridge. Great labour was experienced in bringing up the horse alone, but the money decided to remain blocking the violent, deep, destructive torrent which flows under the bridge through the middle of the glen. They stayed that night in a little town named Piedimonte. Their journey that day was six leagues.

LXXIII. The next day the Earl proceeded over the Alps. Ó Néill remained in the town we have mentioned. He sent some of his people to search again for the money. Though they endured much labour, their efforts were in vain. Because of the snow and ruggedness and ice of the mountain in front of them, they were scarcely able to ride the next day except in the way that is usual when crossing the Alps. There were strong oxen with sleighs yoked to them bringing all of them that could not travel over the hard road. There is a splendid chapel on the very summit of the mountain erected and built in honour of Saint Gotthard. From it that portion of the mountain has taken its name. Near it there is a convenient hostel in which strangers and those who pass the way get supplies to buy. The roads over which they travelled immediately after having departed from that chapel were neither excellent nor such as would be level enough for riding on wild, spirited, untamed horses, but as they descended from the mountain they were icy, stony, narrow and rugged until they reached a town called Airolo. The worst and hardest portion of the mountain is only three leagues long. After that they went through a very beautiful valley until they reached the gate called the Gate of Hell. Over it was written in Italian that no one, under pain of death, should go under it or past it without paying custom. The keeper did not neglect demanding and receiving it. The road was rough, rugged, narrow, and uneven until they reached Faido, and [was crossed by] a hard difficult river. The Earl was there waiting for them in the house of an earl of that country who does kindness and honour to every foreigner and every class of strangers who pass the way. He quickly and readily gave them dinner and provisions. Each of them paid no more than one half-crown at the settlement of their account with the master of the stable for the horses, the chamberlain and servants of the house being not forgotten besides. They remained there that night. Their journey was six leagues.

LXXIV. On the following day they went through a very beautiful valley which had much vines, wheat, crops, produce of every kind, with great wide plains, a very beautiful river, and small streams of spring water. They advanced eight leagues to a fine fortified town called Bellinzona. There are three strong castles with many powerful guards in it, which maintain supremacy and command over the town and all the country in the neighbourhood of the road.

LXXV. The next day they continued to advance through the same valley. They reached another portion of the Alps named Monte Ceneri. There are numerous woods on either side of the road, which was uneven, stony, rough, difficult and hard to travel, although there was no snow on it. There were plenty of vines on the summits and sides of the mountain-range near the road. They came to another very beautiful valley called Lugano. That night they reached a very large town named Capo di Lago, having travelled six leagues.

LXXVI. From there they and their horses went in boats across Lake Lugano, which separates Italy and Helvetia, the country of the Swiss, from each other. The lake is only three leagues in width. They had traversed forty-six leagues of the country of the Swiss, and it was strong, well fortified, uneven, mountainous, extensive, having bad roads, and no supremacy, rule or claim to submission by any king or prince in the world over the inhabitants. In themselves they form a strange, remarkable, peculiar state. They make their selection of a system for the government of the country each year. They have fourteen important cities. Half of them are Catholics and the other half are heretics, and by agreement and great oaths they are bound to one another for their defence and protection against any neighbour in the world who should endeavour to injure them or oppose them in upholding the public good with moderation and appropriateness. The names of the aforesaid cities are Lucerne, Bâle, Valais, Soluthurn, Zug, Schwyz, Zürich, Bern, Uri, Stanz, Glarus, Fribourg, Schaffhausen, and Appenzell. It is said of the people of this country that they are the most just, honest, and untreacherous in the world, and the most faithful to their promises. They allow no robbery or murder to be done in their country without punishing it at once. Because of their perfect honour they alone are guards to the Catholic kings and princes of Christendom.

PEDRO ALONSO O'CROULEY
1740–1817

The son of a Limerick man and an O'Donnell from County Clare,
O'Crouley was born in Cadiz, Spain, and educated at Senlis in France.
Choosing the career of a merchant, he made his first journey to Mexico
at the age of twenty-four, repeating the visit several times in the
course of the subsequent decade. His business interests prospered and
enabled him to assemble a substantial private collection of antiquities,
a catalogue of which he published in 1794. He belonged to several
learned societies, including the Real Academía de Historia (history
was his other main interest). At the time of O'Crouley's journeys, New
Spain was under the control of an able administrator, José de Galvez,
who realised the importance of consolidating its northern frontiers.
(The commandant-general in El Paso, Texas, at the time was Hugo
O'Connor, one of many Irishmen in the service of Spain.) O'Crouley
married, at the age of forty-four, Maria Power, also of Irish ancestry,
and they had nine children. A street in Cadiz is named after him.

REMARKABLE CURIOSITIES

Ignorance judges as fabulous all that is said about the Indies,[1] holding
it to be visionary and the only reality to be money. But if one
considers the enormous extent of land and the different climates that
obtain, one must blame travellers for being careless, even the better-
educated ones, who might discover an immense treasure hidden in
the multitude of plants, springs, rocks, and so on, so little known or
valued; only gold and silver receive undivided attention.

I shall deal in this chapter with those things that have come to my
notice, although for many of them I lack precise detail.

1   The New World.

242

This land abounds in sulphur, nitre, copper, and lead, which are so useful for purposes of war. A person going from the Presidio del Norte into New Mexico will be astonished to find at La Jornada del Muerto[2] a big hill called Las Balas because it is made entirely of stone cannonballs, formed by nature and in all calibres, from small shot to balls for 24- and 36-pounders and larger. They are so perfectly turned and spherical in shape that they would appear to have been cast.

On the shores of the Río Grande del Norte some trees grow that are as vigorous and as big as the largest poplar. The entire trunk of the tree to where the water covers it is changed into the hardest flint, from which the Indians make tips for their arrows and the soldiers make shot for their muskets. The rest of the tree is wood and the branches are very leafy. The leaves are nearly the same in colour as a poplar leaf, although they are an uneven oblong in shape. If one should be curious to try, it would be possible to cut a sliver from which one could make an arrow with a point of flint and a wooden shaft, all of one and the same piece, a rarity to be collected for the King's armoury. The fruit produced by these trees has mangrove-like seedlings a Spanish yard long, or three-quarters that length, which hold swarms of poisonous mosquitoes that in hot weather obscure the sun. Two distinct materials are united in this highly unusual tree: the flint, the petrifaction of common stone which is mineral inanimate; and the wood, the vivifying vegetal element. With wonder one asks how or by what road there passes through this mixed body, stony-hard and earthy, compacted of particles so solid, the nutritious sap, the active and vital principle, that is judged so necessary for the functioning of living things.

In Texcoco and other places there have been found bones, teeth, and the like, that after careful examination proved to be those of giants. I have seen them in Mexico City, in the possession of an interested collector. It is argued that they were of the Toltecs, the first tribe that peopled these dominions and had its capital at Tula.

In the district of Valles, on a mountain spur, two springs were discovered close to each other, one extremely cold and the other very hot and sulphurous. The two combined were found to provide a medicinal bath for cripples and persons afflicted with venereal disease.

2 A long stretch of waterless desert on the east side of the Rio Grande, in New Mexico. Wislizenus, *Memoir* (1848), says that its name refers to 'an old tradition that the first traveller who attempted to cross it in one day perished in it'.

In the district of Cadereita and in a valley called Jaquiapa, at the foot of a large fig tree there is a spring, and it was discovered that on discharging a gun, playing a musical instrument, or throwing a stone, its waters change, growing in volume and flooding the place with pure, clear water.

In the district of Otumba there is an aqueduct made by a Franciscan priest to carry water to this town. It is noteworthy among works of the Kingdom because, on the way, two hills made a very deep canyon and it was necessary to build very high arches midway of it, the spaces half-round at the top and the pillars between them being so tall that a stone thrown with force will hardly reach all the way up, and so free from growth that the noble composition of the aqueduct's frame and structure evokes admiration.

In the district of Cuernavaca, at the town of Atotonil, there is a bath that Hernán Cortés ordered built. It is completely covered with masonry vaults, and in it the waters rise and fall as the bathers wish. The water is so pure and clean that even the finest sand can be seen at the bottom, and so tepid that it has been found beneficial for various infirmities. Baths of the same kind, nicely made, are found on an island called El Peñón, in the Lake of Mexico. Each bath has its own very convenient accommodations for one family. In the centre there is an oratory for common use. Many families come there from the city, with no little benefit to the owner.

In the middle of the main square of the city of Tepeaca there is a fortress-like building that served as a hospice and a defence for the valorous Cortés and his soldiers in the year 1520. Its structure has deteriorated greatly for want of repair. In the district of the same city, at the edge of the town of Aljojuca there is a large lake of almost brackish water. In places it is seventy fathoms deep and it has never been known to increase or decrease. The great lake of Alchichica is nearly twenty leagues long and is bordered on one side by the town of Santa María in this same district and on the other by the town of Perote.

Three volcanoes are known, although no one of them is now active. One is Orizaba and other two [Popocatépetl and Ixtaccíhuatl] are called those of Mexico. The first is covered with ice and snow all year from where one passes it on going to Veracruz. It is so high that it can be seen from the sea at a distance of twenty-five leagues, and it is situated a further twenty-five leagues from the coast.

In the town of Tecali, five leagues from Puebla, a kind of marble is extracted that at the start is easy to work. From it are made altar stones, containers for altar bread, and skylights for churches; they are so transparent that they let in enough light. Also there are multicoloured rocks from which exquisite table tops are made. Another kind of marble was discovered in this diocese in the time of Bishop Fuero. It has veins of colour, violet and other hues. At the bishop's expense a sumptuous chapel with three naves was built at a place called San José de Chiapa. It is worth seeing as its construction is both handsome and massive. The high altar, with two arrangements of columns, is made entirely of this marble. It cost more than 40,000 pesos. Since the site of this chapel is distant from any town, a baptismal font was installed and a chaplain appointed, with an endowment, so that while a town is growing up there he may attend to the spiritual needs of the large farms of the vicinity, which number fourteen.

In the district of Zacatlán de las Manzanas there are deposits of various sulphates belonging to the Duke of Alba and the Duke of Arco.

In the district of the villa of Atlixco, which is five leagues from Puebla, to the west of that city and north of the villa is the famous *ahuehuete* tree, which is a kind of cypress with similarly small leaves. It is very tall, with a rounded head and oval shape. I have seen it and recorded its dimensions as follows:[3] 31 varas round outside at the foot of the trunk; 19 varas round inside (its middle is hollowed); 21 varas round halfway up the trunk; 6 varas vertically from the ground to the first branches; 6 varas in diameter inside (it was burned by lightning and by a fire started by Indians who took refuge there); at the middle inside, 25 varas round and 9⅓ varas in diameter by a measurement accommodated to the unevenness of the ground. There are six openings, the main one being that through which the trunk may be entered; it is on the east side and is 1⅓ varas [44 inches] wide. There is a spring of fresh water inside at which the livestock drink; and town talk affirms, on the evidence of an interested observer, that a dozen horses have been known to go inside for water at the same time.

The fertile and wonderful plain of Tehuacán de las Granadas has a plentiful supply of water to fertilise its lands and plants; but although

3   English equivalents, rounded to the nearest foot, are, respectively: 85 ft., 52, 58, 16, 16, 77, 17.

the waters are soft and taste good, they are nitrous, which accounts for a strange occurrence in their courses, namely, that the ditches and channels through which they pass thicken and harden in such a way that the bordering earth becomes like stone and mortar, and with the passing years it is necessary to change their paths, with the result that the fields come to be like foundations of buildings that resemble ancient ruins. It has the peculiarity that, whereas it hardens earth to stone, it dissolves kidney stones and expels gravel.

The city of Cholula preserves a number of monuments from heathen times. One of them is a height close to the entrance to the city on the east side. It was built by hand by the Indians and had in it a temple for their idols, but now it holds a beautiful chapel dedicated to Nuestra Señora de los Remedios. Here are large textile workshops turning out cottons, coarse woollens, and close-woven ones. The last are scarcely inferior to the lower grades of English manufacture.

The district of Acayucan with its warm and moist climate is so fertile that it yields as many as four harvests of maize a year. One has only to clear away the thickets and poke holes in the ground with the point of a stick. The same is true for kidney beans, which need no plough.

In the city of Pátzcuaro, the former seat of the bishopric of Michoacán, there is a temple that has only one nave although the foundations are laid for five in the form of a hand. It remains in this condition, as the episcopal see and chapter were transferred to Valladolid.[4] If completed it would have been one of the most noteworthy works in America; the old nave, as it stands, is admired by architects for its excellence. It has two winding staircases. The sections of the hewn stone in one are so smoothly fashioned that it is a common amusement of the Indians to take hold of the upper part and let themselves drop, coming down the spiral without bump or risk. The other consists of a tall pillar with two winding staircases placed contrariwise so that two persons going up together come down without seeing each other and leave through different doors.

In this diocese are the best copper mines.

In the district of Maravatío there is a place called Purúa where there is a spring with rare properties. The principal and most unusual of these is that in all its waters when pieces of wood, however small,

4 Now Morelia.

are floated, they undergo a chemical change, attracting a deposit, and with layer by layer of this coating they become like stones, increasing in size until, after a certain number of days, they have a very hard consistency. These bezoar-like stones have excellent sweat-producing powers that have been found beneficial in acute fevers. As the waters of the flowing spring hurry down a slope, descending ladder-like from pool to pool, they twist and turn in a manner most enjoyable to behold. In them the virtues of the bezoar stones retain their value and powers for remedial application. Moreover, the true fraxinella has been found in the countryside here, and then it has been discovered that many deer in these parts develop bezoar stones in their intestines, and in the centre of the stones is found a little ball of fraxinella.

A short distance from the town of Teremendo there is a mountain with a close growth of trees and brambles. Silver ore of superior quality was discovered here. When subjected to the test that miners call the assay by mercury, it showed a high yield of silver in the form of nuggets. The results of more exacting tests did not correspond with these indications, but, led on by old traditions and reports, prospectors have persisted in their quests.

In the year 1712 some of them, searching in this mountain range, discovered in a very deep ravine an entrance that was quite large. Fearful of going in lest there should be animals inside, they first hit on a scheme of setting off firecrackers to drive them out, and in consequence out rushed foxes, big owls, barn owls, bats, and other rapacious birds of the noctural solitudes. After this precaution and, furthermore, carrying lights in their hands, both torches and lanterns, a number of persons went in, and there were discovered some enormous chambers known to heathen times, contained within very strong walls made stronger yet by fire. In the middle of the second chamber there was a bench in the shape of the base of an altar where there was a large number of idols and fresh offerings of copal, and, woven in wool, a number of figures of men and animals, much marvelled at, which were taken out. They examined the strange way in which the walls were built and it was discovered that, for the wall to be of easily worked stone at the base, the builders made a section of wall with a loose piece and piled wood against it which they set on fire. The surfaces then melted and united. In the same way, too, the roof was made without mortar or any other binding material; and the corners were terraced. After a great length of time its conspicuous top came to have thickets and dense forest. The work was discovered in this century owing to hopes of finding the silver that was indicated in the ores of this region.

In the district of Teposcolula and Apoala a hunter roving the forest came upon an eagle of handsome appearance that had two heads. He shot at it and broke a wing and the eagle fell like lead. At the same time three similar birds started up, beating the air with their wings. The hunter ran to his prize and, seeing the dreadful claws and beaks with which it threatened him, its drooping shoulders, and the two perfect heads on their necks, he had not the patience to catch it alive, which would have made it a more acceptable gift, but blasted it with his gun and thereby took from it the life that with care he would have been able to preserve. The priest of that area sent the dead eagle to the Viceroy, the Marqués de Valero, who in turn sent it to Spain. In this area some of the huge eagles that are taken today can lift a lamb and fly with it in their claws. They sustain themselves at no small cost in animals.

In the town of Nopalucan, near Puebla, there occurred in the year 1740 a daily quaking of the earth for about three months. The province of Oaxaca is the most prone to earthquakes, and they are most frequent there, although throughout the entire Kingdom some minor tremors are felt every year.

In the town of Córdoba there are more than fifty mills for grinding sugar cane, manned by many Negro slaves.

Shortly after the capture of Mexico City, the great Cortés, amongst other presents, sent a large culverin of silver to the Emperor Charles V, who was also King Charles I of Spain. He called it 'the Phoenix,' and on it he had this inscription engraved:

> Ave nació sin par,
> yo en serviros sin segundo,
> y vos sin igual en el mundo.

> A bird born without equal,
> none excels me in serving
> you, unequalled in the world.

The fecundity of the women in all this Kingdom, particularly where the climate is temperate, is well known. In Puebla I have seen a white woman who with one man alone had forty-eight children, twins at each of the twenty-four births; many trustworthy people of the town have testified to this. In the same city there was a brother in the convent of C—— who had not slept for many years; not since, he being then a novice, they awakened him by giving him a fright and a scolding. A very strange case is that of Doña —— of the city of —— who for many years was subject to retention of urine and was at times on the verge of death from this malady. Lately, for nine years to the present she has not made water at all, to the wonder of the doctors.

Amongst Indians, idlers, and poor people, one finds a number of rare accomplishments. I have actually seen in Mexico City a flea leashed with a gold chain[5] composed of links so thin and light that it does not keep the creature from leaping, pricking, and running as if it had been loose. The same skill produced little gold boxes as watch-charms that were no bigger than a large bean and had a lock and hidden key and, within, a needle-case with needles, scissors with steel blades, and other exquisite objects.

Worth noting, finally, is the method some of the Indians use to catch the ducks that are so plentiful on many lakes. They throw large gourds into the lake and leave them there so that the ducks get used to seeing them and will not shun them. When the ducks come, the Indians cover their heads with hollow gourds, in which they have made two holes to see through, and, up to their necks in the lake, approach the ducks, which, now familiar with the sight, are unsuspecting. The Indians catch them by the feet and tie them to their waists. Then they leave with their game, procured at small cost.

Hunting jaguars and pumas is done with small dogs, which tree the animals and pester them with continuous barking; and while their attention is fixed on the dogs, they are shot at, or, perhaps, lassoed from the nearest tree.

The *grana*, or cochineal,[6] the most highly valued product in this Kingdom – the only place in America where it is produced, – is made chiefly in the diocese of Oaxaca. The cultivation of the little creature requires much care and tedious attention. It feeds on the *nopal*, a plant made up of joints studded with spines like those of the prickly pear. It puts forth flowers and flesh-coloured fruit, and there are various ways of killing the little creatures its fruits produce, which make the black, mottled, ash-coloured, or reddish cochineal.

5 The MS adds that its length is 'de a ¼,' but omits to say one-fourth of what unit of measurement.
6 A dyestuff made from the dried bodies of females of a scale insect.

LIAM O'FLAHERTY
1897–1984

An Aran Islander who wrote with equal facility in Irish and English,
O'Flaherty's reputation rests on his short stories, many of them vivid
evocations of island life, and on novels such as *The Informer* –
successfully filmed – and *Famine*. Intended initially for the priesthood,
he was sent to school and university in Dublin, but on discovering that
he had no vocation, he joined the Irish Guards in 1917 under his
mother's name of Ganly. He fought at the Somme and, after being
invalided out, travelled extensively, supporting himself with a wide
variety of menial employment, until his return to Ireland and his
involvement in the 1922 Civil War on the Republican side. During the
1920s and 1930s O'Flaherty produced a large body of fiction which
earned him a solid popular reputation. His brief espousal of
Communism in the late 1920s is reflected in his travel book *I Went to
Russia*. This extract is from *Two Years* (1930), an account of the travels
that followed his war service.

ON THE BEACH

I doubt if there is any place in the world as beautiful as Rio de
Janeiro. From the moment our ship entered the narrow neck of its
gorgeous harbour I was entranced. Across the smooth bay, littered
with ships and pretty boats, lay the city, rising in terraces, with
majestic mountains behind, and the great sugar-loaf, like a stupendous
monument, on the left. Trees and tropical plants everywhere.
Everything resplendent with brilliant sunlight. No dirt, no smoke,
seemingly no slums. Astonishing, like a fairy tale. Facing this
phenomenon of beauty, I forgot that I was penniless, that my nostrils,
my eyes, and my finger-nails were blackened with coal dust, that my
clothes were shabby, that I was an unknown and unwanted stranger.

It seemed to lie before me, waiting for ravishment. I wanted to jump from the ship's side and swim ashore, lest one extra moment of my life should be wasted before I began the enjoyment of this miraculous city.

I saw a great sign facing the shore: 'Bebam Antarctica.' Certainly, I was going to drink Antarctica, and every other possible drink. I was going to live there in a continual ecstasy of unimaginable pleasures. The whole crew was almost equally excited. Some had been there already, and knew that it is more comfortable to stand in the rain without an overcoat beside the wall of a ruined factory than to stand in golden moonlight on a warm night outside the brilliantly lit windows of a great house, where there is a riot of merry-making, of wine-drinking, and love-making, and gluttonous feasting. But sailors are easy to please, and they always expect the impossible.

At first we lay at anchor in the harbour, and a fleet of tiny boats came around us, offering to sell us oranges and pineapples. They also had bottles of gashasa, which is a native whisky of great power. This they offered to us secretly. It was amusing to bargain with them in pidgin Portuguese: 'Quanto costa the oranges? Too much. Quanto the bloody pineapples?' But we bought nothing. We remained at anchor all that night, greedily watching the brilliant lights of the city. We could hear music from the shore. It was wonderful seeing the seemingly endless row of lights spreading out to the left towards Tres Jardines, or whatever the suburb is called.

Lucy, leaning over the rails by my side, said in a hoarse whisper: 'It's all one big whore-house. I wish I were ashore.'

That night in the fo'c'sle, everybody talked of women, women, women. I really felt very exalted, in the same way that I felt when for the first time I saw from the deck of the steamer *Duras* the yellow houses of Salthill drift along as we approached the ancient town of Galway. I was then a little boy at my mother's side. It was sunset in summer. She pointed ahead over the ship's prow, and said:

'Look. There's Galway. Do you see it?'

I was unable to answer her with excitement. I just clutched at her dress and blushed, and stood on tiptoe, keeping very close to her side, and looked in awe at the dun pile of grey stone houses rising above the shimmering waters of the bay.

That was the first, this was the last time I experienced such a mixed feeling of awe and romance. Now one town is the same as another to

me, each person intrinsically as disappointing as the previous one I
have met. The visible world and the movements of man upon it have
both become completely absorbed by my imagination, which has
gone farther than reality to create its needed harmony and only looks
out upon reality with a frown, and seizes upon its various aspects
with remote and critical interest, merely to imagine harmony more
vividly by contrast with disappointing reality. How unhappy that
makes one! How pleasant it is to look at the world with the amazed
eyes of a child, crowing with glee on sight of a butterfly's wings!
How pleasant it is to remain a child, and shout hurrah at the sight of
one's country's flag, or to laugh immoderately and sincerely at a
bawdy story told by a commercial traveller! The rash ecstasies of the
inward-gazing intellect exact a heavy toll in the form of consequent
depressions, whereas simplicity and ignorance always look outward,
and feed healthily upon the giant stores of the earth's phenomena.

Next morning we drew alongside the pier, and a gang of workmen
came aboard to unload the ship. We set to work overhauling the
boilers. We were not allowed ashore until evening. The Brazilian
workmen were astonishing creatures. They worked naked to the
waist, chattering all the time. There seemed to be no order among
them. They were nearly all coloured. The Portuguese among them
looked utterly decadent, but the negroes were of a fine physique, and
merry of disposition. At meal-time I talked to some of them. They
were very interested to know what Europe and North America were
like. Had I seen snow? What was it like? Did people die of the cold in
the north? They were like children, but without the delicate beauty of
children. They repelled me. The gorgeous city began to lose its glitter
as soon as I came in contact with its inhabitants. The loungers on the
quays were even more decadent than the workmen. They had
withered faces, and their movements were slow. They looked
dissipated.

But I was determined to hold fast to my romantic vision, and I told
myself that the mere scum of a city's population hangs around
docks. Beyond, in the magnificent thoroughfares, I was going to
meet glorious types of humanity, worthy of such a splendid city.
Would evening never come?

It came at last. I dressed, bade goodbye to the ship, and went
ashore. I had eighteen shillings and sixpence in my pocket; not an
enormous sum with which to set forth into a foreign country in

search of adventure. I changed it for Brazilian money at a money-changer's booth near the docks, and headed for the city. In a short time, after passing through a few shabby side streets and ruins, I reached the Avenida Centrale. Then, indeed, it seemed that my dream had come true, for the loveliness of that thoroughfare overwhelmed me. I walked up and down its whole length several times before I could leave it. Then, being weary and thirsty and lonely, I cut into a side street and wandered along, hoping to meet some sailor-men. As I was standing uncertainly at a corner, a newsboy came up to me, looked at me, and then said:

'Rua Vasco da Gama?'

'Eh?' I said.

'Johnny want plenty . . . ?' he said with a grin.

I was exceedingly mortified. It seemed to me that by going to sea I had become physically branded, and that henceforth, whenever I went ashore anywhere, corner-boys would rush up and show me the way to a brothel, such being the only place fit for a seafarer's company. I made a kick at him, but he dodged nimbly aside, and said in broken English he would show me the way for two hundred reis. I tried to hunt him several times, but he clung to me with great persistence, and at last I gave him a penny to get rid of him. He was very grateful, told me how to get to the Rua Vasco da Gama, what sort of women were there, and what they did with sailor-men, illustrating everything with obscene gestures. Then he dashed off yelling the name of his newspaper at the top of his voice. A perfectly happy little scoundrel.

I was ashamed of admitting to the ragged newsboy that I really wanted to go to the brothel quarter; but as soon as he had gone, I eagerly used the directions he had given me. Yet I had no intention of having any physical relations with the harlots. That is the attitude of the vast majority of men towards the social disease of harlotry. It is extremely rare to find a man who has not had some sort of relation with a harlot in his life; yet it is equally difficult to find a man who will admit publicly that he has had such relationship. It is an interesting form of hypocrisy, but a perfectly natural one, in no manner reprehensible. No man deliberately sets out to have relations with a harlot, except in case of actual physical necessity, drunkenness, or curiosity. Sailors, students, and soldiers are the general mainstay of the common sort of harlotry, simply because these groups of individuals are generally poor, unknown socially, and vigorous in health. Being unable to afford wives, or expensive mistresses, and not having sufficient capital and address to procure themselves satisfaction by seduction, they purchase cheap loves. Drink adds its quota to the harlot's earnings from among the most diverse classes, from clergymen to scavengers. Finally there are men who, rendered perverse by the dullness of their family life, seek in a brothel the excitement of the senses which is denied them at home.

Harlotry is almost everywhere looked upon as an obscene profession, yet it is hard for an honest and clear-thinking man to see why it is so. It is quite easy to understand why women who are not professional harlots are opposed to professional harlotry, since under social conditions that recognise the rights of private property, the harlot is a poacher on the rights of marriage, which, in turn, is the respectable woman's chief means of livelihood. The harlot, to put it crudely, retails what the respectable woman sells wholesale for a fixed annuity, and various other emoluments, personal and social. Again, the harlot leads a riotous life, and if she is intelligent, attractive, and well versed in her art, prospers considerably, and has numbers of handsome lovers without doing any unpleasant work, while the righteous wife has to labour and be content.

The anger of celibates is also understandable. They object to the ease with which unchaste men can procure the satisfaction of their carnal lusts without incurring the burden of a family. So also is the anger of rustics and uncouth mountainy beggars, who never have an opportunity of visiting a brothel, owing to their remoteness from civilisation and their poverty. But the reproving attitude of the average civilised man is less easy to understand.

There is, of course, the question of disease. It is a fact that harlots are the chief carriers of sexual diseases nowadays.

There is also the fact that, in general, harlots manage their affairs very badly by robbery, and a callous treatment of their customers. That also is the fault of society, which persecutes the harlot with one hand while it tolerates her with the other, thus making her skittish in her code of honour and imbuing her with a stupid anger against those that traffic with her.

The one healthy reason why all decent men should object to the harlot is because she is barren, as a rule, whereas the most beautiful instinct in man is that which impels him to seek immortality through procreation. For that reason alone harlotry as a profession must be allowed to incur odium. But on the other hand, there are certain women who are born harlots, promiscuous by nature, without the maternal instinct, gay, witty, and intelligent. For such women there should be allowance made in an intelligent and well-ordered society.

As it is, the harlot is a dull and objectionable trollop, worthy of all the contempt she receives; and since she is a portrait of the worst feature of woman-in-society, respectable women gain nothing by spitting at her because she is cheaper than they. The difference may often be merely a difference of price.

In any case, I think, personally, that the harlot is a mean, scavenging, lying, thieving, filthy and odious being; but she attracts me as an artist, in the same way that criminals and other objectionable human types attract me, to arouse that remorse of conscience which is the necessary prelude to a bout of creative energy.

I soon reached the Rua Vasco da Gama. I was pleasantly surprised to find it quite different from the brothel quarter in Dublin, which we were in the habit of visiting, crowds of us, when I was a student. In Dublin, the brothel quarter was a disgustingly sordid place, and half the men that came there used it as a shebeen purely and simply. It was a merry place, with personality and a great demonish charm, and at least one of the hostesses was almost a national figure. There was no glitter, hardly any refinement, and a great deal of humanity and turmoil. But instead of being calculated to arouse sensual desires, unless a man was utterly drunk or foreign to the most primitive instincts of delicacy, its appearance aroused thoughts of hell and eternal damnation.

Here, by the benevolent favour of a sunny climate, the whorish quarter looked gay and voluptuous on the surface. The houses were pretty, with painted shutters on the window openings. The cobbled street surface was clean. The women, leaning out of their windows, in various stages of nudity, with extraordinary expressions on their countenances, a mixture of greed and lust, while a mixed horde of men wandered up and down outside, also in the throes of restless passion, all gave the street the appearance of a deliberately constructed tableau. For the most part, the men were of a fine physique, although shabbily dressed, being nearly all seafarers. The women were gaudily dressed, though they wore little. Some were handsome. Others were grotesque, being swollen by idleness, alcohol, and disease.

I walked along this strange market-place gloomily, blushing when, at each window, I was invited by a low hiss and a mumbled, hoarse whisper, to enter, and taste of some woman's delights. I was still very young, with the northern suspicion of soft pleasures still strong in me. Whereas I might have paid the most unseemly woman in the street for her companionship, I would not have paid the most beautiful for her body. And that is, as a general rule, the main reason why men pursue love affairs of this sort. They are lonely, and have no other means of becoming intimate with women. The instinct that drives men to whores is often more worthy than the instinct which drives many men to the marriage altar or registry office. A good many men marry for money and other base motives. In the other case, many men pay money and run the danger of disease for the sake of feeling human, having a woman's arms about them, just as they had their mother's arms about them in infancy.

As I was walking along, an old woman caught me by the arm, and pulled me into a doorway.

'Where do you come from, sonny?' she said.

I told her. She began to stroke my hair. She had a kindly face, and a soft, friendly voice. She was an Englishwoman, about sixty years of age, but well-preserved, and in no way injured by the sort of life she had led.

'What are you doing here?' she said. 'Looking for a nice girl?'

'No,' I said. 'I'm just walking about.'

Two girls ran out into the hall, from a room on the right. One was wearing a dressing-gown and green wooden slippers. She had beautiful dark hair, that lay down her shoulders and her back.

'Here's a young man from your country, Kitty,' said the old woman.

The young girl was a little drunk. She looked at me, laughing at first, and then she threw her arms about me, and burst into tears. The old lady spoke to her severely.

'All right,' said the girl. 'Come on, boy. Come and talk to me.'

'No,' I said, resisting her. 'I really don't . . .'

She dragged me along the corridor. The other girl, a fat, unhealthy-looking woman, with dark eyes, and dyed hair, began to talk to the old woman excitedly in Portuguese. We went into the room on the right. She closed the door, and drew the curtains on the window. Then she put me sitting on the bed, and sat beside me. The room was rather shabby, but clean. I felt extremely embarrassed, largely because the girl had burst into tears, and because she was Irish and beautiful, and slightly drunk. Or was it mad?

She looked at me fiercely for half a minute without speaking. Her lips quivered. There were tears still in her eyes.

'What part of Ireland do you come from?' I said, not because I wanted to know, but just for the sake of breaking the strange trance which had taken possession of her.

I hate hysterical women.

'I come from Dublin,' she said.

That was obviously a lie. She spoke with a Liverpool accent, and was probably a native of some country place in Ireland, gone originally to Liverpool as a servant or a waitress, and then become a street woman. She was about twenty years of age.

'How long have you been out here?'

'Tell me about Ireland,' she said irrelevantly.

Her eyes wandered all over me.

'Really!' I said, 'you shouldn't have brought me in here, because I . . .'

'Listen,' she said.

She looked towards the window. Then she put her arms around my neck, looked at me intensely, and said:

'Kiss me.'

I stared at her foolishly for a moment. Then she suddenly jumped to her feet, her eyes shone, she laughed coarsely, and said:

'I'll sing you an Irish song. Listen:

She lived beside the Anner, at the foot of Slieve na Mhan,
A gentle Irish colleen, she was fairer than the swan.

'How much money have you got? Tell me.'

She rushed over to the bed, and, breathing heavily, she tried to fondle me. She had now assumed the manner of a professional whore. Greed shone in her eyes, and her mouth was cruel.

'I have no money,' I said. 'I told you I . . .'

'Oh! Go away then,' she said harshly.

She jumped from the bed, pulled aside the curtain, and sat at the window, to entice the passers. I felt extremely embarrassed, and took two milreis from my pocket. I offered them to her. She took no notice, so I put them on the dressing-table beside her. She still took no notice.

'Goodbye,' I said. 'I hope you have good luck.'

She looked at me coldly, but said nothing. I left the room. As I went out, the old woman in the hall took no notice of me whatsoever. I hurried away, and began to curse most violently under my breath. All this had made me feel dreadfully lonely and unhappy. I went into a little café, sat down at a table, and ordered a bottle of beer. There were two natives on a little platform making music, with a melodeon and a violin. A crowd of sailors stood about the place, drinking and talking loudly. Here, also, I saw beachcombers for the first time.

While I was drinking my beer near the doorway, two extremely ragged men came along. They halted on the pavement near my chair, and one of them spoke to me. He wore a cotton singlet without sleeves, a ragged straw hat without a crown, dungaree trousers, and wooden slippers. His young face was blotched and pimpled. His eyes were bloodshot and extremely melancholy. His companion looked healthier and better dressed, wearing a complete suit of dungarees, with a sweat rag round his throat. A rough fellow, with a stout neck and tattooed hands. The young man spoke with an American accent.

'What do you want?' I said.

'Give me a stone, for Christ's sake,' he said.

'A what?'

I did not know then that 'stone' was beachcomber's jargon for the Brazilian coin approximating in value to two English pennies.

The waiter rushed over, and threatened the beachcombers with his fist. They moved away. I finished my beer, and left the café. I followed them. A little distance away I saw them halt, and argue. Then they separated. The fellow in the dungaree suit went off waving his arm at the American. The latter stood uncertainly, staring into the gutter, extremely abject in appearance. I came up to him and said:

'Hello, boy! Wasn't it you asked me for something just now?'

He looked at me mournfully, and said:

'Yep. I bummed you for a stone just now.'

'Well!' I said. 'You must forgive me. I didn't know what you meant. Would you like to have a drink?'

'I'd like a cigarette,' he said. 'Have you got an American cigarette?'

'I've got English tobacco and papers. Can you roll one?'

'That's fine. If you like we'll go an' have a drink at a joint I know. It's better down there than here. Are you on a ship?'

'Just left one.'

'Damn silly. It's a son of a bitch to be on the beach here. I've been here a month. It's goddam awful. Is your ship gone yet?'

'No. She just docked this morning.'

'Then get back on her. Did you have an idea of getting a job?'

'No. I have no idea at all. I'm just wandering around. I might go up country.'

'Can't do it. I've been. Unless you're an engineer. It's no good here.'

We walked along downwards towards the docks. We went through the Praga Quinze Novembre, past the ferry landing-place, up some side streets towards the Marine Barracks. Here we met other beachcombers wandering about, each looking more deplorable than his mate. We were now in a slum quarter, where most of the people were coloured.

'My name is Foster,' said the American. 'I come from Newport, Virginia. I got a mother and two young sisters at home. They depend on me more or less. See what a mess I've made of myself. It's just like that. At home, when I used to see a bum goin' along dirty and drunk, I used never to think that he was once decent, with a nice home and people. I guess that's just how you look on me now, but maybe in a week's time you'll just begin to rot away just the same as me. It's the climate, here, see, that makes ye go quicker and sink lower. I got the wind up proper. The only thing is to get drunk and stay drunk. Then in a little while they put ye in the bughouse, and ye pass out.'

He told me he had come down here on a job for the tramway company, I think, as far as I can remember. Then he went to live with a Frenchwoman, and got into trouble. I was not interested in what he was or how he got into his present condition; for the reason that he seemed to me very romantic and a new specimen, full of colour. One is very selfish when one is not just sentimental. Surgeons take joy from mangled limbs and gaping skull wounds.

We turned into a small square, the centre of which was a wilderness of rubble and weeds, walled on one side by a row of ruined houses, and on another by a blank wall. A little to the right from where we entered, two policemen with drawn swords were lounging outside the door of a café. When Foster saw the police, he drew back instinctively for a moment, and then went on. We entered the café. Over the door I saw written Casa do Machaco, the monkey-house. It was a queer place, rather like a London coffee bar in Soho, but the customers were much more odd than anything seen in Soho. There were a number of coloured harlots, dandified Brazilian white men, coloured workmen, beachcombers, and sailors. We sat down at a little table where there was another beachcomber sitting alone.

'This is Tramcar Reilly,' said Foster. 'Been on the beach here for years. He can tell you the ropes.'

'Two years,' said Reilly. 'You American?'

'No,' I said.

'He's a European,' said Foster.

'What? A limejuicer?' said Reilly.

'Let's have that drink, buddy,' said Foster wearily. 'I've got the shivers.'

I ordered three glasses of gashasa. Then I examined Reilly with the same astonishment with which I had examined Foster. If anything, he was even more extraordinary. He was a little fellow, with very small blue eyes, a perfectly bald head, pale cheeks, and a large, furtive mouth. He wore a shabby Panama hat, a linen shirt, from which one sleeve was missing, and dirty linen trousers. His feet were bare. There were bandages on his right leg above the ankle. His hands were like those of a diver, blotched and swollen.

Reilly and Foster began to discuss their day's experience. Reilly had spent most of the morning begging fresh bandages for his leg at the hospital. Then he begged his dinner at a *pension*, and received very little, because they would not allow him to enter the premises for the purpose of washing dishes owing to the ulcer on his leg; for fear of contagion. His bad luck continued during the afternoon, for in three hours' street begging, he received only a penny and three cigarettes. Furthermore, a woman tried to get him put in charge, but the policeman refused to arrest him, knowing that if he got locked up the state would go to unnecessary expense treating him for his ulcer. Finally, he got struck by a docker for sneaking a glass of gashasa in the café.

Foster had better luck. He got twopence from a priest early in the morning. Then he got a milreis from a devout woman who was coming from Mass. Instead of going to a *pension* to beg his dinner, he got drunk on the money he had begged, and then slept for the rest of the day on a waste plot near the docks. Now he was feeling very badly.

I was deeply impressed by the serious manner in which they discussed their work. I asked them where they lived.

'How d'ye mean?' said Reilly. 'D'ye mean have we got rooms? No, sir. The Brazilian sky is a fine an' dandy roof. Only for this goddam leg, though, I'd be up country right now. I had a good job up there, only for the lousy nigger women. I was doing fine.'

'What were you doing?'

'Ran a gambling joint in a camp. Jesus! What a country! Regular cannibals up in the forests here, man-eating animals, all sorts. Still! Some good stuff among those nigger bitches. I ain't sorry. Get up there again as soon as my leg gets better.'

'Listen, Reilly,' said Foster, after we had drunk three glasses each, 'you'll never leave here until ye rot. Nobody ever leaves here once he goes barefoot. A bum told me that, an' it's true. Honest to God.'

He got very melancholy, and began to snigger. He was so besotted with alcohol that he got drunk immediately. Reilly, on the other hand, seemed to become tensely insane. His eyes darted about, and he kept moving restlessly. I was too nervous, so drink had no effect on me.

'No, sir,' said Reilly, 'I intend as soon as my leg gets all right, to go up country, and make another stake. I'm going to lay off this dope. When I make my little pile, I'm going right back to Chi, and get myself a saloon or a dance hall. You fellahs don't know Chi? No. Jesus! I was a goddam fool to leave that burg. Still, I'll have more sense when I get back.'

'Listen, Tramcar,' said Foster in a doleful voice. 'You know damn well every bull from Maine to Oregon is lookin' for you. How did you get that name, Tramcar? You goddam thief! I never stole nothin'. I got a good American mother in Newport. See? I'm not a lousy bum like you. I'm a sailor-man.'

I ordered some more drinks. The two of them got more and more quarrelsome, until finally Foster struck Reilly on the skull with a glass. A general fight started, because Reilly, throwing a glass at Foster, struck, by mistake, a monkey that was hopping about on a perch in a corner of the room. The monkey was the mascot of the place, and was useful to the management for the purpose of attracting custom, as it had been taught to do various obscene tricks. A number of natives dashed in on the beachcombers, and one fellow struck at me with a chair. I avoided the blow, and answered with a kick to the stomach. The fellow lay down moaning.

Then I rushed for the door. At that moment two policemen were coming in with drawn swords, but I took them unawares, and as I dashed out between them they lost their balance, and fell against tables, one on either side. I got around the corner before anybody had time to leave the café.

I was so frightened by my experiences in this place, and so disappointed with the city, that I decided to return to the ship, so I made for the docks as fast as I could; but when I reached the quays and saw the ship in the distance, I hesitated. I began to walk up and down the quays, wondering what I should do. In the distance I could hear the braying of bugles. The city's revels were at their height.

It was nearly midnight.

BERNARD SHARE
1930–

When the author first visited Tahiti in 1956, the only means of access
was by Tasman Empire Airways flying-boat from Fiji or by sea. Nine
years later, Polynesia was another, and far less appealing, world. Chez
Rivnac had been swallowed up by the new airport, and the islands
had become just another round-the-world tourist destination. The
French nuclear test programme both actually and symbolically wrote
the final chapter. This evocation of prelapsarian Tahiti is from
The Moon is Upside Down (1962).

HEARTS ARE TRUMPS

There were four of us playing – if that is the right word: Werner, a
German who spoke no French and no Tahitian; Tavi, a formidable
Tahitienne with an astonishing grasp of English invective, and Mona,
whose toothless grin belied his somewhat sinister appearance. The
game appeared to be an original blend of Rummy, Pontoon, Snap
and Russian Roulette. No one offered to explain any rules, but the
procedure seemed to hinge upon the fact that one could collect or
discard any card at any time in any manner, if it seemed likely to be
to one's advantage.

It soon became clear also that the object was not to win, but to
avoid losing. The difference was subtle but important. The first
person 'out' (and therefore, presumably, the winner) had his success
acknowledged only by a polite smile. Then the game began in earnest,
increasing in tempo until someone was left holding a fistful of assorted
cards which he had not been able to slam on the table quickly
enough. At this point the game ended, amid shrieks of laughter,
catcalls and jeers of 'You Lose!' from Tavi, directed at the unfortunate
victim who paid the penalty of defeat by being obliged to deal the

next hand with such of the cards as could be retrieved from wherever they had been flung in the excitement of the climax.

We were all in the drinking-cum-dancing space of the Hotel Rivnac, a Grade A name disguising an unorganised assembly of thatched huts beside the lagoon and about 15 kilometres from Papeete in an anti-clockwise direction. Rivnac, as it was generally known, was presided over – 'managed' gives a misleading impression of purposefulness – by an Alsace Frenchman, his French wife and their mutual and semi-mutual children, and was sheltering when I knew it representatives of at least six European nations communicating in any one or two of as many languages. There was Laris, the dark, smoulder-eyed Greek who preferred to talk Arabic when he could; there was Werner, the German who had learnt his Australian English in New Guinea and who was working off the effects of two or three years' partial celibacy by sleeping with a different Tahitian girl every night of his five weeks' stay. There was Bill, the Sudeten German who spoke his English with an accent acquired in Drogheda, Ireland, and his Spanish with hissing Chilean sibilants; there was Vicki, born in Greece, educated in Hungary, re-educated in Germany and in a large London hospital (where she learned, not very accurately, *cad é an t-am é* and a couple of other Irish phrases), married first to a Welshman and then to an English music-hall artist (*son mari est magicien!* – I was told by one of the Tahitian girls soon after my arrival); and there was Peter, Balliol and the Stock Exchange, ex-naval-officer, straight out of the pages of Maugham and Conrad, living in a state of perpetual tension with a 15-year-old from Moorea, still with the manner and attitude of the Mess or the Common-room. Then there were the genuine Tahitians who more or less lived round about – Tavi, who came from Bora Bora, Teva, Vahiné, Lulu (who also liked to be known as Henry Coventry, because, as he told us proudly, his father was an Englishman); Santiao the boxer, revered as a travellin' man because he had been to New Caledonia, Fati, a girl as plump as her name who turned up beside me in bed one night quite unannounced. . . . We were an odd lot: preaching and boasting, arguing in half the tongues of Europe and the mangled tongues of Polynesia, most of us without immediate aim or purpose, neither coming nor going, forgetting in the moon and the bath-water warmth of the lagoon and the Algerian wine and the endless, endless music of the *cocoleles* anything we chose to forget, and remembering only when memory took us by surprise.

Te Manu Pukarua, te rua Puka manu . . . the words of the nonsense-song, all about a bird of Pukarua (an island) and some *pommes de terre* vibrate like a bead curtain behind all my memories of Rivnac. I had arrived there quite by accident, on the last leg of a circuit of the island by bicycle (at least I was on a bicycle and my friend Maurice the builder on a *motocyclette*, a distinction which I quickly came to regret) and we had stopped at Rivnac for lunch. As soon as I saw this collection of motley huts and equally motley people on the edge of the lagoon I decided to transfer myself from the small hotel in Papeete where I had been staying, and went back into town to collect my baggage and pile it on top of Mr Opeta's heavily-laden bus which made two journeys a day between Papeete and Punaauia. Vicky, whose magician-husband had been left behind in Sydney while she learnt Tahitian dancing for a night-club act in Hong Kong, soon winkled me out of the whole hut which I had precipitately and expensively rented and into the other half of hers, where we developed a practical domestic arrangement which only occasionally broke down over such questions as whose turn it was for the big bed (the other being quite unsuitable for entertaining) and whose turn it was to go and pick the lemons and mangoes for lunch.

Under a copy of the *Reader's Digest* for July, 1936, badly stained with lizard droppings, which I unearthed in the corner of the hut, I found a first edition, in English, of Aldous Huxley's *Eyeless in Gaza*. Now, it is only through the rather oblique process of remembering the science-fiction overtones assumed by that novel as I read it in between glimpses of the coral bed and its fruit-drop fish and a social visit from Tavi or one of the others, that it is at all possible to recapture the complete other-worldliness which for me was to prove the long-lingering result of contact with even such a modified Polynesian society as that of Tahiti. The dog which falls with such grisly effect from the sky in chapter 12 to spatter the lovers with the blood of guilt and inhibition would fall in vain on Punaauia, for there was nothing there to establish any link between this microcosmic Eden and the world in which Helens and Anthonys lumber their love-making with the inescapable implications and consequences of civilised society. It was not so much that I was revelling in the life of the noble savage (I was still eating steak, drinking wine, and carrying a typewriter) as that I was suddenly made aware of the distance that still divides Polynesia from Paris or London, a distance which must in its own way be as great as it was when Captain Wallis's crew first bought Tahitian favours with ship's nails in 1767. I found myself meditating every action and profession of Huxley's characters as if it was all quite new to me, as if I were re-learning painfully the postures of social behaviour. Writing this as I am, once more embedded in a civilising stream, it sounds facile and naive, but there in Punaauia, as Vicki sat contentedly in the sun with three of her favourite admirers, all of them watching a fourth fishing out on the reef, I had to make a conscious and unpleasant effort of will to remind myself that Huxley had anything to do with me, or that I had not been sitting around in this old pair of shorts on this beach all my life, nibbling windfall bananas and watching the dense, black rainclouds gathering on the 7,000 foot peak inland. The sensation has an edge of irritation just because it has been so confidently and frequently predicted, and no one likes to feel he is falling for a well-worn tourist trick; so one is rather surprised that the effect of Polynesia takes so long to dwindle and vanish, if it ever does. For a way of life which is at once hedonistic and intensely irritating it can exercise a profoundly modifying effect on one's whole outlook. Back in Australia it was some weeks before the calculations and full-dress emotion of Bach or Beethoven made any sense at all, some time before Sydney girls stopped looking chalky and puppet-like. And it was even longer before anyone could get out of me the anecdotes of Tahitian sex-life they all wanted to hear. Then the cynics told me that sex was the only thing I really remembered it all for; and in a way, of course, they were right.

Ever since the prospecting voyages of Wallis and Cook brought back excited accounts of the Polynesian attitude to this pastime a great deal, probably too much, has been written about it from every point of view. If one is an honest tourist sex is the thing one must sample in Tahiti as wine in France or poteen in Ireland, and it has the advantage of being both cheaper than the former (the immediate cost is nil) and more legal than the latter, since the French have, administratively speaking, left this manifestation of Polynesia relatively undisturbed. Sex is almost impossible to write about in this context without sounding either smug or libidinous, and it is almost equally difficult to shake oneself free of one's conditioning and attempt to look at it as the Tahitians themselves do – as enjoyable a pastime as downing a pint or cheering a football team. The Tahitian language has words in plenty for even the more recondite of sexual refinements (*Amuhua* I have in my home-made student's vocabulary as *soixante-neuf; ammure* – ditto, *version féménine; utupapa* – *papillons d'amour*) and their frequent appearance in ordinary conversation is marked by a total lack of embarrassment or self-consciousness. By the time one has acquired sufficient of the language to follow, one is no longer shocked or indecently curious: the biggest shock is the discovery that one's own ideas on the matter which one had always thought of as liberal are about as constrained and artificial as a Victorian waistline.

But enough of this 'one'. In matters of sex the generalisation is rarely interesting or acceptable, and last night's passion looks strangely absurd in the morning, even in Tahiti. I was lucky perhaps in my fortuitous measuring-rod, Huxley; unlucky that in common with many Europeans I was always a little self-conscious about it all, self-conscious even about the fact that I was trying not to be self-conscious. There was Werner, with his determined and deadening debauch; Laris, with his beautiful half-Tahitian, half-Chinese French officers' wives; my building friend, and his girl who appeared out of the night at the Tropiques hotel, evidently all part of the room service and not on the bill – were we all indulging ourselves for the same reasons? The paradox of the situation, and of course fruitful material for the moralist, was that one discovered depressingly quickly the truth of the dictum about forbidden fruit, even in this matter. Only Peter, with his desperate possessiveness for the 15-year-old Janine, seemed to be involved in a 'real relationship' in the European sense of the term, and it was perhaps significant that he was the only genuinely unhappy person amongst us.

One of the hardest things to assess, from the standpoint of the casual visitor, is the exact meeting-point between the European and Polynesian worlds. The Polynesians of Tahiti are about as racially pure as the Gaels of Galway, but for all their Chinese and English and French admixtures they are far from being racially equivocal or nondescript. The Polynesian 'way of life' in Tahiti is not observed on the surface, certainly not in the joking hula dances which the girls put on for the pop-eyed tycoons of the Matson boats; but you cannot spend a week on the island without coming up against a subtle

challenge to your ingrained way of thinking everywhere you turn. In
Papeete there are to be found the usual customs and manners, and
the usual riff-raff, that fill the gutters of any seaport in the world
when the bars stop serving drinks, but the 15 kilometres to Punaauia,
past the little white signboard marking Gauguin territory, take you
into a world which, if not quite the primitive paradise of the story
books, is different enough to make you want to come to some sort of
terms with it and discover how these people live with such obvious
zest and lack of concern for the morrow. There is the antique custom,
still intermittently in force, of what's thine is mine – extending at
least to minor possessions. One night in the dance-bar at Rivnac   I
was reddening my pipe with one of my last five matches when one of
the Tahitian boys leant over and without a word filled my box from
his own. It is only fair to add that shortly after that someone 'borrowed'
a relatively expensive tin of meat I had bought at the Chinese shop as
a special treat. There are unannounced lady visitors in the middle of
the night; and, on the other hand, there was the romantic swain who
drank half a bottle of Eau de Cologne (a dramatically fin-de-siècle
gesture) because someone else had replaced him in Vicki's affections.
There were the stories of the confusion created on one of the small
islands by the presence of a Presbyterian mission on one end and a
Roman Catholic on the other; and there was the Catholic priest,
never, unfortunately, adequately identified, who would not marry a
Tahitian couple until they had lived together for 15 years.

Little of this would interest the professional anthropologist, being
as it is evidence not so much of a way of life as of a makeshift
compromise between two conflicting worlds. In this compromise,
however, lies the seductive appeal as well as the disappointing
features of present-day Tahiti. Is there a bare minimum of civilisation
which even the escaper will cling to? Is environment and tradition
sufficiently strong to preserve some vestiges of the Polynesian outlook
even in the face of tourism and Coca Cola? In Tahiti at present one is
still conscious that the clash and the contrast of two different
approaches to the bases of living exists and has real meaning. Its
power is greater in that it is shouted from no rooftop and paraded in
no manifesto, but implicit in the spontaneous offering of a *cocolele* or
a night of love. Historical prophecy is a barren pastime, but Tahiti as
a way of life will almost certainly be near its end when the sympathetic
visitor – as distinct from the day-tripper who never gets outside

Papeete – finds a price tag on either of these items.

One of the many stories they told me in Rivnac (they grow as numerous and as tall as the coco-nut palms) concerned a European living on a remote island of the Society group – of which Tahiti is a member – who felt that civilisation was leaving him a little too far behind. To redress the balance he decided to dress for dinner every evening, and thereafter greeted his native girl at the appropriate time splendidly attired in a black tie – a bronzed torso and a pair of grubby shorts completing the ensemble. Listening to such yarns, usually told by other Europeans with a slightly bitter twist, I came to realise something of the fatal fascination of the Tahitian compromise, and how very easy it would be to dream and drift oneself into this condition of suspended animation, living and partly living in a sunlit, laughing hell of one's own making, the echoes from the frightening but tantalising world outside booming and receding like the surf on the wicked crenellations of the coral reef. Even so, there were many times when I would not have complained had the customs of a Tahitian yesteryear spirited away my return ticket.

PETER SOMERVILLE-LARGE
1929–

The author of one of the best available short histories of Dublin, Peter
Somerville-Large is related to Edith Somerville, co-author of the 'Irish
RM' stories. Educated at Trinity College Dublin, he worked at various
occupations in the Middle East and Australasia, including a spell as
lecturer in the Royal Military Academy in Kabul, before turning to
travel writing. His books in the genre encompass journeys to the
Yemen and Iran, as well as several unconventional excursions in
Ireland. This extract from *To the Navel of the World* (1987), the record of
a journey largely by recalcitrant yak through Nepal and Tibet, typifies
his unheroic and self-deprecating approach to the discipline. He was
accompanied by 'a tall, handsome Anglo-Irish girl [Caroline] who
insisted on introducing me to everyone as Uncle'.

VISA

In Kathmandu Caroline collected her mail. 'Look what I've got –
your Tibetan visa.' First the good news – there were strong rumours
that Hong Kong visas would no longer be valid at the Nepal–Tibetan
border. Up until now foreigners were allowed to use them because of
a loophole in the law – they were valid for the whole of China, and
Tibet was technically a part of China. But the Chinese wanted to
regulate visitors more closely. They did not want a string of
impoverished trekkers, but wealthy tourists bearing loads of hard
currency.

Everyone we asked agreed. 'Hong Kong visa no good.'

'Forget about them, the border's closed. The Chinese have got
wise, and are turning back everyone.'

Still we persisted against all advice. Caroline had a friend, another
one of the new Tibetan entrepreneurs who have made a significant
contribution to the Nepali economy over the last twenty years. He

and his family manufactured carpets, sending them back to Tibet among other places.

'We have a Land-Rover going up to the border tomorrow taking some carpets and seven lamas. If you wish you can join them. They are very nice fellows.'

The Land-Rover collected us next day beside the gompa at Bodnath where it picked up the lamas and a nun for good measure. Bulbous shaven heads shone in the sun like lumps of old leather as we twisted and trundled northward along the new Chinese road. We travelled all day until evening, when we reached a steep valley. Small villages with little terraced fields around them lay clear of the rocks, while a river poured its way down like a spurt of beer released from a bottle. The valley narrowed to a gorge; overhead the sky was blue, but down here everything was in shadow.

Deep in the gloom was Tatopani, the Nepalese customs post, a scrapheap of a town full of flimsy huts. We got down from the Land-Rover which instantly vanished. Everyone left us, the seven lamas, the nun, the driver and his long rolls of carpet strapped to the roof of his vehicle. We were left on our own to be followed by some ragged children and dogs pausing to sniff garbage. A cold wind blew down from Tibet.

We camped in an inn, a derelict place with mud walls, a few benches and very little food – another foretaste of Tibet. Bed was the draughty dormitory upstairs with no glass in the window, no lights and sacks stretched across holes in the floor. Two strangers joined us; I could see their silhouettes in the dark. In the morning they turned out to be a couple of cheerful Nepalese who found Caroline an object of great fascination. She did look striking, lying back wearing her bandana and black silk gloves, like a picture I had once seen of Edith Sitwell posed like a recumbent ecclesiastic on top of a tomb.

In the gloom of the morning we could see how the place had been hurriedly thrown together to accommodate workers on the new road camped all round in squalid little huts made of matting. We waited for hours, despairing of leaving the dreary scene until suddenly the Land-Rover with lamas screeched to a halt a few yards from where we sat in a coffee house of almost unbearable filth.

Once more we were climbing up the gorge where men and women were breaking stones with hammers, building culverts and carrying baskets of earth under the supervision of Chinese engineers in blue uniforms and round straw hats. The occasional old-fashioned lorry with a rounded snout painted olive green rumbled past. We crossed the still-unfinished skeleton of Freedom Bridge which divided Nepal from Tibet. It had been completed some years ago, but then had broken up during heavy monsoon rains. On the far side of the gorge a waterfall splashed down and higher up were patches of cleared land and a few stone huts. Through vapoury mist mountain peaks glistened in the sky.

We reached the border town of Zhangmu, a contrast to Tatopani with its brand new lines of flat-roofed white houses and a large building with a flag waiting to receive visitors. We drove through the entrance on to a concrete ramp where a Chinese soldier stood waiting.

Caroline said, 'I'll do the talking.'

We hung around reading the large pictorial display outside the custom building showing pictures of achievements that had taken place since National Liberation. Time passed; I watched two more soldiers and a girl walking down the road carrying steaming bowls of rice. The lamas had long passed through the far end of the building and vanished. Two more officials in Mao suits sauntered down the road, their arms entwined like lovers.

Caroline said, 'They don't get proper sex until after thirty. During the Cultural Revolution that sort of thing was not allowed, but now it goes along with the Responsibility System.'

A girl in uniform approached. 'Please sign visitors' book.'

The small office was spotless with a comfortable sofa and chairs, a large map of China and Tibet, and a bowl of plastic flowers. After we had completed forms declaring amounts of money and duration of proposed stay, Caroline went to the little window that overlooked us carrying our passports. Although I knew she had lived in China and spoke the language, it was still a pleasant surprise to hear her burbling away. I remembered the opinion of the missionary who considered mastering Chinese was a task for people with bodies of brass, lungs of steel, heads of oak, hands of spring-steel, eyes of eagles, memories of angels and life spans of Methuselah.

The two officers in their smart blue uniforms were also impressed, but not impressed enough.

She called back, 'They say the destination is not marked in.'

'What does that mean?' I knew well enough. Hong Kong visa no good. The young man with the opaline face as round as a moon shrugged his shoulders. A soldier brought us cups of tea with lids on to console us.

We were not the first travellers to be denied entry into the secret land, nor would we be the last. As we stood forlornly beside our baggage, another Land-Rover drove up from the Nepali side. Beside the driver sat a bushy-haired African dressed in a kaftan.

'Hi, man! You going to Tibet?'

Joseph came from Mauritius and was on a world trip. He also had a Hong Kong visa; a journey to Tibet was a side visit. 'A crazy place, man.'

We watched him go up to the window and hand his passport to the same bland-faced official. After a few minutes it was returned politely. How infuriating it would have been if they had allowed him through.

'Hey . . . this is the latest visa . . . who do they think they are? I've paid good money to hire this jeep, man!' The Chinese officials could have been idols or stones.

Joseph's bad luck was a stroke of fortune for us, since we could share his jeep back to Kathmandu. Now that he was returning he did not seem to worry. He had made a big effort to get over, and okay, the visa was a piece of crap and there were other places to see. He was heading towards the stews of Bangkok. Hour followed hour as we sat bunched in the back nibbling some tasty cookies he offered us while the familiar road slithered past. At seven we were back at the Kathmandu Guest House, not feeling well; we were dizzy, the world turned in circles and my legs had become putty. The cookies had been laced with marijuana.

Next day we had headaches and shattered hopes. But by midday we had evolved a plan which was utterly illegal. It centred on the fact that there was very little wrong with our passports, just the lack of a name. The officials at Zhangmu had told Caroline that they needed a destination written in by their embassy in Kathmandu. The words 'Good for Lhasa' would be sufficient.

Possibly the dope helped us along. 'Why don't we get George to doctor them?'

George was a Hong Kong Chinese, one of a select group of foreigners at the Kathmandu Guest House whose mysterious comings and goings aroused envy among those tied to plebeian group treks. The dreaded independent travellers, immune to package deals, hated by the agencies, included some exotics who were pointed out with

awe. A man with a black spade beard was said to have travelled
around Dolpho. A German girl who went barefoot had spent the
winter in a distant gompa with her Nepalese lover. There was the
German who had walked through Cambodia, and the two Finnish
girls who had hitch-hiked across Afghanistan. There was George. He
and a few carefully selected companions had a scheme to bicycle into
Tibet on inflatable mountain bikes with eighteen gears.

George's Chinese calligraphy was exquisite. We persuaded him to
help us without much trouble, perhaps because his own plans were
as daft as ours. We lent him a pen and the operation took a minute.
He examined his handiwork with pride. 'I think that should do. I've
written in "Good for Zhangmu and Lhasa".'

'Wonderful!'

One day later we were on our way again in a Land-Rover which
was decorated with a board on which was painted HARRY'S JOURNEY.
It was an anxious time and we didn't speak much as we drove past
skeins of paddy fields with the occasional group of trekkers trudging
down the road bearing their rucksacks.We drove through the familiar
mountains, through the gloom of Tatopani until HARRY'S JOURNEY
was moving into the People's Autonomous Republic of Tibet. With
each hairpin bend the idea of presenting our forged visas seemed
less good.

Once again our bags were tumbled out and the same soldier
looked on. Once again I watched Caroline go up to the same window
and talk Chinese. I could see that a different official was peering at
George's ideograms. For some time nothing happened and there was
just the cheep of voices and unexplained silences. Then an officer
came out and directed our baggage to the main hall to be examined.

We quickly paid off our driver, and then we were sitting on a
bench in the empty customs hall on the correct side of the border.

I was suffused with such a warm golden feeling that I failed to
notice a jeep roaring up containing four senior army officers. They
assembled inside the office talking and occasionally looking out of
the window in our direction. The place smelt of disinfectant; minutes
passed. Then an official appeared and handed back our passports.
We were free to go.

Next to the customs was a new hotel waiting for the expected
hordes of tourists. We had seen the manager two days ago strolling
arm in arm with his friend.

'Good evening. You wish to spend night?'

'That sounds fine.' I looked at the comfortable chairs, the spotless disinfected passages and a group of Chinamen in blue Mao jackets waiting to serve us. With a good meal in mind, we went down to the kitchen which was full of women in white surgical robes where we found there was nothing to eat at all.

Caroline said, 'I despair of you, Peter. Perhaps you think that getting through the customs was a piece of cake. And who did all the talking? We can't possibly stay here. You realise it will only take a phone call to the embassy in Kathmandu to make someone realise that something is wrong with our visas. Anyway, I asked – a bed in this place is thirty pounds a night.'

After a jar of tea we left carrying our bags. There are no porters in the People's Republic. Although we had pared down everything, the loads were immense, Caroline's rucksack, zip bags and camera equipment, my large rucksack and the unwieldy duffle bag marked mendaciously ANNAPURNA EXPEDITION containing the tent, food, medicine and other useful things. A few steps filled me with bad thoughts about all the weary miles ahead.

Beyond the hotel the road turned up the hill in a series of dusty loops away from the neat line of customs house, hotel and bank to where the rest of Zhangmu was jumbled together in a collection of huts just like its sister town down the road on the other side of the border. We hoped to find a lorry and put a distance between ourselves and the frontier, but we immediately faced problems. In Nepal people still enjoy meeting and helping foreigners, but here we found any attempt to enter into a commercial travelling arrangement met with no, no, no. Staggering under our bags, we climbed the hill to more houses, barracks, and more lorries packed with timber or soldiers staring down. No lifts. Higher up and at the town's end were two lorries whose backs were covered with tarpaulin, indicating a long journey ahead. Once again Caroline tried fruitlessly to negotiate a price. It began to rain, then to hail and the road turned to mud.

'We must find a bed. We'll have to try again tomorrow.'

Just before dark we managed to obtain accommodation in a room full of broken beds, empty except for a Japanese couple huddled together on a stained mattress trying to keep warm. Wind poured through cracks and the roof leaked, making puddles on the floor. We were charged the equivalent of two pounds a night; it was not worth a penny more. Stomach trouble compounded my misery and during the night I had to leave my dirty bed countless times to stumble past the creaking door out into the rain and wind to crouch in mud. In the morning I felt like a ghost, my stomach a sieve, pains racking my body. Caroline gave me a couple of her pills.

We struggled from the hut with our luggage into the steep shanty town where wisps of malodorous mist hung above the gorge and clung to the pea-green jackets of soldiers. Soldiers were all over the town, strolling about in the damp, a multitude of bright green uniforms, baggy blue trousers, boots and red enamel stars on peaked caps. Here on the frontier the People's Army seemed unoccupied and bored. Not everyone by any means was working on the road; there were no proper shops to go into or cafés or other garrison amusements. A ceaseless procession of lads in green walked up and down the corkscrew hill, pausing to look down into the forests of Nepal. There seemed to be mighty few Tibetans.

I searched out the driver who had hinted the night before that his lorry was leaving, and he might, just might, take on extra passengers for huge sums of money. But he and his companions were fast asleep. Carrying our bags down the spiralling street once again, we felt increasing despair.

Two cars swept around a bend on the way down to the customs post and we had time to glimpse some Caucasian faces. Abandoning our bags we ran down the hill in pursuit. At the hotel we found two Italians covered in dust and a young Scottish couple.

The Scottish pair told us how they had rented their van with great difficulty in Lhasa in order to see more of Tibet. The problem had been the driver. Throughout the journey he had ignored them and taken no notice of any requests they made. During every repeated breakdown of his tin-can vehicle he had infuriated them with his rudeness. He gave an extra dimension to the concept of rudeness.

Anthony's clipped Scots vowels came through clenched teeth. 'If you've ever really hated anyone, double that again, and you'll get some tiny indication of the way I feel about that bastard!'

The Italians were continuing their journey down to Kathmandu, 'Thank God we leave Tibet! Thank God we go to Nepal! Thank God!' But miraculously Anthony and Jean were returning to Lhasa since their exit visas only permitted them to leave Tibet through China. There were eight seats in the van.

'You realise it's not very comfortable. Bump, bump until your ass is splitting.'

'Oh we don't mind!' We arranged to meet in an hour.

When we returned with our baggage a crowd had gathered round the van, and in among the spectators Anthony and the driver were facing each other and shouting. In his hand Anthony waved the distributor cap he had torn from the engine. 'He's a bastard!' The roar was an octave deeper than the driver's Chinese cries, 'Bastard! Now he says he must have special permission to bring us back.'

'Why?'

'You can speak Chinese, for Christ's sake! Tell him that unless we go now I keep the fucking distributor!'

The driver spoke to Caroline in the tones of a hoarse budgerigar. 'He says it is forbidden to go back.'

'Then I'll break up his fucking car!' Anthony was hopping up and down. 'I'm not letting him get away with this after all we've suffered! He can go the police or whoever. I don't mind! I don't mind, I tell you! He's not getting his machine back.'

Caroline began loading our luggage.

The row ended abruptly. The driver consented to go back to Lhasa with his passengers. Anthony returned the distributor, the crowd wandered off. To my amazement and great joy we were driving up the hill past the shacks of Zhangmu. I remembered the manta that Nhuche had composed before I left Kathmandu invoking success on my journey. He told me that its mystifying refrain 'Lalasu Thochhe' meant 'Yes, Sir . . . Thank you.' It had set us on our way, but would it help us any more? My stomach rumbled and I had a sensation of frailty like the man in Cervantes' story who believes he is made of glass.

WALTER STARKIE
1894–1976

A fellow academic, A.J. Leventhal, wrote of him: 'Our professor, like Borrow, found his way to Spain, but unlike him took a fiddle instead of a Bible for company.' Professor of Romance Languages and Literature at Trinity College Dublin from 1926 to 1943, Walter Starkie was a director of the Abbey and Gate theatres, translator of *Don Quixote* and author of critical studies of Spanish and Italian writers. It was, however, his wanderings with his fiddle among the gypsies of the Balkans and of Spain that supplied the material for his most successful books, and his *Raggle Taggle* (1933), from which this episode in Huedin, Romania, is taken, was followed by several others in similar vein. Starkie spent the war years in Madrid as head of the British Institute, taught at Madrid University from 1948 to 1956 and was subsequently professor in residence at the University of California. The amatory episodes in his books did not recommend them to the puritan Ireland of his day, though some, according to McDowell and Webb's history of Trinity College were 'rumoured to have been inserted by his wife in order to liven up the narrative'.

VAGABONDING WITH ROSTÁS

As we were walking down one of the crowded streets my two girls gave a whoop and started to run after a man who was entering a shop. Catching him by the coat they swung him round and with many gesticulations pointed at me. The man came up and bowed deferentially. He was a most sinister figure and one who brought back to my mind all the recollections of the Borrovian Gypsy heroes. He was tall of stature, though he walked with bent shoulders and kept his eyes fixed on the ground. His face was walnut colour and his bushy eyebrows gave him a Satanic expression. When he looked at you, his queer opal-coloured eyes shone with a malevolent glint and a deep gash across his forehead gave him an expression of fierceness.

When I spoke to him in Romany he immediately began to fraternise with me. Under his arm he carried a fiddle in a bag and as soon as I uttered the *bashavav* he handed it to me.

Playing in the street in fair-time is not an easy task, for each moment you are liable to be crushed under some cart. As soon as I started to play 'Hullamszó Balaton' and 'Lyuk, Lyuk' his eyes brightened, for he was a Hungarian Gypsy. He seized the fiddle from my hands and started a *lassu*. Soon we became excited rivals and a competition took place to show who knew the biggest number of Hungarian melodies: I very soon had to confess myself defeated, and to cover up my deficiencies I played 'Emer's Farewell' and the song of the Irish Wheelwright, but this would not satisfy Hungarian Gypsies, who are the most notorious chauvinists in the world as far as music is concerned. Any music other than Magyar does not arouse more than a contemptuous shrug of the shoulders from them. However, at the end of each outburst of fiddle-scraping he thrust the instrument into my hands and willy-nilly I had to saw away to the best of my ability.

It was curious to watch the effect of our music on the solemn-eyed peasant men and women who stood round us gaping with astonishment to see a perfectly normal, fair-haired stranger excitedly fiddling with a disreputable-looking Gypsy. The peasants found it hard to understand that any normal white man should ply the trade of the Gypsy. The cunning Gypsy seized the chance of cheap publicity and probably monetary gain: he therefore encouraged the crowd to approach and as I played he beat time loudly with his feet. As for the ragged Gypsy girls, they flitted about around us like may-flies.

It was a motley assembly: some men who were dressed in the white costume of the field labourers stood there with their scythes; others wore enormous-brimmed straw hats such as are worn by the harvest workers; there were old women laden with jars and baskets of water-melons. On all sides bright-eyed brats of children tumbled in the dust and scampered like cats as we played on and on.

The heat was suffocating: the streams of perspiration rolled down my face on to the fiddle and trickled into the f. holes; all life seemed to be melting from me as I responded to the dictatorial Rostás. At last he made me understand that our performance might be continued at greater length in a bar near by, and so off we went, followed by some of the crowd, to a dirty, evil-smelling bar where I stood a round of drinks to the friends of Rostás. Other Gypsies came in and swelled our party, and fiddle-playing started again with greater fury of concentration. This time when I played Hungarian tunes some of the others improvised an accompaniment to the solo.

I noticed that as a rule the violinists who accompany the *Primás* do not possess real bows. Any lithe stick suffices and across this they stretch black horsehair, but they keep it very slack so that they can play across the four strings of the fiddle at once and produce a crude harmony.

As usual in all those feasts of music the peasants did not need much rhythmic stimulus to react. Within five minutes the whole room was trembling beneath the stamp of the dancers. Nowhere in the world is the effect of music more immediate than in these countries. It is as if some god of rhythm entered the bodies of those people and possessed them to the exclusion of every other emotion in life. There is a proverb which says that you can make a peasant drunk on a glass of water and a Gypsy fiddler. This is certainly true of the peasants in Transylvania. The music has the effect of *Katharsis* in the lives of these people. It is the necessary outlet for emotions that would otherwise be starved in the rough work of the earth. All those peasants fraternised with my friend Rostás as long as they were under the influence of the Deus rhythmicus, and one gawky, bearded man put his arms affectionately around him as he filled his glass. And yet I imagined to myself the expression of contempt with which he would greet him at other hours of the day when life was normal and the Gypsy was relegated to his position of slave to the Magyar. As for myself, I found the attentions of some of the women rather embarrassing: one eight months gone with child and carrying with difficulty her enormous bulk came up to me and gave me a kiss that resounded like a smack through the bar. Everyone laughed at this naïve expression of pleasure, but I had visions of a dark, scowling husband lurking in wait for me. The young girls were more restrained and kept up an incessant chatter among themselves.

Before I left the café all the Gypsies insisted on my examining and trying their instruments. Pathetic sights they were, those poor Transylvanian fiddles: they had been for many years subjected to every change of weather. Sometimes as the vagabond minstrel played, the sun would beat down like a furnace upon his instrument and melt the varnish; other days the rain poured ceaselessly and the soaked violin croaked out its misery to the world. Gypsies never put their fiddles in cases, but in a shabby old bag, and as they carry it you may see part of the bow protruding. And yet those poor instruments, when touched by the thyrsus of the god of rhythm, respond as if they possessed in the grain of their wood a particle of that magic which gave to the Cremonas their golden tone. No matter how badly a Gypsy may play, once he becomes excited by the audience to do his best, then he can make his instrument resound with a wild untutored music.

All that he does is the result of intuition and tradition; the printed page of music is to him a marvel, for he has never learnt to decipher it. When I showed Rostás some music I had in my pocket he looked at it suspiciously as though it were some secret spell. But my wonder was greater than that of Rostás, for I found that his ear was much more perfect than mine: if he heard a melody played twice or three times he would play it perfectly and his companions would forthwith improvise a harmony.

Rostás never allowed a melody to remain in its primitive state: if I sang him an Irish tune he would cock his head on one side and listen gravely; then he would take up the fiddle and introduce arabesques of the most complicated kind until my poor, simple Irish tune became like a berouged street-girl of southern Europe. It was useless to argue with him about such matters of taste, for he was completely convinced of the superiority of his Tzigan artistry over that of a mere *busnó*. However, I liked Rostás and I determined to go out vagabonding with him.

I have very rarely met a Gypsy whose eyes did not blaze with covetousness when he caught sight of a silver coin. In the villages the traveller, as a rule, is pestered by the Gypsy mendicants who demand charity and curse you all the while under their breath in Romany: in the cafés the Gypsy musicians flaunt the plate beneath your nose after every piece they play.

Not so Rostás! Never once did he demand money from me when we were on the tramp together, but when he had gathered together his friends he would call the waiter over and would give the order in a lordly manner. When it came to the hour for paying and I would pull out my purse, Rostás would make a solemn, deprecating gesture as though I had committed an impropriety by such an action.

I never omitted to pay the bill in spite of that mute protest of my friend.

Rostás had many points of delicacy and a dignity that is rare in his race. When we used to perform in cafés or in bars he would always pass round the plate himself so as to spare my feelings, and I appreciated this.

In all my wandering with Gypsies I have always made it a rule not to ask for shares in the spoils, and they have invariably respected my motives. I was the stranger and it was a privilege for me to be taken temporarily into the wandering tribes and become a student of their mysteries.

I am sure the ancestors of Rostás must have been those Counts of Little Egypt who wandered through Europe surrounded by slaves to do their bidding. The Gypsy chief was always the strongest and the handsomest of the tribe and he held office by virtue of his magnetic personality. It was such a man who under the name of Duke Panuel emblazoned his coat of arms on some of the cathedrals of Western Europe. Rostás had a great deal of the arrogance of the Gypsy chief. With me he was calm and watchful: he accepted with great dignity the presents I made him, the meals I paid for, but always with the impression that he was doing me a great favour.

Our conversation was never very consequent, for my knowledge of Transylvanian Romany was limited to certain isolated words describing general things. It was only when we held our fiddles in our hands that communion of spirit was possible. His face did not lead me to expect deep confidences, for it seemed to have a shutter closed down over it except on certain occasions when he became exalted. The scar on his forehead, his flashing eyes, his cynical expression set him apart from the frankly-gay Gypsies I had met in Hungary.

We set out from Huedin one morning at eight o'clock.

Even at that hour the roads were dusty and the sun a furnace. It was all I could do to keep up with the long stride of Rostás, and at last I insisted on a halt when we had walked ten kilometres. The country was bewitchingly beautiful at this time of the year, for the smell of the harvest was in the air and everywhere we saw the fields full of white-robed peasants working. The plain with its fertile crops undulated away into the distant horizon with its blue mountains. Along the roads we met many a cart laden with peasants returning slowly from Huedin: in some cases the men were full of Bacchus and were lurching forward on the seats shouting out songs. At the back of the carts sat girls in costume laughing and cracking jokes with the peasants as they passed by.

A little farther on we came across a band of ragged Gypsies labouring in a field: they were darker than Rostás and had shaggy, black beards. It was easy to arouse their interest by a few phrases such as 'Shukar rakli' or 'pi mol'.

At various places on the way we drank from fresh springs to relieve our thirst, but in spite of all these rests I was a sorry, footsore figure when we arrived at Almás at six-thirty in the evening.

Rostás led me straight to his own house, which was down a lane just at the outskirts of the town. It would be decidedly optimistic to call it a house, for it seemed to have been constructed of all the old pieces of wood and tin that could be found on a scrap-heap. The whole construction looked as if it was just going to crumble in ruins and was only holding itself aloft out of a sentiment of jaunty pride.

There was only one room and no regular chimney to let out the smoke. Inside we found a very ugly old hag whom he presented as his mother, a younger good-looking but very slatternly woman, his wife, and their children whose ages varied from seven to two years. I was fascinated by the appearance of the old hag: she reminded me of the *gule Romni* referred to so often by Dr Wlislocki in his book on the Transylvanian Gypsies. She seemed incredibly old and her face was so furrowed by wrinkles that the skin seemed to be in limp strips. Her chin was very prominent and her mouth gaped open with toothless gums. Only her dark eyes recalled to me the fact that Rostás was her son.

When we entered the hovel she was crouching down over the fire stirring a pot. She came up and scrutinised my face most carefully and then she went and said something in Hungarian to Rostás and her daughter-in-law. She approached again and passed her hands over my clothes. Finally Rostás must have reassured her, for she beckoned me to sit down by the fire. Meanwhile the small children stood like statues in the corner and gaped at me as if I had been an apparition.

The wife was a handsome woman of the strong and passionate kind. She was big and well-developed and her face was strongly chiselled like that of an athlete. Her skin was like beautifully-polished wood with a certain golden quality about it. There was something panther-like in her movements and when she walked she rolled her hips in a way that suggested the Gypsies of Andalucía. Her hair too was striking, owing to its blue-black colour. If Rostás was arrogant in manner his wife was ever so much more imperious and there was an intensity in her gaze that frightened me. She too was a queen in spite of her ragged smock, showing half of one naked breast, and her bare legs.

The supper was not a kingly one. The old hag served up a kind of broth with great tough pieces of gristle in it: it was so tasteless that irresistibly my mind, as I chewed the meat, strayed to thoughts of dog or horse. After the repast Rostás said it was time to go down to some of the cafés and play, and though I was weary and footsore I followed him from one café to another. It was not a good evening for wandering minstrels as there were few peasants about, and I think the earnings of Rostás did not amount to more than a few lei. At last we turned back to the hut, and when we arrived I found that the company had increased. The sister-in-law of Rostás and her husband were seated with the family.

Soon afterwards we all settled down for the night. There were no beds in the hovel and everyone had just to lie on a few skins and straw on the ground. I have slept in more uncomfortable quarters, but I was not prepared for the promiscuousness of our resting-place. The hovel was not more than 18 feet by 12 feet, and in that space a family of eight people had to sleep. I lay in one corner and near me lay the sister-in-law and her husband, then on the other side lay Rostás, his wife, the old mother, and farther away two children were ensconced, while above our heads in a hammock arrangement swung the baby of the family.

The ground was very hard and the skins were smelly. The atmosphere was stifling, and in addition I began to feel the first fierce onslaught of those voracious beasts that haunt the Gypsies. It is curious that they postpone their chief attack until the silent watches of the night when you lie motionless. Then when you are just slipping off into slumber they start their attack by the slight stinging sensation they inflict. A few minutes later you are like Gulliver in Lilliput –

delivered gagged and bound to the executioner. The activity of those beasts is surprising and their intelligence worthy of Swift's Lilliputians, for when you scratch fiercely they lead you to believe that you have annihilated them. For a moment you think you are free and your body tingles gratefully, but then the slight itching starts in some different spot and works up again to a climax of irritation. My neighbours all this time seemed blandly unconscious of the destruction that was taking place: I suppose hundreds of years of acquaintance with those hosts gives immunity.

The room was pitch dark now, for the fire had burnt low. On one side I heard the stentorian snores of the old woman: on the other I heard a low conversation between Rostás and his wife. The whole scene seemed unreal to me: I could not realise that I was sleeping amid Gypsies in Transylvania. Gradually I slipped off into a queer dreamland, where I seemed to wander aimlessly for centuries through dim forests surmounted by queer animals. I was playing a flute and at each note all sorts of queer little green goblins hopped out in front of me. But as soon as I stopped playing they faded away into thin air and I continued my wandering. I did not know how long I had been dreaming, but it seemed centuries when I suddenly awoke with a start, feeling a hand moving over my body. It was no sluggish hand, for it travelled straight towards my inside pockets as though its owner was quite certain what the quest should be. For a moment I allowed its explorations to continue, then suddenly when it was descending on my purse in my trousers pocket I caught hold of it with a firm grasp and held on tight.

There was a smothered explanation and a suppressed laugh: it was the sister-in-law who evidently thought that her talent for *ustilar pastesas* might be tried with profit upon me.

Poor, misguided girl, if she had only known that when the *busnó* goes on Gypsy trips he leaves the bulk of his money and valuables under lock and key in the nearest big town, for he is superstitious enough to believe that one should not tempt Providence.

Finding that she had failed, the girl became affectionate and tried to cuddle up against me. She whispered words of invitation and put out her arms and tried to draw me within their embrace. It was an embarrassing moment for me: Love knows no fury like a woman scorned, but there was also the peril of her husband who might be lying awake on her other side.

Even if I had been tempted circumstances required a strict
neutrality, and at the risk of playing the part of a rather middle-aged
Joseph, I firmly rejected her advances. Perhaps my ideas concerning
the jealous nature of Gypsy husbands did not apply to Transylvania.
I knew that in Spain ever since the days of Borrow the fidelity of
Gypsy wives has been proverbial and *Lacha ye trupos* or corporal
chastity is considered the most perfect possession of a woman.
Nobody, however, gives the Gypsies of the east of Europe credit for
being very chaste. In fact, throughout Roumania we meet an immense
number of Gypsy flower-sellers who will also sell their bodies for a
few lei. I may relate that the sister-in-law's husband was grey-haired,
but he was grim-looking and I was sure he would be a dangerous
rival for any inexperienced Don Juan to encounter. After this little
aventure I found it impossible to sleep in the confined space of the
hovel, for the smell of unwashed bodies mingled with the scent of
onions and rotten fish seemed at this hour of the night to increase
rather than to diminish in intensity.

I got up noiselessly and slipped out of the hut.

Outside, it was fairyland: the moon shone brightly and the sky was
still starry, but gradually the ghostly green light of dawn was creeping
across the sky and putting out the fairy lamps one by one. There was
not a sound anywhere. Occasionally the bark of a dog miles away
seemed to bring back to the earth my roving spirit. I started to walk
through the country which at this hour in the queer half-light seemed
to be crawling with phantoms. Every tree when it rustled was stirred
by some goblin, and I saw shadows hurry across the moonlit road. At
this hour just before the dawn the silence became wellnigh unbearable,
for all nature seemed to hold back and the heart-beat of the world
stopped for the fraction of a second.

There was a sense of preparation as though every living thing
drew in its breath so as to salute with a cry of joy the coming of the
dawn. I now understand why the Provençals and the Catalans
composed their beautiful *aubades* or songs of the dawn under the
influence of this magic hour of mystery just before the splendour is
about to appear.

As I saw the light increase in brightness and the green tints blush
to red, I longed for a band of musicians to salute Aurora in song.
Among the Gypsies a red dawning would seem to bode ill if we may
believe the Gypsy poem:

Full moon, high sea,
Great man thou shalt be;
Red dawning, cloudy sky,
Bloody death shalt thou die.

The Gypsies still attach supernatural attributes to the moon in Hungary and Roumania. In the latter country there are a host of superstitions connected with Diana, for it is under her light that fairies and witches carry out their revels and they are implacable to anyone who disturbs them when they are dancing in the moonlight. There is even a phrase for a man who fell ill—'*naiso ie na vilnisko Kolo*'—'he stepped on a fairy ring.'[1] In Roumania also they tell the sad story of the shepherd boy Stanko, who played on a flute by moonlight and became so absorbed in his playing that he did not heed the Ave Maria bell. He saw a *vila* or fairy sitting on a hedge and she was as fair as could be. She never left him but haunted him awake and sleep. There she was—a white, unearthly spectre, gradually drawing him into the shadow of death by her magic. No magician was able to break the spell and the poor youth wasted away. Some days he would be found bound to a tree and he said she had beaten him because he would not follow her. At last they found his body in a ditch where he had been drowned.

These were the thoughts that were surging in my mind as I walked along, and the red dawn when it came acted as a beneficent deity who cleans away the vapours and cobwebs of the mind.

1 Leland, *Gypsy Sorcery*.

FRANCIS STUART
1902–

Born in Queensland, Australia, of Ulster parents, but brought up in
County Meath and the North of Ireland from infancy, Francis Stuart
at eighteen married the daughter of the revolutionary Maud Gonne
and was active on the Republican side in the Civil War, being
captured and imprisoned. He began writing novels in the 1930s,
producing some dozen, as well as several plays, before the outbreak of
World War II. In 1940 he left Ireland to take up a position at the
University of Berlin and spent the remaining war years in Germany,
broadcasting to Ireland between 1942 and 1944 in support of
continuing Irish neutrality. In 1945 he was arrested by French
occupation forces, but no charges were brought. Following his release
in 1946, he lived in Germany, France and Britain before returning to
Ireland in 1958. His reputation rests largely on the novels of this latter
period, many of which draw upon his wartime experiences. This
extract from a postwar diary was first published in 1950.

FROM THE JOURNAL OF AN
APATRIATE

Aug. 10, 1945: At last, with the series of jolts that I was now accustomed
to, the train moved slowly into the Gare de l'Est. There was some
more delay and an air of uncertainty as the repatriates stood around
in the station with their luggage and two French women in uniform
did not seem to know what to do with us. A young man with painted
finger nails strolled up and taking charge of the weary travellers,
herded us into some ancient green buses. Thus we came to the rue
Leonardo da Vinci off the Place Victor Hugo. Here in this narrow,
fashionable street several large houses had been converted into
reception camps by simply filling their rooms, whose ceilings were
richly moulded and whose doors were elaborately panelled, with
rows of the usual double-tiered beds.

AUG. 11: The first proper meal for three years. Meat stewed in red
sauce, and a pile of macaroni. While a little Jewess next to me began

scraping the sauce from her portion of meat and examining it suspiciously, I devoured my helping and swallowed a tin mugful of red wine. Each meal now seems better than the previous one, and it strikes me that there is nothing like eating a piece of meat in just this strong reddish sauce and washing it down with a long draught of Algerian wine.

After lunch wandered through the house until I found a room in which were basins and a mirror. The filth of the basins and the fact that the floor of the room was under water did not bother me. When I felt I was sufficiently clean to appear at the consulate, I went to the Yugoslav who sat at the table in the portico and asked him where this was. He spoke in German, the common language of the camp, lazily turning over the leaves of a telephone directory. With his other hand he felt in the drawer of the table, and, bringing out a packet of Gauloise, tossed them to me. This gesture, more than the wooden buckets of wine, more than the pieces of fat lying under the tables, brought it home to me that the seven lean years were at least temporarily over.

When I arrived at the porter's lodge of the consulate I was told that I was too late, the reception hours ending at four. In my meagre French I tried to express an opinion that, as one of the few nationals of this particular country who had been lost and was returning, as it were, to the fold, as a wanderer miraculously appearing out of the wilderness, I was not subject to these petty regulations, and that I wished to have my arrival announced. But the French porter neither followed nor wished to follow the language of this disreputable looking visitor.

AUG. 12: Walked along the avenue Victor Hugo to the Place d'Étoile. Stood there at the edge of the stream of traffic circling round the great grey rock of the Arc de Triomphe. This was the great world, and watching it, the cars and the people in them, I felt a deep distaste of it. Here at last was civilised life again and I felt a complete stranger in the midst of it.

At ten, again presented myself before the porter of the consulate, and after some time in a waiting-room was called by the consul into his office. The first thing that I noticed, after the consul himself, was his black hat with an elegant curl to its brim, hanging on a coat-stand in a corner. This fascinated me more than anything I had yet seen. Imagined him putting it on and getting into his black car and charging around the great rock of the Arc de Triomphe. If he turns out to be civil it will be no harm to have him as an ally in the great, roaring world through which I must pass. Said he would have my case looked into and I am to return this afternoon.

Later: 'You were not interned, Mr X?' the consul asked me after another long wait in ante-room.

'No. Were you?'

'I shall send a cable about the renewal of your passport but, taking all the circumstances into consideration, I am very doubtful about attaining any positive result.'

'How long will that take?'

'Two or three weeks.'

'And what am I to live on meanwhile?'

'You have a bank-account at home, I suppose?'

'No.'

'There you are. In that case your predicament is a very equivocal one. I would not care to take the responsibility of advising you.'

'A thousand thanks.'

AUG. 14: NOTES ON THE CAMP: This is officially run by an effeminate young sergeant who has a room at the top of the house from which he occasionally emerges in beautifully creased uniform trousers and sandals, and pads ineffectually around the drier parts of the building. Most of his work seems to be done by his German girl who, now that the leaves of the big chestnut tree are beginning to turn, queens it in a white rabbit-skin jacket among the shabbily dressed repatriates. She is known as Marcel's girl and, at first, I had been somewhat in awe of her and her mysterious functions, but as I get to know her I find her kind and helpful. The house is really run however by the big Yugoslav with thick wavy hair and a wrinkled, weather-beaten face. It was to him that I spoke yesterday about the possibility of getting a room in a hotel and continuing to eat at the camp (having the day before received the sum of four thousand francs from the consul). To the Yugoslav there was no difficulty at all in the arrangement. Once I had a room he told me I could have my meals in a house just round the corner in the rue Lerroux. (The bugs that infested the camp made this more advisable.)

'You've only got to say a word to Jules and give him a cigarette now and then.'

The house in the rue Lerroux is larger and more palatial than that in the rue Leonardo da Vinci. In the upper parts various officers of the Centre de Rapatriement have luxurious bureaux and in the basement the repatriates eat and the food for the camps in the houses is prepared. It was there I found the little Belgian, Jules, with a round face, and, behind thick glasses, pale eyes perpetually screwed up against the smoke of the cigarette that was always in his mouth. He was presiding over a group of seven or eight repatriates who had just sat down to lunch.

'From the rue Leonardo da Vinci?' repeated Jules, pretending to look into a grubby note-book. I offered him a cigarette, the one hanging from his lip having burnt down to the last few threads of tobacco, and, when he took it, told him to keep the rest of the packet.

'Yes, that's all right,' Jules said out of the free corner of his mouth. Sat down at the table, and before the meal was over found that the dark little fellow next me was a Russian who had been educated at an English Public School and still spoke with an Eton accent. His name was Darykov and he was a refugee in Paris with his Hungarian wife. He spoke of a residence in Cyprus, of British papers which had been cancelled, of children boarded out at a Salvation Army hostel and of all the other eternal complications that were the habitual lot of us apatriates.

AUG. 17: Went yesterday, on Darykov's advice, with him to the Peruvian Consulate, where, he had been told, it was possible to obtain a visa on our Repatriation cards in return for agreeing to work two years as agricultural labourers in a part of Peru which, he assured me, was extremely salubrious. After two hours in queue, nothing came of this.

'You've got to keep worrying them,' Darykov tells me twice a day. He brings new addresses at which to apply. I put the slips of paper into my pocket with the others and do not try to explain my apparent lethargy. I have never believed in trying to force things. The great events come in their own way and time, for me, anyhow. I change the subject, nodding at the rows of inscriptions on the bell indicator: Salle de bain de M. le Baron, boudoir de Mme. la Baronne. I say, for instance: 'Who the devil was M. le Baron, I wonder?'

'Oh, that! Probably the Baron de Rothschild. But have you been

over to number sixty, avenue Foch? That's where the headquarters of
the Ministry for Rapatriés et Déportés are.'

AUG. 20: No news. It seems the only thing left is for me to return
whence I came. But don't know how to set about this.

AUG. 21: Consulted the Yugoslav.

'Yes, it is possible,' he told me. 'All is possible, if you go about it in
the right manner.'

(By now I have begun to see that my immediate future is to consist
in learning to be an apatriate among apatriates, and any clinging to
the idea of being anything else, a writer, for instance, is a useless
struggle against the flow of destiny.)

He paused to hear what an apatriate who had been waiting in the
background wanted.

'Bugs!' he said. 'I know damn well there are bugs here. But I can't
conjure them away, can I? I'm not a bleeding magician. That's Marcel's
business, why don't you go and complain to him, eh?'

'Where is he?' asked the little Bulgarian professor timidly.

'He's where he always is – in bed with that German whore of his.'
He turned back to me.

'You go and speak to Mademoiselle sous-Lieutenant Courcelles
over in the house where you feed. Tell her to put your name down
for the next transport. Only you've got to get hold of her in the
mornings; she spends her afternoons with American sergeants. But
at least she has picked up some English from them so that you can
talk to her in your own lingo.'

AUG. 21: Found Mademoiselle Courcelles in her office. A tall girl
with a mass of fair, reddish hair and a pretty, freckled face. She spoke
English that she had certainly picked up from no United States
sergeants, but had probably learnt in some expensive academy for
girls.

'You're no sooner free than half of you are wanting to go back,' she
said. 'I must go and have a talk with the Americans about you. Come
around again early next week, will you, please? I shall put you on the
list.'

Went away with a certain faith in the young sous-lieutenant and
her list. That such a list existed, that was already something.

AUG. 25: 'I've had an awful lot of trouble over you,' the
Mademoiselle sous-Lieutenant Courcelles told me. 'I don't mean
only over you, but over all who want to go back.'

'The thing is, can we go back?'

'I think so. I've got you on to a transport, only you're German, you understand; you can speak some German, can't you, if anyone asks? You had better be in the rue Leonardo da Vinci tomorrow evening with your luggage at six o'clock.'

'I think there is a possibility of getting to Germany in a few days,' I told Darykov later. I was proud of being on the list, any list was better than none, better than being completely disowned.

'But it's Austria you want to go to, old fellow, isn't it?'

AUG. 26: Yesterday evening, as promised, a bus drove up to the camp and an American lieutenant got out and was presented by Mademoiselle Courcelles with the list. When our little group had climbed in he read out our names and we were driven to the Gare de l'Est. At the station the lieutenant shepherded us to a corner near the barrier, and told us to wait until he returned.

'They will send me to Hungary,' a Hungarian boy said to me anxiously. 'That's what will happen to me. They will send me home.'

'You don't want to go?'

He shook his head.

'Why do you go then? You're not a prisoner?'

Bewilderment on the part of the boy. 'I don't know, but I cannot go back,' he repeated.

'Well, don't go back. There is the exit to the street over there. Take your rucksack and walk through it.'

The boy hesitated a moment and then took up his luggage and walked quickly away through the crowd.

'Where's he gone?' Dr Bogusky, who was in charge of the party, asked.

'He's gone away.'

The Latvian took the list out of his pocket and I looked at it over his shoulder. The sheet was headed: 'To the United States officer in charge, Châlons-sur-Marne' and was a request that those on it should be repatriated to the places indicated against their names. Against my name was that of a town I could not decipher.

AUG. 27: Arrival in Châlons-sur-Marne. Started out with Dr Bogusky to look for the American officer.

Rain was falling as we made our way across a wooden bridge over the river and along a muddy road into the town. Each time we were splashed by the American lorries and jeeps jolting by over the filled-up bomb-craters, Dr Bogusky stopped and carefully wiped the drops from the ends of his grey trousers.

Arrived at a house in a dreary square from whose porch the French and American flags hung limply in the rain. Entered a room whose door was labelled 'Colonel so-and-so' in which, of course, there was no colonel but a couple of women, smoking cigarettes and occasionally moving from typewriter to telephone with the high-heeled French walk.

Again the showing of papers, the flow of French and the sinking of heart.

Watched closely the Latvian as he folded up his papers again, but his thin face was impassive and from the conversation itself I had gathered that nothing could be done until the colonel came in the afternoon. The rain had increased to a downpour and we waited in the hall for it to abate while the doctor told me that the French women advised us to apply to the Displaced Persons' Camp in another part of the town.

Took advantage of the delay to go to the lavatory and clean myself up, not having had an opportunity to wash since Paris. There was a big square of yellow soap on the wash-basin that gave off a foamy lather, a sign of the presence of the Americans more impressive than the limp stars-and-stripes drooping from its staff over the porch. Wrapped the big hunk of soap in a piece of paper and put it in my pocket.

At the office of the Displaced Persons' Camp we were received by yet another girl in uniform, who after a short talk with Bogusky pushed a large book towards him, in which she asked him to sign our names.

'She says we must stay here two or three days while a *laissez-passer* over the frontier is being made out for us,' the doctor said.

SEPT. 4: After a fruitless week of waiting, escaped from the camp in Châlons-sur-Marne and continued the journey with the remnants of group, to Strasbourg.

Here we were directed to the Deuxième Bureau, the office of the French military intelligence, and, while the others waited in the background, Doctor Bogusky and myself went up to the table of an elderly little colonel.

The doctor began his explanation and unfolded his two papers which the officer read. He turned to his adjutant at another table and referred the case to him.

'It is a matter for the Prefect of Police,' said the adjutant. 'Ring up the Prefect and tell him we are sending Doctor Bogusky over to him. It's a special case.' The colonel glanced again at the doctor's papers. 'Doctor Bogusky was of great service, while in charge of the refugee camp at Lagenau, to the French Republic.'

I listened with astonishment. With such a document in his pocket I no longer wondered at the doctor's air of cool superiority. My heart sank as I made my own request to the shiny, pink-cheeked face: I had been of no service to anything and had nothing to show but an invalid passport. The colonel waved me to the table of the adjutant who was ringing up the Police Prefecture.

SEPT. 5: The doctor and I were interviewed by the Prefect, the others sent to another room. Was told my application would be considered and to return in three days. What the doctor was told did not discover, the Latvian preserving a superior silence, on account, no doubt, of his excellent paper. The others had disappeared into one of the many offices of the big building.

SEPT. 7: On going back to the Prefecture no trace of application could be found and was told to wait another couple of days. My French not being good enough to explain prolonged stay in the *rapatriement* hut impossible, was interviewed by a young woman who spoke English, specially called in. She suggested I should come back with her to the Prefecture, where she herself worked, and she would try to trace application.

SEPT. 9: No trace of application. No possibility of staying on in Strasbourg. Return to Paris in company of an apatriate of Polish origin.

SEPT. 10: Return of the raven to the Ark. No branch, nothing. The sous-lieutenant listened sympathetically.

'Come round from time to time. The Americans have a way of doing things when least expected.'

Melkowsky asked that his name should be added to the new list.

'You want to go to Poland?'

'To Germany, my dear lady.'

'En route for Poland?'

'Certainly.'

SEPT. 20: Yesterday a new transport was suddenly reported to be leaving. This time under more propitious auspices. The young sergeant was wandering around in his sandals and beautifully pressed trousers with his German girl, in her white rabbit-skin jacket, hanging on his arm. She told me that this time she was going too.

'And Marcel is coming with us as far as the frontier to see that there is no trouble.'

At supper Melkowsky shuffled in late and brought some rumour that the transport had been postponed.

'Nonsense, I was talking to Mademoiselle Courcelles an hour ago,' an apatriate next to him said. There was a general nervousness among those going on the transport.

'All right, my dear lady, we shall see,' muttered Melkowsky, bent over his plate of beans. He alone seemed indifferent as to whether it went or not.

Disliked Melkowsky at that moment with his jacket smeared with soap and his whole indifferent air, noisily eating his beans and scowling to himself. But a few moments later, Mademoiselle Courcelles appeared with the typed list in her hand.

SEPT. 21: At Metz we waited on the platform while Marcel went off to enquire about some goods trains to which we were to be attached. Saw a fatal similarity with the arrival at Strasbourg. After a long delay Marcel came back and began talking to his girl in a low voice while a little group of apatriates gathered anxiously around him. Girl's raised voice protesting angrily that she refused to go to any camp.

'Only for tonight,' Marcel said, 'you are going on tomorrow morning.'

'I know that tomorrow morning of yours. I'm not going to leave this platform.'

Marcel looked round helplessly, and began to explain to the others that he had been able to find out nothing about any eastbound goods train. In the end a despondent move was made towards the station exit. Marcel, with his girl dragging reluctantly on his arm, followed in the rear. Outside the station the luggage was again piled up and the little crowd stood forlornly around. A lorry backed up to the pavement and its tail-board was let down. We were driven through the town and beyond it across a bridge over the Moselle. Beside the river rose a gaunt barracks built in the shape of a square, and through a gate-way in this the lorry drove and the heavy doors were shut behind it. When the little group of apatriates climbed out we found ourselves in an arch-way under one of the blocks separated from the big inner square by a barbed wire gate through which a ragged-looking crowd was watching our arrival. The sight of the barbed wire and the look of those beyond it, confirmed our forebodings. Flight of Marcel and girl, leaving us to our fate.

OCT. 22: Yesterday, after three weeks in the desolate barracks, we were herded to a platform at the goods station where a long line of cattle trucks were awaiting us. Settled myself in the corner of a waggon. It was cold in the night and in the morning we had only reached Strasbourg, where, in a network of lines somewhere outside the station, there was another interminable delay. A girl came along from truck to truck distributing American Red Cross parcels. Snow had fallen in the night and covered the expanse of tracks. The Yugoslavs climbed down and lit fires beside the train, boiling coffee and heating the various tins from the American packets.

Jumped down and stood between the tracks by a big fire. The American captain in charge of the transport, who had been drunk the night before, emerged from the passenger carriage at the end of the train in which he had his quarters. He agreed that the fact that in over twelve hours we had only travelled from Metz to Strasbourg was very discouraging. He was a small, thick-set American with humorous eyes and he stood there in his military overcoat shivering and sending members of his little staff to enquire what was happening.

Climbed back into waggon where Melkowsky was finishing up his share of the rations that were meant to last the whole day. Sat on the straw and ate a tin of sardines and then the contents of a tin of jam for which I had no more biscuits left to go with.

'Looks like being an early winter,' says Melkowsky.

'Early or late, damn all odds it makes to us. As we do not know where we shall spend it, with whom, or under what conditions, there is no point in worrying over the weather. Worry can only begin when there is some minimum of plan or expectation.'

THEOBALD WOLFE TONE
1763–1798

'Having been a month in this country and made many enquiries,'
Tone wrote from Westchester, Pennsylvania, to his friend Thomas
Russell, 'I am a little more competent to speak my opinion . . . . The
result of my observation is a most unqualified dislike of the people.'
Wolfe Tone, founder with Russell and Napper Tandy of the United
Irishmen in 1791, had sailed from Belfast in May 1795 and remained in
America until the following February when he left for France to
persuade the Directory to invade Ireland in the cause of independence.
The first expedition in 1796 proved abortive, but when news reached
France of the 1798 Rising, Tone succeeded in sailing with a small force
of 3,000 to Lough Swilly, where the French were engaged by a
superior British squadron, and he was captured. He was taken to
Dublin and court-martialled, but though he stood trial in his French
uniform, his appeal for a soldier's death by firing squad was refused
and he took his own life on the morning fixed for his execution. His
aim – 'to substitute the common name of Irishman in place of the
denominations of Protestant, Catholic and Dissenter' – remains to be
achieved. Tone's autobiography, from which this account of his
American visit is taken, was published in the USA in 1826.

OFF TO PHILADELPHIA

We were now at sea and at leisure to examine our situation. I had
hired a state-room, which was about eight feet by six, in which we
had fitted up three berths; my wife and our youngest little boy
occupied one, my sister and my little girl the second, and our eldest
boy and myself the third. It was at first grievously inconvenient, but
necessity and custom by degrees reconciled us to our situation; our
greatest suffering was want of good water, under which we laboured

the whole passage and which we found it impossible to replace by wine, porter, or spirits, of which we had abundance. The captain was tolerably civil, the vessel was stout, and we had good weather almost the whole of our voyage. But we were 300 passengers on board of a ship of 230 tons, and, of course, crowded to a degree not to be conceived by those who have not been on board a passenger ship. The slaves who are carried from the coast of Africa have much more room allowed them than the miserable emigrants who pass from Ireland to America; for the avarice of the captains in that trade is such that they think they never can load their vessels sufficiently, and they trouble their heads in general no more about the accommodation and stowage of their passengers than of any other lumber aboard. I laboured, and with some success, to introduce something like a police, and a certain degree, though a very imperfect one, of cleanliness among them. Certainly the air of the sea must be wonderfully wholesome, for if the same number of wretches of us had been shut up in the same space ashore with so much inconvenience of every kind about us, two-thirds of us would have died in the time of our voyage. As it was, in spite of everything, we were tolerably healthy; we lost but one passenger, a woman; we had some sick aboard, and the friendship of James Macdonnell of Belfast having supplied me with a small medicine chest and written directions, I took on myself the office of physician. I prescribed and administered accordingly, and I had the satisfaction to land all my patients safe and sound. As we distributed liberally the surplus of our sea stores, of which we had great abundance, and especially as we gave from time to time wine and porter to the sick and aged, we soon became very popular aboard, and I am sure there was no sacrifice to our ease or convenience in the power of our poor fellow-passengers to make that we might not have commanded. Thirty days of our voyage had now passed over without any event save the ordinary ones of seeing now a shoal of porpoises, now a shark, now a set of dolphins – the peacocks of the sea – playing about, and once or twice a whale. We had, indeed, been brought to, when about a week at sea, by the *William Pitt*, Indiaman, which was returning to Europe with about twenty other ships under convoy of four or five men-of-war; but on examining our papers, they suffered us to proceed. At length, about the 20th July, some time after we had cleared the banks of Newfoundland, we were stopped by three British frigates – the *Thetis*, Capt. Lord Cochrane; the *Hussar*,

Captain Rose; and the *Esperance*, Capt. Wood – who boarded us, and
after treating us with the greatest insolence, both officers and sailors,
they pressed every one of our hands save one, and near fifty of my
unfortunate fellow-passengers, who were most of them flying to
America to avoid the tyranny of a bad government at home, and who
thus most unexpectedly fell under the severest tyranny – one of them
at least – which exists. As I was in a jacket and trousers one of the
lieutenants ordered me into the boat as a fit man to serve the king,
and it was only the screams of my wife and sister which induced him
to desist. It would have been a pretty termination of my adventures if
I had been pressed and sent on board a man-of-war. The insolence of
these tyrants, as well to myself as to my poor fellow-passengers in
whose fate a fellowship in misfortune had interested me, I have not
since forgotten and I never will. At length, after detaining us two
days, during which they rummaged us at least twenty times, they
suffered us to proceed.

On the 30th July we made Cape Henlopen; the 31st we ran up the
Delaware; and the 1st of August we landed safe at Wilmington, not
one of us, providentially, having been for an hour indisposed on the
passage nor even sea-sick. Those only who have had their wives,
their children, and all in short that is dear to them, floating for seven
or eight weeks at the mercy of the winds and waves, can conceive the
transport I felt at seeing my wife and our darling babies ashore once
again in health and in safety. We set up at the principal tavern, kept
by an Irishman, one Captain O'Byrne O'Flynn (I think), for all the
taverns in America are kept by majors and captains either of militia
or continentals, and in a few days we had entirely recruited our
strength and spirits and totally forgotten the fatigues of the voyage.

During our stay in Wilmington we formed an acquaintance which
was of some service and a great deal of pleasure to us with a General
Humpton, an old continental officer. He was an Englishman born in
Yorkshire and had been a major in the 25th regiment, but, on the
breaking out of the American War, he resigned his commission and
offered his services to Congress, who immediately gave him a
regiment, from which he rose by degrees to his present rank. He was
a beautiful, hale, stout, old man of near seventy, perfectly the soldier
and the gentleman, and he took a great liking to us, as we did to him
on our part. On our removal to Philadelphia he found us a lodging
with one of his acquaintance, and rendered all the little services and

attentions that our situation as strangers required, which indeed he continued without remission during the whole of my stay in America and I doubt not equally since my departure. I have a sincere and grateful sense of the kindness of this worthy veteran.

Immediately on my arrival in Philadelphia, which was about 7th or 8th August, I found out my old friend and brother exile, Dr Reynolds, who seemed, to my very great satisfaction, very comfortably settled. From him I learned that Hamilton Rowan had arrived about six weeks before me from France, and that same evening we all three met. It was a singular *rencontre* and our several escapes from an ignominious death seemed little short of a miracle. We communicated respectively our several adventures since our last interview, which took place in the jail of Newgate in Dublin fourteen months before. In Reynolds' adventures there was nothing very extraordinary. Rowan had been seized and thrown into prison immediately on his landing near Brest, from whence he was rescued by the interference of a young man named Sullivan, an Irishman in the service of the Republic, and sent on to Paris to the Committee of Public Safety by Prieur de la Marne, the Deputy on Mission. On his arrival he was seized with a most dangerous fever, from which he narrowly escaped with his life; when he recovered, as well as during his illness, he was maintained by the French Government; he gave in some memorials on the state of Ireland and began, from the reception he met with, to conceive some hopes of success, but immediately after came, on the famous 9th Thermidor, the downfall of Robespierre, and the dissolution of the Committee of Public Safety. The total change which this produced in the politics of France, and the attention of every man being occupied by his own immediate personal safety, were the cause that Rowan and his plans were forgotten in the confusion. After remaining, therefore, several months, and seeing no likelihood of bringing matters to any favourable issue, he yielded to the solicitude of his family and friends and embarked at Havre for New York, where he arrived about the middle of June 1795 after a tedious passage of eleven weeks.

It is unnecessary to detail again my adventures, which I related to them at full length, as well as everything relating to the state of politics in Ireland, about which it may well be supposed their curiosity and anxiety were extreme. I then proceeded to tell them my designs, and that I intended waiting the next day on the French Minister with such credentials as I had brought with me, which were the two votes of thanks of the Catholics and my certificate of admission into the Belfast Volunteers engrossed on vellum and signed by the Chairman and Secretaries; and I added that I would refer to them both for my credibility in case the Minister had any doubts. Rowan offered to come with me and introduce me to the Minister, Citizen Adet, whom he had known in Paris; but I observed to him that, as there were English agents without number in Philadelphia, he was most probably watched, and consequently his being seen to go with me to Adet might materially prejudice his interest in Ireland. I therefore declined his offer, but I requested of him a letter of introduction, which he gave me accordingly, and the next day I waited on the Minister, who received me very politely. He spoke English very imperfectly and I French a great deal worse; however we made a shift to understand one another; he read my certificates and Rowan's letter, and he begged me to throw on paper in the form of a memorial all I had to communicate on the subject of Ireland. This I accordingly did in the course of two or three days, though with great difficulty on account of the burning heat of the climate, so different from what I had been used to, the thermometer varying between 90 and 97. At length, however, I finished my memorial, such as it was, and brought it to Adet, and I offered him at the same time, if he thought it would forward the business, to embark in the first vessel which sailed for France; but the Minister for some reason seemed not much to desire this, and he eluded my offer by reminding me of the great risk I ran, as the British stopped and carried into their ports indiscriminately all American vessels bound for France; he assured me, however, I might rely on my memorial being transmitted to the French Government and backed with his strongest recommendations; and he also promised to write particularly to procure the enlargement of my brother Matthew, who was in prison at Guise – all of which I have since found he faithfully performed.

I had now discharged my conscience as to my duty to my country; and it was with the sincerest and deepest contristation of mind that I saw this, my last effort, likely to be of so little effect. It was barely possible, but I did not much expect, that the French Government might take notice of my memorial and, if they did not, there was an end of all my hopes. I now began to endeavour to bend my mind to my situation, but to no purpose. I moved my family, first to

Westchester and then to Downingstown, both in the State of Pennsylvania, about thirty miles from Philadelphia, and I began to look about for a small plantation such as might suit the shattered state of my finances, on which the enormous expense of living in Philadelphia – three times as dear as at Paris or even London – was beginning to make a sensible inroad. While they remained there in the neighbourhood of our friend General Humpton, whose kindness and attention continued unabated, I made diverse excursions on foot and in the state wagons in quest of a farm.

The situation of Princeton in New Jersey struck me for a variety of reasons, and I determined, if possible, to settle in that neighbourhood. I accordingly agreed with a Dutch farmer for a plantation of one hundred acres, with a small wooden house, which would have suited me well enough, for which I was to pay £750 of that currency; but the fellow was too covetous, and, after all was, I thought, finished, he retracted and wanted to screw more out of me, on which I broke off the treaty in a rage, and he began to repent, but I was obstinate. At length I agreed with a Captain Leonard for a plantation of 180 acres, beautifully situated within two miles of Princeton and half of it under timber. I was to pay £1,180 currency, and I believe it was worth the money. I moved in consequence my family to Princeton, where I hired a small house for the winter, which I furnished frugally but decently. I fitted up my study and began to think my lot was cast to be an American farmer.

For myself, I believe I could have borne it, and, for my wife, it was sufficient for her that I was with her; her incomparable firmness of mind and never-failing cheerfulness and equanimity of temper sustaining her and me also, whose happiness depended solely on hers under every difficulty; but when we looked on our little children, we felt, both of us, our courage fail. Our little boys we could hardly bear to think of rearing in the boorish ignorance of the peasants about us, and to what purpose give them an education which could only tend to discontent them with the state wherein they were thrown and wherein learning and talents would be useless? But especially our little girl, now eight or nine years old, was our principal uneasiness; how could we bear to see her the wife of a clown without delicacy or refinement, incapable to feel or to estimate the value of a mind which even already developed the strongest marks of sensibility and tenderness? For my own part, the idea tormented me beyond enduring, and I am sure no unfortunate lover in the paroxysms of jealousy ever looked forward with greater horror to the union of his mistress with a rival than I did to the possibility of seeing my darling child sacrificed to one of the boors by whom we were surrounded. I could better bear to see her dead, for with regard to the delicacy and purity of women I entertain notions of perhaps extravagant refinement.

But, to return, in this gloomy frame of mind I continued in for some time, waiting for the lawyer who was employed to draw the deeds, and expecting next spring to remove to my purchase and to begin farming at last, when one day I was roused from my lethargy by the receipt of letters from Keogh, Russell, and the two Simms's, wherein, after professions of the warmest and sincerest regard, they proceeded to acquaint me that the state of the public mind in Ireland was advancing to republicanism faster than even I could believe; and they pressed me in the strongest manner to fulfil the engagement I had made with them at my departure, and to move heaven and earth to force my way to the French Government in order to supplicate their assistance. Wm. Simms, at the end of a most friendly and affectionate letter, desired me to draw upon him for £200 sterling and that my bill should be punctually paid, an offer at the liberality of which, well as I knew the man, I confess I was surprised. I immediately handed the letters to my wife and sister and desired their opinion, which I foresaw would be that I should immediately, if possible, set out for France. My wife especially, whose courage and whose zeal for my honour and interests were not in the least abated by all her past sufferings, supplicated me to let no consideration of her or our children stand for a moment in the way of my engagements to our friends and my duty to my country; adding that she would answer for our family during my absence, and that the same Providence which had so often, as it were miraculously, preserved us would, she was confident, not desert us now. My sister joined her in those entreaties, and it may well be supposed I required no great supplication to induce me to make one more attempt in a cause to which I had been so long devoted. I set off accordingly the next morning (it being this time about the end of November) for Philadelphia, and went immediately on my arrival to Adet, to whom I showed the letters I had just received, and I referred him to Rowan, who was then in town, for the character of the writers. I had the satisfaction, contrary to my expectations, to find Adet as willing to forward and assist my design now as he seemed, to me at least, lukewarm when I saw him before in August. He told me immediately that he would give me letters to the French Government recommending me in the strongest manner, and also money to bear my expenses if necessary. I thanked him most sincerely for the letters, but I declined accepting any pecuniary assistance. Having thus far surmounted my difficulties, I wrote for my brother Arthur, who was at Princeton, to come to me immediately, and I fitted him out with all expedition for sea. Having entrusted him with my determination of sailing for France in the first vessel, I ordered him to communicate this immediately on his arrival in Ireland to Neilson, Simms, and Russell in Belfast, and to Keogh and McCormick only in Dublin. To everyone else, including especially my father and mother, I desired him to say that I had purchased and was settled upon my farm near Princeton. Having fully instructed him, I put him on board the *Susanna*, Capt. Baird, bound for Belfast and, on the 10th of December 1795, he sailed from Philadelphia, and I presume he arrived safe, but as yet I have had no opportunity of hearing of him. Having despatched him, I settled all my affairs as speedily as possible. I drew on Simms for £200, agreeable to his letter, £150 sterling of which I devoted to my voyage; my friend Reynolds procured me *louis d'or* at the bank for £100 sterling worth of silver. I converted the remainder of my little property into bank stock, and, having signed a general power of attorney to my wife, I waited finally on Adet, who gave me a letter in cypher directed to the Comité de Salut Public, the only credential which I intended to bring with me to France. I spent one day in Philadelphia with Reynolds, Rowan, and my old friend and fellow sufferer James Napper Tandy, who, after a long concealment and many adventures, was recently arrived from Hamburg, and at length on the 13th December, at night, I arrived at Princeton, whither Rowan accompanied me, bringing with me a few presents for my wife, sister, and our dear little babies. That night we supped together in high spirits, and Rowan retiring immediately after, my wife, sister and I sat together till very late engaged in that kind of animated and enthusiastic conversation which our characters and the nature of the enterprise I was embarked in may be supposed to give rise to. The courage and firmness of the women supported me, and them too, beyond my expectations; we had neither tears nor lamentations, but, on the contrary, the most ardent hope and the most steady resolution. At length, at four the next morning, I embraced them both for the last time, and we parted with a steadiness which astonished me. On the 16th December I arrived in New York, and took my passage on board the ship *Jersey*, Capt. George Barons. I remained in New York for ten days, during which time I wrote continually to my family, and a day or two before my departure I received a letter from my wife informing me that she was with child, a circumstance which she had concealed so far, I am sure, lest it might have had some influence on my determination. On the 1st January 1796 I sailed from Sandy Hook with nine fellow passengers, all French, bound for Havre de Grace. Our voyage lasted exactly one month, during the most part of which we had heavy blowing weather; five times we had such gales of wind as obliged us to lie under a close-reefed mizen stay-sail; however, our ship was stout. We had plenty of provisions, wine, brandy, and, especially, what I thought more of, remembering my last voyage, excellent water, so that I had no reason to complain of my passage. We did not meet a single vessel of force, either French or English; we passed three or four Americans, bound mostly, like ourselves, to France. On the 27th we were in soundings at 85 fathoms; on the 28th we made the Lizard and, at length, on the 1st of February, we landed in safety at Havre de Grace, having met with not the smallest accident during our voyage. My adventures from this date are fully detailed in the Diary which I have kept regularly since my arrival in France.

JOHN TYNDALL
1820–1893

Educated at the local National School at Leighlinbridge, County
Carlow, John Tyndall worked first for the Ordnance Survey of Ireland,
was a railway engineer from 1844 to 1847, gained his doctorate at
Marburg, Germany, in 1850, was elected a Fellow of the Royal Society
in 1852 and became in the following year Professor of Natural
Philosophy at the Royal Institution in London. A close friend of
Michael Faraday, whose biography he wrote and whom he succeeded
as superintendent of the Royal Institution, Tyndall's own scientific
contribution lay chiefly in his investigations into the properties of
radiant heat. He first visited the Swiss Alps in 1849 and later wrote: 'I
have returned to them every year and found among them refuge and
recovery from the work and the worry . . . of London.' A skilled
mountaineer, he made the first ascent of the Weisshorn in 1861 and
reached a then record altitude on the unconquered Matterhorn of
13,000 feet. This description of a climb in 1858 is from his book *The
Glaciers of the Alps* (1860). Pic Tyndall on the Matterhorn is named after
him, as is Mount Tyndall in New Zealand and a peak in California.

ASCENT OF THE
FINSTERAARHORN

Since my arrival at the hotel on the 30th of July I had once or twice
spoken about ascending the Finsteraarhorn, and on the 2nd of August
my host advised me to avail myself of the promising weather. A
guide, named Bennen, was attached to the hotel, a remarkable-
looking man, between 30 and 40 years old, of middle stature, but
very strongly built. His countenance was frank and firm, while a
light of good-nature at times twinkled in his eye. Altogether the man
gave me the impression of physical strength, combined with decision
of character. The proprietor had spoken to me many times of the

strength and courage of this man, winding up his praises of him by the assurance that if I were killed in Bennen's company there would be two lives lost, for that the guide would assuredly sacrifice himself in the effort to save his *Herr*.

He was called, and I asked him whether he would accompany me alone to the top of the Finsteraarhorn. To this he at first objected, urging the possibility of his having to render me assistance, and the great amount of labour which this might entail upon him; but this was overruled by my engaging to follow where he led, without asking him to render me any help whatever. He then agreed to make the trial, stipulating, however, that he should not have much to carry to the cave of the Faulberg, where we were to spend the night. To this I cordially agreed, and sent on blankets, provisions, wood, and hay, by two porters.

My desire, in part, was to make a series of observations at the summit of the mountain, while a similar series was made by Professor Ramsay in the valley of the Rhone, near Viesch, with a view to ascertaining the permeability of the lower strata of the atmosphere to the radiant heat of the sun. During the forenoon of the 2nd I occupied myself with my instruments, and made the proper arrangements with Ramsay. I tested a mountain-thermometer which Mr Casella had kindly lent me, and found the boiling point of water on the dining-room table of the hotel to be 199.29° Fahrenheit. At about three o'clock in the afternoon we quitted the hotel, and proceeded leisurely with our two guides up the slope of the Æggischhorn. We once caught a sight of the topmost pinnacle of the Finsteraarhorn; beside it was the Rothhorn, and near this again the Oberaarhorn, with the Viescher glacier streaming from its shoulders. On the opposite side we could see, over an oblique buttress of the mountain on which we stood, the snowy summit of the Weisshorn; to the left of this was the ever grim and lonely Matterhorn; and farther to the left, with its numerous snow-cones, each with its attendant shadow, rose the Mighty Mischabel. We descended, and crossed the stream which flows from the Märjelen See, into which a large mass of the glacier had recently fallen, and was now afloat as an iceberg. We passed along the margin of the lake, and at the junction of water and ice I bade Ramsay goodbye. At the commencement of our journey upon the ice, whenever we crossed a crevasse, I noticed Bennen watching me; his vigilance, however, soon diminished, whence I gathered that he finally concluded that I was able to take care of myself. Clouds hovered in the atmosphere throughout the whole time of our ascent; one smoky-looking mass marred the glory of the sunset, but at some distance was another which exhibited colours almost as rich and varied as those of the solar spectrum. I took the glorious banner thus unfurled as a sign of hope, to check the despondency which its gloomy neighbour was calculated to produce.

Two hours' walking brought us near our place of rest; the porters had already reached it, and were now returning. We deviated to the right, and, having crossed some ice-ravines, reached the lateral moraine of the glacier, and picked our way between it and the adjacent mountain-wall. We then reached a kind of amphitheatre, crossed it, and climbing the opposite slope, came to a triple grotto formed by clefts in the mountain. In one of these a pine-fire was soon blazing briskly, and casting its red light upon the surrounding objects, though but half dispelling the gloom from the deeper portions of the cell. I left the grotto, and climbed the rocks above it to look at the heavens. The sun had quitted our firmament, but still tinted the clouds with red and purple; while one peak of snow in particular glowed like fire, so vivid was its illumination. During our journey upwards the Jungfrau never once showed her head, but, as if in ill temper, had wrapped her vapoury veil around her. She now looked more good humoured, but still she did not quite remove her hood; though all the other summits, without a trace of cloud to mask their beautiful forms, pointed heavenward. The calmness was perfect; no sound of living creature, no whisper of a breeze, no gurgle of water, no rustle of débris, to break the deep and solemn silence. Surely, if beauty be an object of worship, those glorious mountains, with rounded shoulders of the purest white – snow-crested and star-gemmed – were well calculated to excite sentiments of adoration.

I returned to the grotto, where supper was prepared and waiting for me. The boiling point of water, at the level of the 'kitchen' floor, I found to be 196° Fahr. Nothing could be more picturesque than the aspect of the cave before we went to rest. The fire was gleaming ruddily. I sat upon a stone bench beside it, while Bennen was in front with the red light glimmering fitfully over him. My boiling-water apparatus, which had just been used, was in the foreground; and telescopes, opera-glasses, haversacks, wine-keg, bottles, and mattocks, lay confusedly around. The heavens continued to grow clearer, the thin clouds, which had partially-overspread the sky, melting gradually away. The grotto was comfortable; the hay sufficient materially to modify the hardness of the rock, and my position at least sheltered and warm. One possibility remained that might prevent me from sleeping – the snoring of my companion; he assured me, however, that he did not snore, and we lay down side by side. The good fellow took care that I should not be chilled; he gave me the best place, by far the best part of the clothes, and may have suffered himself in consequence; but, happily for him, he was soon oblivious of this. Physiologists, I believe, have discovered that it is chiefly during sleep that the muscles are repaired; and ere long the sound I dreaded announced to me at once the repair of Bennen's muscles and the doom of my own. The hollow cave resounded to the deep-drawn snore. I once or twice stirred the sleeper, breaking thereby the continuity of the phenomenon; but it instantly pieced itself together again, and went on as before. I had not the heart to wake him, for I knew that upon him would devolve the chief labour of the coming day. At half-past one he rose and prepared coffee, and at two o'clock I was engaged upon the beverage. We afterwards packed up our provisions and instruments. Bennen bore the former, I the latter, and at three o'clock we set out.

We first descended a steep slope to the glacier, along which we walked for a time. A spur of the Faulberg jutted out between us and the ice-laden valley through which we must pass; this we crossed in order to shorten our way and to avoid crevasses. Loose shingle and boulders overlaid the mountain; and here and there walls of rock opposed our progress, and rendered the route far from agreeable. We then descended to the Grünhorn tributary, which joins the trunk glacier at nearly a right angle, being terminated by a saddle which stretches across from mountain to mountain, with a curvature as graceful and as perfect as if drawn by the instrument of a mathematician. The unclouded moon was shining, and the Jungfrau was before us so pure and beautiful, that the thought of visiting the 'Maiden' without further preparation occurred to me. I turned to Bennen, and said, 'Shall we try the Jungfrau?' I think he liked the idea well enough, though he continuously avoided incurring any responsibility. 'If you desire it, I am ready,' was his reply. He had never made the ascent, and nobody knew anything of the state of the snow this year; but Lauener had examined it through a telescope on the previous day, and pronounced it dangerous. In every ascent of the mountain hitherto made, ladders had been found indispensable, but we had none. I questioned Bennen as to what he thought of the probabilities, and tried to extract some direct encouragement from him; but he said that the decision rested altogether with myself, and it was his business to endeavour to carry out that decision. 'We will attempt it, then,' I said, and for some time we actually walked toward the Jungfrau. A grey cloud drew itself across her summit, and clung there. I asked myself why I deviated from my original intention? The Finsteraarhorn was higher, and therefore better suited for the contemplated observations. I could in no wise justify the change, and finally expressed my scruples. A moment's further conversation caused us to 'right about,' and front the saddle of the Grünhorn.

The dawn advanced. The eastern sky became illuminated and warm, and high in the air across the ridge in front of us stretched a tongue of cloud like a red flame, and equally fervid in its hue. Looking across the trunk glacier, a valley which is terminated by the Lötsch saddle was seen in a straight line with our route, and I often turned to look along this magnificent corridor. The mightiest mountains in the Oberland form its sides; still, the impression which it makes is not that of vastness or sublimity, but of loveliness not to be described. The sun had not yet smitten the snows of the bounding mountains, but the saddle carved out a segment of the heavens which formed a background of unspeakable beauty. Over the rim of the saddle the sky was deep orange, passing upwards through amber, yellow, and vague ethereal green to the ordinary firmamental blue. Right above the snow-curve purple clouds hung perfectly motionless, giving depth to the spaces between them. There was something saintly in the scene. Anything more exquisite I had never beheld.

We marched upwards over the smooth crisp snow to the crest of the saddle, and here I turned to take a last look along that grand corridor, and at that wonderful 'daffodil sky.' The sun's rays had already smitten the snows of the Aletschorn; the radiance seemed to infuse a principle of life and activity into the mountains and glaciers, but still that holy light shone forth, and those motionless clouds floated beyond, reminding one of that eastern religion whose essence is the repression of all action and the substitution for it of immortal calm. The Finsteraarhorn now fronted us; but clouds turbaned the head of the giant, and hid it from our view. The wind, however, being north, inspired us with a strong hope that they would melt as the day advanced. I have hardly seen a finer ice-field than that which now lay before us. Considering the *névé* which supplies it, it appeared to me that the Viescher glacier ought to discharge as much ice as the Aletsch; but there is an error due to the extent of the *névé* which is here at once visible: since a glance at the map of this portion of the Oberland shows at once the great superiority of the mountain treasury from which the Aletsch glacier draws support. Still, the ice-field before us was a most noble one. The surrounding mountains were of imposing magnitude, and loaded to their summits with snow. Down the sides of some of them the half-consolidated mass fell in a state of wild fracture and confusion. In some cases the riven masses were twisted and overturned, the ledges bent, and the detached blocks piled one upon another in heaps; while in other cases the smooth white mass descended from crown to base without a wrinkle. The valley now below us was gorged by the frozen material thus incessantly poured into it. We crossed it, and reached the base of the Finsteraarhorn, ascended the mountain a little way, and at six o'clock paused to lighten our burdens and to refresh ourselves.

The north wind had freshened, we were in the shade, and the cold was very keen. Placing a bottle of tea and a small quantity of provisions in the knapsack, and a few figs and dried prunes in our pockets, we commenced the ascent. The Finsteraarhorn sends down a number of cliffy buttresses, separated from each other by wide couloirs filled with ice and snow. We ascended one of these buttresses for a time, treading cautiously among the spiky rocks; afterwards we went along the snow at the edge of the spine, and then fairly parted company with the rock, abandoning ourselves to the *névé* of the couloir. The latter was steep, and the snow was so firm that steps had to be cut in it. Once I paused upon a little ledge, which gave me a slight footing, and took the inclination. The slope formed an angle of 45° with the horizon; and across it, at a little distance below me, a gloomy fissure opened its jaws. The sun now cleared the summits which had before cut off his rays, and burst upon us with great power, compelling us to resort to our veils and dark spectacles. Two years before, Bennen had been nearly blinded by inflammation brought on by the glare from the snow, and he now took unusual care in protecting his eyes. The rocks looking more practicable, we again made towards them, and clambered among them till a vertical precipice, which proved impossible of ascent, fronted us. Bennen scanned the obstacle closely as we slowly approached it, and finally descended to the snow, which wound at a steep angle round its base: on this the footing appeared to me to be singularly insecure, but I marched without hesitation or anxiety in the footsteps of my guide.

We ascended the rocks once more, continued along them for some time, and then deviated to the couloir on our left. This snow-slope is much dislocated at its lower portion, and above its precipices and crevasses our route now lay. The snow was smooth, and sufficiently firm and steep to render the cutting of steps necessary. Bennen took the lead: to make each step he swung his mattock once, and his hindmost foot rose exactly at the moment the mattock descended; there was thus a kind of rhythm in his motion, the raising of the foot keeping time to the swing of the implement. In this manner we proceeded till we reached the base of the rocky pyramid which caps the mountain.

One side of the pyramid had been sliced off, thus dropping down almost a sheer precipice for some thousands of feet to the Finsteraar glacier. A wall of rock, about 10 or 15 feet high, runs along the edge of the mountain, and this sheltered us from the north wind, which surged with the sound of waves against the tremendous barrier at the other side. 'Our hardest work is now before us,' said my guide. Our way lay up the steep and splintered rocks, among which we sought out the spikes which were closely enough wedged to bear our weight. Each had to trust to himself, and I fulfilled to the letter my engagement with Bennen to ask no help. My boiling-water apparatus and telescope were on my back, much to my annoyance, as the former was heavy, and sometimes swung awkwardly round as I twisted myself among the cliffs. Bennen offered to take it, but he had his own share to carry, and I was resolved to bear mine. Sometimes the rocks alternated with spaces of ice and snow, which we were at intervals compelled to cross; sometimes, when the slope was pure ice and very steep, we were compelled to retreat to the highest cliffs. The wall to which I have referred had given way in some places, and through the gaps thus formed the wind rushed with a loud, wild, wailing sound. Through these spaces I could see the entire field of Agassiz's observations; the junction of the Lauteraar and Finsteraar glaciers at the Abschwung, the medial moraine between them, on

which stood the Hôtel des Neufchâtelois, and the pavilion built by
M. Dollfuss, in which Huxley and myself had found shelter two
years before. Bennen was evidently anxious to reach the summit, and
recommended all observations to be postponed until after our success
had been assured. I agreed to this, and kept close at his heels. Strong
as he was, he sometimes paused, laid his head upon his mattock, and
panted like a chased deer. He complained of fearful thirst, and to
quench it we had only my bottle of tea: this we shared loyally, my
guide praising its virtues, as well he might. Still the summit loomed
above us; still the angry swell of the north wind, beating against the
torn battlements of the mountain, made wild music. Upward,
however, we strained; and at last, on gaining the crest of a rock,
Bennen exclaimed, in a jubilant voice, 'Die höchste Spitze!' – the
highest point. In a moment I was at his side, and saw the summit
within a few paces of us. A minute or two placed us upon the
topmost pinnacle, with the blue dome of heaven above us, and a
world of mountains, clouds, and glaciers beneath.

CATHERINE WILMOT
1773–1824

The leisurely progress of the Grand Tour had been rudely interrupted by the French Revolution and the Napoleonic wars. With the return of peace, travellers once again flocked to France – among them Stephen, 2nd Earl Mount Cashell, a man of simple rural tastes with a much more urbane and intelligent wife, who was later to get into trouble for befriending the revolutionary Robert Emmet. With the Mount Cashells there travelled Catherine Wilmot, a young Cork lady who had been befriended by the family. In a journal written primarily for the enlightenment of her brother Robert, she cast a sharp eye on the doings both of her noble patrons and the Continental world in which they moved. This extract is headed 'Paris, Hotel de Rome, Rue St Dominique, Fauxbourgs [sic] Saint Germain, 1802. Sunday 19th June, 30 Prariel'. Her subsequent travels took her to Russia and Vienna – journeys of which she has left equally entertaining and perceptive accounts. She died unmarried in Paris on 28 March 1824.

AN IRISH PEER ON THE
CONTINENT

The 5th of this Month we dined at the Thuilleries with Bonaparte. After passing through various Antechambers where were bands of military music, we at length reach'd the room where Madame Bonaparte sat under a canopy blazing in Purple and diamonds. More than two hundred persons were assembled and Bonaparte walk'd about the room speaking politely to everybody. His countenance is delightful when animated by conversation, and the expression in the lower part of his Face pleasing to the greatest degree; his eyes are reflection itself, but so charming a smile as his, I never scarcely beheld. His dress was simple and his air, tho' reserv'd, announcing everything of the polish'd gentleman. The Band struck up on our

315

going into dinner, to which Bonaparte led the way by taking the Regal prerogative of walking out of the room first. Everyone follow'd indiscriminately and both Bonaparte and Madame sat down at the side of the table without any regard to place. Lady Mount Cashell looking beautiful and dress'd in black crape and diamonds was handed in to dinner by the English Minister, and I by General Grouchy,[1] Madame Condorcet's brother, a highly polish'd and pleasing man. He was my Society during Dinner. For on looking to my right hand, who should I see gobbling like a duck but Talleyrand. We however renew'd our acquaintance for two or three minutes, and then I left him, to the destruction of all the poultry he could lay his claw upon. General Grouchy was second in command in the affair of Bantry Bay, on board the 'Fraternité,' and had every intention of snapping the grappling Irons which attached Ireland to England. We laugh'd heartily at the different circumstances under which our acquaintance wou'd have commenc'd had the business succeeded. However I took care to tell him 'had their philanthropic undertaking prosper'd as happily in Ireland as it did across the Alps, I should expect by this time to see our little Island hung up as a curiosity in the Louvre amongst the Italian Trophies.' This would not have been too civil, but that it past in the highest good spirits. He had just been admiring Lady Mount Cashell, and in allusion to that said, 'it was not necessary to go to Italy to look for "Venus's" and "Apollo's",' &c. I was more regaled than I can express by the perfume of oranges and roses which, with a thousand other kinds of Flowers, seem'd to grow out of Moss and artificial Rocks, the entire length of the plateau which reach'd from the top to the bottom of the table. There was a servant to every chair and nothing but Plate was used. The Apartments were hung over with fine Gobelins, and the ceilings painted by the first hands. Grecian statues brought out of Italy ornamented the room where we dined and Musick play'd delightfully during the entire entertainment. After sitting two hours, we return'd into the reception room, drank Coffee and liqueurs, talk'd in côteries, and so departed after having spent an uncommonly amusing day. But I believe there never was a Court more manacled by the observances of Etiquette, than the Thuilleries.

1 Emmanuel de Grouchy, Marshal of France (1766–1847), blamed for his failure to assist Napoleon at Waterloo.

Lady Mount Cashell and I are in the carriage almost every morning at 7 o'clock, and drive off to Tivoli, where the establishment for Bathing is on the most extensive scale. One may have Baths prepared in imitation of every kind of water in the world and drink the factitious ones, with equal effect. We only Bathe in common warm-water. But the Ladies most frequently have their Baths perfum'd with Eau de Cologne, Rose Water, or some perfume of that kind. The little Garden into which every Bath opens is absolutely red with roses, and the women who attend, cleanly dress'd every morning in a white linen jacket and petticoat. It is very much the fashion to Breakfast in the Bath, and we sometimes call for our Cotellette en Papillote, Potage or whatever else we like, for the variety of Déjeuners are inexhaustible. Afterwards we walk frequently in the Publick gardens, which are very fine and a part of the establishment of Tivoli. But it would be endless to describe Publick Gardens, as at present Paris seems but to peep from amongst its green leaves 'like the Devil in a bush'. The Boulevards, which encircle the Town, are thickly planted with high branching trees, under which is an eternal scene of festivity. All the Cafés are out of doors, and a thousand groups of happy looking people, sitting under blossoming Arbours, quaffing lemonade, wine, cider or Beer, and conducting themselves with such chearfulness and decorum, that it is delightful to witness it. The little Cabarets are full of dancers. The Theatres of the People are open everywhere and amusement of this nature purchasable at 5 Sous. Musick breathes universally throughout. The trees on either side of the Boulevard meet like an arch at top, and a thousand Lamps sparkle through the branches. The oratory of Charlatans! the tricks of conjurers! the parti-colour'd limbs of Harlequins that you catch flourishing in the air! the eternal balance of the Network swing-swang! the long bounding of the tight-rope! with a hundred such fooleries, serve to diversify the scene and give an indescribable effect of innocent festivity! Every day we hear of new Gardens where you go to eat ice, and wander thro' Grottos, Temples, close-Alleys, lit with colour'd Lamps and edifices dedicated to the Gods. Frascati is a favourite Retreat and the other night we spent at Tivoli, which is a most superb Garden with every diversified description of entertainment that Fancy can suggest. The Waltzes and Contre-dances, which are seen flitting like Fairy Rings through the illuminated Trees, and the sweetness of the music, give an air of Magic from the shadowings of night and uncertainty of the objects. Ladies in light flowing white veils winding through Seringa walks, and sparkling sheets of water repeating all the scenery. The moon was beautifully bright and the Summer lightning so mingled with fire-works, that 'twas difficult to distinguish the difference. Suddenly the Heavens appear'd open'd, the Thunder broke over our heads, and the fork'd-flashes of lightning gave so livid an effect to every creature that you wou'd have imagin'd a Church-yard was suddenly brought to Life. The Bolts fell from Heaven amongst the crowd, and in a moment, everyone disappeared and flew in consternation to the Houses, as tho' they had relaps'd into their Sepulchres. So far for the fluctuation of Climates. But these French People possess the genius of amusing themselves beyond anything I ever saw, and they mingle throughout their entertainments a spirit of attraction, that bewitches everybody at the time into a total forgetfulness that there exists anything in the world more agreeable, or more delightful than themselves!!!

We have, amongst innumerable Theatres, seen one, where the principal Actors and Actresses are imitated in mechanism, and Vestris dances in wheels and Springs exactly with the same elasticity he does at the Opera House. This exasperates the live performers, to the last degree.

Alli Effendi, the Turkish Ambassador is returning to Constantinople – and the new one is arriv'd. The other evening they gave a Turkish entertainment, at which we were. In the suite of his present Excellency, is a Persian Prince travelling for his amusement. He is the most magnificent looking creature I ever beheld. As I don't choose to plague you with a repetition of either people or places, I will say no more at present. Almost every evening we either visit, or are visited, for morning visits are always paid here in the evening, if it is not a Bull to say so. Kosciusko comes and tumbles on the ground with the children; young De Castor's Tutor comes and talks about the Punic War; Joel Barlow[2] calls and tells us American stories; and twice a week generally we pass the evenings at Miss Williams'.

2 Joel Barlow (1754–1812), distinguished American author and poet; settled in London in 1791, but removed to France two years later, owing to his revolutionary writings being proscribed; died during the Retreat from Moscow.

PARIS, 30TH JULY, 1802. 9 THERMIDOR, HOTEL DE ROME,
RUE ST. DOMINIQUE.

Really, Robert, when one gets domesticated to any place, habit so familiarises novelty that one becomes insensible to its presence. A Month has slipt through my fingers and I feel very much at a loss to account for its expenditure. I am standing before you like the faithless man, who had buried his Talent roll'd up in a napkin, without a word to say for myself in vindication. Did I ever mention the Chevalier de Miller and his brother, who lodged in this Hotel? They are before my eyes continually, and yet I have nothing over interesting to relate about them. The Chevalier is rather romantic, and walks up and down the garden swinging Helvetius' Poems in one hand, and flourishing a white pocket-handkerchief in the other. He at other times, plays the Flute amongst the Apple and Cherry trees, and imagines himself the Frontispiece to a Romance. There is another drowsy man, who appears sometimes in the walk with one leg tuck'd up, and his head under his wing, like a duck when it is asleep; in that attitude he stands for hours together. But really I must mention FitzJames, the Ventriloquist, who exhibits his extraordinary powers of voice so as to possess you absolutely with the belief that you are in the room with hundreds. He hides himself behind a screen and imitates every species of voice, noise, and event, that used to take place in the Popular Jacobinical assemblies during the times of terror. The various gradations of sound, and variety of tones cheat you into the belief of some of the voices being at half a mile's distance, when instantly afterwards, another's voice in a foreign cadence thunders in your ears, and then is soberly reply'd to from behind the wainscot. Really, it is miraculous, and as little Robert[3] says 'I'd rather be a Ventriloquist than anything in the world.'

We have been twice to see the Phantasmagorie, and the children stood the ghosts most marvellously.

The other night at Miss Williams', I was sitting next a gentleman who talk'd to me a vast deal about the pomps and vanities of this wicked world, without much irreverence for them. When on his turning away I ask'd Mr. Stone who that old Beau was, and what was my surprise to hear it was the celebrated De La Crusca whose 'Poems

3 Hon. Robert Moore, Lord Mount Cashell's second son.

to Matilda,' do you remember, Mrs. Trant[4] made us read at Cheltenham.

Monsieur de la Harpe,[5] who educated the Emperor of Russia, is the great friend and Crony of Mr. Stone and Miss Williams. I have seen him there lately, as he is within this month return'd from Moscow, where he went by the Emperor's invitation, to pay him a visit. The accounts he gives of him are delightful; he has such confidence in his Subjects that he goes everywhere without a Guard, and, without the slightest precaution, walks about the streets as a private Man, often saying, if he had occasion to distrust the confidence of his fellow citizens, he would not esteem his life worth preserving. He used to go to La Harpe in the evenings, and after conversing in his Society for hours, return to his palace either on foot, or with the attendance of a single servant to his carriage. La Harpe is a remarkably philosophic looking Man in appearance, about 60 years of age, and with grey, smooth, locks, comb'd over his forehead. He is married to a pretty little young woman, daughter to a Russian Merchant.

The 25th of June, Lady Mount Cashell added a 'Citoyen' to the French Republick; two days after his birth he was presented to the Municipality and his name inscrib'd in the national archives. This ceremony is necessary with everyone born in France, and it may be an advantage in giving him constitutional rights, as long as he lives, if the French have any such to impart, which seems to be much doubted.

14th July was the Confederation des François which was celebrated by a blaze of illuminations. At present Paris is become a little England, 5000 is the calculation this last week.

The other night at Miss Williams' we were introduced to Carnot.[6] I was very much pleas'd at seeing a man of such celebrity. We have also got acquainted with Maria Cosway,[7] who is drawing the Pictures in the Louvre, so as to give an idea of their subjects and arrangement,

---

4 Probably the widow of Dominick Trant, of Dunkettle, Co Cork, MP, who married, 1776, Eleanor, daughter of John Fitzgibbon and sister of John, 1st Earl of Clare.

5 Jean François de la Harpe (1739–1808), distinguished French author and critic.

6 Lazare Carnot (1753–1823), French Revolutionary statesman; displayed great ability in creating the fourteen armies of the Republic.

7 Maria Cecilia Louisa Hadfield, the daughter of an Irish inn-keeper at Florence, married 1781 Richard Cosway (1741–1821), the celebrated miniature painter. She was created a Baroness by Francis I of Austria in 1834, and died four years later.

in small copperplates. That night Lord Holland[8] was there, not unlike you in his appearance. I like his manners extremely. We also renew'd our acquaintance with Kemble,[9] who you know we saw a good deal of in London, and spent a remarkably pleasant evening at his House there. Lady Mount Cashell's confinement will best account to you for the want of incident in this last month, which has not been much spent beyond the precincts of her Bed-chamber.

I forgot to mention Mr. Fox[10] with whom at Miss Williams' we spent the evening. He was paid great compliment and attention, but was rather lourd and maladroit in his address and embarrass'd in his manners. As he did not enter into conversation with those he was presented to, I can only say of him, that the vision I had of the Great Man, disappointed me most dolefully.

PARIS, 30TH AUGUST, 1802 – HOTEL DE ROME; RUE ST. DOMINIQUE, FAUXBOURGS ST. GERMAIN.

15 FRUCTIDOR

Lady Mount Cashell is at length beginning to reassume her usual habits of Life. The Penroses[11] have been in Paris some weeks, and the St. Legers, Mr. Moore[12] of the Co. Tipperary, Mr. Trench,[13] Lord Cloncurry[14] and his two sisters[15] – and various other Irish, so that I sometimes fancy myself at home with you again. We have been seeing various things and some over and over again. The 'Glass Manufactory' in which 600 men are employed, is amongst them. The Hospital for the blind, 'the Observatory,' &c. &c. The 15th of this month there was a public Fête in honour of Bonaparte's birthday and perpetual Consulship. We dined in la Place Vendôme, within which

---

8 Henry Richard Vassall Fox, 3rd Baron Holland (1773–1840).

9 John Philip Kemble (1757–1823), founder of the declamatory school of acting.

10 Rt. Hon. Charles James Fox (1749–1806), eminent statesman and orator.

11 James Penrose, of Woodhill, Co. Cork, married 1794, Louisa, daughter of Robert Uniacke Fitzgerald of Corkbeg, Co. Cork, MP.

12 Stephen Moore, of Barne, Co. Tipperary, MP, a relative of the Mount Cashell family.

13 Richard Trench, Barrister-at-Law (1774–1860), sixth son of Frederick Trench of Woodlawn, Co. Galway, by Mary, daughter of Francis Sadleir of Sopwell Hall, Co. Tipperary. He was father of the gifted and scholarly Richard Chenevix-Trench, Archbishop of Dublin.

14 Valentine, 2nd Baron Cloncurry (1773–1853), the last nobleman to be imprisoned in the Tower of London.

15 Hon. Valentina Lawless, married, 1801, Hon. Sir Francis Nathaniel Burton, GCH, MP; and Hon. Charlotte Louisa Lawless, married, 1803, Edward. 14th Lord Dunsany.

were encircled 103 Pillars, made to represent the departments whose names were severally written in transparencies of Fire. Every column sparkled with different colour'd lamps, and each was united to the other, in a festoon of fire. The Thuilleries look'd like a magician's palace, and all Paris throughout the night, was light as noon day. It is astonishing, how happy these flaming Fêtes make the people! I forgot to mention what is much better worth speaking about, and what we went to see some days before: the distribution of Prizes at the Prytanée François. This is a National military institution, something of the style of Woolwich, where Boys are educated to be officers. We have visited it frequently and the order, regularity, attention and variety of elegant gentleman-like instruction surpasses anything I ever witnessed, in the effects I mean on the manners and characters of the students. Once every year, Prizes are allotted to those who have distinguish'd themselves in different sciences and on this occasion multitudes assemble from all parts to witness the glory of the Victors. All the specimens of drawing, Mathematicks, &c. are framed and publickly exhibited, and the young élèves who have distinguished themselves either in composition or translation, recite their own works in the most finish'd and eloquent manner. The Minister of the Interior, Chaptal, presided, and crown'd with a chaplet of flowers every Hero who pretended to celebrity. To the elevated seat where this ceremony is performed, they were accompanied by a band of Martial music, entirely executed by their fellow students, who likewise lay claim to the premiums and honors which are distributed. When the premium is given, and the crown put on their heads, they are embraced by the minister, who dismisses them with glory amongst their associates where nothing is heard but acclamations throughout the entire place. Certainly the French know how to touch the Master spring of Vanity in this puppet shew of Life, and understand better than any other people how to use the incongruities of humanity, so as to make the result subservient to the happiness and practicability of existence. The elegance of manners of all the élèves in the Prytanée is charming, and is shewn in the gradations from 8 years old to 18. Two young men of this latter age, who were crown'd two or three times during the different examinations, were presented to us; sons of the famous Philangerie who wrote in favor of Liberty, and they in consequence were banish'd from Naples. The French Nation have educated them at this School;

they bear away all the Prizes and, for cleverness, grace and beauty, I never saw their fellows. There are three other National institutions in Paris for Education as well Civil as Military, and ambition is awakened in the same manner by Publick examinations held once a year, where Dunces are absolutely regenerated by the hope of Glory. You can form no idea of the interesting effect of this exhibition! There was one lovely Child about eight years old, who when Chaptal put the Crown on his head, was so enchanted, he burst out crying, and not waiting for the regular formalities threw his hands about his neck and kiss'd him with such affection and for so long a time that there was a general suspension, which at length was interrupted by a thunder of applause from all parts, and the Mother of the little Boy fainted dead away upon the benches. A hundred smelling Bottles leap'd from the scabbards in her defence and the little fellow holding his crown of Flowers tight on his head with both his little red fat hands ran through the crowd until he reach'd the spot where she was sitting.

While I am on the subject of Mothers and sons, I must tell you Lady Mount Cashell has been occupying herself in having her's christened. There has been a glorious junketting of course, the Gossips being, the Polish Countess Myscelska, the American Minister, and Mr. William Parnell. The name of the child is Richard Francis Stanislaus Moore. The Godmother of his is a very amiable Being. She has just arriv'd at that unbounded extent of Aristocracy which always produces the utmost republicanism of manners, and with more than regal revenues, she is the most simple and unpretending of any one in Society; the other day she call'd in here, and saw Lady Mount Cashell eating plain boil'd Potatoes for her luncheon in the middle of the day. She then heard for the first time that *that* was the principal Food of the Irish, and immediately resolv'd on giving Lady Mount Cashell a breakfast in compliment to her country. We went there and literally found nothing but Potatoes dress'd in fifty different fashions. I thought the repast would never have been at an end, such was the torture she had put her fancy to in devising methods to diversify the cookery. She has insisted on Lady Mount Cashell making her a present of a Tree, which Lady Mount Cashell has, choosing an Arbutus as being common in Ireland. She is to take it into Poland with her where she has a little Plantation representative of her Friends and favourites, each having given her the sort of tree most emblematic of their sentiment towards her, and in this place she walks, and imagines herself conversing with all she loves, and likes, in every corner of the world. She has four or five little children, and their education is her chief Hobby-Horse. It is a curiosity to peep into the establishment of her House. She has studied the nature of each child and has provided Tutors according with the disposition, so that there is no end of instructors; every language they are to learn introduces a new inmate into the family, and you really wou'd suppose you were in the Tower of Babel if you were but to spend half an hour in her Drawing Room.

I don't know how to give you any idea of the heat of the weather; within some weeks we have suffered seriously from its enervating effects. We let down the curtains, and sit during the mornings more dead than alive; in the evenings we begin to breathe a little on the Balconys, but scarcely with strength to fan ourselves; mostly we eat Fruit for our breakfasts, but have been advis'd to eat cold-meat, to fortify a little against the exhausting and excessive weakness which we experience from the oppression of the weather. Peaches and grapes and Strawberries and every kind of Fruit are as plentiful here as Blackberries. I am really astonish'd how people in very hot Countrys can possess a single idea!

Within the last week Lord Mount Cashell and Mr. Moore have set out on an expedition to Orleans. We have late in the evenings under the escort of two or three gentlemen, gone Vagabondizing on the Boulevards, and poking our noses into every haunt of the lower order of people. We have been in Cabarets, Cafés, 'Theatres' where you pay a few sous for entrance, in the midst of dancing dogs, conjurers, wild beasts, Puppet Shews, Charlatans, Gangues, and in short every resort where the manners of the people cou'd be characteris'd, and I protest for the motto of the meanest place, you may put Elegant Decorum without the least fear of these expressions being forfeited in the most trifling instance.

The other evening we drove two leagues out of town to see the Château of Meudon. It was built by Francis I; commands an extensive view of the Country and is situated on the summit of a high Hill up which we wound through Purpling Vineyards. From the windows of the Château one sees the fine Woods of Montmorency skirt the distant Hills, the winding of the Seine breaks the Valleys, and the dome of the Pantheon, Gothic Towers of Notre Dame and streaming of the tri-colour'd flag from the Thuilleries, recall to view the finest objects within the walls of Paris. I never saw anything more romantic than it look'd at that moment as a loud thunder-storm broke heavily over our heads, and the mouldering Turrets and old Iron Gates were lit with a thousand colours by the quick fork'd flashes of the Lightning. I felt disappointed at not hearing the rattlings of the Chains of the drawbridge, or the blowing of the Warder's horn, and still more-so at not being greeted by a Valorous Knight in shining Armour, and Feathered Casque. We ventured nevertheless to explore our way through the Square Courts and ruin'd pavements where wildness and neglect mark'd every footstep; the Chapel walls had moulder'd away, and nothing remain'd but the Altar from which issued, instead of the pious dirges of a sainted choir, the natural chorus of a thousand singing Birds which, if you are in an allegoric mood, may serve as a fanciful imagery of the emblematic metamorphose of revolutionis'd Religion. We were oblig'd to hasten away, as the storm gather'd heavily again, and the Castle seem'd fading away like a deepen'd shadow on the dark blue cloud. I am tired of telling about my thunder and lightning, so will take you whisking back by the École Militaire, the Temple of Mars, the boulevards and returning loud under the Gateway of the Hotel de Rome where I will leave you, imagining what else you like, as having occupied us during the last Month, for my memory has got a hole in the bottom of it like an old Purse and I really have not been able to find a farthing's worth since I came to Paris. I ought tho' to mention various people whom I have omitted: Mrs. Opie[16] who writes Poems and novels; Mr. Richard Trench, since married to Mrs. St. George, who is most extremely gentlemanlike and so beautiful that if I was to describe him, you'd fancy it was the Apollo Belvedere in a Second Edition. Kemble has dined here and been in the evening two or three times; Mr. Heathcote who is with him; a Family of Smiths from Gloucestershire, excessively gentle and pleasant people, and endless others, but it would be no amusement to call over a muster roll of their names. Signor Fiore is continually here. He is a Neapolitan and as satirical as a two edg'd knife, nevertheless witty and entertaining. His history is like a fairy tale, but I have not time to hang the separate Labels round each person's neck as really the task would be eternal.

Lady Mount Cashell and I are like walking Arabias with Otto of

---

16 Amelia, daughter of John Alderson, MD, of Norwich, married, 1798, John Opie, the Cornish painter (1761–1807).

Roses, given to us by the Ottoman Ambassador. I never see them, that I don't long to rob them of their shawls, and Eastern treasures. I wish I cou'd describe to you a Parmazan, Count Lenati who is travelling, not for his pleasure, but his improvement, and studying Chemistry and antiquities all day long, but I shan't, nor do more neither, than finish this off with the greatest expedition.

PARIS, 16TH SEPR. 1802. HOTEL DE ROME, RUE ST. DOMINIQUE,
FAUXBURGS ST. GERMAIN.
FRUCTIDOR 29E, AN 10

But one Fortnight remains previous to our bidding adieu to Paris. We have been return'd a week from the beautiful Valley of Montmorency where we were spending some time with the Duke and Duchess of Cauzana; they are Neapolitans, and she is a sweet amiable, and elegant little woman, tho' so delicate in her health that she was scarcely out of her bed the entire time we were with her. The Duke looks like a valiant and right courteous Knight in the days of Chivalry, unnumber'd deeds of glory flash from his eyes, and to relieve the oppressed, and vanquish the oppressor, seems to be emblazon'd in the scroll of his destiny. The extent of this Valley is 13 miles, scatter'd through which there are about 30 villages. Both going and coming back we pass'd through St. Denis which was the burying place of the Kings of France. We walk'd through the Church, and the metamorphosis is strange from the Hungry Grave to a Magazine of Food, to which it is converted at present. Nothing remains but the mere skeleton of the church, which however is magnificent. In the time of the Terror, all the coffins were dug up for the benefit of making bullets of the lead, and as the bones within them were once Kings, the Jacobins destroy'd them and everything belonging to the Church, so that even in the sculptur'd representation of the day of Judgment, over the gateway, all the wicked are going to Hell, and all the good to Heaven, without a single head upon their shoulders!

I found it very interesting attending the publick Courts of Justice. In the Criminal Court I was present at two trials; the process is I have been told something like that in England. I also visited the Court of Cassation where the Queen and Madame Roland were condemned, and a lesser Court for petty offences. Under the Palais de Justice is the Conciergerie. We also went to see the Prison of the Abbey. These names will suggest to your remembrance so many scenes of which they were the theatres that you will not be surpris'd at the melancholy pleasure I took in seeing them.

I have now brought you to the last days of our sojournment in this delightful Town, of which I have given you a very imperfect idea, and but a mere outline of my own intercourse with its amusements, institutions and inhabitants. But as we are to return here again before we go back to Ireland, and perhaps to spend part of another winter, I will promise to make ample compensation. I bid adieu to this charming Town with the sensation of having pass'd through a little existence, and please myself with the idea that I have not lived in vain. I reflect on the variety of novel circumstances which has kept all my character in exercise and console myself with thinking that amongst the acquaintances we have made, intimacy has in some instances changed admiration into the belief of friendship. If in some instances I appear to estimate the state of Society and manners here too highly, I hope you will have the candour to attribute it to the effect of novelty and of that seductive influence which marks the manners of the French. I know your antipathy to this nation, and when contrasted with the sounder morals of the English I do not wonder at your dislike.

GLOSSARY

Amah	A wet nurse (Anglo-Indian).
Barranca	A gorge or ravine (Spanish).
Bashavav	To play the fiddle (Romany).
Busnó	Non-gypsy (term of contempt, Romany).
Calenture	Disease affecting sailors in the tropics, in the course of which delirium causes them to see the ocean as green fields and they try to leap into it.
Capote	A long, shaggy coat with a hood.
Churros	Fritters (Spanish).
Cocolele	A ukulele made out of a coconut (French).
Couloir	A steep mountain gorge or gully.
Djellaba	(or jellaba) A long garment: 'longbearded jews in their jellibees' (James Joyce, *Ulysses*).
Eoganacht	Descendants of Eogan Mór, king of Munster (Irish).
Fraxinella	Cultivated species of dittany, especially *Dictamnus fraxinella*.
Gimberi	(or gimbri) A small Moorish guitar; a player of this instrument (Arabic).
Gompa	A monastery (Tibetan).
Haere mai	Welcome (Maori).
Haic	An oblong piece of cloth worn as outer garment (Arabic).
Koti roa	A long coat (Maori).
Kuscussoo	Couscous – a dish prepared from semolina (Arabic).
Lassu	Slow (Romany).
Mali	A gardener (Hindustani).
Mere pounamu	A stone weapon (Maori).
Mitrailleuse	A breech-loading machine gun.
Mol	Wine (Romany).
Ndalo	(or dalo) The taro plant (Fijian).
Névé	A field or bed of frozen snow (French).
Nome	A territorial division (Greek).
Pakeha	(or pakehaa) A foreigner (Maori).
Shukar rakli	A pretty girl (Romany).
Ta and wiri	Locking and twisting (Maori).
Takini!	Run! (Maori).
Taniwha	A fabled sea monster (Maori).
Taonga	Treasure (Maori).
Taua	Army (Maori).
Tetere	War-trumpet (Maori).
Tino tangata	A good man (Maori).

Toro-toro	The climbing plant *Metrosideros scandens* (Maori).
Ulemas	Authorities on law and religion (Arabic).
Ustilar pastesas	To steal with the hands (Romany).
Utu	An eye for an eye (Maori).
Yanggona	(or yaquona) Kava (*Piper methysticum*) or drink made therefrom (Fijian).

BIBLIOGRAPHY

BIRMINGHAM, George A. *A Wayfarer in Hungary*, London, Methuen,1925

BRYANS, Robin. *Crete*, London, Faber and Faber, 1969

BUTLER, Hubert. *Escape from the Anthill*, Mullingar, Lilliput Press, 1985

BUTLER, William Francis. *The Great Lone Land*, London, Sampson Low, Marston, Searle and Rivington, 1889

COLLIS, Maurice. *Into Hidden Burma*, London, Faber and Faber, 1953

CORRY, John. *A Satirical View of London*, London, 1801

DUFFERIN, Lord. *Letters from High Latitudes*, 11th edn, London, J.M. Dent, 1903 (First published 1857)

FENNELL, Desmond. *Mainly in Wonder*, London, Hutchinson, 1959

GIBBINGS, Robert. *Over the Reefs*, London, J.M. Dent, 1948

GRATTAN, Thomas Colley. *Tales of a Walking Gentleman*, London, 1823

GRIMSHAW, Beatrice. *From Fiji to the Cannibal Islands*, London, Nelson, 1917

HENNESSY, Maurice N. *Africa Under My Heart*, New York, Ives Washburn, 1965

HIGGINS, Aidan. *Ronda Gorge and Other Precipices*, London, Secker and Warburg, 1989

HINKSON, Pamela. *Indian Harvest*, London, Collins, 1941

JOHNSTON, Denis. *Nine Rivers from Jordan*, London, Derek Verschoyle, 1953

KELLY, William. *Life in Victoria*, Vol. II, London, Chapman and Hall, 1859

LEARED, Arthur. *A Visit to the Court of Morocco*, London, Sampson Low, Marston, Searle and Rivington, 1879

LESLIE, Anita. *Love in a Nutshell*, London, Hutchinson, 1952

LYNCH, Hannah. *French Life in Town and Country*, London, Newnes, 1901

M'CLINTOCK, F.L. *The Fate of Sir John Franklin*, 5th edn, London, John Murray, 1881 (First published 1860)

MAC LIAMMÓIR, Micheál. *Put Money in Thy Purse*, London, Methuen, 1952

MANING, Frederick Edward. *Old New Zealand*, Christchurch, Whitcombe and Tombs, 1949 (First published 1863)

MITCHEL, John. *Jail Journal*, Dublin, M.H. Gill, 1913 (First published 1854)

MURPHY, Dervla. *Full Tilt*, London, John Murray, 1965

O'BRIEN Conor. *Across 3 Oceans*, London, Arnold, 1926

Ó CIANÁIN, Tadhg. *The Flight of the Earls*, trans. Father Paul Walsh, Dublin, M.H. Gill, 1916

O'CROULEY, Pedro Alonso. *A Description of the Kingdom of New Spain*, trans. and ed. Sean Galvin, Dublin, Allen Figgis, 1972

O'FLAHERTY, Liam. *Two Years*, London, Jonathan Cape, 1933 (First published 1930)

O'MEARA, John J. (Trans.). *The Voyage of Saint Brendan*, Dublin, Dolmen Press, 1976

SHARE, Bernard. *The Moon is Upside Down*, Dublin, Allen Figgis, 1962

SOMERVILLE-LARGE, Peter. *To the Navel of the World*, London, Hamish Hamilton, 1987

STARKIE, Walter. *Raggle Taggle*, London, John Murray, 1933

STUART, Francis. *States of Mind*, Dublin, Raven Arts, 1984 (First published *Envoy*, 1950)

TONE, Theobald Wolfe. *Life of Theobald Wolfe Tone, edited by his son William Theobald Wolfe Tone*, Washington, 1826

TYNDALL, John. *The Glaciers of the Alps*, new ed., London, Longmans Green, 1896 (First published 1860)

WILMOT, Catherine. *An Irish Peer on the Continent, 1801–1803*, ed. Thomas U. Sadleir, London, Williams and Norgate, 1920

ACKNOWLEDGEMENTS

Grateful acknowledgement is made to:

The estate of George A. Birmingham for permission to quote from
A Wayfarer in Hungary (Methuen, 1925);
Robin Bryans for permission to quote from *Crete* (Faber and Faber, 1969);
Louise Collis for permission to quote from *Into Hidden Burma* (Faber and
Faber, 1953) by Maurice Collis;
Desmond Fennell for permission to quote from *Mainly in Wonder*
(Hutchinson, 1959);
The estate of Beatrice Grimshaw for permission to quote from *From Fiji to
the Cannibal Islands* (Nelson, 1917);
Hamish Hamilton for permission to quote from *To the Navel of the World*
(1987) by Peter Somerville-Large;
HarperCollins for permission to quote from *Indian Harvest* (1941) by
Pamela Hinkson;
Maurice N. Hennessy for permission to quote from *Africa Under My Heart*
(Ives Washburn, 1965);
Hodder and Stoughton for permission to quote from *Across 3 Oceans* (1926)
by Conor O'Brien;
Hutchinson Books for permission to quote from *Love in a Nutshell* (1952) by
Anita Leslie;
Rory Johnston for permission to quote from *Nine Rivers from Jordan* (Derek
Verschoyle, 1953) by Denis Johnston;
Lilliput Press for permission to quote from *Escape from the Anthill* (1985) by
Hubert Butler;
Methuen London for permission to quote from *Put Money in Thy Purse*
(1952) by Micheál Mac Liammóir;
John Murray for permission to quote from *Full Tilt* (1965) by Dervla
Murphy; for permission to quote from *Raggle Taggle* (1933) by Walter
Starkie;
Peters Fraser and Dunlop for permission to quote from *Two Years*
(Jonathan Cape, 1933) by Liam O'Flaherty;
Laurence Pollinger for permission to quote from *Over the Reefs* (J.M. Dent,
1948) by Robert Gibbings;
Raven Arts Press for permission to quote from *States of Mind* (1984) by
Francis Stuart;
Martin Secker and Warburg for permission to quote from *Ronda Gorge and
Other Precipices* (1989) by Aidan Higgins;
Bernard Share for permission to quote from *The Moon is Upside Down*
(Allen Figgis, 1962);

Colin Smythe for permission to quote from *The Voyage of Saint Brendan* (Dolmen Press, 1976), trans. John J. O'Meara.

Blackstaff Press Limited regret they have not been successful in tracing all copyright holders. They apologise for any errors or omissions in the above list and would be grateful to be notified of any corrections that should be incorporated in the next edition or reprint of this volume.